WILLIAM MARSHAL AND IRELAND

John Bradley, Cóilín Ó Drisceoil
and Michael Potterton

EDITORS

FOUR COURTS PRESS

Typeset in 10.5 pt on 12.5 pt EhrhardtPro by
Carrigboy Typesetting Services
FOUR COURTS PRESS LTD
7 Malpas Street, Dublin 8, Ireland
www.fourcourtspress.ie
and in North America for
FOUR COURTS PRESS
c/o IPG, 814 N Franklin St, Chicago, IL 60610.

First published 2017.
Paperback edition 2021, 2025.

A catalogue record for this title is available
from the British Library.

ISBN 978-1-84682-961-1

Printed in England
by CPI Antony Rowe Ltd, Chippenham, Wilts.

WILLIAM MARSHAL AND IRELAND

In memory of John Bradley, Billy Colfer and Emma Devine

Contents

Illustrations

FIGURES

TABLES

PLATES

(between p. 160 and p. 161)

Abbreviations

Acts and letters	*The acts and letters of the Marshal family, marshals of England and earls of Pembroke, 1145–1248*, ed. David Crouch (London, 2015)
AFM	*Annála Ríoghachta Éireann: Annals of the Kingdom of Ireland by the Four Masters, from the earliest period to the year 1616*, ed. John O'Donovan (7 vols, Dublin, 1851; 3rd repr. with intro. by K.W. Nicholls, Dublin, 1990)
AI	*The Annals of Inisfallen: MS Rawlinson B503*, ed. Seán Mac Airt (Dublin, 1951)
Albion	*Albion: A Quarterly Journal Concerned with British Studies* (Boone, NC, 1969–2005)
ALC	*The Annals of Loch Cé: a chronicle of Irish affairs, 1014–1590*, ed. William Hennessy (2 vols, London, 1871; repr. reflex facsimile, Dublin, 1939)
APMDI	*Association for the Preservation of the Memorials of the Dead, Ireland*
ATig.	*The Annals of Tigernach*, ed. Whitley Stokes. In *Revue Celtique*, 16 (1895), pp 374–419; 17 (1896), pp 6–33, 119–263, 337–420; 18 (1897), pp 9–59, 150–97, 267–303 (repr., Llanerch, 2 vols, 1993)
AU	*Annála Uladh: Annals of Ulster, otherwise Annála Senait: Chronicle of Irish affairs, 431–1131, 1155–1541*, ed. William Hennessy and Bartholomew Mac Carthy (4 vols, Dublin, 1887–1907; vol. i ed. Hennessy, vols ii–iv, ed. Mac Carthy)
Avent, 'Chepstow's place'	Richard Avent, 'William Marshal's castle at Chepstow and its place in military architecture' in Turner and Johnson, *Chepstow Castle*, pp 81–90
Avent, 'Gatehouse at Chepstow'	Richard Avent, 'The late twelfth-century gatehouse at Chepstow, Monmouthshire, Wales', *Château Gaillard*, 20 (2002), pp 27–40
Avent, 'Marshal's Chepstow'	Richard Avent, 'William Marshal's building works at Chepstow Castle, Monmouthshire, 1189–1219' in Kenyon and O'Conor (eds), *The medieval castle in Ireland and Wales* (Dublin, 2003), pp 50–7
Avent and Turner, 'Middle Bailey'	Richard Avent and Rick Turner, 'The Middle Bailey' in Turner and Johnson, *Chepstow Castle*, pp 63–70
Ballard, *British borough charters*	Adolphus Ballard, *British borough charters, 1042–1216* (Cambridge, 1916)
BAR	British Archaeological Reports
Bateson, *Borough customs*	Mary Bateson, *Borough customs* (2 vols, London, 1904–6)
Beresford, *New towns*	Maurice Beresford, *New towns of the Middle Ages: town plantation in England, Wales and Gascony* (London, 1967)
Bk Leinster	*Book of Leinster formerly Lebor na Núachongbála*, ed. R.I. Best, Osborn Bergin, M.A. O'Brien and Anne O'Sullivan (6 vols, Dublin, 1954–83)

Bradbury, *Philip Augustus*	Jim Bradbury, *Philip Augustus, king of France, 1180–1223* (London and New York, 1998)
Bradley, 'Anglo-Norman Kilkenny'	John Bradley, 'Anglo-Norman Kilkenny' in John Bradley and Michael O'Dwyer (eds), *Kilkenny through the centuries: chapters in the history of an Irish city* (Kilkenny, 2009), pp 24–45
Bradley, *Discover Kilkenny*	John Bradley, *Discover Kilkenny* (Dublin, 2000)
Bradley, *Kilkenny*	John Bradley, *Kilkenny* (Irish Historic Towns Atlas, 10; Dublin, 2000)
Briais, *Loches*	Bernard Briais, *Loches through history* (Monts, 2012)
Brooks, *Knights' fees*	Eric St-J. Brooks, *Knights' fees in Counties Wexford, Carlow and Kilkenny (13th–15th century)* (Dublin, 1950)
Brown, *Castles from the air*	R.A. Brown, *Castles from the air* (Cambridge, repr. 1992)
CAAR	*Calendar of Archbishop Alen's register,* c.*1172–1534*, ed. Charles McNeill (Dublin, 1950)
Carrigan, *Ossory*	William Carrigan, *The history and antiquities of the diocese of Ossory* (4 vols, Dublin, 1905; repr. 1981)
Cathcart King and Cheshire, *Pembroke Castle*	D.J. Cathcart King and Mark Cheshire, *Pembroke Castle and the town walls of Pembroke* (1987, repr. from *Archaeologia Cambrensis*)
CCD	*Christ Church deeds*, ed. M.J. McEnery and Raymond Refaussé (Dublin, 2001)
CDI, 1171–1251 [etc.]	*Calendar of documents relating to Ireland, 1171–1251* [etc.], ed. H.S. Sweetman and G.F. Handcock (5 vols, London, 1875–86)
Chartae, privilegia et immunitates	*Chartae, privilegia et immunitates: being transcripts of charters and privileges to cities, towns and other bodies corporate [...], 1171–1395* (Dublin, 1829–30; pub. 1889)
CIPM	*Calendar of inquisitions post mortem and other analogous documents preserved in the Public Record Office* [1236–1432] (23 vols, London, 1904–2004), 2nd ser. [1485–1509] (3 vols, London, 1898–1955)
Civil Survey	*The Civil Survey, AD1654–6*, ed. R.C. Simington (10 vols, Dublin, 1931–61)
cllr/s	councillor/s
Clyne, *Kells Priory*	Miriam Clyne, *Kells Priory, Co. Kilkenny: archaeological excavations by T. Fanning and M. Clyne* (Dublin, 2007)
Colfer, *Arrogant trespass*	Billy Colfer, *Arrogant trespass: Anglo-Norman Wexford, 1169–1400* (Enniscorthy, 2002)
comp.	compiler/compiled by
CPCRI, Hen. VIII–Eliz. [1514–75]	*Calendar of the patent and close rolls of chancery in Ireland* [1514–75], ed. James Morrin (Dublin, 1861)
CPR, 1216–25 [etc.]	*Calendar of the patent rolls, 1216–25* [etc.] (London, 1901–)
Crede Mihi	*Crede Mihi: the most ancient register book of the archbishop of Dublin before the reformation*, ed. J.T. Gilbert (Dublin, 1897)
Crosland, *William Marshal*	Jessie Crosland, *William the Marshal, the last great feudal baron* (London, 1962)

Crouch, 'Earley'	David Crouch, 'Earley, John (II) of (*c*.1173–1229)' in *ODNB*, 17, pp 574–5
Crouch, 'Marshal, Sir John'	David Crouch, 'Marshal, Sir John (d. 1235)' in *ODNB*, 36, pp 812–13
Crouch, *William Marshal*	David Crouch, *William Marshal: knighthood, war and chivalry, 1147–1219* (2nd ed., Harlow, 2002)
Crouch, *William Marshal* (2016)	David Crouch, *William Marshal: knighthood, war and chilvary, 1147–1219* (3rd ed., Harlow, 2016)
CS	*Chronicum Scotorum: a chronicle of Irish affairs from the earliest times to AD1135, with a supplement 1141–50*, ed. William Hennessy (London, 1866. Repr., Wiesbaden, 1964)
CSGJ	*Castle Studies Group Journal*
CSMA	*Chartularies of St Mary's Abbey, Dublin, with the register of its house at Dunbrody and Annals of Ireland*, ed. J.T. Gilbert (2 vols, London, 1884–6)
Decies	*Decies: Journal of the Waterford Historical and Archaeological Society* (Waterford, 1976–)
Deeds of the Normans	*The deeds of the Normans in Ireland: La geste des Engleis en Yrlande, a new edition of the chronicle formerly known as the Song of Dermot and the Earl*, ed. Evelyn Mullally (Dublin, 2002)
DIB	*Dictionary of Irish biography*, ed. James McGuire and James Quinn (9 vols, Cambridge, 2009)
Doran, *New Ross*	Linda Doran, 'New Ross in maps: an enduring image, 1590–1900' in Tom Dunne (ed.), *New Ross. Rosponte. Ros Mhic Treoin: an anthology celebrating 800 years* (Wexford, 2007)
Duby, *William Marshal*	Georges Duby, *William Marshal: flower of chivalry* (London, 1986)
'Duiske charters'	'The charters of the abbey of Duiske', ed. C.M. Butler and J.H. Bernard, *PRIA*, 35C (1918–20), pp 1–187
EIMP	*Extents of Irish monastic possessions, 1540–1*, ed. N.B. White (Dublin, 1943)
Excavations 1971 [etc.]	*Excavations 1971* [etc.]*: summary accounts of archaeological excavations in Ireland*, ed. T.G. Delaney (1971–6), Clare Cotter (1985–6), Isabel Bennett (1987–) [1977–84 incorporated in *Journal of Irish Archaeology*, 4 (1987–8) and 5 (1989–90), ed. Conleth Manning and Declan Hurl] (Bray, 1986–)
FAI	*Fragmentary annals of Ireland*, ed. Joan Radner (Dublin, 1978)
fd	founded
FJ	*Finn's Leinster Journal* (newspaper)
Flanagan, *Irish royal charters*	Marie Therese Flanagan (ed.), *Irish royal charters, texts and contexts* (Oxford, 2006)
Fleury and Kruta, *The castles of the Louvre*	M. Fleury and V. Kruta, *The castle of the Louvre* (Dijon, 2000)
Florençon, *The city of Aigues-Mortes*	Patrick Florençon, *The city of Aigues-Mortes* (Paris, 2001)

Gillingham, *Angevin empire*	John Gillingham, *The Angevin empire* (2nd ed., New York, 2001)
Giraldus, *Expugnatio*	*Expugnatio Hibernica: the conquest of Ireland by Giraldus Cambrensis*, ed. and trans. A.B. Scott and F.X. Martin (Dublin, 1978)
Girault, *Loire Valley castles*	Pierre-Gilles Girault, *Loire Valley castles* (Paris, 2014)
Gleeson and Leask, 'Nenagh'	D.F. Gleeson and H.G. Leask, 'The castle and manor of Nenagh', *JRSAI*, 66 (1966), pp 247–69
Goodall, *The English castle*	John Goodall, *The English castle* (New Haven and London, 2011)
Graham, 'Towns of medieval Ireland'	B.J. Graham, 'The towns of medieval Ireland' in R.A. Butlin (ed.), *The development of the Irish town* (London, 1977)
Graves and Prim, *St Canice's*	James Graves and J.G.A. Prim, *The history, architecture and antiquities of the cathedral church of St Canice, Kilkenny* (Dublin, 1857)
Gravett and Hook, *Norman stone castles*	Christopher Gravett and Adam Hook, *Norman stone castles (2): Europe, 950–1204* (Oxford, 2004)
Guy et al., 'Castles of north Munster'	Neil Guy et al., 'Castles of north Munster', *CSGJ*, 23 (2009–10), pp 4–116
Hilling, *Cilgerran Castle*	J.B. Hilling, *Cilgerran Castle, St Dogmael's Abbey etc.* (Cardiff, rev. 2000)
Hodkinson, 'Nenagh'	B.J. Hodkinson, 'Excavations in the gatehouse of Nenagh Castle, 1996 and 1997', *Tipperary Historical Journal* (1999), pp 162–82
Hore, *Ross*	P.H. Hore, *History of the town and county of Wexford: Old and New Ross* (London, 1900)
Hore, *Wexford*	P.H. Hore, *History of the town and county of Wexford* (6 vols, London, 1900–11; repr. Dublin, 1978)
Hulme, 'Château Gaillard'	Richard Hulme, 'The impact of Château Gaillard and crusading on English castle architecture', *CSGJ*, 27 (2013–14), pp 203–33
Hunt, *Figure sculpture*	John Hunt, *Irish medieval figure sculpture* (2 vols, Dublin, 1974)
HWM	*History of William Marshal*, ed. A.J. Holden and David Crouch, trans. Stewart Gregory (3 vols, London, 2002–6)
IHS	*Irish Historical Studies: the Joint Journal of the Irish Historical Society and the Ulster Society for Irish Historical Studies* (Dublin, 1938–)
IMED	*Irish monastic and episcopal deeds, AD1200–1600*, ed. N.B. White (Dublin, 1936)
Innes-Smith, *Pembroke Castle*	Robert Innes-Smith, *Pembroke Castle: birthplace of the Tudor dynasty* (Derby, 1996)
IRC	Irish Research Council
JRSAI	*Journal of the Royal Society of Antiquaries of Ireland* (Kilkenny, later Dublin, 1849–)
Keating, *Foras feasa*	Geoffrey Keating, *Foras feasa ar Éirinn: The history of Ireland*, ed. David Comyn and P.S. Dinneen (4 vols, London, 1902–14)
Kenyon, *Medieval castles of Wales*	J.R. Kenyon, *The medieval castles of Wales* (Cardiff, 2010)

Knight, *The three castles*	J.K. Knight, *The three castles: Grosmont Castle, Skenfrith Castle, White Castle. Hen Gwart moated site* (Cardiff, 1991)
Knight, 'Usk Castle, 1136–1245'	Jeremy Knight, 'Welsh space and Norman invaders: Usk Castle, 1136–1245' in J.K. Knight and Andy Johnson (eds), *Usk Castle, priory and town* (Logaston, 2008), pp 55–78
Leabhar mór na ngenealach	*Leabhar mór na ngenealach: The great book of Irish genealogies compiled (1645–66) by Dubhaltach Mac Fhirbhisigh*, ed. and trans. Nollaig Ó Muraíle (5 vols, Dublin, 2003)
Leask, 'Irish castles, 1180 to 1310'	H.G. Leask, 'Irish castles, 1180 to 1310', *Archaeological Journal*, 93 (1937), pp 143–99
Leask, *Irish churches*	H.G. Leask, *Irish churches and monastic buildings* (3 vols, Dundalk, 1958)
'*Liber Niger*'	'A calendar of the *Liber Niger* and the *Liber Albus* of Christ Church, Dublin', ed. H.J. Lawlor, *PRIA*, 27C (1908), pp 1–93
Long Room	*Long Room: Ireland's Journal for the History of the Book* (Dublin, 1970–)
Ludlow, *Pembroke Castle*	Neil Ludlow, 'Pembroke Castle: discoveries in the outer ward', *Castle Studies Group Bulletin*, 18 (Sept. 2014), pp 2–6
Lynch and Manning, 'Dublin Castle'	Ann Lynch and Conleth Manning, 'Excavations at Dublin Castle, 1985–7' in Seán Duffy (ed.), *Medieval Dublin II* (Dublin, 2001), pp 169–204
MacCotter, *Medieval Ire.*	Paul MacCotter, *Medieval Ireland: territorial, political and economic divisions* (Dublin, 2008)
Mac Niocaill, *Na buirgéisí*	Gearóid Mac Niocaill, *Na buirgéisí, xii–xv aois* (Dublin, 1964)
Manning, 'Clogh Oughter Castle'	Conleth Manning, 'Clogh Oughter Castle, Co. Cavan, and thirteenth-century circular towers in Ireland', *Château Gaillard*, 25 (2012), pp 223–32
Manning, 'Dublin Castle'	Conleth Manning, 'Dublin Castle: the building of a royal castle in Ireland', *Château Gaillard*, 18 (1996), pp 119–22
McNeill, *Castles in Ireland*	T.E. McNeill, *Castles in Ireland: feudal power in a Gaelic world* (London, 2000)
McNeill, 'Squaring circles'	T.E. McNeill, 'Squaring circles: flooring round towers in Wales and Ireland' in Kenyon and O'Conor (eds), *The medieval castle in Ireland and Wales*, pp 96–106
Mesqui, *Châteaux forts*	Jean Mesqui, *Châteaux forts et fortifications en France* (Paris, 1997)
Meyer, *L'histoire*	Paul Meyer (ed.), *L'histoire de Guillaume le Maréchal, comte de Striguil et de Pembroke, regent d'Angleterre de 1216 à 1219* (3 vols, Paris, 1891–1901)
MHFPI	E.B. Fitzmaurice and A.G. Little (eds), *Materials for the history of the Franciscan province of Ireland, AD1230–1450* (Manchester, 1920)
Moore, *AI Waterford*	Michael Moore, *Archaeological inventory of County Waterford* (Dublin, 1999)
Moore, *AI Wexford*	Michael Moore, *Archaeological inventory of County Wexford* (Dublin, 1996)

MRHI	Aubrey Gwynn and R.N. Hadcock, *Medieval religious houses: Ireland* (London, 1970; repr. Dublin, 1988)
MS/MSS	manuscript/s
Murphy, 'Profits of lordship'	Margaret Murphy, 'The profits of lordship: Roger Bigod, earl of Norfolk, and the lordship of Carlow, 1270–1306' in Linda Doran and James Lyttleton (eds), *Lordship in medieval Ireland: image and reality* (Dublin, 2007), pp 75–98
Murtagh, 'Kilkenny Castle'	Ben Murtagh, 'Kilkenny Castle, the Parade, Kilkenny', *Excavations 1997*, pp 102–4, no. 304
n./nn	note/s; footnote/s
n.d.	no date (given)
Neely, *Kilkenny: an urban history*	W.G. Neely, *Kilkenny: an urban history, 1391–1843* (Belfast, 1989)
NGC	National Grid Coordinate(s)
NHI	*A new history of Ireland*, under the auspices of the RIA, ed. T.W. Moody, T.D. Williams, J.C. Beckett, F.X. Martin, F.J. Byrne, W.F. Vaughan, Art Cosgrove, J.R. Hill and Dáibhí Ó Cróinín (9 vols, Oxford, 1976–2005)
NLI	National Library of Ireland
O'Brien, 'Politics, economy and society'	Alfie F. O'Brien, 'Politics, economy and society: the development of Cork and the Irish south-coast region, *c.*1170 to *c.*1583' in Patrick O'Flanagan and C.G. Buttimer (eds), *Cork: history and society* (Dublin, 1993), pp 83–154
ODNB	*Oxford dictionary of national biography*, ed. H.C.G. Matthew and Brian Harrison (60 vols, Oxford, 2004), rev. ed. www.oxforddnb.com
Ó Drisceoil, 'Medieval New Ross'	Cóilín Ó Drisceoil, 'The layout, topography and archaeology of medieval New Ross, County Wexford' (2 vols, MA, UCD, 1996)
O'Keeffe, 'Dublin Castle's donjon'	Tadhg O'Keeffe, 'Dublin Castle's donjon in context' in John Bradley, A.J. Fletcher and Anngret Simms (eds), *Dublin in the medieval world: studies in honour of Howard B. Clarke* (Dublin, 2009), pp 277–94
OKR	*Old Kilkenny Review: Journal of the Kilkenny Archaeological Society* (Kilkenny, 1948–)
OLL	*Ossory, Laois and Leinster* [journal]
opp.	opposite
Ormond deeds, 1172–1350 [etc.]	*Ormond deeds, 1172–1350* [etc.], ed. Edmund Curtis (6 vols, Dublin, 1932–43)
Orpen, 'Castles in Ossory'	G.H. Orpen, 'Motes and Norman castles in Ossory', *JRSAI*, 19, fifth ser. (1909), pp 313–42
Orpen, *New Ross*	G.H. Orpen, *New Ross in the thirteenth century* (Dublin, 1911)
Orpen, *Normans*	G.H. Orpen, *Ireland under the Normans* (4 vols, Oxford, 1910–20; repr. Dublin, 2005)
OS	Ordnance Survey
OSA	Order of Saint Augustine
OSI	Ordnance Survey Ireland

Otway-Ruthven, *Medieval Ire.*	A.J. Otway-Ruthven, *A history of medieval Ireland* (2nd ed., London, 1980)
Painter, *William Marshal*	Sidney Painter, *William Marshal: knight-errant, baron and regent of England* (Baltimore, 1933)
Panouillé, *Châteaux forts*	Jean Pierre Panouillé, *Les châteaux forts dans la France au Moyen Âge* (Rennes, 2015)
Perfect, *Flint Castle*	Vicky Perfect, *Flint Castle: the story of Edward I's first Welsh castle* (Mold, Flintshire, 2012)
Peritia	*Peritia: Journal of the Medieval Academy of Ireland* ([Cork and Turnhout], 1982–)
Praestitis	T. Duffus Hardy (ed.), *Rotuli de liberate ac de Misis et Praestitis* (London, 1884)
PRIA	*Proceedings of the Royal Irish Academy* (Dublin, 1836/40–)
PRO	Public Record Office
PROI	Public Record Office, Ireland
r.	reigned
RAST	*The register of the abbey of St Thomas the Martyr, Dublin*, ed. J.T. Gilbert (London, 1889)
RBO	*The Red Book of Ormond*, ed. N.B. White (Dublin, 1932)
'Register of Kells'	'The register of Kells', ed. N.B. White, in *IMED*, pp 303–13
'Registrum de Dunbrothy'	J.T. Gilbert (ed.), 'Registrum Monasterii de Portu Sancte Marie, Dunbrothy' in *CSMA*, ii, pp 97–208
repr.	reprint/reprinted (in)
rev.	revised/revision
RIA	Royal Irish Academy
RSJB	*Register of the hospital of St John the Baptist without the New Gate, Dublin*, ed. Eric St-J. Brooks (Dublin, 1936)
Schweitz, *Châteaux et forteresses*	Daniel Schweitz, *Châteaux et forteresses du Moyen Âge en Val de Loire* (Tours, 2006)
ser.	series
Shields, 'Walling of Ross'	Hugh Shields, '"The walling of New Ross": a thirteenth-century poem in French', *Long Room*, 12–13 (1976–7), pp 24–33
Simington, *CS Wexford*	R.C. Simington, *The Civil Survey, AD1654–1656, 9: County of Wexford* (Dublin, 1953)
Song of Dermot	*The song of Dermot and the earl*, ed. G.H. Orpen (Oxford, 1892)
Studies	*Studies: An Irish Quarterly Review* (Dublin, 1912–)
Swanson, *British towns*	Heather Swanson, *Medieval British towns* (Basingstoke, 1999)
Sweetman, *Medieval castles*	David Sweetman, *Medieval castles of Ireland* (Cork, 1999)
TCD	Trinity College Dublin
Topographical poems	*The topographical poems of John O'Dubhagain and Gilla na Naomh O'Huidhrin*, ed. John O'Donovan (Dublin, 1862)
Turner and Johnson, *Chepstow Castle*	Rick Turner and Andy Johnson (eds), *Chepstow Castle: its history and buildings* (Logaston, 2006)
UCD	University College Dublin

Unkel, 'Architectural patronage'	Jill Unkel, 'Architectural patronage in Ireland: the early Anglo-Norman lords' (PhD, TCD, 2010)
Ware, *Annals*	[James Ware], *The annals of the affairs of Ireland from the first conquest by the English in the reign of King Henry II unto the end of the reign of Queen Elizabeth*, part 4 of *The antiquities and history of Ireland by the right honourable Sir James Ware, knight* [ed. Robert Ware] (Dublin, 1705)
Warren, *King John*	W.L. Warren, *King John* (New Haven and London, 1997)
Wiggins, *Anatomy of a siege*	Kenneth Wiggins, *Anatomy of a siege: King John's Castle, Limerick, 1642* (Bray, 2000)
Wiles, 'Marshal towers'	John Wiles, 'Marshal towers in south-west Wales: innovation and mimicry', *CSGJ*, 27 (2013–14), pp 181–202

Contributors

JOHN BRADLEY was, prior to his death in 2014, a senior lecturer in the Department of History, Maynooth University.

MIRIAM CLYNE is an IRC post-doctoral research fellow on the 'Monastic Ireland: Landscape and Settlement Project', at Trinity College Dublin, in collaboration with the Discovery Programme and University College Cork.

BILLY COLFER, a graduate of St Patrick's College, Drumcondra, completed his doctoral research on medieval Wexford at Trinity College Dublin. His career as a primary school teacher was spent in the Christian Brothers' School, Wexford. Billy died in 2013.

DAVID CROUCH is Professor of Medieval History at the University of Hull and a Fellow of the British Academy. He has published widely on the social and political history of the period 1000–1300. He was one of the academic team which edited the History of William Marshal, and he is the author of the best-selling *William Marshal*, now in its third edition.

ADRIAN EMPEY is an independent scholar. He has published widely on aspects of Anglo-Norman settlement and the development of the parochial system in medieval Ireland.

GILLIAN KENNY is a curator and a research associate at Trinity College Dublin's Centre for Gender and Women's Studies. Her research focuses generally on women's roles in medieval and early modern European society.

BEN MURTAGH is an archaeologist and architectural historian based in the south-east of Ireland, specialising in the study and survey of medieval and early modern buildings. He conducted extensive excavations on Kilkenny Castle in the 1990s.

CÓILÍN Ó DRISCEOIL is managing director of Kilkenny Archaeology. His research interests focus on urban archaeology.

MICHAEL POTTERTON is a lecturer in the Department of History at Maynooth University.

DANIEL TIETZSCH-TYLER is a self-employed illustrator and heritage consultant who specialises in archaeological reconstruction drawing. Since 1994, his reconstructions have been commissioned for on-site information panels and publication in books and articles by national and local government heritage services, local heritage groups, and individual archaeologists and historians.

Preface and acknowledgments

CÓILÍN Ó DRISCEOIL

In 2008, a conference was organised in Kilkenny Castle to celebrate the 800th anniversary of William Marshal's foundation charter to the city. Prior to the conference the charter had been generally dated to between 1207 and 1211 but through the researches of John Bradley it subsequently transpired that it was issued in 1207. And so although the conference was being held in the wrong year, it was definitely a case of better late than never. For despite William Marshal being one of the most famous personalities of the western medieval world, his Irish career, which spanned a period of some thirty years (1189–1219), has not figured to any great extent in scholarship, on either side of the Irish Sea. Similarly, the significant role played by his wife, Isabel de Clare, daughter of Strongbow, has also received little attention. The purpose of this book, which presents essays arising from the 2008 conference, is therefore to highlight the achievements and legacy of both William and Isabel in Ireland. The essays that follow offer detailed explorations of how both the Marshal and de Clare transformed Leinster during their thirty years of direct involvement with Ireland. They show the Marshal in a new light that differs from his renowned and well-researched role as a courtier, tourneyer and 'flower of chivalry', and instead present him as an empire builder, a magnate, an administrative and economic strategist, and a builder of towns, castles and churches.

To begin with, an outline is presented of the key events in the narrative of William and Isabel in Ireland. The Marshal's celebrity results in no small measure from the fact that his life was recorded in an extended biography – traditionally known as the *Histoire de Guillaume le Maréchal* – that was completed some five years after his death in 1219. The *Histoire* recounts that the Marshal was born around 1146, the fourth son of John Marshal of Hamstead, Berkshire, a down-on-his-luck nobleman. In 1152, during the civil war known as 'the Anarchy', his father John famously refused to surrender to King Stephen despite the king threatening to kill William unless his father surrendered his castle at Newbury. Having survived this episode and his father's subsequent tyranny the Marshal in his youth went on to excel on the tournament circuit in France and the Rhineland, where he became wealthy and very famous. In 1167, he caught the eye of Queen Eleanor, wife of Henry II of England, who brought him into the household of the Plantagenets. He became a master at 'courtliness' and he quickly rose to become an indispensible member of the royal household where he was renowned for his loyalty; his allegiance was copper-fastened by his valour shown when fighting with King Richard the Lionheart on the Crusades and in Normandy. By way of reward, Richard granted the Marshal the hand of Isabel, the daughter of Earl Richard of Striguil (Strongbow) and one of the wealthiest heiresses in the kingdom, with lands in Ireland, England, France and Wales. In August 1189 they married; she was 17 and he was around 42.

Little is known about Isabel for, like most medieval women, her life has gone largely undocumented but the *Histoire* does provide some insights. It makes it clear that there was a great deal of endearment between William and Isabel and also that she was an influential and determined presence in the administration of the Irish lordship. William's marriage to Isabel was, however, unpopular with King John; Leinster had been retained by the king since her father Earl Richard's death in 1176 and John was reluctant, to say the least, to give it up. This was a bone of contention between John and the Marshals and it took another three years before they finally gained control of the lordship. A brief visit was made by the Marshal in late 1200, at which time he probably set in train the foundation of his chief port at New Ross and the development of the lordship of Leinster. At this time he also founded the Cistercian abbey at Tintern *de Voto* in fulfilment of a vow made during a near-death trip by boat from Pembroke. But William's major rupture with John was to happen in Normandy, which John had disastrously lost to King Philip II of France in 1204.With England and Normandy under separate rulers William had to choose which king to follow. The Marshal negotiated an accord with Philip for his Norman lands. To John this was the ultimate treachery and in 1205 he took the Marshal's eldest son as a hostage and humiliated William at court. The Marshal had no choice but to go into exile and this is why he and Isabel came to Ireland in 1207.

The Ireland that met the Marshals was, to Anglo-Norman eyes, the 'wild-west' of Norman Europe: a war-weary land that was precariously governed by the battle-hardened warriors of Strongbow's conquering army. If staying under the radar from King John was the key reason William came to Ireland in 1207, there was the equally pressing need to tame Meiler fitz Henry, the old soldier who had been on the boat with Robert fitz Stephen in 1169 and whom John had made justiciar of Ireland in 1199. Fitz Henry was ambitious, hated the Marshal and was using his connections to John to thwart William's plans for Leinster by retaining extensive lands in Leinster – including Dunamase Castle, Co. Laois – that were rightfully William's. The Marshal declared war on fitz Henry, which enraged John and he was recalled to court where he was humiliated again by an angry king. The Marshal's absence from Leinster left him wide open to an attack from fitz Henry's rebels. But at this point the *Histoire* tells us Isabel stepped into the spotlight. She was undoubtedly respected by the Leinster barons and her presence at Kilkenny would have been a powerful symbol that she used to bolster her husband's position as lord of Leinster. Shortly afterwards, war broke out in Leinster. In what was evidently a pointed attack on one of the 'jewels in the crown' of the Marshal lordship, fitz Henry's first act of war was to burn his new port town at New Ross. After the burning of Ross, fitz Henry went on to besiege a vulnerable Kilkenny Castle. Amid the chaos a heavily pregnant Isabel lowered a messenger from the battlements of the castle to inform her followers in Ulster of her plight; they quickly came to her rescue and routed fitz Henry. Fitz Henry's defeat by a woman was the ultimate humiliation and to rub salt in the wounds Isabel forced his submission to her. Isabel's decisive actions restored her family's grip on Leinster and John had no choice but to permit the Marshal's return to Ireland. The Marshal could now rule Leinster with something approaching full independence, and thus began an enormous campaign of administrative, social and economic transformation throughout the Marshal lordship of Leinster.

A host of military castles were built or rebuilt to underpin the security of the lordship, for example at Ferns (pl. 4), Carlow (pl. 5), Kilkenny (pl. 11), Old Ross and Callan. Likewise, the lordship's spiritual conquest was underpinned by enormous investment in the church: cathedrals, parish churches and monasteries were patronised and supported by the Marshals and their followers. Their patronage was an influential force in the spread of the 'Early Irish Gothic' architectural style throughout Leinster. Examples include the Augustinian priories of St John's and Kells, Kilkenny, the Cistercian houses of Tintern Abbey (pl. 2) and Duiske Abbey (pl. 1), Graiguenamanagh, the cathedrals at Kildare (pl. 3) and St Canice's in Kilkenny (pls 15–18) and new large parish churches at New Ross (pl. 27) and Kilkenny (pl. 22).

But it is in the realm of urban development that the Marshal excelled. A grand plan was set in train to develop, structure and control a new urban network for the benefit of his lordship. Old towns like Kildare, Wexford and Kilkenny were dramatically expanded and new 'plantation' towns such as Thomastown, Inistioge (pl. 24), Naas and Carlow were established at key strategic locations. As capital of the Marshal 'empire', Kilkenny quickly expanded between its cathedral and castle to become the largest inland town in Ireland and in every way a European medieval city, which the Marshal also provided with its own outport at New Ross. New Ross was critical to the success of the lordship because it was the port for a network of markets, boroughs and towns that were strung out along the river catchments of the Nore, Barrow and Suir in the south-east of Ireland. New Ross was also perfectly sited because it allowed the Marshal to bypass King John's port at Waterford and the town can be seen as a striking symbol of the autonomy of the Marshal's Irish empire from royal power. Here we also see the hand of Isabel at work; New Ross was situated on Isabel's ancestral lands, her grandfather's former kingdom, and it is hard to escape the conclusion that she was instrumental behind the scenes.

William and Isabel's seven-year 'exile' in Leinster came to an end in 1213 when the Marshal was brought out of semi-retirement by King John to quell the first barons' war, which he succeeded in doing by being one of the chief architects of Magna Carta. On the death of John in 1216, William Marshal was chosen by his peers in England as protector for the nine-year-old Henry III. On 14 May 1219, the Marshal died at Caversham and he was buried as a Knight Templar in the Temple Church, London (fig. 1.1, pl. 28). At the time the archbishop of Canterbury, Stephen Langton, famously eulogised him as the 'greatest knight that ever lived'. Isabel followed him ten months later after another, final, battle to retain her lands in Leinster. She was buried next to her mother, the great Aoife Mac Murchada, in Tintern Abbey, Wales.

This book has been a long time in gestation and its journey to print has been a rocky road. It is a poignant fact that three people who were centrally involved in the conference and in this book have since died. Emma Devine (d. 2012), the late wife of this writer, archaeologist and museum curator, was the chief organiser of the conference and her drive and energy made it a memorable and enjoyable experience for all who contributed and attended. Billy Colfer (d. 2013) presented a stimulating paper on William Marshal and Wexford at the conference and his essay in this volume is a reminder of the great contribution he made, and the great loss he is, to the study of medieval Ireland. John Bradley (d. 2014), who co-edited this volume and was writing an essay on the Marshal's charter to Kilkenny until he became ill, made a singular contribution to the study of Irish history and archaeology. This book is dedicated to each of their memories.

I thank the contributors for the considerable patience and tolerance they have shown in the protracted process of publishing this book. Each author is also thanked for their stimulating contributions to the conference and for the considerable amount of work they undertook in researching and writing their respective essays. Alexis Bernstorff also presented a paper at the conference. Special mention must go to Ben Murtagh who without hesitation took on the daunting task of finishing John Bradley's essay on the Marshal charter to Kilkenny. I also wish to thank Martin Fanning and the staff of Four Courts Press for their patience, and in particular my co-editor Michael Potterton.

Without the funding provided by Kilkenny Borough Council the 2008 conference would not have been possible and the assistance of Brian Tyrell (Senior Executive Officer, Kilkenny County Council), Cllr Malcolm Noonan, and former Cllrs Pat Crotty and Paul Cuddihy in this regard is gratefully acknowledged. Kilkenny County Council have also contributed generously towards the costs of publishing this book. Those who assisted at the conference are also gratefully acknowledged: Sinéad Marshal, Grace Fegan, Philip Kenny, John Healy, Mary Ó Drisceoil and Ian Hamilton, as well as Ann Teehan and Frank Kavanagh of the Office of Public Works, Kilkenny Castle. I also thank everyone who attended the conference.

The following individuals and institutions are thanked for permission to reproduce illustrations: Airshots; Kilkenny County Council; the National Library of Ireland; the National Monuments Service; the National Museum of Ireland; Niall Colfer; Ordnance Survey Ireland; the Photographic Section, Department of Arts, Heritage and the Gaeltacht; the Royal Irish Academy; the Royal Society of

Antiquaries of Ireland; TRIARC, Trinity Irish Art Research Centre, Trinity College Dublin; and the Old Ross Research Project. Neil Jackman and Abarta Heritage (www.abartaheritage.ie) deserve particular mention for their colour plates. Individual illustration credits appear in the image captions below.

Adrian Empey wishes to thank Philip Kenny (Kilkenny Archaeology) for producing the maps that accompany his essay. He also acknowledges the generous permission received from the late Billy Colfer to utilise his maps showing the development of the Marshal's manors in Co. Wexford (see Colfer, *Arrogant trespass*, pp 48, 73) (fig. 2.2). He thanks Paul MacCotter for permission to use his map of the cantreds of medieval Ireland to construct maps both of the lordship of Leinster (fig. 2.1) and of the medieval county of Kildare (see MacCotter, *Medieval Ireland*, pp 257ff) (fig. 2.5). He notes that fig. 2.3 is based on a map he published in Nolan and Whelan (eds), *Kilkenny: history and society*, p. 85, while fig. 2.4 is based on another of his maps that appeared in McGrath and Nolan, *Carlow: history and society*, p. 162.

Miriam Clyne's essay is based on work undertaken for the National Monuments Service, which resulted in the publication of the monograph *Kells Priory, Co. Kilkenny: archaeological excavations by T. Fanning and M. Clyne*. She expresses her sincere thanks to all those who participated in the project, especially to Conleth Manning and Ann Lynch, senior archaeologists in the National Monuments Service. She is grateful to Daniel Tietzsch-Tyler for contributing a revised reconstruction drawing of Kells Priory to this volume.

Daniel Tietzsch-Tyler would like to thank Jane Fenlon for including him in the recent guidebook project for Kilkenny Castle, and the late John Bradley for discussing the archaeology of the castle and the possible extended layout of the castle. He also thanks Conleth Manning for comments on the initial version of the reconstruction published in the castle guidebook, which led to some changes being made. Finally, he wishes to thanks Cóilín Ó Drisceoil and the late Emma Devine, who convened a stimulating conference on William Marshal in Kilkenny Castle, where the genesis of his essays first appeared in poster format.

John Bradley wished to thank David Crouch for his prompt and insightful responses to his various queries.

Cóilín Ó Drisceoil acknowledges the assistance with producing the figures that accompany his essay from Barry Fitzgibbon and Philip Kenny of Kilkenny Archaeology. Linda Doran is thanked for providing a copy of her study of archaeological investigations in New Ross, as is Catherine McLoughlin for allowing access to her report on excavations at the Bullawn, New Ross. Sinéad Marshal and Tori McMorran of the Old Ross Research Project are thanked for allowing publication of a LiDAR image of Old Ross motte and bailey. Finally, my thanks to my wife Elizabeth and children Béa and Maia for allowing me the time to complete this book.

KILKENNY
11 October, feast day of St Canice

William Marshal in exile

DAVID CROUCH

William Marshal, the fourth son of John Marshal of Hamstead, Berkshire, and grandson of Gilbert, court marshal of King Henry I of England, is fast becoming one of the more famous inhabitants of the Middle Ages. He currently has six modern academic studies devoted to him. Not only that but a writer called Elizabeth Chadwick has written several best-selling historical novels based on his life.[1] The Marshal's celebrity can be accounted for by the fact that he is one of the very few medieval laymen who was the subject of a genuine extended biography in his own day. We know very little of its author, other than that he was a professional poet called John and that he came from the Loire Valley. But we do know that he worked at the commission of William Marshal's eldest son and namesake, that he began his work in 1224 – five years after the Marshal died – and completed his task late in the summer of 1226. The result was over 19,000 lines of French verse telling the story of the elder William Marshal from his birth around 1146 to his death in May 1219.[2] It is one of the tiny number of medieval life stories that we can reconstruct, and that in itself is why William Marshal is so very important to students of the Middle Ages. He is the nearest we can get the aspirations, ideas and confusions of a medieval man.

Of course, William Marshal was not 'typical' as a medieval person. It was no ordinary man who could call forth the effort and expense to commission an extensive biography, as he did. He died after acting for nearly two years as regent for the boy-king Henry III of England, and after successfully repulsing a French

1 T.J. Jarman, *William Marshal, first earl of Pembroke and regent of England* (Oxford, 1930); Sidney Painter, *William Marshal: knight-errant, baron and regent of England* (Baltimore, 1933); Jessie Crossland, William the Marshal: the last great feudal baron (London, 1962); Georges Duby, *Guillaume le Maréchal, ou le meilleur chevalier du monde* (Paris, 1984), trans. Richard Howard as *William Marshal: flower of chivalry* (London, 1986); Thomas Asbridge, *The greatest knight* (London, 2015); David Crouch, *William Marshal* (3rd ed., Harlow, 2016). Elizabeth Chadwick's enjoyable historical romances are: *The greatest knight: the story of William Marshal* (London, 2006); *The scarlet lion* (London, 2007). 2 The edition used here is *History of William Marshal*, ed. Anthony J. Holden and David Crouch, trans. Stewart Gregory (3 vols, London, 2002–6), hereafter, *HWM*. There is still much of value in the earlier edition, *L'Histoire de Guillaume le Maréchal, comte de Striguil et de Pembroke, régent d'Angleterre de 1216 à 1219*, ed. Paul Meyer (3 vols, Paris, 1891–1901). For an analysis of authorship, genre and purposes of the *History*, see David Crouch, 'Writing a biography in the thirteenth century: the construction and composition of the "History of William Marshal"' in David Bates, Julia Crick and Sarah Hamilton (eds), *Writing medieval biography, 750–1250: essays in honour of*

invasion of England that had nearly succeeded in displacing the Plantagenet dynasty from the throne of England and combining England with Capetian France. Nor was that all. In his youth, and indeed up until his fortieth year, William Marshal was a renowned sportsman and team manager, a giant on the tournament circuit of northern France and the Rhineland in the 1170s and 1180s. For his level of talent there were stupendous rewards in the sport. His transfer fees, retainers and profits in ransoms were sufficient for him to begin the impressive rebuilding of his Welsh fortress of Chepstow in 1190.[3] Though with barely one landed estate to his name, the Marshal was already a wealthy man in 1186.

Therefore we have to approach the Marshal with care. Attempting to read the medieval character from William Marshal – as some have done – is a risky business. In a number of ways he can be seen to have been different from his peers. He was an abnormally accomplished man physically and a tactical genius in his chosen sport. He was a warrior by profession. It is true that most men of his class and day embraced warrior ideals, but others of his peers pursued more active careers as administrators, landowners or legal specialists. The Marshal was unusual in being so *decidedly* a captain and a knight. The Marshal was not a man of any intellectual accomplishments, as far as we can tell. His biographer gives us little evidence that the Marshal had ever been put to learn his letters and if he had been functionally literate it was probably only in vernacular French. In 1183 his clerk had to read to him letters he had received from correspondents at his former lord's court. Such a low level of literacy was, in fact, unusual among his class.[4] The ideal of a nobleman in the late twelfth century was that he should be a singer or musician of some sort, be literate in French and Latin, and be a raconteur and courtier, a poet if possible, a hunter, a sportsman and – naturally – a horseback warrior. But some of the Marshal's peer group went further in their intellectual aspirations. They collected and commissioned books, some even wrote them, and aspired – like Robert II of Leicester, Henry II's chief justiciar – to acquire knowledge of philosophy, theology, history and astronomy.[5] Earl Robert also liked to correspond with the leading minds of his day. He was not the sort of man with whom the Marshal would have had much in common. Apart from the fact that he sang quite well and told a good story, William Marshal only had the warrior skills. He did not apparently much enjoy hunting, judging by the lack of interest in his woodlands in both his charters and his biography. So he was by no means a typical product of the twelfth century. His career and life story do illustrate for us much about the reactions and aspiration

Professor Frank Barlow (Woodbridge, 2006), pp 221–35. 3 For the rebuilding programme at Chepstow *c.*1190, immediately after Marshal's acquisition of the honor of Striguil, see the dendrochronological dating of the timber of his new gatehouse: Richard Avent and Daniel Miles, 'The main gatehouse' in Rick Turner and Andy Johnson (eds), *Chepstow Castle: its history and buildings* (Logaston, 2006), pp 51–62. 4 For literacy and the twelfth-century aristocracy, see Martin Aurell, *Le chevalier lettré: savoir et conduite de l'aristocratie aux xiiè et xiiiè siècles* (Paris, 2006), pp 47–114; David Crouch, *The English aristocracy, 1070–1272: a social transformation* (New Haven, 2011), pp 249–50. For the letter incident, see *HWM*, i, lines 5898–918. 5 Paul Hayward, 'The earls of Leicester, Sygerius Lucanus and the death of

1.1 Purbeck effigy traditionally assigned to William Marshal in Temple Church, London (photograph: Cóilín Ó Drisceoil).

of his day, however, and among those aspirations is the motive for what brought him to Kilkenny in the thirteenth century, as I propose to explain.

It may seem an obvious point, but there was no career path for a man, let alone a woman, in the 1160s; there was no job market for William Marshal to launch himself into. His parents had done their best for him. In his puberty he was sent to Normandy to be trained as a knight in the household of his mother's kinsman, the lord of Tancarville. He received a first-class military training, but on his knighting at the age of twenty, the rest was up to him. He fought his first skirmish under his cousin's banner in 1166, and went to his first tournaments in 1167 in the Tancarville colours. But soon afterwards Tancarville downsized his retinue and young William was advised to find a new opening. Cast adrift, he was lucky to get a post in the household of his maternal uncle, Earl Patrick of Salisbury. But his career there was brief, for his uncle was assassinated in Poitou soon after the Marshal joined him. It was at this point that good fortune intervened, for he was retained by Queen Eleanor of England after his performance in his uncle's defence. After that he was a made man, for the rest of his career was to be in the various royal households of the Plantagenets, as household knight and captain.[6]

Seneca: some neglected evidence for the cultural agency of the Norman aristocracy', *Speculum*, 91 (2016), pp 328–55. **6** See Crouch, *William Marshal* (2016), pp 23–59.

Such a man as William Marshal was going to be driven his entire career by the fragility of his livelihood. He was remarkably career-minded. He learned as a boy that his natural charm, good looks and affability earned him friends, so he developed his social skills further. He became a studied and effective courtier. The ability to excel in the environment of the princely court was a skill that twelfth-century men and women consciously pursued; naturally so, as success at court was the best available means of personal advancement. Historians have only recently begun to come to terms with the idea that some medieval people were sophisticated enough to modify their behaviour self-consciously for their own ultimate benefit. We call the phenomenon 'courtliness', and however you regard him, William Marshal was a starred graduate in its school of advancement, as his biography makes clear enough.[7]

There are in fact twelfth-century publications which could easily have been given the subtitle: *How to succeed at court and make influential friends*. The earliest of them are called *Ensenhamens* ('instructions'), and derive from southern France. The first surviving one for men was written around 1170 by an Aquitainian aristocrat and enthusiastic tourneyer called Arnaut-Guilhem de Marsan, who can be proved to have been part of the circle of the young William Marshal and must have met him, at court or on the tournament field, at the outset of his career.[8] They belonged to a shared thought world and the ideal knight of Marsan's *ensenhamen* might very well have served as a template for the behaviour of the young Marshal. Marsan's intent was to define the ideal conduct of an aristocratic knight. In some ways this is trivial. For instance, his hair should be well-cut and clean; no stubble and the moustache kept short; his clothes if not expensive should at least be well-chosen; his cloak should match his tunic. He should not be over the top in his gestures, and should always be bright and alert, with no slack-jawed vacuity about him.

Others of Marsan's injunctions are more to do with lordship than appearance. No man should play the game of knighthood if he does not have the resources for it; otherwise he will just look pitiful, because it is expensive. Squires should be well-selected; they should be charming, educated and well-dressed, like high-level PAs recruited from a good business school. All the servants should be well-trained, especially those who keep the door of his hall, and a lord should make his home hospitable to all his guests. He should never make the mistake of removing himself from his guests into his private chambers. At the same time, however, he should be sure never to be too close to his inferiors, but sit apart in the best seat and never himself serve at table.

7 See principally C. Stephen Jaeger, *The origins of courtliness: civilizing trends and the formation of courtly ideals, 939–1210* (Philadelphia, 1985) and, for Britain, Crouch, *English aristocracy*, pp 204–7. 8 See, generally, Don A. Monson, *Les ensenhamens occitans: essai de définition et délimitation du genre* (Paris, 1981). For an edition and translation (by Gerard Gouiran) of Marsan's work into modern French, see Jacques de Cauna, *L'Ensenhamen ou code du parfait chevalier du troubadour gascon Arnaut Guilhem de Marsan* (Mounenh en Biarn, 2007), pp 64–95.

In the aristocratic sports, which were more relevant to William Marshal, our model knightly lord should be in control of himself. In playing dice he should bet handsomely and cheerfully, showing no emotion if he starts losing. He should have the best horses and equipment for war and the tournament. His armour and weapons should be carefully selected and his heraldry depicted on shield, banner, saddle and saddle trapper. Hardiness was the important thing to demonstrate. Cuts must be heavy and strong; when the lance breaks you should sweep out your sword and ride straight in whether you have one or two opponents. Whatever you do, do not get captured because that can be prohibitively expensive. And if our knight can be successful in all this, then he will attract and seduce the ladies.

The world of Marsan's *ensenhamen* is almost entirely secular, as indeed is the world of William Marshal's biography ... where the name of God is chiefly taken in vain. Though an educated man, Marsan has little to say about the spiritual or ethical dimension of being a knight. His little tract is a pragmatic exercise in making friends and influencing people in the same way a successful business man will write a handbook on how to succeed and make money, or in Marsan's case, succeed with women, for sex is for him the big payoff. That was not the case with the Marshal biography where the payoff is political success and cash, but then the young Marshal had to climb higher than Marsan, for he had to come from a lower circle of the aristocracy.

The Marshal did everything according to the book. He was modest and cheerful. He told jokes against himself. He was always loyal and true to his current lord. He presented a low profile to avoid the malice of those who would try to subvert and undermine him – his rivals at court. He knew that he had to acquire and amass resources, because in his earliest days as a knight when his horse was killed he was reduced to selling the only decent cloak he had. He did not want to look pitiful, and the tournament field was his salvation, for there he found fame, employment and rewards. He always fought hard and intelligently and was rarely captured for ransom. When he was wealthy he employed the best and brightest squires, offering liberal hospitality to his friends.

As a result, William Marshal – mostly – prospered at the royal courts of Plantagenet England. He could play the game well. There were hiccups when he got the balance wrong. In 1182, when he was tournament manager for the Young King Henry, the eldest son of Henry II of England, he came under a cloud because he had become too keen on his own profit in meetings, and had failed to attend to his principal duty of leading the knights who kept the king safe from capture and ransom on the field. His enemies delightedly attacked him in the area which was critical for a successful courtier – his reputation for steadfast loyalty. The Marshal had enough enemies to mount a whispering campaign against him and his royal master began snubbing him. Eventually, at the Christmas court of 1182 at Caen in Normandy, he was forced to leave the Young King's household, but made the most of it by taking a post in the Flemish tournament team, for a hiring fee of astonishing value. But with some adroit manipulation and patience, the Marshal found his way back into favour with the king in a few months, though the young man's death not long afterwards soured the Marshal's victory over his enemies.[9]

William Marshal got on best with intelligent lords who themselves knew how to play the courtly game. He seemed to get on best in his career with three particular royals: Queen Eleanor of Aquitaine, Henry II and Richard the Lionheart, though it has to be said that in the year 1190, when the Marshal himself looked back on his career up to that date, it was his young lord, the late, glamorous and handsome Young King whom he singled out as the lord he had loved most. Which brings us to the lord he loved least, King John. John was neither self-controlled, reliable, trustworthy nor measured. No revisionism will ever make John into an admirable ruler; in fact the current trend in historiography is to confirm his place as one of the worst rulers Britain ever had, perhaps particularly because he had undoubted gifts, which he squandered.[10] He was personally objectionable – yet in a bizarre twist – he had a concern to be seen as humanitarian, righteous and ethical in his rule as king. But this was not how contemporaries saw him. For one French writer, who was in England during the last year of John's reign, the king was dishonest, lecherous, envious and a spendthrift:

> He set his barons against each other whenever he could. He was delighted when he saw them at each other's throats. He hated all *preudommes* through envy; he was most unhappy when he saw a good deed done for anyone. He was brimming with bad qualities: he was always spending too much; he was much given to gluttony and feasting whenever he might.[11]

William Marshal lived to regret his powerful advocacy of John's candidature for the throne on King Richard's unexpected death in April 1199, though it took a while for the magnitude of his error to sink in. In fact William Marshal – with an eye to the future – can be detected to have been cosying up to John as early as 1190. Indeed William's elder brother, John Marshal II of Hamstead, was John's seneschal; dying in the defence of John's castle of Marlborough against King Richard in 1194.[12] Within five years of John's coronation, King Philip of France had conquered Normandy and would go on to seize the Plantagenet dynasty's heartland in the Loire Valley. King John retreated to England early in December 1203, and this is when the Marshal's problems began. He had done well out of John's rule so far. He had been created earl of Pembroke and confirmed in his wife's inheritance. Isabel, daughter of Earl Richard of Striguil, brought with her several claims. The first was to the earldom of Pembroke, which had belonged to

9 Crouch, *William Marshal* (2016), pp 49–59. **10** For two recent academic studies on the king and his reign, associated with the centenary of Magna Carta, see Stephen Church, *King John and the road to Magna Carta* (London, 2015); Marc Morris, *King John: treachery, tyranny and the road to Magna Carta* (London, 2015). **11** *Histoire des ducs de Normandie et des rois d'Angleterre*, ed. Francisque Michel (Paris, 1840), p. 105. **12** For William Marshal's support for John before 1199, see Crouch, *William Marshal* (2016), pp 88–96.

her grandfather and had been suppressed in 1153. King John revived it for William Marshal in 1199 at his coronation. There were two other claims which were to cause him grief and were ultimately to blame for his exile from the court, centre of his emotional and political life. The first was Leinster, conquered by Anglo-Norman adventurers led by Isabel's father. The problem with Leinster was that it had been retained in royal hands since 1176, under the distant overlordship of John as lord of Ireland. John had been reluctant to give it up on the Marshal's marriage to Isabel, and William had not been able to exert much control there. It was a continuing source of tension between the Marshal and the king, and a worry for the Marshal's reputation as a lord of men.

The third inheritance the Marshal got with his wife was the complex of estates her father had acquired from his Clare and Giffard ancestry. This was in fact to be the cause of the Marshal's downfall, because it included substantial estates in Normandy, and in 1204 the duchy would submit to its new lord, King Philip II of France. The Marshal was among many great barons whose estates spanned the English Channel. With England and Normandy under two different rulers, they had to choose which king to follow. If they chose England, then their Norman lands were forfeit. Some barons were willing to take the hit, and King John was willing to compensate some of them in England for their losses. But William Marshal was not happy to do that. Most of his active career had been on the Continent. He clearly loved France. So when in April 1204 the Marshal was sent as part of an embassy to negotiate with King Philip about terms for a ceasefire, he took the opportunity to do some negotiating on his own part.

It is possible to work out how this disaster unrolled, and to see that the Marshal really asked for it. It is clear that John was willing to compensate the Marshal for his Norman losses by grants at Cilgerran and Castle Goodrich in the Welsh marches, which were pushed his way in the spring and summer of 1204. Nonetheless, once in Normandy the Marshal negotiated a private truce with King Philip, surrendering one of his Norman castles in return for a year's truce, at the end of which, if John had failed to recover Normandy, he undertook to do homage to the king of France for his Norman lands. The agreement was written down and sealed, and indeed still survives in the French archives. It committed the Marshal to something which was not unprecedented in medieval political arrangements – simultaneous homage to two lords – but which in the circumstances of 1204 to an oversensitive and suspicious king could well look like treachery. John was just such a king. So when the Marshal returned to England he had an irate John to deal with. The Marshal simply tried to look innocent and claimed it was done with the king's leave. This John denied and threatened the Marshal with a trial for treason, but the quarrel died down for the time being. John had too much else to worry about in 1204 and probably hoped the Marshal's Welsh gains might change his mind.

However in June 1205, by which time the homage had become due and been given, the quarrel reopened with a vengeance. The king apparently had grumbled but allowed the homage to be made to Philip, and so the Marshal became Philip's man for his lands in France. When John assembled an army to attack the French in Poitou subsequently, the Marshal refused to serve in it against his liege lord in France. Had he done so his Norman lands would have been forfeit. But John had *not* given him permission to do exclusive homage to King Philip. It is possible that the Marshal had lied to him, and he certainly had misled him. In Portsmouth, awaiting boarding, King John lost it with his former ally. He launched accusations of conspiracy at the Marshal, calling on the surrounding barons to make a judgment against him. They preferred not to be involved, and the furious king demanded that his household knights take the matter in hand by a duel. But again, they were reluctant. The Marshal may now have been in his sixtieth year, but he was still fit and strong.

So in 1205, although he had weathered his open arguments with the king, the Marshal's star began to wane. The king demanded and got his eldest son, a boy of fifteen, as hostage for his behaviour, and the flow of favours towards him dried up. He lost control of the office of sheriff of Sussex, which had been held by his family since 1190. He hung on at court for six months or so, but after John left on campaign for France in 1206, William Marshal was not summoned back. His exile from court had begun.[13]

The Marshal's biography is evasive about why he should have decided to cross to Ireland in February 1207, and one wonders why. It says that, deprived of the court, the Marshal travelled his estates in England and Wales and then sought leave to visit 'his fine and extensive holdings' in Ireland, where he had yet to visit because the king had refused him leave to go, but now John granted it, albeit unwillingly. Now this is odd in several ways. The oddest thing is that the Marshal had in fact already been to Ireland. As I have proved elsewhere, he was in Ireland between September and December 1200, when he had taken homage of his men, begun the foundation of two abbeys and the borough of New Ross, and met the Augustinian canon, Hugh le Rous, the future bishop of Ossory, who became closely engaged in the government of the liberty. Not only that but there are clear indications in a surviving letter between husband and wife that when he departed Ireland in 1200, he left his wife, Countess Isabel, behind him to oversee the rule of Leinster. She could have stayed there with their younger children till as late as 1203.[14] So the issue in 1207 was not a need to take the opportunity of a first visit to Leinster. The biographer is lying, so as to make John look more unreasonable than he really was; a frequent concern of his. But I think there was even more to it. The writer wants to make the Marshal an innocent victim not just of the king's capriciousness, but of the treachery of his men. Because he knew, as everyone knew, that within a year, the Marshal would be in a life-and-death struggle with his own vassals. Why not make the Marshal look good in 1207 and his vassals look bad by pretending that he had wandered innocently among them, like Caesar into a Senate House full of men with knives under their togas?

13 For this episode, see Crouch, *William Marshal* (2016), pp 109–16. 14 Crouch, *William Marshal* (2016), pp 102–5. For the exchange of letters between William and Isabel, see *The*

My feeling is that the Marshal was by no means the innocent in 1207 that his biographer pretends. He had been making attempts to get to grips with Leinster as early as 1190 when he sent a household knight by the name of Reginald (or William) de Quetteville in a failed attempt to take more effective possession of his wife's inheritance. But when he himself arrived there on the wings of a storm in the autumn of 1200 he appears to have somehow set in motion the events that would lead to catastrophe in 1207. Nor did he lose touch thereafter with Ireland. In the winter of 1203–4 we find him in conference with the bishop of Ossory at his castle of Hamstead in Berkshire, and in 1204 the Marshal despatched his nephew and closest councillor, John Marshal of Hockering, to Leinster, probably to add weight to the Marshal administration there after the return of Countess Isabel to his side. A surviving instrument of September 1205 finds John Marshal busy about his uncle's business in the rule of Leinster.[15]

If the Marshal needed to go to Ireland in 1207 it was for several reasons. The most alarming is that King John had begun to reveal the worrying depth of his ambitions for Ireland. One of Marshal's closest allies at court was William de Braose, a great nobleman and leading baron of the Welsh March. Just like Marshal, Braose had been a major supporter of John's accession and had done very well out of it. The king had made him a grant in 1203 of the lordship of Limerick and Munster, at a considerable price. But Braose had paid very little of the debt before 1206, because he was high in the king's favour. The favour dried up that year as the king began to develop a new royal policy for Ireland, which was to roll back the liberties of the great Irish marcher lordships, beginning with the Braose lordship of Thomond and Limerick. Gratitude was not one of John's virtues. His proxy in this confrontation was to be the Anglo-Welsh baron, Meiler fitz Henry, who would seem at first sight to have been an unlikely convert to the king's cause. Meiler was of very royal, if illegitimate, descent, a second cousin both of King John and of the Welsh prince of Deheubarth, Rhys ap Gruffudd. His Christian name was, in fact, a Welsh one. As a young man he had been prominent in the conquest of Leinster, and he had reaped the benefits in reputation and lands, gaining extensive lordships in Leinster and Meath. In the long period of royal custody of Leinster he seems to have established an ascendancy over the Anglo-Irish baronage, one which is reflected both in the writings of his cousin, Gerald of Wales, and in the historical epic, the *Geste* of the English in Ireland. Most importantly, he gained the favour and confidence of his cousin John, lord of Ireland. And on John's succession as king in 1199, it was Meiler whom he chose to be justiciar of Ireland, and found him in the end to be a rather more aggressive agent of change than he was expecting.[16]

acts and letters of the Marshal family, marshals of England and earls of Pembroke, 1145–1248, ed. David Crouch (London, 2015), no. 54. **15** For the Hamstead meeting, see *Acts and letters*, no. 53; for the seneschalcy of John Marshal in Leinster, see *RAST*, pp 337–8. **16** For Meiler and King John and their respective ambitions, see Marie Therese Flanagan, 'Henry II and the kingdom of Uí Fáeláin' in John Bradley (ed.), *Settlement and society in medieval Ireland*

William Marshal would have been all too aware of the problem represented by Meiler after his visit to Ireland in 1200, for the justiciar was nothing if not personally ambitious. There is some reason to believe that the two loathed each other. To Meiler, the Marshal would have been an intruder into the community of the March of Dublin, a courtier and toy soldier of but modest lineage. To the Marshal, Meiler would have been a troublesome vassal, difficult to deal with because of his warrior prestige, royal connections, mixed allegiances and independent power as justiciar of Ireland. Meiler was also ambitious and willing to use his influence with King John to further his position. When, in 1204, the Marshal sent his nephew to act as his seneschal in Leinster, it may have been because Meiler took the lordship of Uí Failge into his hands in January of that year on the death of his cousin Gerald fitz Maurice, despite its being part of Leinster. Meiler was still holding it in 1207, along with the imposing castle of Dunamase in Loígis (Laois), which he had enjoyed since 1181, though his title to it was contestable by the lord of Leinster.

In February 1207 with the court unfriendly and the king turning against his friends, the Marshal seems to have decided to go to Ireland to confront Meiler and solve the continuing problem he represented. We can suggest this because the first evidence of his activity is in a letter addressed to King John in May 1207 by a body calling itself 'the barons of Leinster and Meath' petitioning him to restore Uí Failge to its lord. It seemed that this body had confronted Meiler personally with its demand and backed it up with the letter to the king. The Marshal and his allies in the Lacy family are noticeably absent from the letter, but William was lord of Leinster and Walter de Lacy was lord of Meath, so these barons were their tenants. Also, if Uí Failge was to be restored, it was to William Marshal.[17]

The king was enraged by the letter as we know from the surviving reply that he dictated. He absolutely refused to countermand something the justiciar had done in answer to his writ, and he followed up this with a mandate recalling William Marshal to the royal court in England. The Marshal was reluctant to go, but found he had no choice. The king issued orders to the leading Irish barons of Leinster and Meiler himself to come to England to receive a piece of his mind over the business. The Marshal biography backs up this interpretation of events. It vividly portrays the Marshal taking leave of the pregnant countess – his wife – at the castle of Kilkenny and confiding her to the protection of his military household and tenants. It implies he knew that once he was gone, the justiciar's men would launch an assault on his lands. There is therefore little doubt as to why the Marshal went to Ireland or what he did when he got there. He had

(Kilkenny, 1988), pp 229–38; Seán Duffy, 'John and Ireland' in S.D. Church (ed.), *King John: new interpretations* (Woodbridge, 1999), pp 238–42; and, most revealingly, Colin Veach, 'King John and royal control in Ireland', *English Historical Review*, 129 (2014), pp 1051–78. **17** For the letter, see *Rotuli Litterarum Patentium in turri Londonensi asservati*, ed. Thomas Duffus Hardy (London, 1835), p. 72.

declared war on his rival, the usurping Meiler fitz Henry. But to do so also put him at odds with the king, who was inciting Meiler's actions.

William Marshal was punished for his presumption. The king used the court against him. His return to the royal court at the palace of Woodstock in October 1207 was not what he might have wanted. He had come with a large body of his Leinster tenants and as soon as they reached the court the king ruthlessly humiliated the Marshal by securing their help and assistance by means of bribes of lands and privileges. Even the Marshal's nephew, John, went over to the king, leaving his uncle utterly alone and unsupported. The Marshal's biographer says nothing of this: he dare not because those men were still alive and powerful when he was writing. What he does tell us about is the valiant defence of Kilkenny and Leinster from Meiler's forces by the men the Marshal left behind.[18] To compound the Marshal's woes the king allowed Meiler to return to Ireland in January 1208 while the Marshal had to kick his heels insulted, isolated and humiliated at court; 'nobody would talk to him', says the biography, 'for fear that, if the king found out he had, he would bear him ill-will'.[19] Meiler carried royal writs to the Marshal's seneschals to return to England, no doubt so he could have a free hand in his war. Despite this the Marshal bore himself as a very icon of courtly self-control, impressively so due to the lack of news from a storm-bound Ireland. When news did come, it was good for him. His wife had negotiated an alliance with the Lacy brothers, Walter and Hugh, whose great liberties of Meath and Ulster were also threatened by King John's new policy, and who were willing to help destroy the king's proxy, Meiler fitz Henry. The Marshal military household, reinforced by allied knights and infantry from Ulster, withstood a siege of Kilkenny, defeated Meiler and devastated his lands, capturing and imprisoning him and his knights. Meiler was forced to surrender Dunamase and his son to the countess to secure his release, and submit to the judgment of her court on his seizures of land. The victory went to the Marshal therefore, or rather to his wife, her allies and the accomplished warriors he had left with her. The king at this point chose to sacrifice Meiler to his enemies, since he had proven to be a broken reed and perhaps too mercenary to be a faithful royal servant, even in an age of self-interest. The Marshal was once again sent into exile from the court, and returned to Ireland where he was to remain till the crisis of the Barons' War in 1213.[20]

And these were the circumstances by which William Marshal came to Kilkenny in 1207 in his sixty-first year. My belief is that he learned a lot from the subsequent events. He came to Ireland as a man whose skills had been demonstrated in the arenas of combat which were – in different ways – the battlefield and the royal court. He may have proved himself adept in both, but

18 Crouch, *William Marshal* (2016), pp 122–8. **19** *HWM*, ii, lines 13798–800. **20** Crouch, *William Marshal* (2016), pp 129–32; Colin Veach, *Lordship in four realms: the Lacy family, 1166–1241* (Manchester, 2014), pp 130–6.

not till 1207 had he had to play the high game of politics. What he had learned by 1208 was that there were a range of other skills needed to occupy the position he had done since 1189. He had to rule men and defend his own lands, while simultaneously playing the game of high politics with a losing hand at court. His success in this at such a late stage of his career was the most impressive thing about it, more impressive than his defence of England against the French invasion in 1216. And it is clear to me that his conduct in the minority of the child king Henry III owed a very great deal to what he had learned in the desperate days in Leinster ten years earlier.

In the meantime, in exile from the court, William Marshal ruled Leinster, though no longer with a free hand. As part of the settlement of 1208 he was obliged to accept John's agenda and surrender the unrestricted marcher privilege he had previously enjoyed in Ireland.[21] He was no longer trusted by the king. That same year his second son, Richard, approaching the age of knighthood, was demanded of him as a further hostage. Also in 1208 the Marshal was again in the firing line for sheltering a desperate William de Braose, when he fled to Ireland after a failed insurrection in the Marches of Wales. In 1210, the Marshal was once more humiliated by being forced to appear in Pembrokeshire before the king, as he prepared his great army to invade Ireland and destroy the power of the Lacys, the Marshal's former allies and now mounting a defiant rearguard action to preserve their privileges.[22] Marshal could protect neither Braose nor the Lacys, but he did survive. And finally, in 1212, when King John was in trouble on all fronts, scared of assassination, invasion and rebellion, William Marshal was at last taken back into royal favour, and his exile from the court ended. He had not wasted his time in Leinster. Marshal was a builder: castles, churches and boroughs were endowed and regulated. This is another aspect of his abilities which he manifested late. One wonders indeed how much of this industry was owed to his wife – who comes very much to the fore in the biography in the Irish years and who, after his death, was briefly revealed as a political operator of determination and subtlety (see Kenny, below).[23]

That really is the final point which needs to be made here. Before 1207, William Marshal was a man of the court, whose fortunes depended on his relationship with his lord the king, and the skills and support he could bring. In Kilkenny he learned that what was equally important was his relationship with others: his tenants, councillors, advisers and indeed the wife from whom he derived his lands. If Marshal had an impact on Kilkenny's development, Kilkenny likewise had an impact on his and, ultimately, on Plantagenet England's.

21 *Acts and letters*, pp 479–81. **22** David Crouch, 'The complaint of King John against William de Briouze (*c.*September 1210)' in Janet Loengard (ed.), *The England of King John and Magna Carta* (Woodbridge, 2010), pp 168–79; Colin Veach, 'King John and royal control', pp 1051–78. **23** Crouch, *William Marshal* (2016), pp 143–9.

The evolution of the demesne in the lordship of Leinster: the fortunes of war or forward planning?

ADRIAN EMPEY

To say that the great Anglo-Norman lordships of Ireland were modelled according to some predetermined seigniorial prototype would be an overstatement. That, however, is not to say that they were the random product of a conquest that was made up as events unfolded. True, the process of the conquest itself was contingent on too many variables to admit a predetermined plan. Certain areas were more amenable to intensive settlement than others. Strategic alliances might result in concessions to Irish septs in border and highland zones, or stubborn resistance could yield more favourable terms where military solutions were not optional. Yet when all is said and done, it is clear that Anglo-Norman lords in Ireland, possessing territorially compact lordships, were in a position to impress their designs on them, much as their predecessors in Wales had done.[1] This stands in marked contrast to the Norman settlement in England, where Anglo-Saxon landholding systems and embedded customs were long established, and where successive confiscations in the reign of William the Conqueror produced widely dispersed forms of tenancy-in-chief. Robert of Mortain, for example, held almost eight hundred estates scattered across twenty shires.[2] In other words, except in border areas, Norman lordships in England resembled loose territorial federations of scattered estates, one of which served as an honorial centre. By contrast, the great lordships of Ireland like Leinster (fig. 2.1), Meath and Ulster consisted of territorial blocs within which everyone – with the single exception of the tenants of the crosslands – was ultimately subject to a single overlord.

The element of timing, moreover, conferred an additional measure of uniformity upon the diversity of Anglo-Norman lordships in Ireland. A.J. Otway-Ruthven noted that 'by the later twelfth century the new Anglo-Norman society [in Ireland] was already settling on lines that precluded that ready adoption of alien custom which had been so marked a feature of Norman conquest in both Wales and Italy.'[3] She also noted that in Ireland the knight's fee 'seems to have been a considerably more precise unit than it was in England'.[4]

1 See R.R. Davies, *Conquest, coexistence and change: Wales, 1063–1415* (Oxford, 1987), pp 95–100. 2 H.R. Loyn, *The Norman conquest* (London, 1967), p. 124. 3 A.J. Otway-Ruthven, *A history of medieval Ireland* (2nd ed., London, 1980), p. 102. 4 Ibid., p. 107. For a more detailed discussion of knight service in Ireland, see A.J. Otway-Ruthven, 'Knight service in

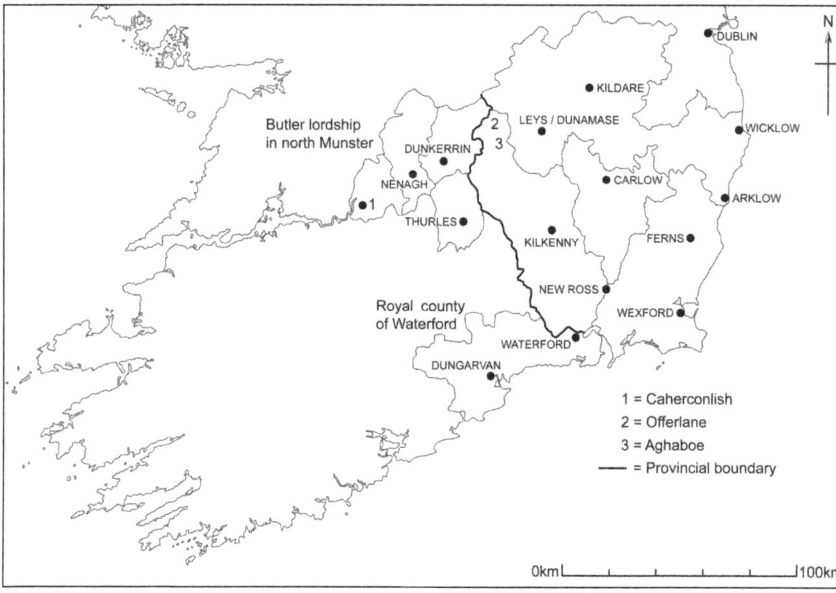

2.1 Lordship of Leinster, *c.*1225 (map: Philip Kenny, Kilkenny Archaeology). Map outline based on Paul MacCotter, *Medieval Ireland*, appendix 2, by kind permission.

The effect of legal, feudal and seigniorial developments in the course of the twelfth century profoundly affected the shape of the settlement in Ireland. The introduction of common law ensured that royal law was imposed not only on royal counties but on the great liberties as well, thereby producing a very different outcome from the conquest of south Wales at the end of the eleventh and in the early twelfth century. Just as the mechanisms of royal authority that developed in England were transposed ready-made to Ireland, so too the mechanisms of seigniorial authority were transmitted to the lordships all the way down the feudal food chain, whether they related to the terms of feudal tenure, town charters, manor courts or forms of seigniorial administration. Much the same can be said about the ecclesiastical institutions imported by the Anglo-Normans: the post-Gregorian uniformity exhibited by the parochial system associated with manors and towns in areas of Anglo-Norman settlement in Ireland is particularly striking.[5] While the main impact of these twelfth-century developments was to prevent the sort of institutional fusion that occurred in

Ireland' in Peter Crooks (ed.), *Government, war and society in medieval Ireland* (Dublin, 2008), pp 155–68. This essay was originally published in *JRSAI*, 89 (1959), pp 1–15. 5 See Adrian Empey, 'The layperson in the parish: the medieval inheritance, 1169–1536' in Raymond Gillespie and W.G. Neely (eds), *The laity and the Church of Ireland, 1000–2000: all sorts and conditions* (Dublin, 2002), pp 14–15; idem, 'The origins of the medieval parish revisited' in H.B. Clarke and J.R.S. Phillips (eds), *Ireland, England and the Continent in the Middle Ages and beyond* (Dublin, 2006), pp 29–50.

post-Hastings England, south Wales and Italy, they also provided ready-made and time-tested models of practice that could be immediately applied to the administrative and institutional needs of the new Irish lordships.

We get occasional glimpses of background policy making, even if no blueprint existed. We know, for example, from the charters of Kilkenny, Carlow,[6] Cooleagh and Callan that through the agency of one of his leading barons, Geoffrey fitz Robert, the Marshal decreed a rent of one shilling per burgage in his towns within his Irish lordship. In so doing, fitz Robert was merely applying a long-established customary charge, but it is significant that the charters allude to his activities in the first decade of the thirteenth century. Indeed, that he applied a charge sanctioned by custom in this particular instance serves to underline the fact that the Marshal and other Anglo-Norman lords in Ireland sought to exact the maximum return from the rights and prerogatives that belonged to them in right of lordship. This principle motivated kings no less than their tenants-in-chief: John, in his capacity as lord of Ireland, pressed his rights as overlord to the extreme limit by circumscribing the jurisdiction of the great liberties, exploiting his feudal prerogatives and ensuring that royal oversight of the Irish church was absolute, even within the liberties. Indeed, his confrontation with his barons occurred precisely along the fault-lines where their feudal prerogatives clashed. The comparison may be pressed further. In the course of the thirty-nine years that John was lord of Ireland (1177–1216), he paid only two visits to his lordship – in 1185 and 1210. From the perspective of this essay, John was himself a major landholder, having an extensive royal lordship, particularly in Munster and Leinster. This means that many of his plans for Ireland were devised at a distance and carried out by his agents on the ground. Such circumstances required regular consultation as well as a more careful consideration of key issues than might have been the case had John been on the spot. Exactly the same was true of the Marshal and especially of Theobald Walter, who spent very little time in Ireland, but whose lordships, as we shall see, bear the hallmarks of careful planning.

Certain considerations had to be addressed in the course of creating lordships of the kind that were established in Ireland around the end of the twelfth century. First and foremost, the lord had to determine how much territory he must retain in demesne, where he should locate his *caput* or *capita*, to which all services due from his tenants and vassals would be attached. Thus the careful location of castles was a priority not only for the future security of the lordship, but equally because the organisation and exploitation of demesne land was the single most important source of revenue. While the agriculturally advanced forms of manorial organisation that are apparent in many late thirteenth- and early fourteenth-century extents existed only in more rudimentary forms in the late twelfth century, the fact remains that if territorial provision had not been

6 Mac Niocaill, *Na buirgéisí*, ii, pp 138, 134; *Ormond deeds, 1350–1413*, nos 92, 441.

made in the course of the initial settlement for the development of demesne lands it could not have occurred after the lordship had been subinfeudated. What is striking about these later extents is the scale of the arable demesne, reflecting wider trends in estate management elsewhere in western Europe in the second half of the twelfth century.[7] The remarkable productivity of the Bigod demesnes in Carlow in the closing decades of the thirteenth century provides unambiguous evidence that the lessons of thirteenth-century manuals on agricultural management, such as those composed by Walter of Henley and Robert Grosseteste – whose *Rules* may have been composed for Margaret, widow of the earl of Lincoln, who married William Marshal, earl of Pembroke, in 1242 – had been absorbed and applied.[8] A second consideration was the disposition of the tenements – military, urban, free and servile – supporting corresponding populations of knights, burgesses, free tenants and betaghs. The distinction between these two fundamental components of lordship is perhaps best expressed by the terms *Grundherrschaft* and *Gutsherrschaft*. *Grundherrschaft* (overlordship) refers to seigniorial oversight exercised primarily over estates with no demesne component, having to do with the exaction of rents and services of various kinds. *Gutsherrschaft* (estate management), on the other hand, denotes estates over which the lord exercised direct administrative control, and from which he received revenue in the form of profits of cultivation.[9] The kind of lordships we encounter in Ireland are essentially a mixture of the two, with the overwhelming proportion of territory falling into the *Grundherrschaft* category. Thus, for example, in the Butler lordship of Eliogarty, only 8,268 out of 120,000 statute acres were reserved in demesne at the beginning of the fourteenth century.[10]

There was much more to this planning process than drawing lines on putative maps, not least because Anglo-Norman lords had to utilise pre-existing borders, frequently in the form of *tuatha* and townlands, as a basis for territorial division in the absence of any source of information like a Domesday survey of Ireland. Within the demesne itself, the lord had to apportion significant allotments of land in burgage tenure for his urban foundations. Indeed, the lordship of Leinster provides a most compelling illustration of just how soon after conquest

7 M.M. Postan, *The Cambridge economic history of Europe, 1: the agrarian life of the Middle Ages* (2nd ed., Cambridge, 1966), pp 291–339. 8 Margaret Murphy, 'The profits of lordship: Roger Bigod, earl of Norfolk, and the lordship of Carlow, 1270–1306' in Linda Doran and James Lyttleton (eds), *Lordship in medieval Ireland: image and reality* (Dublin, 2007), pp 75–98. See also Elizabeth Lamond, *Walter of Henley's* Husbandry *together with an anonymous* Husbandry, Seneshuaci *and Robert Grosseteste's* Rules (London, 1890), pp xlii–xliii. 9 Postan, *The Cambridge economic history*, p. 576. 10 See C.A. Empey, 'Medieval Thurles: origin and development' in William Corbett and William Nolan (eds), *Thurles, the cathedral town: essays in honour of Archbishop Thomas Morris* (Dublin, 1989), pp 31–9; C.A. Empey, 'The Anglo-Norman settlement in the cantred of Eliogarty' in John Bradley (ed.), *Settlement and society in medieval Ireland: studies presented to F.X. Martin OSA* (Kilkenny, 1988), pp 207–39.

this process was undertaken: even before Strongbow's death in 1176 we have firm evidence that burgage allotments existed in his manors of Kilkenny, Kildare, Ferns and Wicklow.[11] We cannot imagine that these fledgling urban foundations had progressed very far within a period of two or three years since their conquest and occupation: they can have been little more than military settlements, but plans were already in place and boundaries had been drawn up.[12] Such considerations aside, the lord then had to determine what services were due from various categories of tenants within the seigniorial manor: free tenants (farmers who held their lands for fixed terms in return for rent); customary tenants like cottiers; and servile tenants like betaghs. He had to determine the levels of jurisdiction to be exercised by borough courts and the manor court. He had, moreover, to decide how to dispose of the tithes of his tenants, whether they should be retained for the use of the parish priest, or whether they should be assigned to a monastic foundation. If he wanted to found a monastery to provide for the spiritual interests of his family, then he had to decide how much land or how many tithes he was prepared to invest in it, not to mention his particular choice of monastic order. He might also opt to retain the more important advowsons in his hand, less for financial advantage than as a means of exercising patronage. And in the case of the liberties, such as Leinster, the lord retained the considerable judicial profits of royal jurisdiction, which he had to protect from the encroachment both of royal courts and of the courts of his own tenants. Thus the successful exploitation of his potential seigniorial rights demanded skill, vigilance, strict administrative oversight and a determination to extract every possible advantage from them. Failure to lay claim to them was an open invitation for others to do so, resulting in their permanent alienation by virtue of established custom and precedent.

But what of the outworking of the *Grundherrschaft* element, which included the great territorial mass of the lordship – about fourteen fifteenths in the case of the lordship of Eliogarty, and doubtless similar proportions elsewhere? Lordship, in a fundamental sense, was less about the management of real estate

11 See Strongbow's charter to the Hospital of St John of Jerusalem *c.*1175 in the appendix.
12 Presumably a Hiberno-Norse town already existed at Wicklow, and there may have been pre-Anglo-Norman ecclesiastical settlements of a proto-urban description at the other sites. Whatever the nature of such communities, the term 'burgage' can only mean that Strongbow intended to reconstitute them along Anglo-Norman lines, thereby ensuring that those who held their tenements by burgage tenure were integrated into the structure of the lordship by rendering specific services. To what extent these new communities overlaid the previous ones is unclear. However, it is clear that the new town of Kilkenny did not include whatever community may have existed on the crosslands of St Canice's Church. Strongbow's charter talks about burgages in 'the town of Kilkenny' and 'the church which is opposite the church of St Kenni on the other side of the water on the east side'. The boundary was formed by the River Bregagh, which subsequently divided the Hightown of Kilkenny and the Irishtown of Kilkenny. The church seems to be St Mary's, which lies to the south-east, which clearly implies that parish and borough already coexisted before Strongbow died.

as conceived in modern proprietary terms, and more about exploiting varying levels of lordship over distinct classes of tenant that were expressed in terms of personal allegiance and tenure. In this sense every class within the territorial confines of the lordship was bound directly or indirectly to the lord by ties of allegiance. Where no such bond existed, as in the case of the tenants of the crosslands, there was no lordship. For this reason the lands of the church located within the liberties were eventually formed into distinct royal counties. Careful consideration had to be given not only to the immediate defensive requirements of a conquered territory, but also to its future security needs. More than that, the lord had to satisfy the land hunger of his household knights both by way of reward for their services in the course of the conquest, and because he needed a reserve of experienced men to administer the lordship as seneschals, sheriffs or constables. The creation of strategically placed fiefs was one way of satisfying these requirements, but long-term security considerations required a network of seigniorial castles as much to overawe his vassals as to protect exposed frontier zones. A striking example of frontier castles is provided by the construction of three castles by Henry II and John at Lismore, Ardfinnan and Tibberaghny, at points along the perimeter of the royal demesne.[13] In the case of the Leinster lordship, the retention of castles at Callan, Offerlane, Dunamase and Ferns seems to be a result of similar consideration. Agreements with Irish septs located within the lordship likewise had to be thought through. Such situations arose either as a result of alliances at the time of the conquest, or because it was logistically impossible to assimilate them in remoter areas. What forms of military service would be required of them? What kind of tenurial arrangements were to be fixed? How were disputes to be resolved where non-feudal tenures and two disparate legal systems came into conflict? The Butler-O'Kennedy agreements of 1336, 1356 and 1358, although they reflect shifting balances of power, were nevertheless almost certainly the consequence of repeated attempts by the earls of Ormond to recover and enforce arrangements of a kind that derived from the circumstances of the original conquest.[14] The endowment of monastic foundations likewise had to be determined as part of the original design of subinfeudation: Cistercian foundations in particular required a heavy commitment of land. Finally, jurisdictions had to be defined: who owed suit at the lord's court? In the case of the great liberties, who owed suit at the county court? And what legal competence was to be assigned to vassals' manorial jurisdictions and to corporate towns? Such issues lay at the heart of feudal and

13 The original medieval county of Waterford included the diocese of Lismore north of the Suir: see C.A. Empey, 'The settlement of the kingdom of Limerick' in J.F. Lydon (ed.), *England and Ireland in the later Middle Ages: essays in honour of Jocelyn Otway-Ruthven* (Naas, 1981), pp 1–5; idem, 'County Waterford, 1200–1300' in William Nolan and T.P. Power (eds), *Waterford: history and society* (Dublin, 1992), pp 131–3. 14 C.A. Empey, 'The Norman period: 1185–1500' in William Nolan and Thomas McGrath (eds), *Tipperary: history and society*

seigniorial lordship in terms of *Grundherrschaft*, and therefore could not be left to chance or circumstance, still less to an undefined future: once custom and precedent became established, it became virtually impossible to recover such prerogatives. It is for this reason that the liberty courts required holders of jurisdictions to show by what warrant they held them.[15]

The degree to which Anglo-Norman lords were unconstrained by whatever structures existed in their territories prior to conquest can be paralleled precisely by the freedom with which they reconfigured the church in terms of parishes, rural deaneries, the monastic orders and the designation of the tithes of their tenants. The overlay of manors with parishes and cantreds with rural deaneries has been well established by a number of studies.[16] Even more remarkable is the fact that it is possible to reconstruct with precision the borders of the lordship of William de Burgh on the basis of the tithes he granted his Augustinian priory in Athassel.[17]

I

Since there is no contemporary documentary evidence to show that Anglo-Norman lords designed their lordships according to carefully articulated guidelines, the best course of action is to attempt to reconstruct the original design on the basis of surviving thirteenth- or fourteenth-century extents. These may be taken to be reliable guides to the original subinfeudation because once the territories of the lordship were enfeoffed there was no possibility of going back to the drawing board: the rules of custom and inheritance ensured their permanence. Tenements might be forfeited, escheated or even exchanged, but they could not be reshaped. Besides, the survival of a number of charters of enfeoffment, as well as monastic grants, makes it possible to cross-check later extents in a sufficient number of instances as to warrant confidence in such a strategy by reducing or eliminating the element of speculation.

This being the case, a comparison of a selection of lordships should reveal something of their original design, despite the passage of time since the conquest. By comparing three lordships so reconstructed it should be possible

(Dublin, 1985), pp 86–9. **15** See, for example, the earl of Ormond's summons to the liberty court of Tipperary in 1432: 'We order you throughout your bailiwick, both in cities, boroughs and market towns as elsewhere within the said liberty, to have published and proclaimed that all those who by charter of the kings of England or in any other way claim any liberties within our liberty shall be there before the said seneschal to show what kinds of liberties they claim to have and by what warrant': *Ormond deeds, 1414–1509*, no. 102. **16** See, for example, A.J. Otway-Ruthven, 'Parochial development in the rural deanery of Screen', *JRSAI*, 94 (1971), pp 111–22. I have demonstrated the relationship between the rural deanery and the cantred in numerous articles, including those already cited in this essay. See also MacCotter, *Medieval Ire.*, passim. **17** Empey, 'Settlement of the kingdom of Limerick', pp 6–8.

to see how lords in differing circumstances attempted to frame their territories so as to exact the utmost benefit from their seigniorial prerogatives. It should therefore be possible by such a process of historical triangulation to see what factors may have been present in the Marshal's mind when he sought to impose some shape on his enormous lordship in Leinster. For our immediate purposes, we will first look at the Butler and royal lordships in Ireland, before returning to Leinster.

II

Thanks to the survival of a series of early fourteenth-century manorial extents for the cantredal *capita* of Nenagh, Caherconlish, Thurles and Dunkerrin[18] it is possible to reconstruct in some detail the process of subinfeudation that followed the grant of five-and-a-half cantreds in north Munster to Theobald Walter, ancestor of the earls of Ormond, and his uncle, Ranulf de Glanville, by John, lord of Ireland, on the occasion of his visit to Ireland in 1185.[19] More than that, we are fortunate to have extents for two of his three *capita* in the lordship of Leinster: Gowran and Tullow.[20] Only Arklow is lacking a surviving extent.[21]

The remote origins of these *capita* are traceable directly to John's grant to Theobald in 1185. Four of the five named cantreds were reconstituted after the conquest as seigniorial centres: the cantred of Elikaruel (Elyocarroll), subsequently framed by the manor of Dunkerrin; the cantred of Eliogarty by the manor of Thurles; the cantred of Ewermund (Ormond) by the manor of Nenagh; and the cantred of Woedeneoicadelan (Owney) by the manor of Caherconlish.[22] The cantreds can be reconstructed in outline on the basis of the rural deaneries, and because of the equation of manor and parish it is consequently possible to superimpose the information yielded by the fourteenth-century extent on this more primitive ecclesiastical framework. This procedure yields best results in areas that were not wholly or extensively engulfed by the Gaelic recovery in the later fourteenth century, resulting in the twelfth- and thirteenth-century place-names being largely effaced. In the context of the grant to Theobald Walter, the cantred of Eliogarty provides the best opportunity for reconstruction, as it did not suffer from the effects of the Gaelic recovery in the fourteenth century to the same extent as the more northerly cantreds of Ormond and Elyocarroll.

18 Nenagh, 1338: *CIPM*, viii, no. 184; Caherconlish, 1300: *RBO*, pp 154–8; Thurles, 1303: *RBO*, pp 69–83; Dunkerrin, 1305: *RBO*, pp 147–54. **19** See *Ormond deeds, 1350–1413*, no. 426. **20** Gowran, 1306: *RBO*, pp 34–41; Tullow, 1303: *RBO*, pp 1–9. **21** The extent attributed to Arklow in *RBO*, pp 10–12, is certainly an error. The lands in question appear to belong to the manor of Castledermot. **22** See Empey, 'Settlement of the kingdom of Limerick', p. 3.

We are, besides, extremely fortunate having Theobald's charter of the fief of Drom, a dependent manor of Thurles, issued probably between 1190 and 1195, which provides the nearest thing we can get to a twelfth-century blueprint for settlement in the cantred:

> Theobald Walter ... grants to Gilbert de Kentewell and his heirs for homage and service of the fee of five knights in Helyohokerdi [Eliogarty], to wit the tuath of Kenelfenelgille [Drom] ... towards the east as far as the said tuath extends towards the tuath where the castle of Durles [Thurles] is situated, and so extending to le Bernhely [Bernane-ely] as far as the tuath extends; and so from the land of Gilleshodian towards the north ... to the tuath of Kerketeni [Templemore] ... to have and to hold ... with tol and thaem and infangenthef, judgment of fire, water and battle ... by the service of one knight for all services, customs and exactions.[23]

What we have here is first-hand evidence of a scheme of settlement at a very early stage in the planning process. We can already discern the prime components of the finished product as revealed in the extent of Thurles in 1303.[24] The seigniorial unit is the cantred of Eliogarty. The unit of subinfeudation is the tuath that in the course of time will become the manorial and parochial unit, but which at this time is little more than the defined territory of the individual fief. At this point military considerations are uppermost in Theobald's mind. The seigniorial castle at Thurles is the hub of the fief-holding network in the cantred. Three fiefs are mentioned by name: Drom, Templemore and Bernane-ely.[25] The tuath of Thurles is reserved to Theobald in demesne, wherein he will determine the layout of his town and demesne lands. The feudal relationship established by the prescription of knight service will involve more than military obligations: Gilbert and his heirs will be obliged to do suit regularly at Theobald's court in Thurles, to render counsel when required, and to marry only with his consent. If he dies before his heir has achieved majority, his fief will be administered by Theobald's officers until he is 21 years of age, to be restored after rendering due homage and fealty. The competence of Gilbert's manorial court is also defined by this charter.

Gilbert was almost certainly one of Theobald's household knights who, having borne the brunt of fighting in the course of the conquest of north Munster, was rewarded with this grant in acknowledgment of his services. His fief was bounded in the east by a larger fief, Loughmoe, which Theobald had granted to his son-in-law, Thomas de Hereford.[26] In this way we are afforded a

23 *Ormond deeds, 1172–1350*, no. 34. 24 *RBO*, pp 69–83. 25 Bernane-ely seems to have been a sub-fief of Drom, not directly held of Thurles: see Empey, 'Anglo-Norman settlement in the cantred of Eliogarty', p. 215 and n. 24. 26 See Eric St-J. Brooks, *Knights' fees in Counties Wexford, Carlow and Kilkenny* (Dublin, 1950), p. 80.

brief glimpse of the nexus of feudal and family allegiances – a veritable 'band of brothers' – that underlay the unfolding of a plan of settlement.

We cannot say how long it took to colonise these seven *capita* with their dependent settlements. The experience of the early modern settlements in Ulster and elsewhere would suggest several decades. What is clear is that the format of settlement discernible in Theobald's grant in Eliogarty was reproduced schematically in all seven cantreds in Theobald's lifetime, even if developments on the ground may have been more protracted. It is tempting to speculate whether his uncle, Ranulf de Glanville, who accompanied Theobald to Ireland in 1185, may have been the *éminence grise* behind the plan. Ranulf, it should be remembered, was chief justiciar of England, 1180–9, and was succeeded after a short interval in 1193 by Theobald's brother, Hubert.[27] Administrative gifts were not lacking in the family circle.

Apart from the symmetry of the plan, its primary effect was to reserve all the services of military tenants in his extensive lordship – considerably in excess of the twenty-two required by John's charter – to Theobald and his successors.[28] This arrangement stands in marked contrast to the subinfeudation patterns in Leinster and Meath, where many fiefs were held intermediately of the tenants-in-chief of de Lacy or Strongbow: for example, in 1312 the fiefs of Aghaviller, Kilcurl and Derrynahinch owed military services to the lord of the manor of Knocktopher, Co. Kilkenny, rather than to the lord of the liberty of Kilkenny (in succession to Strongbow).[29] In Theobald's arrangement, such services would have been rendered directly to him. This meant not only that he commanded the services of all fiefs in his lordship, but also that he enjoyed the financial benefits of the scutage tax that would otherwise have been substantially dispersed among his chief tenants. It also meant that when a minority arose, it was Theobald, not a mesne lord, who reaped the profits of the tenement as long as the minority lasted. A long minority could yield significant profits.

III

The organisation of the royal demesne in Ireland provides an instructive illustration of how the exercise of lordship contributed to the design of the settlement. Henry II's intervention was occasioned by the death of Mac Murchada, which raised the future status of Leinster in an acute form. The

27 Hubert effectively ruled England during the king's long absences. He resigned the justiciarship in July 1198. 28 In the manor of Thurles alone, 25 fees were held by 17 military tenants, by the service of 6¼ knights: see Empey, 'Anglo-Norman settlement in the cantred of Eliogarty', p. 210. 29 *RBO*, pp 128–9. The original feoffee of Knocktopher seems to have been Griffin fitz William, brother of Raymond le Gros: see Brooks, *Knights' fees*, pp 249–52. It was held by the service of 1¾ knights of the lord of Leinster. He was therefore almost certainly enfeoffed by Strongbow.

homage and allegiance of Strongbow needed to be underwritten by a significant royal presence on the ground in Ireland. What followed Strongbow's submission was as much a demonstration of royal asset-stripping as it was of realpolitik. In retaining the Norse kingdoms of Dublin, Wexford (for a time) and Waterford, Henry provided not only for the strategic presence of royal garrisons, but also the means to support them through the territorial exploitation of their hinterlands in the form of the later counties of Dublin and Waterford. Henceforth, the king was an Irish magnate among others. The shiring of Munster, Desmond and Uriel under John's lordship vastly extended that seigniorial base.[30] This post-Henrician territorial extension was the direct consequence of John's refusal to grant palatine jurisdiction either to the lords of Munster or to the de Verdons in Uriel.[31] By excluding the crosslands in the regrants of Ulster (1205), Meath and Leinster (1208) John ensured that even those bishops whose mensal lands were situated within the liberties were unambiguously his tenants, subject to his courts and to the courts of none other. Royal revenues in Ireland were consequently derived from the exploitation of prerogatives of lordship, for example the profits of justice, the fee farms of royal cities, revenues from the lands of tenants-in-chief in the king's hand during minorities, and from episcopal lands *sede vacante*. To these may be added the profits of demesne manors in the vicinity of Dublin and the Honor of Dungarvan.

Compared to the lordship of Leinster, the royal demesnes were modest if far from insignificant. What distinguishes them from other seigniorial manors is the absence of the military component, of which the manor of Dungarvan is a striking example. Comprising six of the eight cantreds of the medieval county of Waterford (Owath, Athmethan, Dungarvan, Slefgo, Obride and Ohynws), it encompassed an area of about 200,000 statute acres.[32] The royal county of Waterford, with certain significant exceptions along its western, northern and eastern limits, was virtually a manor. The manorial demesne was composed of the castle, manor and town of Dungarvan, but in place of military tenants, who elsewhere occupied the most important dependent manors, we find only rent-paying free tenants. In other words, the strictly feudal tenant class was conspicuous by its absence. The military concerns that were uppermost in Theobald's mind when he was framing the settlement in the cantred of Eliogarty are nowhere visible in this context. The reason, of course, is not far to seek: the king was interested only in maximising his revenues. He had no need to provide for knight services on his own demesnes since this responsibility was charged to his tenants-in-chief. Large fiefs took up too much space and produced no rental

30 See Empey, 'Settlement of the kingdom of Limerick', passim. 31 Significantly, John's grant to Theobald Walter in 1185 specifically excluded 'the crosses and donations of bishoprics and abbeys and dignities which belong to the royal crown, which I have retained to myself': *Ormond deeds, 1350–1413*, no. 426. 32 See Empey, 'County Waterford, 1200–1300', passim.

return. This is not to say military considerations were completely ignored: we have already noted that Henry II and John made provision at an early stage in the conquest for the construction of castles at Lismore in the west, and at Ardfinnan and Tibberaghny in the north. Besides, the progress of the conquest in Munster essentially removed the external danger of hostile Irish attacks. It is therefore reasonable to conclude that in circumstances where military considerations were subordinate to other needs John was free to plan his lordship of Dungarvan with a view to yielding the maximum revenue. And so it proved: in 1259 Edward, lord of Ireland, granted Dungarvan to John fitz Thomas in return for a highly profitable annual rent of 500 marks. Like Theobald, John was clearly in a position to impose his designs on his extensive demesne in Co. Waterford, unconstrained by tenurial traditions and customs of the kind that would have rendered such a design impossible in Anglo-Saxon England in the previous century.

IV

By comparison with the lordships of Theobald and the king, discerning the original design of the demesnes of the lordship of Leinster presents a greater challenge for three reasons. First, Strongbow's premature death in 1176 meant that he had relatively little time at his disposal other than to pacify the Irish and reward his leading household knights. Second, the disruption created by Henry II's muscular intervention in the affairs of Leinster by cutting off reinforcements, seizing Strongbow's lands outside Ireland, by depriving him of Dublin and Waterford with their respective hinterlands, as well as withholding Wexford until 1173, must have disrupted the process of organising his immense lordship. The loss of Waterford, in particular, bore heavily on him because it was the gateway to the Leinster interior. It is not surprising that the Marshal eventually compensated for its loss by founding New Ross, as Wexford was too remote from the Leinster heartland to serve as a springboard for trade and settlement. It is true, of course, that the loss of these coastal cities must have given an additional urgency to the search for locations for alternative seigniorial capitals, which may well explain why Strongbow pressed ahead with the creation of boroughs at Kildare, Kilkenny, Wicklow and Ferns before he died in 1176.[33] Third, the effects of the long minority that extended from Strongbow's death until William Marshal finally wrested seisin from John around 1190 must be factored in.[34] This did not of course mean that the settlement of Leinster was put

33 See appendix and n. 12 above. 34 See David Crouch, *William Marshal: knighthood, war and chivalry, 1147–1219* (2nd ed., Harlow, 2002), p. 70. John held Leinster as a wardship during this period. He was eventually compelled by Richard to surrender his wardship as the result of an encounter with the king which Crouch places in the winter of 1190. See also G.H.

in cold storage for fifteen years. Quite the contrary, for we know that John used the interval to his own advantage by awarding fiefs in Leinster to his followers. It was during this period that Theobald Walter was granted the lordships of Arklow, Gowran and Tullow, which he was allowed to retain as a condition of John's restoring Leinster to the Marshal.[35] The consequence of this confused history is that it is difficult to determine in detail which demesne manors were created by Strongbow in his lifetime, by John during the minority of Isabel, or subsequently by the Marshal either directly in the course of successive visits to Ireland, or indirectly through his agents after 1190. The resulting picture is inevitably more conjectural than in the case of Theobald's lordship or the royal demesnes. The challenge of unravelling it so far as the evidence will allow must now be addressed.

The situation facing Strongbow after his submission to Henry II was complicated not only by the need to establish seigniorial *capita* in the interior following the crippling loss of the coastal cities, but also to sort out relations with the Mac Murchadas. Resolving a triangular relationship involving Diarmait as king of Leinster, Henry II as king of England, and Strongbow as lord of Leinster and heir to Diarmait was never going to be easy. Diarmait's death in 1171 and the subsequent revolt by his brother Murchad Mac Murchada added to the complications. From our perspective, the location of the earl's seigniorial centres depended to a considerable degree on how the territorial aspect of this relationship was resolved, not least in the case of Ferns, which was originally a Mac Murchada base. In the case of the other great lordships, the Anglo-Norman lords were not allies of the resident king, still less his heirs in feudal right of their wives. When, however, the dust settled after the uprisings that followed Diarmait's death, Murchadh's son Muircheartach was recognised by Strongbow as king of the Uí Chennselaig, while Domnall Mac Murchada Kavanagh, the other claimant to the title, was appointed seneschal of the Irish of Leinster.[36]

Given these constraints and lack of time, Strongbow had consequently little opportunity to organise his demesne lands before his death in 1176. Indeed, Giraldus Cambrensis tells us that before the intervention of Hugh de Lacy in Leinster in 1181–2 few castles had been built there in marked contrast to Meath.[37] It looks as if the Mac Murchadas gave Strongbow a free hand in disposing the territories of their long-standing enemies and more recent opponents, as long as such grants did not trespass on the Mac Murchada heartland. While we can reconstruct the territorial outline of a significant number of Strongbow's grants to his leading vassals, particularly in the medieval counties of Kildare, Wexford, Carlow and, to a lesser extent, Kilkenny,[38] it is not

Orpen, *Ireland under the Normans* (4 vols, Oxford, 1911), ii, pp 202–3. 35 Crouch, *William Marshal*, p. 70; Orpen, *Normans*, ii, p. 203. 36 For an excellent discussion of this relationship, see Emmett O'Byrne, *War, politics and the Irish of Leinster, 1156–1606* (Dublin, 2003), pp 12–15. 37 Giraldus, *Expugnatio*, p. 195. 38 Orpen, *Normans*, i, pp 367–95;

easy to determine in detail what lands he retained, or intended to retain, in demesne. In view of the dearth of contemporary references to his demesnes, it is tempting *faute de mieux* to assume too readily that the Marshal essentially built his demesne on the foundations laid by Strongbow.

However, the arrangements made in 1177 by Henry II at the Council of Oxford for the government of Leinster following Strongbow's death, as recounted by Wendover, should give us pause for reflection.[39] It is surely significant that Henry chose the coastal towns as the administrative hub of the lordship, not whatever seigniorial castles and demesnes that may have existed in the interior. Kilkenny is not mentioned in Wendover's account, which suggests that at this time it was not sufficiently important to serve as a platform for seigniorial government. (Carlow was not at this point part of the demesne.) Henry consequently divided the lordship into three custodial spheres. First, Hugh de Lacy was granted the city of Dublin, the 'land' [*terra*] of Offelan, the 'land' of Offaly, Kildare with its appurtenances, and Wicklow with its appurtenances: in effect, the territories that later comprised the medieval county of Kildare. The terminology is curious. The word *terra* is applied only to Offelan and Offaly, whereas other terms – such as 'services', 'tenements' or 'fiefs' – could have been employed. Kildare, on the other hand, was an ecclesiastical centre, while Wicklow was a Norse settlement. The implicit distinction is between land in the march, as yet only partially subdued, and more settled areas. If that is the case, then it is likely that Strongbow had already taken steps to establish Kildare as the ecclesiastical and seigniorial centre of northern Leinster.[40] Indeed, it is inconceivable that he would have contemplated granting an episcopal centre to one of his vassals.[41] Second, Henry granted to William fitz Audelin the custody

Brooks, *Knights' fees*, passim; Billy Colfer, *Arrogant trespass: Anglo-Norman Wexford, 1169–1400* (Enniscorthy, 2002), pp 35–52. MacCotter's *Medieval Ireland* is an essential reference work for identifying the territorial basis of Strongbow's grants. **39** *Chronica magistri Rogeri de Houedene*, ed. William Stubbs (4 vols, London, 1868–71), ii, pp 133–5. **40** A number of verses in *The deeds of the Normans in Ireland* indicate that Kildare was Strongbow's base, where he normally resided when not campaigning: see *Deeds of the Normans*, lines 2693–6, 2767–70, 2787–94. Giraldus Cambrensis says that de Lacy and the two royal representatives sent to Ireland in 1181 took Kildare and the adjoining territory away from Meiler fitz Henry and gave him in exchange the *provincia* of Leis (Giraldus, *Expugnatio*, p. 194). This does not mean that Kildare had been granted to Meiler as a fief, though he may well have been Strongbow's constable there. In the context of the strengthening of Leinster's defences by de Lacy, the substitution of Leis makes clear sense. **41** Two of the four seigniorial centres of the lordship were subsequently situated at episcopal centres: Kildare and Kilkenny. While this symbiosis raises some interesting questions, it is noteworthy that neither Leighlin nor Ferns became the seat of shire government. Leighlin may have been unsuitable because it was not located strategically on the Barrow. Unlike Kilkenny, the episcopal seat did not migrate to the seigniorial centre in Carlow. Ferns had none of the advantages presented by Wexford, which combined access to the sea with the command of the Slaney estuary. It may be noted in passing that dispossessing the Mac Murchadas of Ferns was absolutely necessary in order to nullify their influence over the see.

of Wexford, Arklow, Glascarrig, the *terra* of Gilbert de Boisrohard,[42] the *terra* of Fernegenel,[43] Ferns 'with its appurtenances', the whole *terra* of Hervey de Montmorency between Wexford and the estuary [*aquam*] of Waterford, the service of Raymond le Gros in Idrone, the service of Raymond le Gros in Forth (Co. Carlow), the service of Uthmorthi of Leighlin,[44] the tenement of Machtaloe,[45] and other places.[46] In so far as it is possible to map this custody, it seems that fitz Audelin was responsible for the part of Leinster that lay in the dioceses of Ferns and Leighlin, which could be accessed directly by sea or by the River Barrow. As fitz Audelin was the senior member of the triumvirate,[47] it is reasonable to conclude that his share of the lordship represents its seigniorial core around the time of Strongbow's death, with Wexford as its caput. Third, Robert le Poer, the king's marshal, was granted the city of Waterford, with 'all the land which is between Waterford and the river which is beyond Lismore', and 'the whole land of Ossory with its appurtenances'.[48] Robert was therefore charged with the custody of whatever settlements existed opposite Waterford or could be accessed by the River Nore. We do not hear of particular 'services' or cantreds within Ossory, as in the case of the de Lacy and fitz Audelin custodies, nor do we hear anything of Kilkenny itself. Wendover therefore leaves us with the impression that Strongbow had not advanced the settlement of Ossory very far in spite of having issued a number of speculative grants there.[49] Thus the

42 Strongbow granted Gilbert 'Offelimy by the sea', which included Kilmuckridge and probably the eastern part of the deanery of Shermale: see Colfer, *Arrogant trespass*, p. 44; MacCotter, *Medieval Ire.*, p. 253; Brooks, *Knights' fees*, pp 42–3. 43 Strongbow granted Fernegenel to Maurice de Prendergast to hold by the service of ten knights. For this extensive fee, see Colfer, *Arrogant trespass*, pp 43–4; MacCotter, *Medieval Ire.*, p. 251; Brooks, *Knights' fees*, pp 145–51. 44 Orpen considers that Uthmorthi is not a personal name but a reference to the cantred of Omurthy, on the border of Kildare and Carlow. However, as the deanery of Omurthy lies in the diocese of Kildare, this makes no sense: Orpen, *Normans*, ii, p. 386; see also MacCotter, *Medieval Ire.*, pp 177–8. 45 This seems to be a reference to the Mac Dalbeig territory of Ofelymth, later the cantred and manor of Tullow: see O'Byrne, *War, politics and the Irish of Leinster*, pp 29–30. 46 'Et Leis terram Gaufridi de Costentin, et totam terram Otueldi' (*Chronica magistri Rogeri de Houedene*, ii, p. 134). It is unclear from the incomplete Latin construction whether this means the land of Geoffrey de Costentin in Leis in the north-western corner of the diocese of Leighlin. If so, we have no corroborative evidence to suggest he held lands there. I cannot identify Otueldi. 47 He was Henry's *dapifer* or steward in Ireland: see Marie Therese Flanagan, *Irish society, Anglo-Norman settlers, Angevin kingship: interactions in Ireland in the late twelfth century* (Oxford, 1989), pp 298, 301–2. 48 'Totam terram quae est inter Waterforde et aquam quae est ultra Lismore' (*Chronica magistri Rogeri de Houedene*, ii, p. 134). Although Waterford was almost certainly not a county at this stage, the grant clearly intends the whole area of Waterford reserved in demesne, which was in effect the dioceses of Waterford and Lismore: see Empey, 'County Waterford, 1200–1300', pp 131–2. 49 The cantred of Iverk was granted by Strongbow to Milo fitz David sometime before 1176: see Brooks, *Knights' fees*, pp 264–5; the cantred of Knocktopher may have been granted to Griffin fitz William, brother of Raymond le Gros, about the time Raymond enfeoffed him of Fynnore and Kells in Forth (ibid., pp 626, 249–52); and, finally, Strongbow granted the 'half vill of Aghaboe' and all of the half cantred in which it was situated, as 'Ochelli Dermot [*sic*] had held it' to Adam de Hereford (Orpen, *Normans*, i, pp 394 5; Brooks, *Knights' fees*, p. 202).

impression of 'a work in progress' yielded by the carving up of Leinster into three custodial spheres at the Council of Oxford in 1177 accords well with Giraldus's affirmation that before the de Lacy campaigns in 1181–2 there were few castles in Leinster.[50]

V

Trying to trace the development of Leinster during the long custodial interval between the death of Strongbow in 1176 and the marriage of William Marshal to Isabel de Clare, heiress of Leinster, in 1189, presents formidable difficulties. Clearly things did not stand still. At a minimum the major fief-holders must have extended their control over their fiefs, by securing their borders, intensifying settlement and developing their demesnes. We know from Giraldus Cambrensis that Hugh de Lacy, together with John de Lacy, constable of Chester, and Richard de Pec, who had been dispatched to Ireland by Henry in 1181, built numerous castles throughout Leinster including one in Forth Onolan, one in Castledermot and one on the Barrow near Leighlin.[51] Hugh resumed this programme of incastellation on his return to Ireland later in the year by building castles at Timahoe, Norragh and Oboy.[52] All of these castles, however, were associated with fiefs held by the barons of Leinster, and not with Strongbow's demesnes as such. Their location suggests that their strategic purpose was to protect the colonial areas of the later medieval county of Carlow and Kildare from the inroads of the turbulent midland septs. It seems likely that Hugh was acting as much in his capacity as custodian of Leinster as in his capacity as Henry's *custos* in Ireland. This leaves us with the problem of ascertaining what was occurring on Strongbow's demesnes. In general, long wardships did not work for the benefit of a custody, because custodians saw them as an opportunity to pillage the demesnes in their keeping. The practice of farming out such wardships at exorbitant rates meant that the lessee had to recover his money by fair means or by foul, resulting in the indiscriminate asset-stripping of the demesne lands.[53] Such excesses were not new in the twelfth century, but John's demands, particularly for reliefs, were ruinous.[54] How John as lord of Ireland

50 Giraldus, *Expugnatio*, p. 195. 51 For a discussion of the location of this castle, see Colum Kenny, 'New Leighlin: an Anglo-Norman settlement' in Thomas McGrath and William Nolan (eds), *Carlow: history and society* (Dublin, 2008), pp 213–34. 52 Giraldus, *Expugnatio*, p. 195. 53 The abuse of wardships was one of the major grievances expressed by the barons in Magna Carta, coming almost at the head of the list. Chapter 4 of the charter insists on the exaction of 'reasonable revenues' and 'reasonable services', without destruction and waste of men and materials (*sine destructione et vasto hominum vel rerum*). Elaborate provisions are made in the chapter for the correction of such abuses. 54 William de Braose was ruined by the imposition of a fine of 5,000 marks for relief of the honor of Limerick: see J.E.A. Joliffe, *The constitutional history of medieval England from the English settlement to 1485* (4th ed., London,

dealt with the Leinster demesnes is unknown, but it is hard to believe that he or his agents were models of responsible wardship given the reputation he acquired later as king of England. What we know for certain is that he lost no opportunity to reward his followers with grants of fiefs in Leinster during the minority. According to the epic *Histoire de Guillaume le Maréchal*, commissioned by William Marshal's eldest son shortly after his father's death, John refused to give up the custody of Leinster in 1189, until compelled to do so by King Richard. His reluctance was ostensibly because he wished to secure the grants of land that he had made to his men while Leinster was in his custody. 'That cannot be', said the king, 'for what would then remain to him, seeing that you have given all to your people?'[55] Richard was, however, prepared to make an exception in the case of John's butler, Theobald Walter, who had been granted large territories in Leinster around Arklow, Tullow and Gowran, provided Theobald held them in chief of the Marshal and not of John. We do not know what others John had rewarded in this way, but it is likely that the dispute in 1207–8 between the Marshal and John's agent in Ireland, Meiler fitz Henry, was occasioned by the taking of Gerald fitz Maurice's lands in Offaly into the king's hand sometime early in 1207. What seems to have been at issue here was an implicit claim by John to have the wardship of Gerald's Leinster tenements, although in January 1204, shortly after his death, the justiciar had been commanded to deliver the custody of his lands and heir to William Marshal. It looks as if John, having initially waived his claim to prerogative wardships within Leinster, now had second thoughts on the matter.[56] The loss of such custodies would have constituted a serious setback for the Marshal, not only because many of his leading Leinster tenants held lands of the king outside Leinster, but also because the privilege of retaining such wardships was shared by the holders of high jurisdictions elsewhere in England and Wales. The fact that John conceded this claim in the re-issue of the charters of both Leinster and Meath in 1208 not only points to it as having been a recent bone of contention, but also suggests that it had become too firmly established by custom in the Irish liberties to be revocable.[57] Besides, the loss of such custodies by the Marshal carried the additional danger of the ultimate alienation of important tenements, as indeed occurred in the case of the service of William de Burgh's lordship of Castle Amory, which was originally due to Theobald Walter.[58] Thus the dispute over John's grants to his followers in Leinster during the minority, as well as the issue

1961), p. 256. 55 Quoted by Orpen, *Normans*, ii, p. 203. See Paul Meyer (ed.), *L'histoire de Guillaume le Mareschal* (3 vols, Paris, 1891–1901), lines 9581–618. For a more recent edition and translation, see *HWM*. 56 See Otway-Ruthven, *Medieval Ireland*, pp 77–8. Prerogative wardship was a claim by the crown to the custody of all the tenements of a tenant-in-chief, whether or not they were held directly of the king. 57 In marked contrast to the 1208 charters, no mention is made of prerogative wardships in the Ulster charter issued by John to Hugh de Lacy only three years previously: see James Mills and M.J. McEnery (eds), *Calendar of the Gormanston register* (Dublin, 1916), p. 189. 58 See Empey, 'The settlement of Limerick', p. 6.

of prerogative wardships, point to the conclusion that the integrity of Strongbow's lordship was under severe threat, perhaps even of actual dissolution, at the hands of John and his henchmen. For these reasons it is unlikely that much, if anything at all, was done in these years to extend the limits of Strongbow's demesnes. That task almost certainly fell to the Marshal, and to the Marshal alone.[59]

VI

In attempting to reconstruct the Leinster demesnes in the period following William Marshal's gaining possession of his Irish lordship, which can hardly have occurred earlier than 1190, we must be conscious of the thinness of the ice that we have to traverse. As we have seen, we know nothing about the demesnes during the long minority, not to mention their status in Strongbow's lifetime. More insidious is the temptation to assume that the details revealed in the partition of Leinster in 1247 provide a reliable guide to the disposition of the demesnes half a century earlier. Territorial descent over more than half a century is not a simple matter of tracing a direct lineage, notwithstanding my earlier insistence about the necessity of the lord having to make provision for his demesnes at the outset. The 'x' factor in such an equation includes forfeitures, escheats, alienations, purchases and territorial exchanges. A good example of such an exchange occurred sometime in the episcopate of Hugh de Rous, bishop of Ossory (1202–18). Hugh granted to William Marshal 'his vill of Achebo [Aghaboe], together with all appurtenances and all claims to his lands … in the cantred of Achebo', to hold in fee of the bishop. In exchange William agreed to render annually two wax candles to the cathedral on the feast of St Canice, besides sixteen ploughlands in several locations. William also exchanged the patronage of the churches of St Mary, Kilkenny, and St Patrick's (Donaghmore), for the patronage of St Canice's, Aghaboe (pl. 23), together with its dependent churches.[60] Similarly Carlow, which was to become a pivotal defensive and administrative hub of the Marshal lordship of Leinster, must have been acquired by purchase, exchange or even forfeiture. It was originally part of the Clahull lordship of Obargy. Sometime before the death of Archishop Cumin in 1198, John de Clahull requested the archbishop to institute Turstin to a moiety of the church of St Comgall of Catherloc, among other churches in Obargy.[61] While this explains why Carlow is not mentioned in the Council of Oxford, we do not

59 In this respect, Orpen seems over-optimistic in crediting Strongbow with the creation of demesne manors at Carlow, Odogh and Castlecomer, all of which seem to belong to the Marshal period, although he is cautious about the inclusion of Kilkenny: Orpen, *Normans*, i, pp 374–7. **60** See *IMED*, pp 213–21. **61** See *CAAR*, p. 26. I am grateful both to Dr Kieran O'Conor and Dr Margaret Murphy for drawing my attention to the significance of this deed. See also Adrian Empey, 'The medieval county of Carlow, 1169–1245: the formative years', *Carloviana: Carlow Historical and Archaeological Society*, 63 (2015), pp 156–60.

know when or how it came into the Marshal's possession. It is possible that de Clahull supported Meiler fitz Henry's revolt against the Marshal in 1207–8, in which case forfeiting an important strategic point controlling the upper reaches of the Barrow may have been the price of regaining his lord's favour. Prime examples of consolidation of the seigniorial demesne by simple escheat are the important manors of Forth in Carlow, Carbury in Kildare and Greatisland in Wexford.[62] Given the late arrival of the Marshal on the Leinster scene, it seems likely that these various means of strengthening his tenuous hold on Leinster were actively pursued by him in an effort to set his house in order. In these circumstances the simplest way of reconstructing the Marshal's demesnes is to use the partition of 1247 as our historical base line, but to proceed with caution, registering possible problems.

How soon after inheriting Leinster did the Marshal set about this task? Like King John, he spent only two periods in Ireland, the first at the end of 1200, and the second for most of 1207–8.[63] While it is very likely that these visits were defining moments in the reconfiguration of the lordship, we cannot suppose that he was inactive either before 1200 or between visits. As we have seen in the cases of both Theobald Walter and John, much work on the ground was necessarily carried out by their lieutenants in the course of such prolonged absences. Besides, the Marshal had to reward his household knights for their services. Since their expectations would certainly have included rewards in the form of land grants, it is inherently improbable that he could have ignored them during the period 1190–1200. It is therefore likely that the core members of his *mesnie*, Geoffrey fitz Robert, Thomas fitz Anthony, John de Earley and William Mallard, were granted lordships in central Ossory not long after 1190, and that their progress provided a solid platform for the Marshal's intervention in 1200.[64] Traces of the closeness of such allegiances are visible in fitz Robert's charter to

62 Forth reverted to the Marshal on the death of Raymond le Gros, who died sometime between 1190 and 1200, and who had no heir. Greatisland was the caput of Hervey de Montmorency's lordship of Uí Bairrche, which embraced Shelburne and Bargy (for its tenements, see *CIPM*, iv, pp 307–8). Hervey died without an heir, first having assumed the habit of a monk in Christ Church, Canterbury, around 1178. It is not known when he died – estimates vary from *c.*1185 to 1205 – but in any case his lordship would have been escheated either by John as custodian of Leinster before 1190, or by William Marshal after that date. Meiler fitz Henry was granted Carbury by Strongbow, and likewise died without an heir in 1220, when it reverted to William Marshal II. 63 Crouch, *William Marshal*, pp 87–9, 100–15. 64 O'Byrne, following Carrigan, believes that the Mac Gilla Pátraics were expelled from Upper Ossory around 1192: O'Byrne, *War, politics and the Irish of Leinster*, pp 41–2. Given the hostility between the Mac Murchadas and the Mac Gilla Pátraics, the Marshal could well have been influenced by Countess Isabel to pursue the family feud. The Graces, who settled in Tullaroan and Offerlane, were certainly the Marshal's men: see Brooks, *Knights' fees*, pp 72, 227. However, Carrigan rests his case largely on 'the Dublin copy of the Annals of Innisfallen', which apparently states that a castle was erected in Kilkenny in 1192 (Carrigan, *Ossory*, i, p. 70), which is not supported by the Rawlinson MS, edited by Seán Mac Airt in 1951 and repr. 1977. Carrigan presumably consulted the manuscript in Trinity College Dublin

his Augustinian priory of Kells, probably issued shortly after his prior, Hugh de Rous, was elevated to the see of Ossory *c.*1202. Hugh is the first witness. While Hugh was doubtless safeguarding the interests of his former priory, the priory must have been in existence for several years before he became bishop, which provides a firm indication that fitz Robert was established in the lordship of Kells well before the Marshal's first visit to Leinster in 1201. The charter also informs us that the foundation was made 'by counsel and consent, and for the soul of my lord William the Marshal, who is chief lord of the aforesaid country, and who has confirmed by his charter the abovesaid house and all my donations and grants made to it'.[65] The Marshal must have been instrumental in securing Hugh's election, no doubt on fitz Robert's personal recommendation. Naturally, such parvenus cannot have been welcomed by the earlier settlers, whose long dominance in Leinster was now subject to challenge: when push came to shove in the war between the Marshal and Meiler fitz Henry in 1207–8, it was this new element that stood by Countess Isabel when the Marshal was a diplomatic prisoner in John's court. Fitz Henry, a leading Leinster tenant of Strongbow's generation, received most of his support from the old guard.[66] Such men must have been galled by the prospect of subordination to John Marshal and Geoffrey fitz Robert, who governed Leinster alternately in the interim between William's two visits.

There are indications that rapid progress was being made in Kilkenny itself. Sometime between 1202 and 1205 Theobald Walter was forced to make reparation to Hugh, bishop of Ossory, in the parish church of St Mary, Kilkenny, for lands he had wrongfully seized from the previous bishop.[67] We know too from the *Histoire de Guillaume le Maréchal* that Countess Isabel and the Marshal's men held Kilkenny Castle in the war with fitz Henry.[68] All of this suggests that Kilkenny was firmly established by the beginning of the thirteenth century, however modest its beginnings in Strongbow's lifetime, and however exploitative the interim years of minority misrule. The parish church of St Mary in particular could not have existed before the town it was designed to serve.[69] While the castle may not have been completed, it was sufficiently strong in 1207 to resist fitz Henry, a veteran warrior with an impressive track record. While it is possible that its fortification stemmed from the Marshal's first visit six years previously, it is reasonable to speculate that it was begun not long after the

(TCD MS H.1.7). **65** *Ormond deeds, 1172–1350*, no. 30. **66** This point is well developed by Crouch, *William Marshal*, pp 100–15. **67** *Ormond deeds, 1172–1350*, no. 23. **68** Meyer (ed.), *L'histoire de Guillaume le Mareschal*, iii, line 13808. **69** St Mary's was the parish church of the Hightown, close to the castle. Whatever function 'the church of St Kenni' – later the cathedral of St Canice – may have fulfilled before the Anglo-Norman conquest, it is clear from Strongbow's charter that 'the church which is opposite the church of St Kenni on the other side of the water [the River Bregagh] on the east side' [St Mary's] was already functioning as the borough church. In this respect the borough of Kilkenny conforms to the general pattern of post-conquest Anglo-Norman urban parishes: see Empey, 'Origins of the medieval parish

Marshal had gained seisin of Leinster. Finally, if we locate the foundation of the abbeys of Duiske (pl.1) and Tintern (pl. 2) near or around the turn of the century, as Crouch argues, we cannot doubt that he devoted less time and energy to the development of his demesne lands.[70] Various estimates have been placed on the foundation date of the priory of St John the Baptist, Kilkenny, but the general consensus is somewhere between 1202 and 1212.[71] Its foundation formed part of the Marshal's spiritual portfolio in Leinster, and must therefore be regarded as a key element in his plan to shape his Irish lordship according to his design. There is therefore a strong probability that the Marshal sought to impose his design on Leinster fairly insistently, whether or not he was physically present. He owed as much to his wife, whose mind can never have been far from the challenge of consolidating her vast inheritance.

VII

Rather than list the demesnes as they appear in the partition of 1247, it is easier to gain an overview of their distribution by grouping them according to their respective medieval counties.

Co. Wexford (fig. 2.2)

- The manors of Old and New Ross
- The manor of Greatisland
- The seigniorial caput: Wexford town and castle
- The manor of Rosslare
- The manor of Carrick
- The manor and castle of Ferns
- The manor of Taghmon
- The manor of Bannow (Clonmines)

That there is a significant concentration of demesne manors in Wexford is unsurprising, given that most of these manors were accessible by sea and consequently more immediately exploitable, not to mention their strategic possibilities. The main exception to this maritime bias is Ferns, where we have

church revisited', p. 40. **70** Crouch, *William Marshal*, p. 88n.39. While he is justified in questioning how much influence the Marshal could have exerted in Leinster between 1190 and 1200, pointing to the apparent failure of his Irish deputy, Reginald de Quetteville, I suspect he may be too pessimistic in regard to the development of Kilkenny city and castle (cf. pp 70–1). As none of the Leinster barons had any claim on the site, it is entirely possible that progress of sorts could have occurred on the Marshal's demesne lands where the barons had no direct interests at stake. **71** See *MRHI*, p. 182. For some reason, Crouch makes no reference to the priory, although he discusses the foundations of Duiske and Tintern: Crouch, *William Marshal*, pp 210–14.

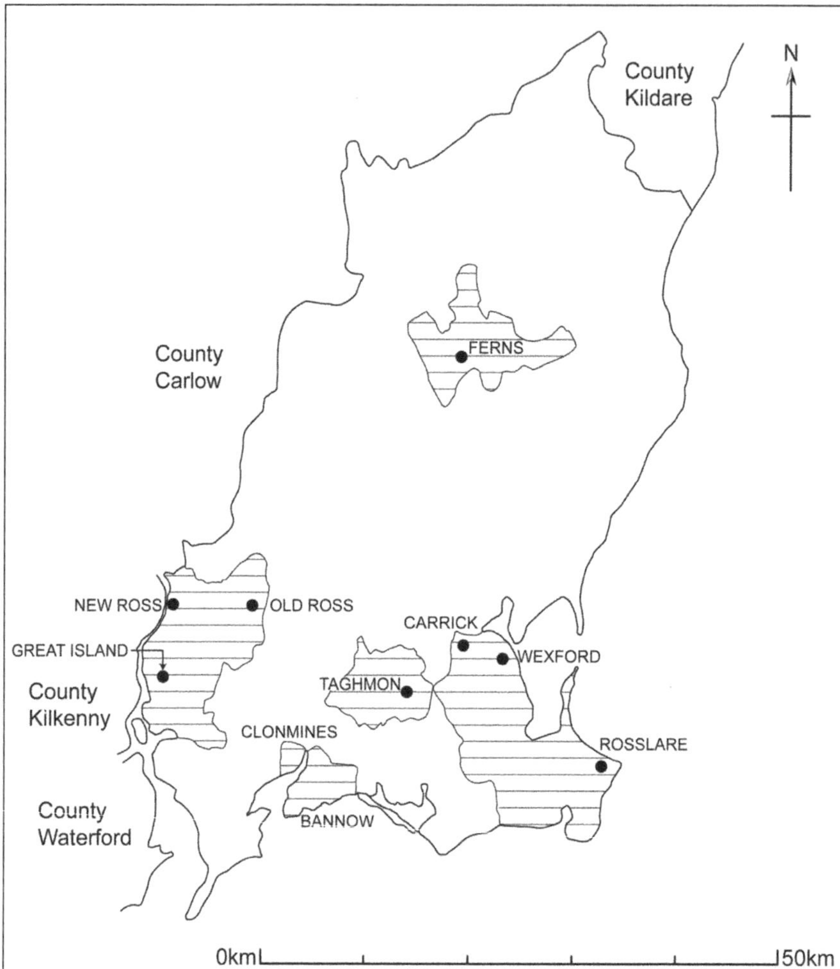

2.2 Marshal demesnes in medieval Co. Wexford (map: Philip Kenny, Kilkenny Archaeology). Map outline based on Billy Colfer, *Arrogant trespass*, p. 48, by kind permission.

already noted that Strongbow founded a town sometime before his death in 1176. Since it was the seat of the bishop of Ferns he could not, for reasons of *Kirchenpolitik*, permit the bishop to be controlled either by his own vassals or, even less, by the Mac Murchadas.[72] He had, besides, to register a seigniorial presence as close as possible to the Mac Murchada heartland for sound strategic and political reasons. The burning of Ferns, an important centre of Mac

72 In the absence of any clearly established royal assertion of lordship over bishops whose temporalities lay within the confines of the great liberties before John's interventions around the beginning of the thirteenth century, the king seems to have taken a laissez-faire attitude to ecclesiastical policy outside the royal demesne. The first Anglo-Norman bishop of Ossory,

Murchada power, by the rebel Muircheartach Mac Murchada in 1172 or shortly thereafter may have given Strongbow the opportunity to occupy it permanently.[73] The fact that he established a borough there means that he intended to stay: this was a strategic as distinct from a tactical decision. In any event, the construction of the imposing castle there was almost certainly on the Marshal's initiative, although it may have come at the cost of expropriating episcopal land.[74] Similarly, the founding of New Ross was clearly integral to the Marshal's town-founding policy across his lordship. It may be noted in passing that the Marshal invested the tithes of New Ross in his new Augustinian foundation, the priory of St John, Kilkenny.[75] As already noted, the loss of Waterford to Henry II meant that a port on the Barrow-Nore-Suir estuary was an essential entrepôt for the trade of the Leinster lordship. The adjacent manor of Old Ross, probably founded by Strongbow, provided an excellent platform for such a development, as it seems to have extended as far as the estuary.[76] Given the rapid growth of New Ross as the major entrepôt for the lordship, Strongbow's siting of the original settlement at Old Ross about ten kilometres inland makes sense only if he depended on Waterford as the gateway to the Barrow and the Nore, even after it had been taken in the king's hand.[77]

In general, it looks as if the Marshal's demesnes in Co. Wexford were for the most part Strongbow's creation, but the siting of New Ross and the building of a major castle at Ferns (pl. 4) together point to a new strategic plan for the government of Leinster after the long years of the minority and political drift. The castle of Ferns was clearly integral to the Marshal's castle-building programme, even if he may not have envisaged Ferns as the seigniorial caput of the county. The proximity of Wexford to Pembroke made it an ideal location for a maritime seigneury, not to mention its strategic position at the mouth of the River Slaney. More likely he intended Ferns to contain the Mac Murchadas. As

Hugh de Rous, consecrated *c.*1202, was previously prior of Geoffrey fitz Robert's priory of Kells. He was almost certainly appointed with the Marshal's approval. In this context I think it is fair to say that until the crosslands were subjected to direct royal control, the lords of the liberties exerted authority over the bishops in a fairly direct manner. 73 See O'Byrne, *War, politics and the Irish of Leinster*, p. 13. 74 See Orpen, *Normans*, iii, pp 54–5. The long and bitter dispute between the Marshal and Ailbe, bishop of Ferns, certainly involved claims about church lands in or around Ferns, which suggests that the construction of the castle at Ferns by the Marshal was the major source of contention. For an account of the dispute, see Orpen, *Normans*, iii, pp 29–31. The seigniorial castle of Kildare was also built on episcopal property. In 1329 the manor of Kildare was charged with an annual rent of 10 marks *pro situ castri de Kildare* (see Gearóid Mac Niocaill (ed.), *The Red Book of the earls of Kildare* (Dublin, 1964), p. 109; cf. p. 131). This suggests that Strongbow had the agreement of the bishop to build his castle there. 75 See *EIMP*, p. 180. 76 For a fuller account of the Marshal demesnes in Co. Wexford, see Colfer, *Arrogant trespass*, pp 35–82. 77 That Old Ross was the site of the first settlement is strongly suggested by the existence of a motte-and-bailey castle there. In 1307 there were 59 burgages in Old Ross, supported by 5 carucates in burgage tenure: *CIPM*, iv, no. 434, p. 307. It would seem that Strongbow had no great ambitions for the borough, as the number of burgages was appropriate for a modest rural borough.

it was also the episcopal seat, the castle served as a salutary reminder to successive bishops of the seigniorial presence in their midst. The fact that the see did not migrate to Wexford, unlike the transfer of the see of Ossory to Kilkenny, made this solution all the more desirable. As for the borough of New Ross, the Marshal's plan to make it the commercial capital of Leinster is underlined by his astonishingly generous provision of 506 burgages.[78] Its significance can be measured in comparison with the relatively modest allocation of 160 burgages each to Carlow and Ferns.[79] The fact that he did not intend to use New Ross as a seigniorial capital serves only to underscore his economic intentions. He clearly sought to build a town on such a scale as to equal, if not to surpass, the royal city of Waterford. The persistent rivalry between the two towns in the succeeding centuries was inevitable.[80] At the risk of repetition, it must be emphasised that the designation of burgages at the time of the urban foundation provides the most unambiguous measure of the founder's expectations. Did he intend it to be a rural borough designed to meet the immediate needs of a particular castle and manor? Or did he intend it to be large enough to serve a greater administrative or strategic need? Did he intend it to be a major focus of trade for an entire lordship with no particular administrative or manorial concerns? It may also be observed that both Carlow and Ferns, equally important (albeit for different reasons), were allocated the same number of burgages. All this suggests that the Marshal had a coherent plan for the restructuring of Leinster, and did not resort to ad hoc measures.

VIII

The construction of powerful castles at Carlow and Kilkenny was clearly part of a wider strategy to control access to the interior of Leinster by securing the key riverine routes. Not to have secured them was unthinkable. While a motte was constructed at Kilkenny in Strongbow's lifetime, it was destroyed *c*.1173.[81] Strongbow's founding of a borough there may have been part of an ensuing programme of reconstruction. Notwithstanding their subsequent role in the governance of the lordship, Kilkenny was not mentioned in the arrangements for the government of Leinster at the Council of Oxford in 1177, neither was it mentioned by Giraldus Cambrensis, who visited Ireland twice in the 1180s. Strongbow understood the strategic value of Kilkenny, which is not to say that

78 In 1307 the burgesses rendered £25 6*s*. 8*d*. for burgage rent: *CIPM*, iv, no. 434, p. 306. We know the rent was fixed at a rate of 1*s*. per burgage. As the rent was invariable, we can be certain that the total rent was fixed at the time New Ross was laid out. Ferns had 160 burgages in 1324: *CIPM*, vi, no. 518, p. 326. No charter has survived for Ferns, but one must have been issued in the Marshal's lifetime. **79** *CIPM*, no. 434, p. 304. **80** See Eamonn McEneaney, 'Waterford and New Ross trade competition, *c*.1300', *Decies*, 12 (1979), pp 16–24. **81** See Orpen, *Normans*, i, p. 376.

he envisaged it as a major seigniorial centre. There is therefore good reason to credit the Marshal with making the vital connection between the site and its possibilities as a seigniorial seat in the context of a comprehensive plan for the government and administration of his vast lordship. But there is another factor to be considered. The Marshal had not only to find suitable unconquered territory within Leinster for rewarding his own household knights, upon whose loyalty he depended not only to govern Leinster in his absences, but also to provide dependable military support of the kind they offered Countess Isabel when Meiler fitz Henry went on the rampage in 1208. Central and northern Ossory alone had that potential to meet these expectations. As we have seen, only southern Ossory appears to have been subinfeudated – specifically the cantreds of Iverk and Knocktopher – in Strongbow's time. It is possible that Theobald fitz Walter had begun to settle the cantred of Oskelan, granted to him by John during the minority, but if that is so the settlement cannot have advanced very far by 1190, given that Theobald arrived in Ireland only in 1185. He was therefore not part of the Strongbow generation of Leinster barons. Whether Strongbow's grant to Adam de Hereford of 'half the vill of Achebo and the entire half (*totum dimidium*) cantred in which the vill is situated' – subsequently confirmed by the Marshal – in the far north of Ossory took effect in the 1170s may be doubted, considering its exposure to attack from barely subdued midland septs.[82] Presumably the other half of the cantred belonged to the bishop before the exchange with the Marshal sometime after 1202. Thus the Marshal had a relatively free hand in making provision both for his household knights and for expanding his demesne in Ossory, without neglecting strategic considerations at the same time. The consequence of this situation is that nowhere is 'the Marshal Plan' more evident than in the settlement of central and northern Ossory.[83]

It is possible to reconstruct the demesnes in Kilkenny (fig. 2.3) by identifying them in the partition of Leinster in 1247, and, less certainly perhaps, from later records relating to the de Clare purparty:

- The borough of Kilkenny
- The profit of the county of Kilkenny
- The manor of Danesfort
- The manor of Locmadran [*recte*: Loghmeran]
- The manor of Odogh
- The manor of Kumbre [Castlecomer]
- The manor of Aghaboe
- The manor of Callan

82 For this grant, see Orpen, *Normans*, i, pp 394–5; *Ormond deeds, 1172–1350*, nos 1, 37. For the de Hereford lands, see Brooks, *Knights' fees*, pp 201–9. 83 In the absence of surviving charters, it is impossible to be certain about the pattern of enfeoffments in the three northern cantreds of Odogh, Galmoy and Aghaboe. However, it is noticeable that Brooks's study of the

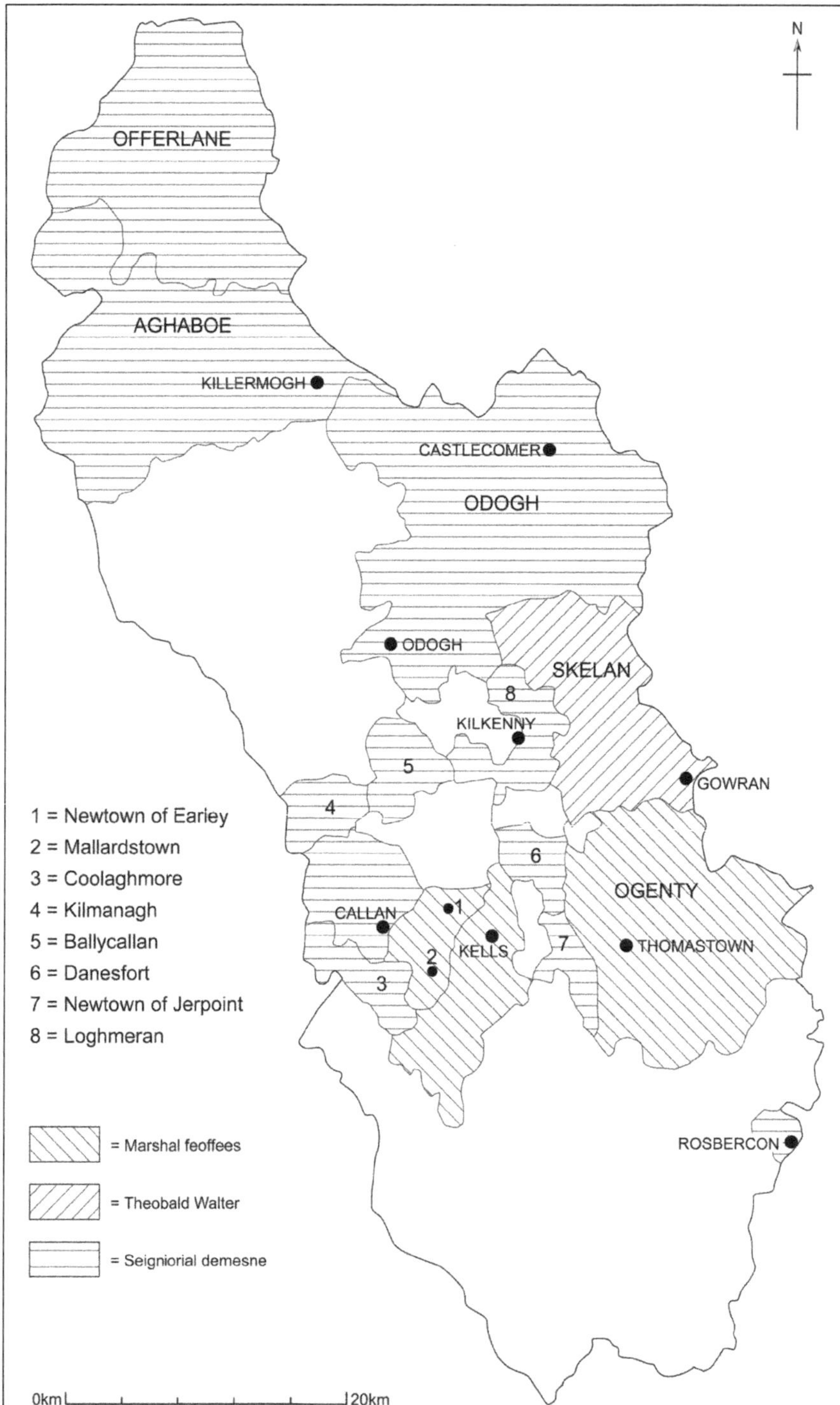

2.3 Marshal demesnes in medieval Co. Kilkenny (map: Adrian Empey, digitised by Philip Kenny, Kilkenny Archaeology).

There seems to be a number of absentees in this list when it is compared to those that appear in the inquisitions post mortem relating to the de Clare purparty in 1307. These include the manors of Coolaghmore, the Newtown of Jerpoint, Ballycallan, Kilmanagh, Rosbercon, Fermoyle, Killermogh, Clontibret and Offerlane.[84] Some, if not all, of them certainly belonged to the Marshal era. The town of Somertoun (*alias* Coilleagh), now Coolaghmore, had a charter from Gilbert Marshal, which was a confirmation of William's charter because it mentions the ubiquitous Geoffrey fitz Robert.[85] Similary, the charter of the town of Rosbercon granted by Gilbert de Clare in 1294, while making no reference either to the Marshal or to Geoffrey, almost certainly represents a confirmation of an earlier charter of William Marshal as we know of no other feoffee in Rosbercon besides the de Clares and their successors.[86] It seems likely that Gilbert inherited Rosbercon as part of the Marshal inheritance. The important castle and lordship of Offerlane also belonged to Gilbert in 1290, again probably for the same reason.[87] Perhaps it represented the lands ceded to the Marshal by Hugh de Rous. Furthermore, the fact that these manors do not occur in later feodaries suggests that they were tenements of manors held in demesne from the outset, such as Offerlane, Aghaboe and Odogh. Whatever militrary services were due to them seem not to have fallen within the scope of the feodary lists, possibly because they would have been recorded in manorial extents, none of which has survived. We know, for example, that Adam de Hereford owed the service of knights for his lands in Aghaboe. Perhaps they were subsequently attached to the Marshal's manor of Aghaboe. If Odogh was the caput of the cantred of the same name, as seems likely, then the Marshal exercised immediate lordship over most of the northern part of the medieval county.

Thus the picture that emerges from the Marshal settlement of central and northern Ossory is fairly clear. The nerve centre of settlement, Kilkenny Castle, was protected by a screen of important fiefs held by his household knights: to the south lay the lordships of Thomas fitz Anthony (Thomastown), Geoffrey fitz Robert (Kells), William Mallard (Mallardstown) and John de Earley (Earlstown). To the east lay Gowran – the lordship of Theobald fitz Walter (comprising the cantred of Oskelan) – whom the Marshal would have known

feoffees in this area of the medieval county of Kilkenny – particularly names like Syward (Glashare), Devereux (Acheteyr), William de St Leger (Rosconnell) and William le Gras (tenant of Offerlane) – seem to be associated with the Marshal rather than with Strongbow. Others were connected with the Marshal's leading vassals, such as Odo Archdeacon, who seems to have married a daughter of Thomas fitz Anthony. Others can be linked with grants or charters relating to the Marshal's religious foundations: Brooks, *Knights' fees*, pp 176–232.
84 See C.A. Empey, 'County Kilkenny in the Anglo-Norman period' in William Nolan and Kevin Whelan (eds), *Kilkenny: history and society* (Dublin, 1990), pp 77–8. 85 *Ormond deeds, 1350–1413*, no. 92. 86 *Ormond deeds, 1172–1350*, no. 314. It is not included in Brooks's exhaustive study of knights' fees in Wexford, Carlow and Kilkenny (Brooks, *Knights' fees*), which suggests that it was never held by a feoffee owing knight service. 87 *CDI, 1285–1292*, no. 620.

through his long association with Theobald's brother Hubert.[88] He must have been satisfied with the sincerity of Theobald's fealty or he would not have agreed to it. More importantly, Theobald had no ties with the first generation of Leinster that owed their lands to Strongbow, although Theobald's links with John had the potential of divided loyalties. To the west, running up to the border of the county of Munster, the Marshal located the important castle and manor of Callan, flanked by two demesne manors, Coolaghmore and Kilmanagh. While the progress of the Anglo-Norman settlement in Tipperary reduced the defensive significance of Callan with its imposing motte-and-bailey castle, the relative security of these demesnes ensured their future prosperity.

The north of the medieval county of Kilkenny presented greater challenges not only because it was less deeply settled by the Anglo-Normans, as the size of the northern parishes would immediately suggest, but also because the indigenous Irish septs, the Mac Gilla Pátraics of Upper Ossory and the O'Brenans of Odogh, retained their distinctive social systems. The Anglo-Norman hold on these regions was tenuous from the outset, depending heavily on military outposts in places like Offerlane, Aghaboe and Castlecomer. Much of the north was to be lost in the course of the Gaelic reconquest in the first half of the fourteenth century.[89] The Marshal clearly grasped the importance of Offerlane and Aghaboe as military outposts on his north-western frontier, exposed as they were both to attack from without – the Irish of the Slieve Bloom Mountains certainly feature as a constant danger from the late thirteenth century onwards, not to mention the midland septs – and to subversion from within by the resident Mac Gilla Pátraics. Certainly there is no evidence that he attempted to settle the northern reaches of Ossory in depth, as there were almost no towns founded in the northern cantreds.[90] That said, it is also true that significant remnants of the settlement in the cantred of Odogh endured throughout the later Middle Ages, albeit in the form of a march.

In retrospect, the Marshal settlement of central Ossory proved to be remarkably enduring by comparison to other centres of his power: Ferns was lost around 1360; while Carlow became so exposed to attack that the Irish of Leinster burned it repeatedly in the later fourteenth century.[91] In the case of Kilkenny, the outer ring of the Marshal's settlement held firm. In spite of losses in the north,

88 The fact that the Marshal was content to confirm fitz Walter in his Leinster fiefs may owe something to the importance of his brother Hubert, bishop of Salisbury in 1189–93, and subsequently archbishop of Canterbury, 1193–1205, and chief justiciar of England, 1193–8. Theobald was raised in the household of the great Ranulf de Glanville, chief justiciar of England, *c.*1180–9, and subsequently became attached to John's household. **89** See Empey, 'County Kilkenny in the Anglo-Norman period', pp 89–91. **90** A town was founded in the manor of Odogh, and another in the episcopal manor of Durrow. **91** See Colfer, *Arrogant trespass*, p. 219; Otway-Ruthven, *Medieval Ireland*, pp 287, 309–11. For Carlow, see Linda Doran, 'Medieval settlement hierarchy in Carlow and the "Carlow Corridor", 1200–1550' in McGrath and Nolan (eds), *Carlow: history and society*, pp 173–212.

Kilkenny was never attacked and burned, and in general urban and manorial society in the centre and south of the county enjoyed relative stability and continuity in the fifteenth century.[92] In addition to its military durability, it should also be noted that in Kilkenny the Marshal added about 100,000 acres to the demesne.[93] It was largely on the basis of the surviving elements of the Kilkenny demesne that the earls of Ormond reconstructed their power base in the late fourteenth century following a succession of catastrophic losses in their north Munster heartland.

IX

The demesnes in the medieval county of Carlow (fig. 2.4), identified in the 1247 partition, are as follows:

- The town of Carlow
- The profit of the county of Carlow [*corpus comitatus*]
- Dunganstown [Ballidunegan]
- The lordship of Forth
- The manor of St Mullins [Tamulyn]
- The lordship of Oboy

The interesting aspect of this inventory is that most of the demesnes in 1247 were the product of escheats that had occurred since Strongbow's original settlement. The cantreds of Forth and Idrone were granted by Strongbow to Raymond le Gros, who enfeoffed his nephew William de Carew of the larger cantred of Idrone, including St Mullins.[94] Raymond, who retained Forth, died without heirs sometime between 1190 and 1200, with the result that this important lordship reverted to the Marshal and his heirs. By contrast, the manor of St Mullins, which was held in chief of the Marshal by Richard Talun, was still in the possession of the same family in 1301.[95] It seems, therefore, that in 1247 it was held in demesne only by reason of the minority of a tenant. The same seems to be true of the lordship of Oboy, originally granted by Strongbow to Roger de Bigarz, but which descended eventually to the de Hastings.[96] Dunganstown, a small manor close to Carlow, was held by the de Hydes, so it too may be the product of a minority in 1247.[97]

92 See C.A. Empey, 'The Anglo-Norman community in Tipperary and Kilkenny in the Middle Ages: change and continuity' in Gearóid Mac Niocaill and P.F. Wallace (eds), *Keimelia: studies in medieval archaeology and history in memory of Tom Delaney* (Galway, 1988), pp 449–67, esp. pp 459 ff. 93 Empey, 'County Kilkenny in the Anglo-Norman period', p. 78. 94 Brooks, *Knights' fees*, pp 60–1. For St Mullins, see Orpen, *Normans*, i, p. 387. 95 Brooks, *Knights' fees*, pp 77–8. 96 See Orpen, *Normans*, iii, p. 105. 97 See Brooks, *Knights' fees*, p. 25.

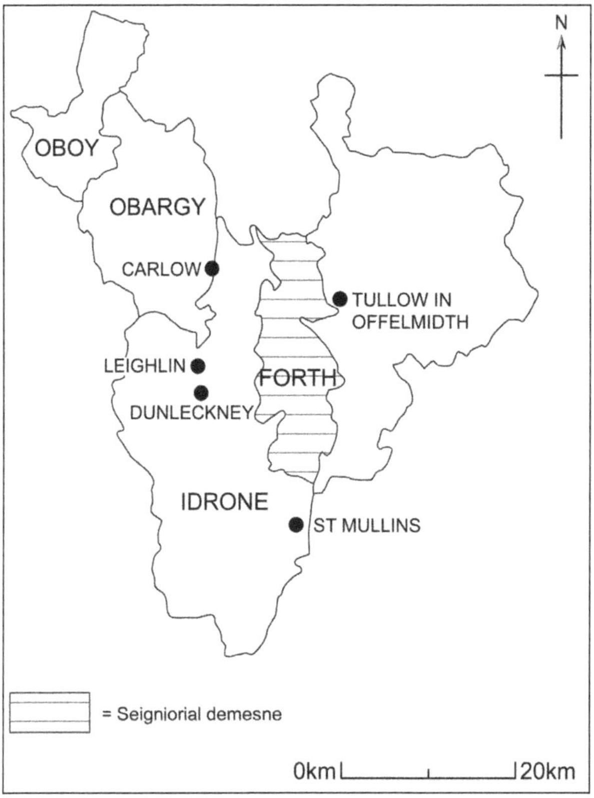

2.4 Marshal demesnes in medieval Co. Carlow (map: Adrian Empey, digitised by Philip Kenny, Kilkenny Archaeology).

The most remarkable aspect of the settlement in Co. Carlow is that Strongbow seems to have been content to carve up the (later) medieval county among his leading vassals, Raymond le Gros in particular. He did not build a castle in the episcopal centre of Leighlin, and even more remarkably he built no castle on the Barrow. Of the five cantreds in the county, he granted two to Raymond (Idrone and Forth), one to Jordan (Offelmidth), one to Roger de Bigarz (Oboy) and one to John de Clahull, his marshal (Obargy).[98] Had Raymond not conveniently died without heirs about the time that the Marshal got seisin of Leinster, the demesne would have been very small indeed. The addition of the lordship of Forth, when combined with the subsequent acquisition of Carlow, significantly transformed the balance of seigniorial power within the county.

98 See Adrian Empey, 'The liberty and counties of Carlow in the high Middle Ages' in McGrath and Nolan (eds), *Carlow: history and society*, pp 153–71, esp. p. 155. Jordan appears to have held Offelmidth before John granted it to Theobald fitz Walter, perhaps as a speculative grant only. John de Clahull was, of course, Strongbow's feoffee, not the Marshal's, as I incorrectly stated on p. 155.

X

The evolution of the medieval county of Kildare (fig. 2.5) is particularly complex because it was not confined within the borders of the diocese. At the eastern extremity were the lordships of Wicklow and Arklow in the diocese of Glendalough, adjoining the cantred of Omurthi in the diocese of Kildare. The western extremity included the cantred of Leys situated in the diocese of Leighlin. This eccentric arrangement of territory was rooted in the territorial horse-trading between Henry II and Strongbow. Wicklow and Arklow effectively represent all that Strongbow was able to recover from Henry II in the dioceses of Dublin and Glendalough following Henry's intervention in 1171–2.[99] The wrangling between the Marshal and John over the services of Theobald Walter, among others, might have resulted in the separation of the manor of Arklow from the lordship of Leinster had the Marshal not insisted on retaining Theobald's homage and fealty for the lands he held there. More significant in relation to the formation of the Leinster demesnes was the triangular contest between the Marshal, Meiler fitz Henry and King John in 1207–8, involving a protracted dispute over the cantred of Leys, the caput of which was Dunamase. In 1177 the king granted the custody of 'the land of Leys belonging to Geoffrey de Costentin with its appurtenances' to William fitz Audelin as part of arrangements made at Oxford for the custody of Leinster.[100] Geoffrey therefore appears to have held Leys as a fief from Strongbow, although no mention is made of a minor. Henry, however, found an opportunity in 1181 to grant it to fitz Henry – presumably as a custody if Geoffrey had an heir – by way of compensating fitz Henry for the loss of the custody of Kildare Castle.[101] According to Giraldus Cambrensis, Henry's representatives in Ireland 'took away from fitz Henry Kildare and the adjoining territory, which had been given to him by the earl, and on behalf of the king gave him in exchange the province of Leis [Laois], a hostile, difficult and wooded region'.[102]

It looks very much as if fitz Henry, who held important tenements elsewhere in the medieval county of Kildare, had been acting as Strongbow's constable of the castle of Kildare.[103] Thus fitz Henry was granted Leys not *in feodo*, but

99 See in particular Marie Therese Flanagan, 'Henry II and the kingdom of Uí Fáeláin' in Bradley (ed.), *Settlement and society in medieval Ireland*, pp 229–39. **100** *Chronica magistri Rogeri de Houedene*, ed. Stubbs, ii, p. 134. **101** Flanagan, 'Henry II and the kingdom of Uí Fáeláin', p. 236. **102** Giraldus, *Expugnatio*, pp 194–5. **103** The sheriff of Dublin accounted for various sums from the lands formerly held by Meiler fitz Henry in Kildare in 1211–12, which were now in the king's hand. These were the cantred of Leis, the cantred of Conal, the cantred of Karbri and the castle of Dunmalc, which is clearly a misreading of 'Dunmasc' or Dunamase. He also had held a certain *pars* in the cantred of Aghaboe: see Oliver Davies and D.B. Quinn, 'The Irish pipe roll of 14 John, 1211–1212', *Ulster Journal of Archaeology*, 4 (supplement) (1941), pp 16–17. Carbury, Oldconnell and Naas were subdivisions of the cantred of Offelan: see MacCotter, *Medieval Ire.*, pp 174–6.

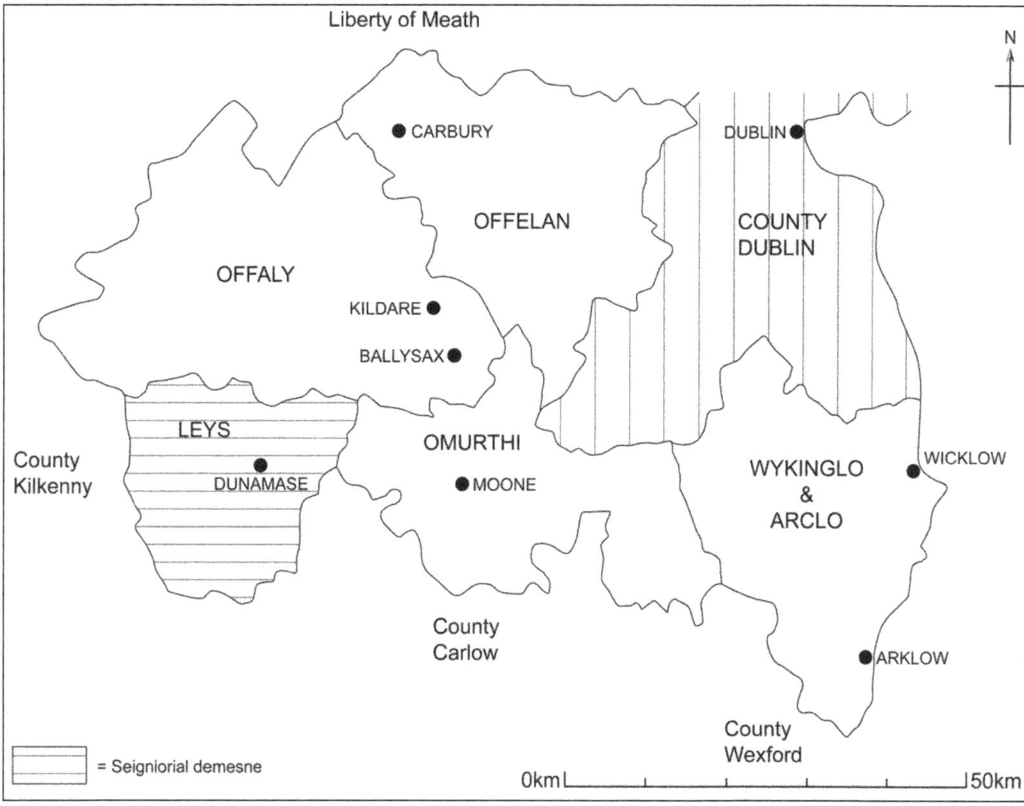

2.5 Marshal demesnes in medieval Co. Kildare (map: Philip Kenny, Kilkenny Archaeology). Map outline based on Paul MacCotter, *Medieval Ireland*, appendix 2, by kind permission.

merely as a custody to be held during the pleasure of the king. In short, the cantred of Leys, which included Dunamase, was part of the original Leinster demesne. Precisely why they were not surrendered to the Marshal when he became lord of Leinster is not evident. It seems likely that the Marshal's efforts to recover them underlay the outbreak of hostilities between fitz Henry's and the Marshal's men in 1207–8, and that they were exacerbated by a dispute between the Marshal and the king over the issue of the wardship of Gerald fitz Maurice's lands in the cantred of Offelan.[104] The second Leinster charter in 1208, which settled the issue of prerogative wards in favour of the Marshal, did not immediately produce the restoration of Leys and Dunamase, which remained in the king's hand in 1211–12 for no discernible reason. The Marshal was still struggling to wrest control of Dunamase from the justiciar in 1215 and 1216,[105] even though 'the king had restored it to him *as his right*'.[106] This temporising was

104 See Otway-Ruthven, *Medieval Ireland*, pp 77–8. **105** *CDI, 1171–1251*, nos 644, 647, 664, 684, 685. **106** Ibid., no. 674. The italics are mine.

by no means over when in May 1216 the king commanded the justiciar 'to cause Earl William Marshal to have all the fees which fitz Henry held of the earl' within the justiciar's bailiwick, but only if fitz Henry should die or adopt a religious habit.[107] Sometime after this fitz Henry retired to his Augustinian foundation of Greatconnell, which most likely provides the latest opportunity for the handing over of Dunamase. It was certainly included among the demesne manors belonging to William Marshal II when he died in 1231.[108]

Thus the Marshal's crowning achievement in the medieval county of Kildare was the successful recovery of significant elements of Strongbow's original demesne in the face of the overt defiance of Meiler fitz Henry, sometimes acting in collusion with the king himself, and in spite of foot-dragging by successive justiciars in Ireland. Had he been unsuccessful, the demesne lands in Kildare would have been much smaller than in Wexford, Carlow or Kilkenny. Without fitz Henry's lands in Leys, Dunamase and Carbury, only the manor and castle of Kildare, Moone[109] and the minor manor of Ballysax (in the deanery of Kildare) would have survived.[110] Finally, although the manor of Wicklow was originally held in demesne by Strongbow, he clearly had second thoughts about its value, granting it instead to Maurice fitz Gerald.[111]

Thus the composition of the demesne in the medieval county of Kildare (fig. 2.5) about the time of the Marshal's death amounted to

- The castle and manor of Kildare
- The cantred of Leys with the manor and castle of Dunamase
- The manor of Carbury
- The manor of Ballysax
- The manor of Moone

XI

Three questions lie at the basis of this enquiry. First, to what extent were the Leinster demesnes the product of careful seigniorial planning as distinct from hit-and-miss opportunism or the random outcome of marcher warfare? Second, what contribution did William Marshal make to the final shaping of the demesne? Third, how does the organisation of the Leinster demesnes compare with other Anglo-Norman lordships in Ireland?

The answer to the first question is important for two reasons. First, it is clear that the circumstances of the Anglo-Norman 'conquest' of Ireland were

107 Ibid., no. 691. **108** Ibid., no. 1872. **109** The town of Moone was granted a charter by William Marshal, the younger, which was probably a re-issue of one granted by his father in the first decade of the thirteenth century: see Orpen, *Normans*, iii, p. 101. **110** These are listed in the 1247 partition. **111** *Deeds of the Normans*, lines 3090–3.

significantly different from the conquest of England, where the settlement patterns and legal structures of Anglo-Danish society were of a very different order, with the result that one aristocracy replaced another by means of piecemeal confiscations. Such a process resulted in lordships that were commonly dispersed over several counties, unlike the territorially compact lordships of the kind that emerged in Wales and Ireland. Second, whereas in England it was possible to settle a numerically small military aristocracy by adapting the previous systems of landholding, in Ireland towns, manors, legal structures and systems of governance had to be created where none existed before, at least of the kind that could readily be adapted to the requirements of lordship as the Anglo-Normans understood it. In such a context, planning was the *sine qua non*. There was, besides, a significant influx of non-military settlers to be accommodated: freeholders, customary tenants, and town-dwellers, of a kind that seem to have been largely absent in 1066.[112] In this respect the exploitation of the new lordships in Ireland can be understood against the broader background of European colonisation in the twelfth and thirteenth centuries, inviting comparison in particular with the colonisation of the eastern borderlands of Germany.[113]

As previously noted, mapping the demesne-making process in Leinster suffers from the serious difficulty that Strongbow had little time in which to shape his demesnes, not only because he died within seven years of arriving in Ireland with a handful of followers, but also because of the distractions of war and the struggle with Henry II. By contrast, Theobald Walter had two decades in which to stamp his authority on his lordship, while John – as lord of Ireland and later as king – had three, beginning with his arrival in Ireland in 1185. While both men were in Ireland for relatively short periods, they were nevertheless successful in constructing lordships to serve their individual needs. That this was accomplished largely by agents, who would certainly have had their instructions, seems to be a virtually inescapable conclusion. There is no reason to believe that their lieutenants were 'professional' agents like the German *locatores*. Rather they were trusted members of their respective *mesnies*, who were as experienced in the management of their lands as they were in the art of war.

So how are we to estimate Strongbow's distinctive contribution to the formation of the Leinster demesnes? Was the choice of his demesnes the result of careful consideration, designed to fulfil a range of strategic, economic and governmental choices; in short, the product of forward planning? There is no

112 See C.A. Empey, 'Conquest and settlement: patterns of Anglo-Norman settlement in north Munster and south Leinster', *Irish Economic and Social History*, 13 (1986), pp 5–31. **113** See Anngret Simms, 'Überformung eines keltischen Siedlungsraumes am Rande Europas durch externe Kolonisationsbewegungen' in Juergen Hadgedorn, Juergen Hövermann and Hans Juergen Nitz (eds), *Gefügemuster der Erdobefläche: d. genet. Analyse von Reliefkomplexen und Siedlungsräumen: Festschrift zum 42. deutschen Geographentag* (Göttingen, 1979), pp 285–312.

doubt that he made a significant contribution to their formation, particularly in Wexford and Kildare. He was also engaged actively in an attempt to colonise his demesne manors by founding towns at Kildare, Wicklow, Ferns and Kilkenny, and no doubt elsewhere. Wexford very probably received a charter from him, although he did not found it. What is not certain is whether he intended some or all of these towns to serve as the future seigniorial hubs of Leinster. The fact that Kildare, Kilkenny, Carlow and Wexford were later to serve that purpose in the Marshal period does not prove that Strongbow had the same vision: the division of Leinster into four counties lay some decades in the future. Curiously, he made no provision outside Dublin for monastic foundations of the kind that the Marshal was to create. There can therefore be no final determination of such questions because of the dearth of documentary evidence. All one can say is that it was a work in progress, cut short by his death, and that his choice of demesnes provided a solid foundation on which the Marshal was later to build. That he achieved so much in such a short time is astonishing, when one bears in mind the protracted struggles of the plantations in the sixteenth and seventeenth centuries.

In response to the second question, how are we to estimate the Marshal's achievement, given that he was lord of Leinster for thirty years in relatively peaceful circumstances? His greatest achievement lay in the successful recovery of so much of his vast inheritance after an extended and disruptive custody, when the lordship was at the mercy of John and his henchmen. His insistence on retaining prerogative wardships was important for maintaining his hold on vassals who were also tenants-in-chief in respect of lands held of the king outside Leinster, thereby halting the steady erosion of their allegiances. He recovered much of the demesne in Kildare as a result of a fierce struggle with fitz Henry, all the while in the face of obstruction by the king and his justiciars. His settlement in Co. Kilkenny proved not only to be a significant addition to the Leinster demesne, but also to be an enduring strategic achievement. More than that, the endowment of two significant monastic foundations in Kilkenny and Graiguenamanagh was in a sense part of his demesne too, because they were resourced from lands and tithes reserved to him. The Marshal was very probably responsible for the subdivision of Leinster into four counties, which was certainly prompted by a need to streamline the government of the lordship.[114] The creation of a system of counties consequently increased the importance of the towns of Kilkenny, Carlow, Kildare and Wexford as administrative as well as

114 We know for certain that a sheriff existed in Kilkenny sometime between 1202 and 1214, and that a county court existed in Wexford in 1204, which presupposes the existence of a sheriff: see A.J. Otway-Ruthven, 'The medieval county of Kildare', *IHS*, 11 (1959), p. 185. It is therefore very likely that Carlow and Kildare were shired around the same time.

as strategic centres. In this context, it seems certain that the Marshal was responsible for the construction of their castles as a means of strengthening his administrative grip on vassals whose loyalty was at best equivocal.

While his achievement in Leinster is indisputable, the question remains as to how much forward planning went into it? It may be suggested that here the evidence is stronger. At the very least the involvement of Geoffrey fitz Robert in fixing the burgage rent in the demesne towns suggests a policy that was implemented from the centre. The founding of New Ross has all the appearance of a grand plan, as the number of its burgages clearly indicates. In sum, the struggle to retain prerogative wardships, the recovery of potentially alienated demesnes, the extension of the demesnes in central and northern Kilkenny, the development of demesne towns, and the strengthening of the sinews of administration all point to a determined plan to re-establish seigniorial authority in Leinster on a firm footing. The success of such a policy depended in the end on substantially increasing the revenue of the lordship, most of which derived from the seigniorial demesne.

Finally, how does Leinster compare with other Anglo-Norman lordships in Ireland? As this study has considered only two examples by way of placing Leinster in context, no final answer can be given on the basis of a limited sample. However, a provisional answer would suggest that for all the complications, discontinuities and conflicts of interest involved in the formation of the Leinster demesnes, they owed rather more to policy and planning than to chance and circumstance. Certain elements stand out. First, Strongbow's maritime demesnes, particularly Wexford, Wicklow and Rosslare, were the key to maintaining the link with his Welsh lordships. Second, securing the riverine routes leading into the interior of Leinster was strategically vital. Even if there was no settlement in New Ross, the territory of the manor of Old Ross certainly had the potential of commanding entry and exit to the Barrow and Nore, while further upstream the new settlement in Kilkenny was significant. Carlow too was destined to emerge as a major seigniorial centre. Third, Strongbow established a seigniorial presence in or near the episcopal sees, thereby ensuring that none of his vassals was in a position to exercise undue influence over them. Finally, his town-founding activity provides unambiguous evidence that he intended to colonise and develop his demesnes, looking beyond immediate strategic considerations. That said, the provisional nature of Strongbow's achievement is indicated by his apparent failure to establish readily identifiable administrative centres. There was no Trim or Nenagh in evidence, even if Wexford may have fulfilled that role on the periphery for the time being. The disruptive interlude of the minority meant that such a task had perforce to wait until the Marshal had established himself firmly as lord of Leinster. For a man so deeply immersed in, and distracted by, the affairs of England and France, this represents an achievement as remarkable as it was enduring.

APPENDIX
STRONGBOW'S GRANT TO THE HOSPITAL OF JERUSALEM, *c.*1175

Earl Richard to the poor of the hospital of Jerusalem and the brethren serving God there. Grants 40 carucates of land and 4 burgages viz. at Kiolkenni, the church which is opposite the church of St Kenni at the other side of the water on the east side, with 10 carucates of land lying next about, and one burgage in the town of Kilkenni; and at Kildaran, the church which is called Kilmelin, with 10 carucates lying next about and extending to the town of Kildaran, and one burgage in the same town; and at Fernes, 10 carucates between the town of Fernes and the great water in the south part of the town, and a burgage in the same town; and at Wikingelo, Innesboithin with 10 carucates lying next about and a burgage in the town of Wikingelo next the bridge in the lower part of the way. He also confirms all gifts made by his men to the said brethren.

Witnesses: Raimund son of William, Griffin his brother, Walter Bluet, Milo de Cogan, Maurice de Prendergast, Hugh de Clahul, John his brother, Robert de Taidene, William Chaplain, Nicholas the clerk.

Abstract from *The calendar of ancient deeds and muniments preserved in the Pembroke Estate Office, Dublin* (Dublin, *c.*1891), pp 11–12. No editor is named.

Kells and its priory

MIRIAM CLYNE

The founder of Kells borough and priory, Geoffrey fitz Robert, was an important household knight of William Marshal. Geoffrey, who, like the Marshal, came from Wiltshire, was already a retainer for his overlord by 1188 and the relationship was to endure.[1] The two men were related by marriage because Geoffrey was an uncle of William's wife, Isabel, daughter of Earl Richard de Clare (Strongbow). In 1189, Geoffrey married Basilia, sister of Richard and widow of Raymond le Gros.[2] The biography of William Marshal, the *Histoire de Guillaume le Maréchal*, written soon after his death in 1219, refers to Geoffrey as he 'who serves me well and faithfully'.[3] When William Marshal gained possession of Leinster, he rewarded Geoffrey fitz Robert by granting him the cantred of Kells and land at Dysart to the south-east (fig. 3.1).[4] Besides these properties in Kilkenny, Geoffrey held the cantred of Grean in Limerick and lands in the cantred of Offa in Tipperary.[5] Following William Marshal's visit to Ireland in 1200, he appointed his loyal friend as seneschal of Leinster, an office where the knight received cash payments for his duties, and Geoffrey was later to serve a second term in this position.[6] Geoffrey was one of four hostages brought to England by King John, where he was held for his lord at Hereford Castle, but shortly before he was due to be released, he took ill and died in 1211.[7]

THE BOROUGH

Geoffrey fitz Robert established a town on the King's River, a tributary of the Nore, at Kells, 12km south of the Marshal's caput at Kilkenny (fig. 3.1, pl. 6). Kells was the manorial caput for Geoffrey's lordship, where the castle – his administrative centre and residence – was located, and a military garrison was established. It has been estimated that construction work on the castle began in

1 Crouch, *William Marshal*, pp 73, 145, 148, 151. 2 Ibid., pp 175, 219. 3 *HWM*, ii, lines 13505–6. 4 Paul MacCotter has published a different assessment of the cantreds of Co. Kilkenny, where he states that the feudal baronies of Kells, Erley and Knocktopher probably formed a single cantred whose name is not preserved: see MacCotter, *Medieval Ire.*, pp 179, 184. 5 C.A. Empey, 'The Augustinian priory of Kells: an historical introduction' in Clyne, *Kells Priory*, pp 1–11 at p. 3. 6 Crouch, *William Marshal*, pp 88–9, 172. 7 *HWM*, ii, lines 14448–62, 14483–6.

3.1 Medieval county of Kilkenny (after Empey, 'County Kilkenny in the Anglo-Norman period', p. 85, fig. 4.1) (© National Monuments Service).

1192 or 1193 because this would have been a priority for the lord of Kells.[8] The original charter for the borough, which has not survived, would have been drawn up soon afterwards, but the charter of Geoffrey's heir, William, has been preserved.[9] The borough of Kells was designed on quite a grand scale. Its layout was similar to other Anglo-Norman towns with a castle, streets with burgage plots, a market place, a mill, a parish church and a religious house, which were all established at the same date (fig. 3.2).

8 C.A. Empey, 'A case study of the primary phase of Anglo-Norman settlement: the lordship of Kells', *OKR*, new ser., 3:1 (1984), pp 32–40 at p. 36. 9 *CPCRI, Hen. VIII–Eliz.* [1514–75], pp 425–6; Mac Niocaill, *Na buirgéisí*, i, pp 129–30.

3.2 Kells Priory, showing existing Anglo-Norman features (© National Monuments Service) (extract from Ordnance Survey six-inch map, 1948. © Ordnance Survey Ireland/Government of Ireland Copyright Permit MP003816).

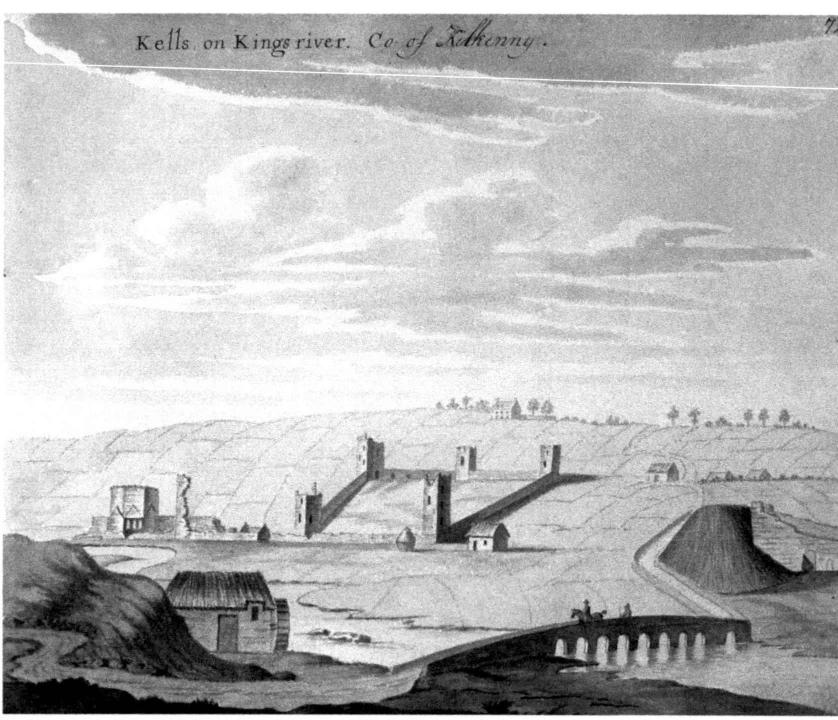

3.3 Gabriel Beranger's eighteenth-century view of Kells, showing motte on right (reproduced by permission of the Royal Irish Academy © RIA).

The castle

The motte-and-bailey castle was erected at the northern edge of the settlement on a natural island, which is no longer obvious because over time the channel on the southern side has silted up (figs 3.2–3.3).[10] Most of the circular flat-topped motte has been destroyed with only the western part surviving.[11] It was a large motte by Irish standards and its summit was probably enclosed by a wooden palisade, with a tower inside for refuge. Adjoining the western side of the motte, the bailey or bawn was enclosed by a masonry wall, which was originally over 5m in height. The bailey wall may be secondary, replacing a timber palisade, which was built before the early fourteenth century as the castle was not maintained by the absentee lords who succeeded after the fitz Robert line died out.[12] There are no visible remains of structures on the bailey, suggesting that these were entirely of wood or possibly timber-framed. Domestic buildings probably consisted of a hall, kitchen and larder, as noted in extents for other Irish sites.[13] There was a chapel at Kells Castle which is mentioned in the charter for the priory (fig. 3.4).[14] The manorial court, or hundred, held at Kells was provided for in the existing town charter, dating from 1211 to 1216, and the courthouse was most likely at the castle.[15] As well as the centre for administration and justice, the court was a source of revenue because tenants paid the lord for business transacted there. Access to the island and castle from the north was by a ford, or possibly a bridge, over the King's River (figs 3.2–3.3). The castle gate, referred to in the priory charter, was probably on the road leading from the river (fig. 3.4).[16]

The town

Geoffrey fitz Robert refers to 'my new town' in the extant charter for the priory of 1204–6 (fig. 3.4).[17] In his town charter of 1211–16, William (Geoffrey's heir) states that his father had established the town, and by this time it would appear that the borough was well developed with an expanding population.[18] As part of the colonisation process, Geoffrey fitz Robert, like other Anglo-Norman lords, brought in immigrant settlers, most of whom probably came from England. The settlement was located to the south of the castle, where it is named 'Kelletowne' on William Petty's seventeenth-century map.[19] This is where the present village of Kells is situated (fig. 3.2). Kells was not enclosed by a wall or earthen

10 Clyne, *Kells Priory*, pp 21–3. **11** For an analysis of the motte's stratigraphy, see T.B. Barry, E. Culleton and C.A. Empey, 'Kells motte, Co. Kilkenny', *PRIA*, 84C (1984), pp 157–70 at pp 160–1 and fig. 2. **12** Empey, 'The priory of Kells: an introduction', p. 5. **13** Empey, 'A case study', p. 37; Barry et al., 'Kells motte', p. 164. **14** *Ormond deeds, 1172–1350*, p. 15, no. 30; *IMED*, p. 1. **15** *CPCRI, Hen. VIII–Eliz.* [1514–75], p. 426; Mac Niocaill, *Na buirgéisí*, i, p. 129. **16** *Ormond deeds, 1172–1350*, p. 15, no. 30; *IMED*, p. 2. **17** Ibid. **18** *CPCRI, Hen. VIII–Eliz.* [1514–75], pp 425–6; Mac Niocaill, *Na buirgéisí*, i, pp 129–30; see also Clyne, *Kells Priory*, p. 25. **19** William Petty, *Hibernia delineatio: atlas of Ireland* (London, 1685; repr. Shannon, 1969), map 14. **20** Avril Thomas, *The walled towns of Ireland* (2 vols, Dublin, 1992), ii, pp 243–4.

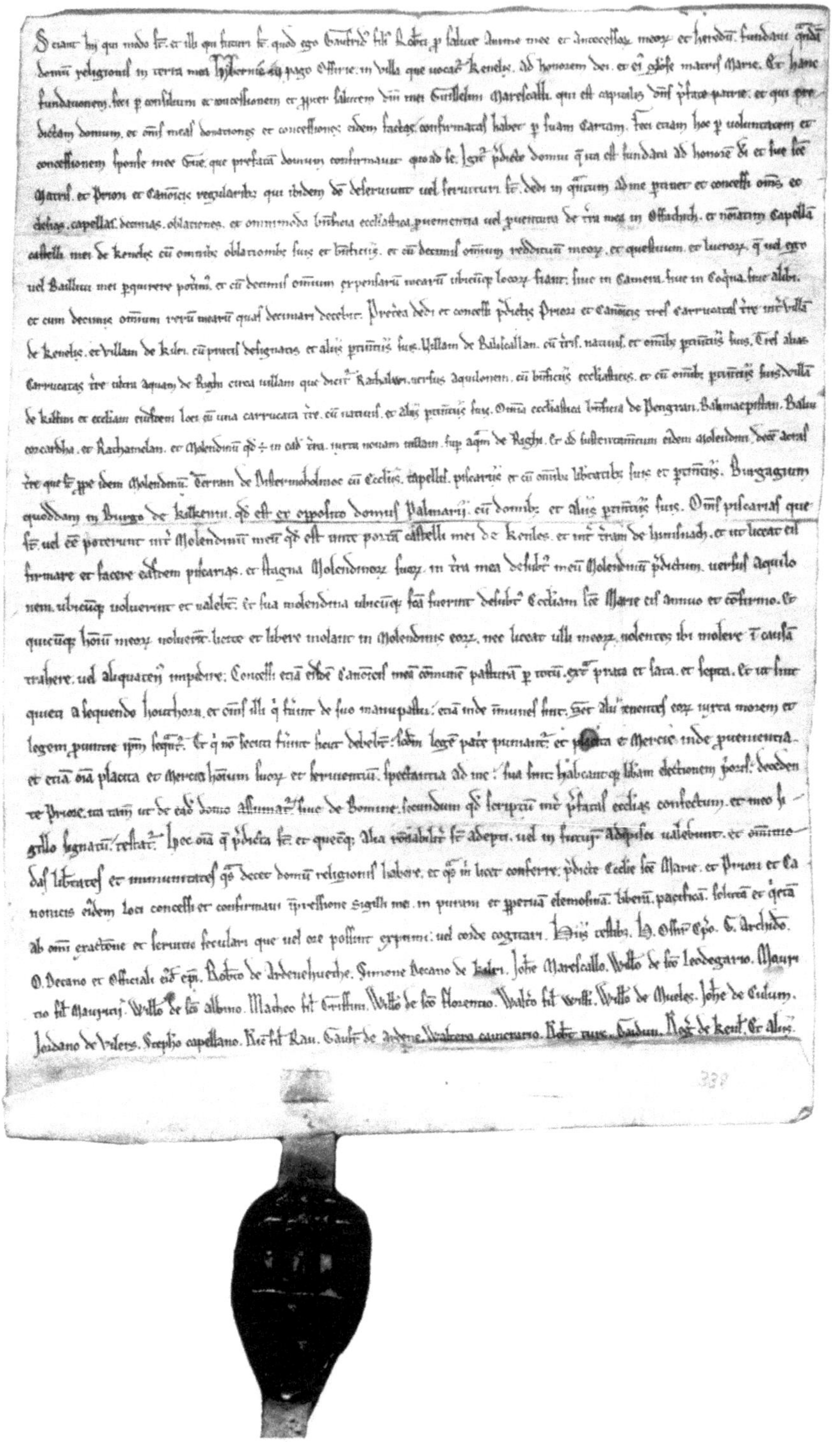

3.4 Kells Priory: Geoffrey fitz Robert's foundation charter, 1204x6) (NLI, D38) (image reproduced courtesy of the National Library of Ireland).

rampart.[20] It would seem that the medieval town was more extensive than the present village and that it had occupied the land in the bend of the river to the west of the priory. The property boundaries on the OS map would appear to reflect the narrow burgage plots fronting the streets (fig. 3.2). Fourteenth-century documents also state that the settlement extended eastwards to the priory.[21] It has been calculated from the rents of 1346 that there were seventy-one burgage plots where the burgesses had their dwellings.[22] None of the houses has survived, probably because most of them were built of timber and clay. The burgesses were granted timber for the construction of their houses on William fitz Geoffrey's lands at Castle Eve west of Kells in the early thirteenth century (fig. 3.5).[23] Deeds relate to a house of stone and to a large storehouse with a substantial rent of 40*s*.[24] The layout of the street plan at Kells, like many other Anglo-Norman towns, was linear – there was a long main street and other streets at right-angles (fig. 3.2).[25] Their names – 'Le Hargrowstret', 'Common Street', 'Mid-Street' and 'Royal Road' – have been recorded.[26] A roadway, defined by a hollow-way, ran from the town centre past the priory continuing eastwards to join the present road (fig. 3.2). It would have linked Kells with the routes to south-east Ireland and the medieval ports of New Ross, Rosbercon and Waterford. Kells had a market where local produce was sold and imported goods purchased. It was probably held at the crossroads in the town, a place where there was adequate space to conduct trade. The cross base, possibly thirteenth century in date, has not survived in its original position, but is in a field to the south-east of the medieval town (fig. 3.2).

THE MANOR

The manor of Kells was the economic unit (its size approximating to the post-Reformation civil parish) within which Geoffrey fitz Robert reserved lands for his demesne that provided for his household (fig. 3.5). Farm buildings would have been located at the castle, which was also the centre for the lord's demesne. Barns or granaries, storehouses, stables and other animal houses are listed in the extents for Irish manors.[27] The land on the western side of the island at the castle

21 *Ormond deeds, 1172–1350*, p. 278, no. 661; p. 279, no. 662; p. 283, no. 673; p. 296, no. 696. 22 C.A. Empey, 'Conquest and settlement: patterns of Anglo-Norman settlement in north Munster and south Leinster', *Irish Economic and Social History*, 13 (1986), pp 5–31 at pp 21–3. 23 *CPCRI, Hen. VIII–Eliz.* [1514–75], p. 426; Mac Niocaill, *Na buirgéisí*, i, p. 129. 24 *Ormond deeds, 1172–1350*, p. 270, no. 637; p. 274, nos 648–9; p. 279, no. 665; p. 296, no. 697. 25 John Bradley, *Walled towns in Ireland* (Dublin, 1995), p. 31; Tadhg O'Keeffe, *Medieval Ireland: an archaeology* (Stroud, 2000), p. 193. 26 *Ormond deeds, 1172–1350*, p. 274, no. 649; p. 296, no. 696; *Ormond deeds, 1350–1413*, pp 17–18, no. 31; *Ormond deeds, 1413–1509*, p. 173, no. 189; Richard Lahert, *The history and antiquities of the parish of Dunnamaggan, including a full history of the great monastic foundation of Kells in the diocese of Ossory* (Tralee, 1956), pp 69–70. 27 Empey, 'A case study', p. 37n.30; Barry et al., 'Kells motte', p. 164n.41.

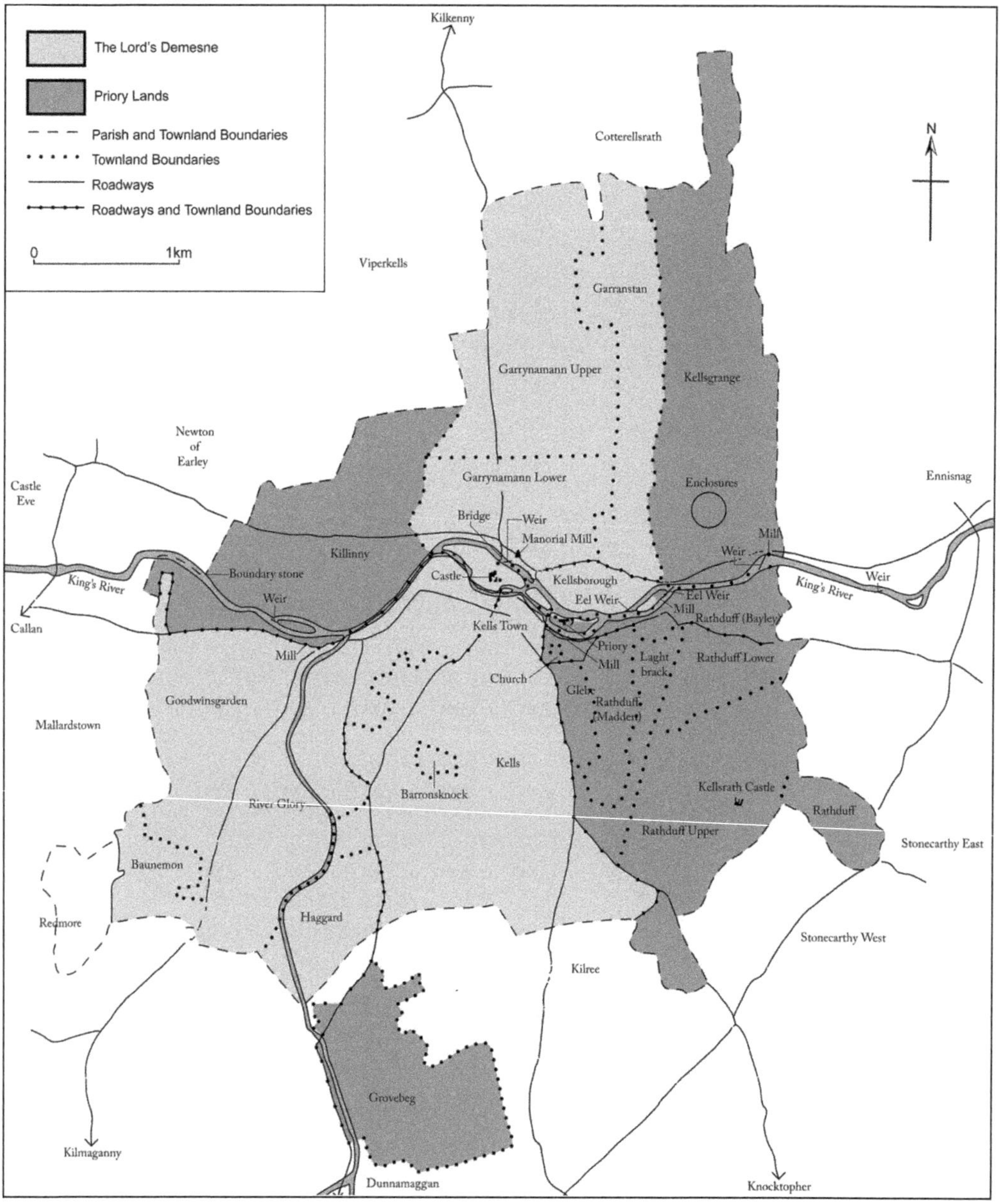

3.5 Map of Kells manor and parish (© National Monuments Service) (based on Down Survey composite map 1655 and © Ordnance Survey Ireland/Government of Ireland Copyright Permit MP003816).

was known as 'bawn meadow' and the eastern part was granted as common pasture to the burgesses of Kells (fig. 3.2).[28] Most of the demesne lands were in Kells parish, comprising roughly three-fifths of the area (2,320 statute acres).

28 *CPCRI, Hen VIII–Eliz.* [1514–75], p. 426; Carrigan, *Ossory*, iv, p. 55; Mac Niocaill, *Na buirgéisí*, i, p. 129.

Additional land was owned by the lord of Kells at Castle Eve to the north of the King's River and west of Kells (fig. 3.5).[29] At the south-west of the manor, the western part of Baunemon was not demesne land and it was part of Redmore belonging to the burgesses of Kells town (fig. 3.5).[30] Much of Kells manor had good agricultural land, and in the charter for the priory, Geoffrey fitz Robert's demesne is described as having 'meadows, sown lands and enclosed spaces'.[31] Possibly up to half of the demesne lands were arable and the remainder comprised pasture, meadow and turbary.[32] The main exports from areas colonised by the Anglo-Normans were cereals, wool and hides.[33] Work was carried out by unfree tenants who were required to give labour service to the lord.[34] Both free and unfree tenants, who were the immigrant settlers and the Gaelic Irish who were absorbed into the manorial system, could lease land.[35] Geoffrey fitz Robert mentions 'my mill towards the north' and 'my mill, which is before the gate of my castle' in the charter for the priory (fig. 3.4).[36] He was referring to his corn mill, which tenants were obliged to use and paid a tax to their lord for the privilege of doing so. Mill sites usually remain the same because of the considerable resources required in their construction and ongoing maintenance.[37] Also, their number was restricted by law and rights were attached to them. Gabriel Beranger's view shows the eighteenth-century mill powered by a vertical wheel on the site of the present mill at Kells on the north bank of the river, which probably had been the site of the manorial mill (figs 3.2–3.3, 3.5).

THE RELIGIOUS HOUSE

While the Anglo-Norman conquest of Ireland was taking place, reform of the Irish church was ongoing.[38] The new lords played a significant role. Growth in the number of reformed monasteries continued at a rapid pace after the invasion with a second wave of foundations in the latter part of the twelfth century

29 *CPCRI, Hen. VIII–Eliz.* [1514–75], p. 426; Mac Niocaill, *Na buirgéisí*, i, p. 129. 30 Lahert, *The history and antiquities of the parish of Dunnamaggan*, p. 66. 31 *Ormond deeds, 1172–1350*, p. 15, no. 30; *IMED*, p. 2. 32 *CPR, 1345–8*, p. 261; *Calendar of the Gormanston register*, ed. James Mills and M.J. McEnery (Dublin, 1916), p. 128. 33 T.B. Barry, *The medieval moated sites of S.E. Ireland: Counties Carlow, Kilkenny, Tipperary and Wexford* (BAR, Brit. Ser. 35; Oxford, 1977), pp 25, 32. 34 Mark Hennessy, 'Manorial organisation in early thirteenth-century Tipperary', *Irish Geography*, 29:2 (1996), pp 116–25 at p. 117; T.B. Barry, 'The chronology and development of medieval rural settlement in Munster', *Journal of the Cork Archaeological and Historical Society*, 105 (2000), pp 191–8 at p. 193. 35 Barry, *Medieval moated sites*, pp 30–1. 36 *Ormond deeds, 1172–1350*, p. 15, no. 30; *IMED*, p. 2. 37 Colin Rynne, 'The Patrick Street watermills: their technological context and a note on the reconstruction' in Claire Walsh, *Archaeological excavations at Patrick, Nicholas and Winetavern Sreets Dublin* (Dingle, 1997), pp 81–101 at p. 87. 38 For ecclesiastical reform and its impact in Ireland in the late eleventh and twelfth centuries, see Aubrey Gwynn, *The Irish church in the eleventh and twelfth centuries*, ed. Gerard O'Brien (Dublin, 1992); M.T. Flanagan, *The transformation of the Irish church in the twelfth century* (Woodbridge, 2010).

continuing into the thirteenth. As well as introducing immigrant settlers to populate his borough at Kells, Geoffrey fitz Robert sought English clergy to colonise his new religious house. This move would provide further stability on his newly established manor as he could be assured of their loyalty. Geoffrey brought in Augustinian canons and he acted unusually in this regard because many of the communities at existing ecclesiastical sites in Ireland adopted the Rule of St Augustine and were not colonised from foreign monasteries.[39] According to the Register of Kells, Geoffrey fitz Robert found it difficult to persuade an English monastery to colonise his new religious foundation at Kells.[40] As an interim measure, he installed four secular priests at the existing church – St Kieran's – to the south of the priory (fig. 3.2), to provide the liturgy for the inhabitants of the town and manor. Eventually, four canons from the prestigious Augustinian priory at Bodmin in Cornwall came to Kells. The canons from Bodmin went on to become distinguished churchmen. Reginald de Aclond was the first prior, Hugh le Rous, the next prior, was installed as bishop of Ossory in 1202, Alured became prior of Inistioge and Algar was later a bishop in Lombardy.[41] Le Rous was an influential churchman not only within his own diocese of Ossory, but over much of the lordship of Leinster as a close relationship developed between the bishop and William Marshal. He played a leading role in assisting the Marshal to found the Cistercian houses at Tintern (pl. 2) and Duiske (pl. 1).[42]

Kells Priory was founded in 1193 or soon afterwards.[43] The foundation charter, preserved with the Ormond deeds, can be dated to between 1204 and 1206, and is probably not the original as it indicates that at least part of the priory church was then constructed (fig. 3.4).[44] It contains *pro anima* requests. Geoffrey fitz Robert states that he founded the monastery

> for the sake of my soul and that of my ancestors and heirs … this foundation I have made by council and consent, and for the soul of my lord William the Marshal who is chief lord of the aforesaid country and who has confirmed by his charter the above said house and all my donations and grants made to it.

It was necessary for Geoffrey to obtain confirmation from his overlord because the priory was on William Marshal's land and it was as his dutiful knight that the lord of Kells commemorated the Marshal.[45] By this time, Geoffrey was married to his second wife, Eva de Birmingham, and her consent to the foundation was

39 See *MRHI*, pp 153–200. **40** 'Register of Kells', p. 311. **41** Ibid., p. 312; Empey, 'The priory of Kells: an introduction', p. 5, appendix 1, p. 9. **42** Crouch, *William Marshal*, p. 152. **43** Empey, 'The priory of Kells: an introduction', p. 3. **44** *Ormond deeds, 1172–1350*, pp 14–18, no. 30; *IMED*, pp 1–3; Empey, 'The priory of Kells: an introduction', pp 4–5. **45** Crouch, *William Marshal*, p. 162.

also confirmed in the charter. The charter stipulates that the prior of Kells must be freely elected and chosen from among the community there or from Bodmin, a proviso that had already been agreed with the mother-house.

The site granted for the priory was an island adjoining the river at the eastern edge of the town (figs 3.2, 3.3). The land here had been associated with the church in preceding centuries because an early medieval ecclesiastical site was located close by, which was dedicated to St Ciarán of Saighir, patron of the Osraige.[46] The introduction of Augustinian canons and the construction of their monastery beside and on land that most likely had belonged to the former ecclesiastical site shows how the reformed priory supplanted the older church system.

Geoffrey fitz Robert allocated lands for the priory within the manor of Kells amounting to almost 1,600 statute acres (fig. 3.5). These lands are listed in his charter. The prior and canons were granted the lands with its betaghs or serfs (*nativi*) adjoining the monastery to the east and south, which was the home farm managed directly from the priory.[47] On the north bank of the King's River and contiguous with the home farm, the second inherited property granted was Kellsgrange, named as 'Rathalwi' in the charter. The third property at Killinny (originally a lesser grant of the church there with ten acres of land from Baldwin de Hamptonsford) was located to the north-west on the opposite side of Kells town. In addition, the monastery was granted rights to common pasture on the lord's demesne. The lord of Kells divided his manor into the lands he retained for himself and the remainder he gave as an endowment to his new religious house (fig. 3.5). Rights to construct corn mills were included in the charter, which would have produced a significant amount of revenue thereby enhancing the monastic economy. Water-powered mills were required for grinding corn grown on the priory estate, which was in a predominantly cereal-growing area. Besides a mill at the priory itself, each of the three farms of land had a mill on the King's River (fig. 3.5).[48] Geoffrey fitz Robert granted the fisheries on a long stretch of the river from his mill near the castle eastwards as far as Ennisnag beyond the monastic estate. Religious observances ensured that fish was an important factor in the monastic diet. In 1541 there were three weirs on the river within the priory estate.[49] The canons had eel weirs, and salmon may have been trapped at the others.[50] Both species were regarded as high-status food in secular and monastic households in medieval Ireland. Furthermore, the lord of Kells

46 Pádraig Ó Riain, *A dictionary of Irish saints* (Dublin, 2011), pp 172–3. 47 The parcel of land at Grovebeg (fig. 3.5) comprising approximately 233 statute acres was a later acquisition recorded at the Dissolution in the extent of 1541 and in subsequent surveys: *EIMP*, p. 188; Conleth Manning, 'The 1653 survey of the lands granted to the countess of Ormond in Co. Kilkenny', *JRSAI*, 129 (1999), pp 40–66 at p. 55. 48 Mervyn Archdall, *Monasticon Hibernicum; or, An history of the abbies, priories and other religious houses in Ireland* (Dublin, 1786), pp 364–5; *EIMP*, pp 188–9; Manning, 'The 1653 survey', p. 55. 49 *EIMP*, p. 188. 50 Clyne, *Kells Priory*, p. 37.

donated land at Dysart with its fisheries and also its churches (fig. 3.1).[51] Geoffrey also granted a burgage in William Marshal's caput at Kilkenny to the canons. Kells Priory was patronised by William Marshal in 1203. His endowment comprised land (400 statute acres) at Ardaloo, north of Kilkenny (fig. 3.1), and another property south of this, its location described as 'between the land of Andree Larcier and Kilkenny'.[52] Another generous benefactor was Matthew fitz Griffin, lord of Knocktopher, who granted five knights' fees at 'Killaleth' and Tullylease in Cork and other lands in Desmond.[53]

As the community at Kells were canons, they could undertake parochial duties. Payment of tithes and the development of a parish structure were further steps taken in church reform. Subinfeudation following the Anglo-Norman conquest provided the framework for territorial organisation, whereby in most cases the newly formed manor became the parish, and the tithes and advowsons were usually granted by the lords to the dioceses or religious houses.[54] Ecclesiastical tithes were a lucrative source of income for Kells Priory. Geoffrey fitz Robert's charter granted the benefices of the churches and chapels on the monastic lands. The priory church was the parish church of Kells where the Augustinian community provided pastoral care for the townspeople and those living in the hinterland. The canons were also to conduct services in the castle chapel and they were granted all of the benefices in Geoffrey's lands in the cantred of Offa in Tipperary. Impropriations at later dates were granted by other knights and deeds dating to the thirteenth century demonstrate that thirty-five such benefices were appropriated by Kells Priory.[55] By the time Kells Priory was dissolved in 1541 it had become the wealthiest monastery in the medieval county of Kilkenny.[56]

THE EXCAVATIONS

Archaeological excavations were directed at Kells Priory by the late Thomas Fanning in the 1970s and in 1980 for the National Monuments Service, which was then part of the Office of Public Works. In 1996, the tower house adjoining

51 *IMED*, p. 2. 52 'Register of Kells', pp 301–2. 53 Ibid., pp 304–5. 54 For studies on Anglo-Norman parish formation and administration, see A.J. Otway-Ruthven, 'Parochial development in the rural deanery of Skreen', *JRSAI*, 94 (1964), pp 111–22; Mark Hennessy, 'Parochial organisation in medieval Tipperary' in William Nolan and Thomas McGrath (eds), *Tipperary: history and society* (Dublin, 1985), pp 60–70; C.A. Empey, 'The layperson in the parish: the medieval inheritance, 1169–1536' in Raymond Gillespie and W.G. Neely (eds), *The laity and the Church of Ireland, 1100–2000: all sorts and conditions* (Dublin, 2002), pp 7–48; Patrick Nugent, 'The dynamics of parish formation in high and late medieval Clare' in Elizabeth FitzPatrick and Raymond Gillespie (eds), *The parish in medieval and early modern Ireland: community, territory and building* (Dublin, 2006), pp 91–123. 55 'Register of Kells', pp 302–13; Carrigan, *Ossory*, iv, p. 65. 56 *EIMP*, pp 188–93; Empey, 'The priory of Kells: an introduction', p. 4.

the chancel was investigated by the author. The excavations, which included the complete church and most of the domestic ranges, are the largest undertaken on an Anglo-Norman monastery in Ireland. Not alone has the work enabled the interpretation of the buildings, the collection of finds (close to 18,000 artefacts) has provided information on the furnishings and on day-to-day life at the priory.[57]

The buildings

In the thirteenth and fourteenth centuries the priory was contained within a monastic precinct and the main buildings comprised the church and two domestic ranges (figs 3.6, 3.7, foreground). The architecture is early Gothic based on the Early English style. The design for the priory, in accordance with the standard Benedictine plan arranged around a central cloister positioned to the south of the church and surrounded by the domestic ranges, was undertaken by a professional then known as a master mason.[58] It is likely that he collaborated with the patron, Geoffrey fitz Robert, and with the four canons who came to Kells from the mother-house at Bodmin. It is possible that the master mason too was from south-west England.

Water management was of prime consideration when designing a monastery. The watercourse, or channel, along the southern boundary of the precinct was used for a number of purposes – it formed a moat and it powered the mill (fig. 3.6; Tietzsch-Tyler, 'Kells', this volume, figs 4.2–4.3). A major discovery in the excavations was the stone-lined main drain in the south of the precinct (figs 3.6, 3.8). There is no doubt that this engineering scheme was designed from the outset, when account of the ground slope and existing watercourses would have been taken into consideration. The drain route was established before the claustral ranges were designed because the east range extends beyond the south range in order to accommodate the drain (fig. 3.6). The misaligned position of the rere-dorter implies that the drain was already built beforehand. The drain was constructed to channel water for flushing the rere-dorter latrines and to carry away the sewage. It fed off the moat and entered the precinct under an arch at the south curtain wall. The drain crossed the lower courtyard and then it ran beneath the east range and rere-dorter. From here on the drain was not investigated and it continued across the eastern precinct to exit under a postern gateway and empty into the open channel and moat outside the eastern curtain and into the King's River (fig. 3.6).

Construction of a monastery usually began with the most important building, the church. The eastern end was built first and when the chancel was complete, worship could take place. The chancel may have been erected by the time

57 Detailed results of the investigations at the priory with specialist reports have been published in Clyne, *Kells Priory*. 58 Nicola Coldstream, *Medieval craftsmen: masons and sculptors* (London, 1991), pp 12–18.

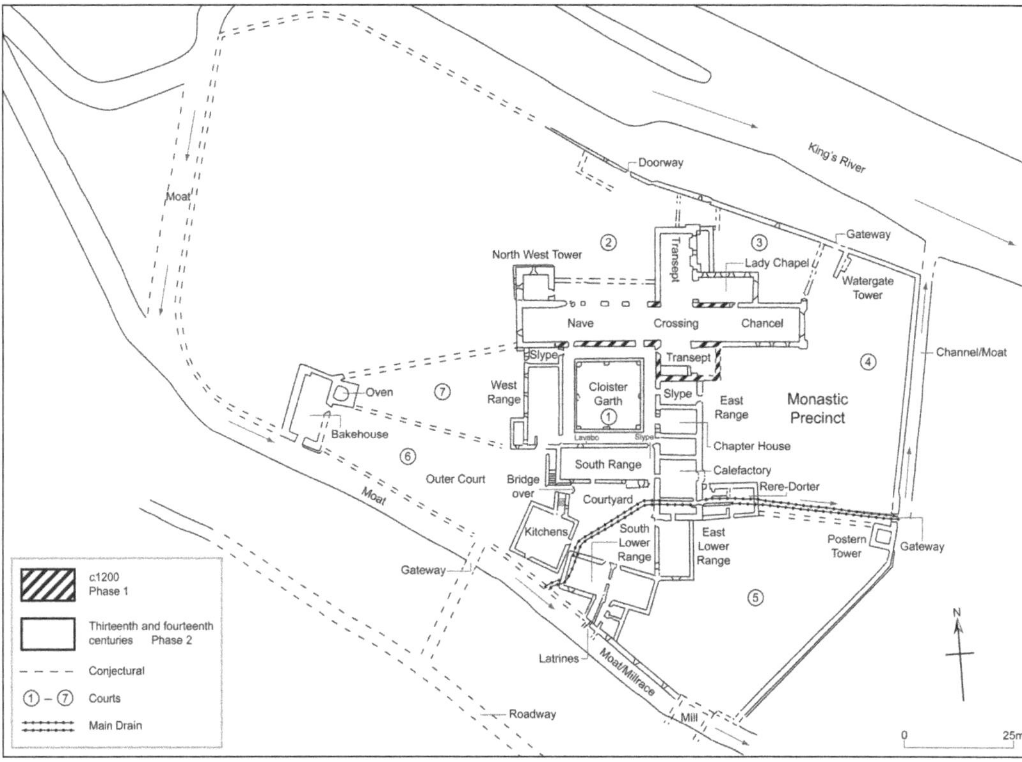

3.6 Kells Priory: plan of priory in thirteenth and fourteenth centuries (© National Monuments Service).

3.7 Kells Priory: view from north-west (© National Monuments Service Photographic Unit).

3.8 Kells Priory: main drain in courtyard, post-excavation, from north-east (© National Monuments Service Photographic Unit).

Geoffrey fitz Robert's charter was drawn up in 1204–6 because it refers to St Mary's Church. It was undoubtedly completed when Hugh le Rous, bishop of Ossory and former prior, was buried there in 1218.[59] The remains of the primary church revealed in the excavation had a cruciform design, comprising the chancel, the nave with the crossing in between leading to a transept north and south, each with a chapel entered through an archway (fig. 3.9). The timber roof was covered with slates, and the ceramic tiles placed along the ridge, although manufactured locally, were copied from Cornish tiles, suggesting that workmen were recruited from the neighbourhood of Bodmin.[60] It would appear from the limited size of the first chancel (fig. 3.9) that it was envisaged that the priory would accommodate only a modest number of canons.

59 Archdall, *Monasticon Hibernicum*, p. 362; Carrigan, *Ossory*, i, p. 279. 60 Joanna Wren, 'The roof tiles' in Clyne, *Kells Priory*, pp 225–34 at pp 226, 231.

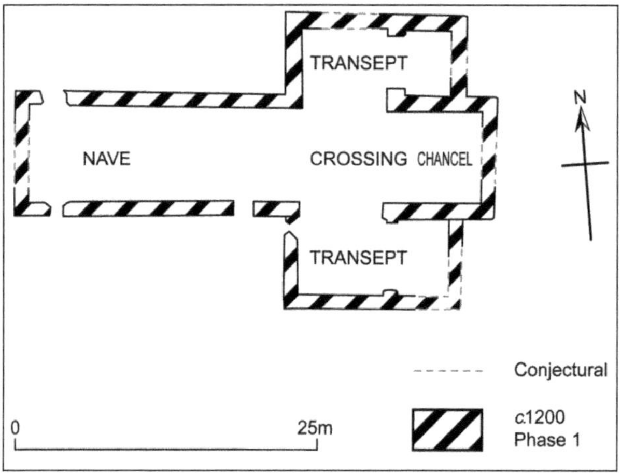

3.9 Kells Priory: plan of primary church (© National Monuments Service).

Work on the claustral ranges commenced in the early thirteenth century while building was still underway on the primary church as the masonry is continuous into the east range. This building originally had five rooms on the ground floor, each the width of the range (fig. 3.6). The two rooms beside the church were probably used for administrative purposes. The slype, or corridor, connecting the cloister with the eastern precinct was quite spacious with seating along the walls suggesting that the room also functioned as a parlour and prior's office. The community would have assembled in the morning in the chapter house and the masonry remains of the benches where the canons sat were uncovered. An opening, or window, which was not glazed, was positioned each side of the doorway from the chapter house to the cloister so that the proceedings taking place in the room could be attended from outside in the ambulatory.[61] The largest room in the range was the calefactory, or warming room, with its fireplace where the canons carried out chores or perhaps where they were allowed to read and meditate during the winter months.[62] The canons' dormitory was on the upper floor and the stone stairs by which they accessed the church at night was in the transept. It was usual to have latrines on the southern end of the range at dormitory level, but evidence for this did not survive at Kells.[63] The main drain passes through the room below on the ground floor and there were possibly latrines here before the rere-dorter was added. There were small rooms in the rere-dorter at ground level suggesting that, although it was not the normal arrangement, latrines were situated here. The sluice, which would have been fitted with wooden gates for flushing the latrines, was situated where the main drain entered the rere-dorter.

61 Roger Stalley, *The Cistercian monasteries of Ireland* (London and New Haven, 1987), pp 163–4. **62** Ibid., p. 169. **63** C.J. Bond, 'Water management in the rural economy' in Roberta Gilchrist and Harold Mytum (eds), *The archaeology of rural monasteries* (BAR, Brit. Ser. 227; Oxford, 1989), pp 83–111 at p. 93; J.P. Greene, *Medieval monasteries* (Leicester, 1992), pp 119, 121, fig. 2.

3.10 Kells Priory: lavabo, post-excavation (© National Monuments Service Photographic Unit).

The south claustral range was next in the constructional sequence. During the monastic occupation, the ground floor was one large room, probably used mainly as a store or buttery (fig. 3.6). There was a wooden staircase at the western end leading to the refectory on the upper floor. This was a bright room with many windows, which had glass with painted designs. The pulpit, where a member of the community read from the scriptures during meals, was in an alcove approached by stone steps (in the south wall at the eastern end) and behind the reader's desk there was a large window of three lights. All religious orders insisted on the washing of hands before meals, and this took place at the lavabo beside the doorway leading to the refectory in the south range (figs 3.6, 3.10). It has a stone basin built into a recess but the upper part is broken and, accordingly, the method of water supply is not known. Waste water was normally conducted into a drain, often the main drain, but the disposal system for the Kells lavabo was a stone-lined soak-away, located in the ambulatory floor beneath. Most of the ground floor in the west – or cellarer's – range comprised a large room where food, drink and other provisions were stored. Its design incorporated two doorways at the southern end, one for convenient access to the refectory and the other for allowing items to be brought in through the main gateway to the precinct (fig. 3.6; Tietzsch-Tyler, 'Kells', this volume, fig. 4.2). The upper floor may have been the prior's quarters in the thirteenth and fourteenth centuries.[64] After the ranges were constructed, the cloister

64 Ibid., p. 9.

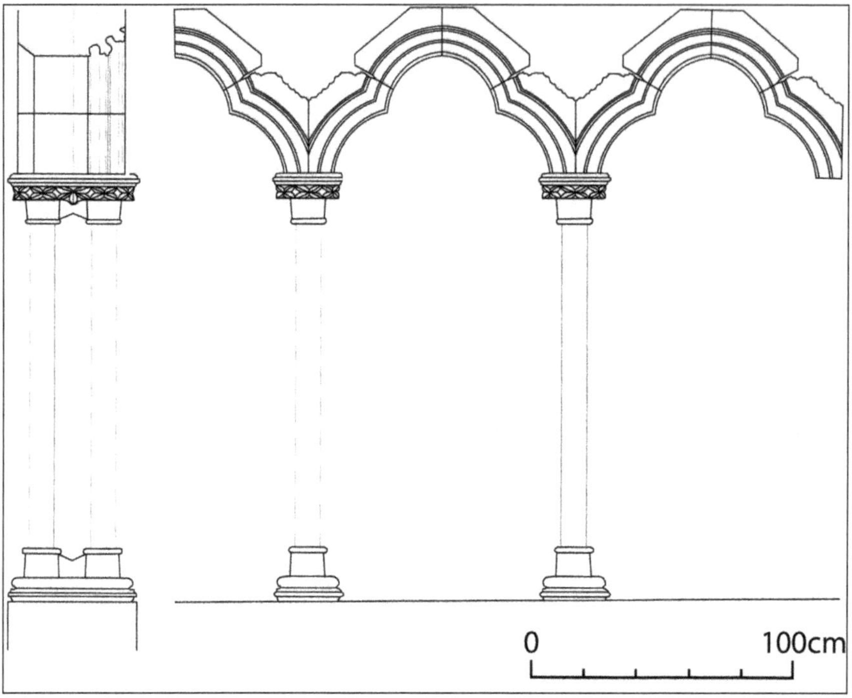

3.11 Kells Priory: elevation and section reconstruction drawings of cloister arcade (after Montague, 'The cloister arcade').

ambulatories were built by the mid-thirteenth century.[65] A low wall supported a carved limestone arcade, which even in its fragmented state is important as it is one of only a few Irish examples of this date (fig. 3.11). It was an elegant architectural feature with slender double column-shafts, capitals ornamented with botanical motifs and dogtooth designs, supporting cusped trefoil arches. The beauty of the arcade was enhanced by the colour contrast on the highly polished black shafts against the matt, pale grey surfaces of the other stonework.

In the thirteenth century the priory was enclosed by a high curtain wall, with towers placed on the inside, built inside the moat (figs 3.6–3.7). It would appear that the western part of the precinct was larger than its present size and the land on the north-west and west was incorporated to form a sub-rectangular enclosure (1.5 hectares/3.7 acres). The eccentric layout of the lower ranges, consisting of single-storey buildings arranged around a courtyard, implies that they post-date the south precinct wall and that they were not part of the original design for the priory (fig. 3.6). Although the results from the excavations were not conclusive, it is likely that the south range was the priory infirmary. The

65 John Montague, 'The cloister arcade' in Clyne, *Kells Priory*, pp 187–206.

3.12 Kells Priory: decorated dish (© National Monuments Service Photographic Unit).

main building was found to have two rooms, probably a chapel and a hall with a fireplace where the inmates were accommodated. A passageway led from the hall to outside the precinct where latrines were situated straddling the moat. The kitchens were in the west lower range, a detached structure so as to reduce the risk of a fire spreading to other parts of the priory (fig. 3.6). They were located behind the south claustral range and food was conveyed to the refectory on the upper floor by a stone staircase supported on a bridge over the courtyard gateway. Deposits in the kitchens and in domestic refuse dumped in the courtyard produced a large quantity of pottery dating from the late twelfth to the fourteenth century.[66] Most of the vessels were Irish and comprised mainly cooking pots, storage jars and jugs. Approximately half of them were manufactured locally, including a decorated dish (fig. 3.12), and others originated within the lordship of Leinster. There were also some unusual items such as a condiment dish, probably for spices, and two small bowls that may have held salt. The amount of imported wares was small. Ham Green sherds were from a jug that was probably brought to the priory with the canons from Bodmin. Jugs from the Saintonge region, north of Bordeaux, came with wine. The same deposits provided useful data on diet – on the cereals, meats and shellfish consumed. Beer, bread and porridge made from the cereals (barley, wheat and oats) were

66 Clare McCutcheon, 'The medieval pottery' in Clyne, *Kells Priory*, pp 316–42.

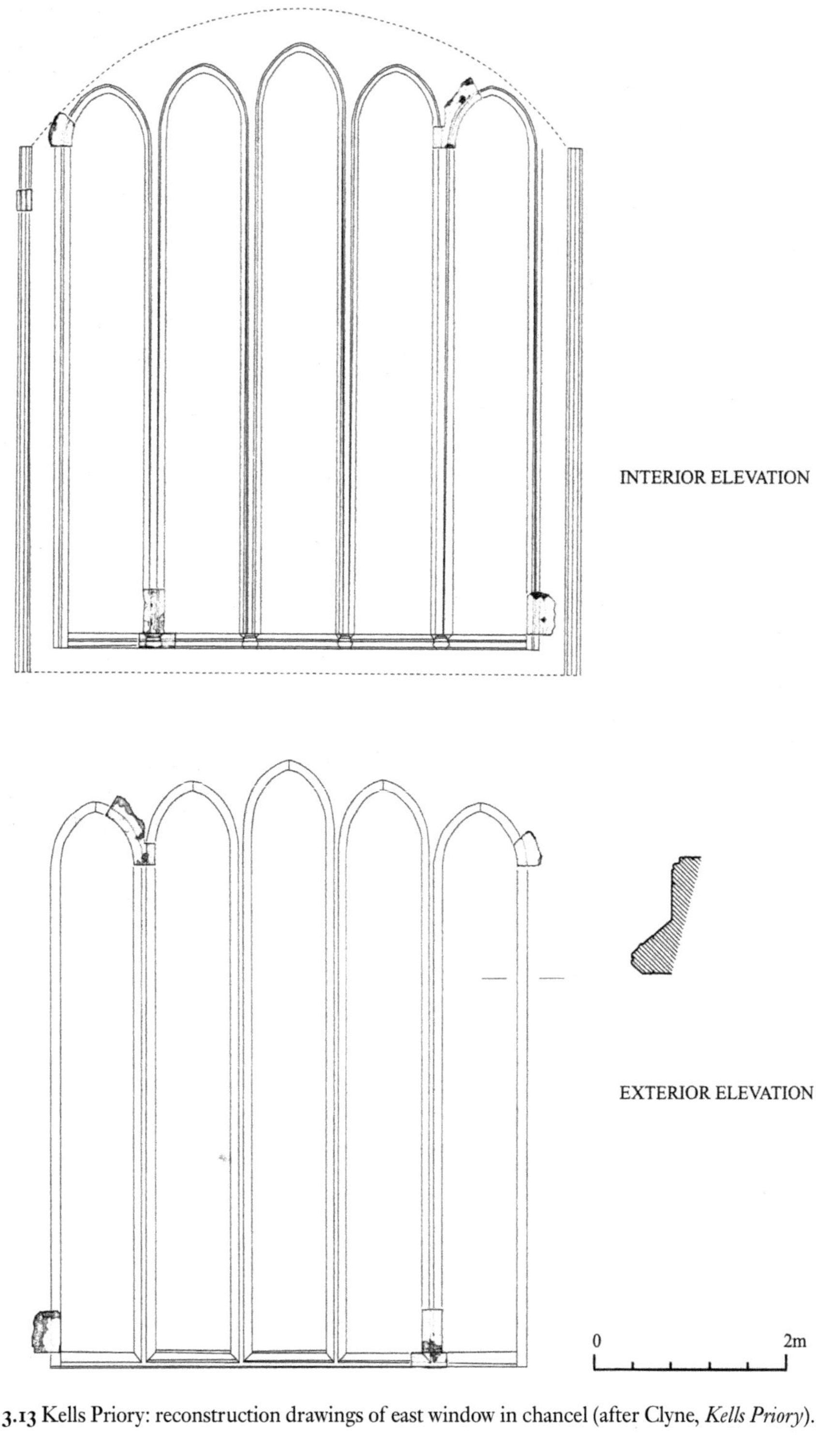

3.13 Kells Priory: reconstruction drawings of east window in chancel (after Clyne, *Kells Priory*).

3.14 Kells Priory: wall-painting fragment with figure (© National Monuments Service Photographic Unit).

part of the staple diet in a monastery, and at Kells there was also evidence for vetches, peas, nettles and hazelnuts.[67] Faunal remains included the common domestic animals of cattle, sheep/goat and pig, and as many of the animals were mature when slaughtered, it can be suggested that meat was bought in instead of the animals being reared on the priory estate.[68] Bird bones were recovered and the kitchen account of 1382 for Kells Priory records that domestic fowl was then being purchased comprising an unspecified number of capons and seventy-two geese.[69] Oyster, cockle, mussel and whelk were part of the monastic diet and their presence shows that the priory already had trade connections with the coastal ports during the early period of occupation.[70]

Enlargements to the church were ongoing by the mid-thirteenth century (fig. 3.6), perhaps made possible by the revenue acquired from new impropriations at this time.[71] This building work reflects a population expansion in the town and an increase in the religious community at the priory. The nave was extended probably when the west claustral range was under construction. Furthermore, an aisle was added to the nave and a tower erected at the north-west corner, which may have been a belfry. The chancel was subsequently increased in size. The great east window collapsed and the blocks were recovered in the excavations, both inside and outside the chancel, enabling a reconstruction on paper (fig. 3.13).[72] It had five bluntly pointed graded lights with roll-and-

67 Michael Monk, 'The plant remains' in Clyne, *Kells Priory*, pp 483–4. **68** Finbar McCormick, 'The faunal remains' in Clyne, *Kells Priory*, pp 477–82. **69** Empey, 'The priory of Kells: an introduction', appendix 2, p. 11. **70** McCormick, 'The faunal remains', pp 477–9. **71** 'Register of Kells', pp 302–13. **72** Clyne, *Kells Priory*, pp 161–5.

3.15 Kells Priory: window glass (after Moran, 'The window glass').

chamfer mouldings. Limestone was used for the weight-bearing elements and sandstone for the arches.

The walls inside the church had a smooth plaster finish and they were painted in bright colours. Ireland's damp climate is not conducive to the preservation of wall paintings and the fragments from Kells are a rare survival. It is likely that the primary decorative scheme dates to the thirteenth century and was composed of a false ashlar masonry pattern interspersed with figures (fig. 3.14).[73] Colours were the standard range for the medieval period. Red and yellow were predominant, and by mixing lime white or carbon black, the palette was extended to deep red, pink, orange and pale yellow. Only the windows in the church and the refectory had panels containing painted and stained glass. The large collection from Kells (1,517 fragments) is very important in the study of Irish medieval window glass.[74] Enough fragments were found from a nave window to reconstruct a complete grisaille panel with roundels of botanical motifs (fig. 3.15), very like those on windows in Lincoln and Salisbury cathedrals. Designs were painted in

73 Karena Morton, 'The wall painting fragments' in Clyne, *Kells Priory*, pp 206–25. **74** Josephine Moran, 'The window glass' in Clyne, *Kells Priory*, pp 261–316.

3.16 Kells Priory: suggested arrangement of tile designs in thirteenth-century tile pavement (after Campbell, 'The floor tiles').

3.17 Kells Priory: suggested reconstruction of fourteenth-century tile pavement (after Campbell, 'The floor tiles').

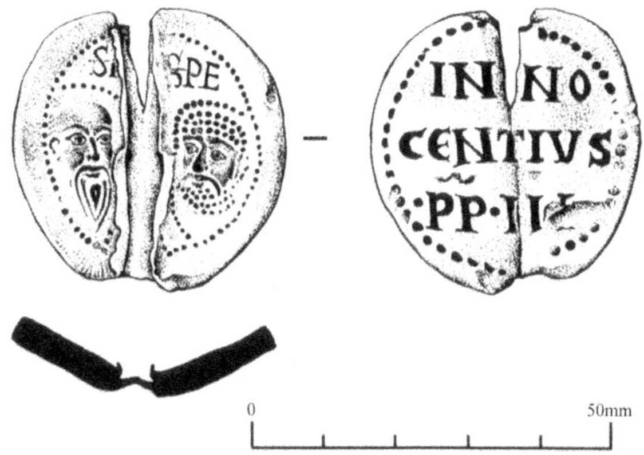

3.18 Kells Priory: lead seal matrix of Pope Innocent III (artist Patricia Johnson, © National Monuments Service).

brown or red on white glass. There were also panels with figures and an inscription may have come from a window depicting St Peter. Coloured glass was blue, red, yellow, green, turquoise and brown. It is probable that the coloured glass, and perhaps also the white glass, was imported from the Continent, possibly from Flanders or Lorraine.

The church had tiled pavements, whereas the floors in the domestic buildings were made of pebbles set in mortar. At the high altar in the chancel, there was an elaborate mosaic pavement. A chapel, built onto the north of the chancel, was probably dedicated to Our Lady (fig. 3.6), where the mortar bedding with tile impressions was preserved in the sanctuary.[75] In the thirteenth-century pavements, the inlaid designs in yellow contrasted with a brown background, with yellow corner tiles and the composition framed with brownish-green tiles.[76] The pavements included designs with addorsed lions, diagonal stripes and foliate spray, bordered by plain tiles (fig. 3.16). Floor tiles were manufactured at the priory in the thirteenth century as the kiln waste was found in the area inside the north precinct wall.[77] It would seem that, in the fourteenth century, the tiles were made elsewhere when the floor in the nave was re-tiled. Reconstruction suggests that panels were laid diagonally with contrasting light and dark colours of yellow, dark-greenish brown and black (fig. 3.17).[78] Decorated tiles include lion rampant and double-headed eagle and the pavement was framed by a border with vine-scroll pattern.

The finds

Aspects of daily life at the priory are indicated by the assemblage of artefacts. A number of finds relating to script and manuscripts are included.[79] The lead seal, or bulla, of Pope Innocent III (1198–1216) with SS Peter and Paul depicted on

75 Clyne, *Kells Priory*, pp 89–90, 504, pl. 3.4. **76** Kieran Campbell, 'The floor tiles' in Clyne, *Kells Priory*, pp 234–61 at pp 234–50. **77** Ibid., pp 256–8; Clyne, *Kells Priory*, pp 88, 106. **78** Campbell, 'The floor tiles', pp 250–6. **79** O.M.B. Scully, 'The non-ferrous metal

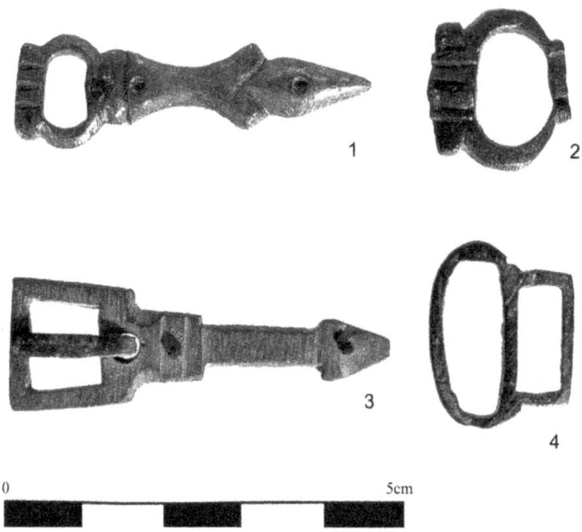

3.19 Kells Priory: copper-alloy buckles (© National Monuments Service Photographic Unit).

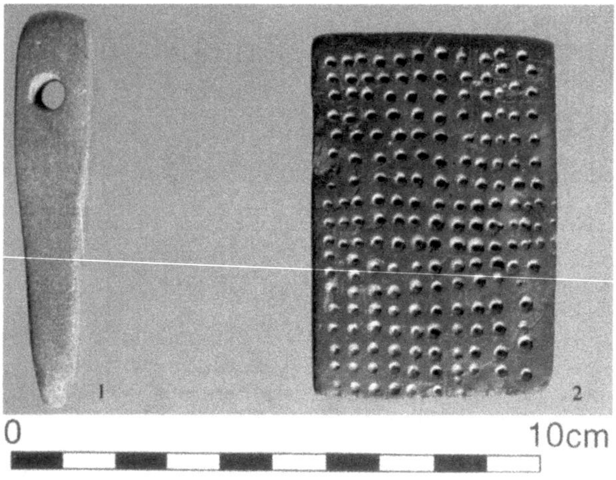

3.20 Kells Priory: stone artefacts: hone and needle punch (© National Monuments Service Photographic Unit).

the reverse (fig. 3.18) was attached to a letter dispatched soon after the priory was founded. There are simple lead points for writing and marking out lines on parchment. Copper-alloy mounts are believed to have ornamented book covers as well as having been attached to other items. Small buckles may have been used to fasten books (fig. 3.19) and it has been suggested that the so-called 'strap-ends' were bookmarkers because of their frequency on religious sites.[80] Sewing is represented by needles, a thimble and a stone needle punch for pushing needles through thick materials (fig. 3.20).[81] A bodkin for threading lace in

artefacts' in Clyne, *Kells Priory*, pp 383–405 at pp 390–1, 393, 397–402. **80** Ibid., pp 397–8. **81** Ibid., pp 387–8; O.M.B. Scully, 'The ferrous artefacts' in Clyne, *Kells Priory*, pp 353–80

3.21 Kells Priory: copper-alloy key (© National Monuments Service Photographic Unit).

garments was found.[82] Buckles and cast buttons were worn by those living at the priory.[83] Personal hygiene is represented by a tiny ear-scoop with a toothpick at the opposite end.[84] Bone combs, one double-sided and another single-sided, were recovered.[85] The tabernacle on the high altar may have been locked by the large copper-alloy key, which had traces of silvering on it (fig. 3.21), while there were other ordinary iron keys.[86] The large numbers of iron knives were used for a variety of purposes and the stone hones were for sharpening them (fig. 3.20).[87] Socketed candlesticks and stone lamps (for burning liquid fuel or for holding a pottery vessel for liquid fuel) provided light in the priory.[88] The playing of music at the priory during the earlier period of occupation is indicated by the bone tuning pegs from a fiddle, small harp or psaltery-type instrument.[89] Activities undertaken on the monastic estate are represented by iron tools including axes for felling trees and fish hooks, which were to be expected due to the proximity of the river.[90]

at pp 354–5; S.W.J. McCutcheon, 'The small stone artefacts' in Clyne, *Kells Priory*, pp 424–33 at pp 429–30. **82** Scully, 'The non-ferrous artefacts', pp 395–6. **83** Ibid., pp 396–402. **84** Ibid., pp 395–6. **85** M.F. Hurley, 'The bone artefacts' in Clyne, *Kells Priory*, pp 415–23 at pp 415–17. **86** Scully, 'The non-ferrous artefacts', pp 389–90; Scully, 'The ferrous artefacts', pp 363–6. **87** McCutcheon, 'The small stone artefacts', pp 424–8; Scully, 'The ferrous artefacts', pp 366–72. **88** McCutcheon, 'The small stone artefacts', pp 428–9; Scully, 'The ferrous artefacts', pp 354–5. **89** Hurley, 'The bone artefacts', p. 418. **90** Scully, 'The

DECLINE

Kells with its priory developed rapidly after its foundation about 1193 and prospered throughout the thirteenth century. The large number of coins recovered in the excavations, including a hoard of ten coins dating from 1180 to 1247, suggests that commerce was thriving during this period.[91] A decline in fortunes in the following century is also reflected as few coins of this date were found. This was part of a greater economic downturn occurring over much of Europe that witnessed a reversal in many economies from expansion to contraction associated with an extraordinary drop in population caused by climatic deterioration followed by famines and a series of waves of bubonic plague.[92] At a local level, there were additional difficulties that had an impact on Kells in the first half of the fourteenth century.[93] After the failure of the fitz Robert line, a succession of absentee lords followed. The Bruce army was in the Kells area in 1317 and ten years later the town was laid waste during the conflict with Desmond. It is difficult to estimate the size of the town of Kells and the number of dwellings there by the fifteenth century, but there is no doubt that its importance, and possibly also its population, had diminished.

The priory came under the control of local families and was to remain so until the Dissolution.[94] The architecture dating to the final century of monastic occupation reflects the secularisation of the priory. A major building programme began in the mid-fifteenth century when a strongly fortified castellated enclosure (1.08 hectares/2.7 acres) was constructed on the southern side of the monastic precinct (figs 3.3, 3.7, in background). It is referred to in documents as the 'Prior's Vill' and more recently as the 'Burgess Court' and is the only complete surviving example of such a late medieval enclosure at an Irish monastery.[95] The Prior's Vill was a large bawn where tenants and stock were protected inside the high curtain wall with mural towers or machicolations at vulnerable points. The enclosure was not excavated, but it is known from documents that tenants lived there, leasing a tower house and a plot of land where they probably had animal houses and other buildings.[96] The roadway to the town centre was incorporated within the enclosure and its gateways were positioned on the roadway. As well as the building of the Prior's Vill, considerable work was undertaken on the monastic precinct wall when fortifications were added and some of this work may have continued into the sixteenth century. A new south gateway with a bridge over the moat was constructed and the largest tower house at the priory was

ferrous artefacts', pp 356–8. **91** Michael Kenny, 'The coins, tokens and jetons' in Clyne, *Kells Priory*, pp 406–14 at pp 406–11. **92** For a study of economic development and contraction in medieval Europe, see N.J.G. Pounds, *An historical geography of Europe* (Cambridge, 1990). **93** Empey, 'The priory of Kells: an introduction', pp 5–6. **94** 'Register of Kells', p. 312; Empey, 'The priory of Kells: an introduction', appendix 1, p. 9. **95** See Clyne, *Kells Priory*, p. 54. **96** *IMED*, p. 43; *EIMP*, pp 188–9.

erected overlooking and defending the gateway (fig. 3.7). A defensive tower house was built inside the precinct adjoining the chancel, which was possibly the prior's residence. In contrast to the earlier period of occupation when the economy of the priory was linked to Anglo-Norman colonisation and contacts, artefacts dating to the fifteenth and first half of the sixteenth century do not provide evidence for outside trade and even the once-flourishing local ceramic industries are not well represented.

CONCLUSION

William Marshal, like other great Anglo-Norman lords, controlled his large territory by dividing it among a number of his loyal knights, who founded manors and towns, thereby providing for the future security of the lordship of Leinster. One of these men, Geoffrey fitz Robert, established his manor and town at Kells, which he laid out according to standard Anglo-Norman practice, with his castle, settlement and religious house. The borough developed very rapidly after its foundation in the late twelfth century and it continued to prosper throughout the thirteenth century. Upstanding archaeological remains at Kells, combined with documentary evidence, verify that this was the town's most affluent period, as well as enabling a reasonably clear picture of its layout. The lord of Kells went to some lengths to colonise his new monastery with English clergy whom he could depend on. They provided pastoral care in his manorial parish and they widened their sphere of influence by accepting impropriations in other lordships in eastern and southern Ireland. The investigations at Kells Priory have provided an understanding of its structural development and they relate not only to the economy of the priory itself, but to the town, its hinterland and the medieval lordship of Leinster.

Kells Priory, *c.*1500: a fortified monastic house

DANIEL TIETZSCH-TYLER

The publication in 1993 of a popular history and visitor's guide to Kells Priory in Co. Kilkenny centred on a reconstruction drawing of the priory as it might have appeared towards the end of the fifteenth century.[1] Preparation of a new edition of that book followed the recent publication of the results of extensive archaeological excavation at the priory.[2] Though the original reconstruction drawing was included in the archaeological monograph, it has been amended since to take into account the latest archaeological evidence (fig. 4.1).

Having wrested the lordship of Leinster from Prince John, William Marshal granted the manor of Kells to Geoffrey fitz Robert, one of his close retinue of household knights.[3] There he erected a motte-and-bailey castle on an island in the King's River and established the Anglo-Norman borough of Kells on the adjacent south bank of the river. In *c.*1193 he founded an Augustinian monastery alongside his new town, with the priory church to serve as parish church for the town. While fitz Robert's town has declined into a sleepy village and his castle has been reduced to a remnant of a motte and a short length of the stone wall that later enclosed its bailey, the priory remains as a substantial ruin just east of the village.[4] Covering several acres of riverside meadow, it is one of Ireland's finest national monuments though also one that remains relatively little known.

The new priory was established on a low island in the King's River, between the main channel to the north and a narrow channel to the south. The latter was already in use as the priory millstream by *c.*1204.[5] From shortly after its foundation Kells Priory was served by four Augustinian canons brought over from Bodmin in Cornwall. Work on the priory buildings was well advanced by *c.*1204 following the usual pattern of commencing with the chancel at the east end of the church, extending westwards to the two transepts and the nave.[6] Alongside the church, work on the monastic ranges progressed in a clockwise manner around the cloister, starting with the east range, which is contemporary

1 Daniel Tietzsch-Tyler, *The Augustinian priory of Kells, Co. Kilkenny: an exploration (a visitor's guide and explanation)* (Stonyford, 1993). 2 Clyne, *Kells Priory*. 3 C.A. Empey, 'The sacred and the secular: the Augustinian priory of Kells in Ossory, 1193–1541', *IHS*, 24 (1984–5), pp 131–51 at pp 139–40. 4 T.B. Barry, E. Culleton and C.A. Empey, 'Kells motte, Co. Kilkenny', *PRIA*, 84C (1984), pp 157–70. 5 C.A. Empey, 'A case study of the primary phase of Anglo-Norman settlement: the lordship of Kells', *OKR*, new. ser., 3:1 (1984), pp 32–40 at p. 37. 6 *IMED*, p. 2.

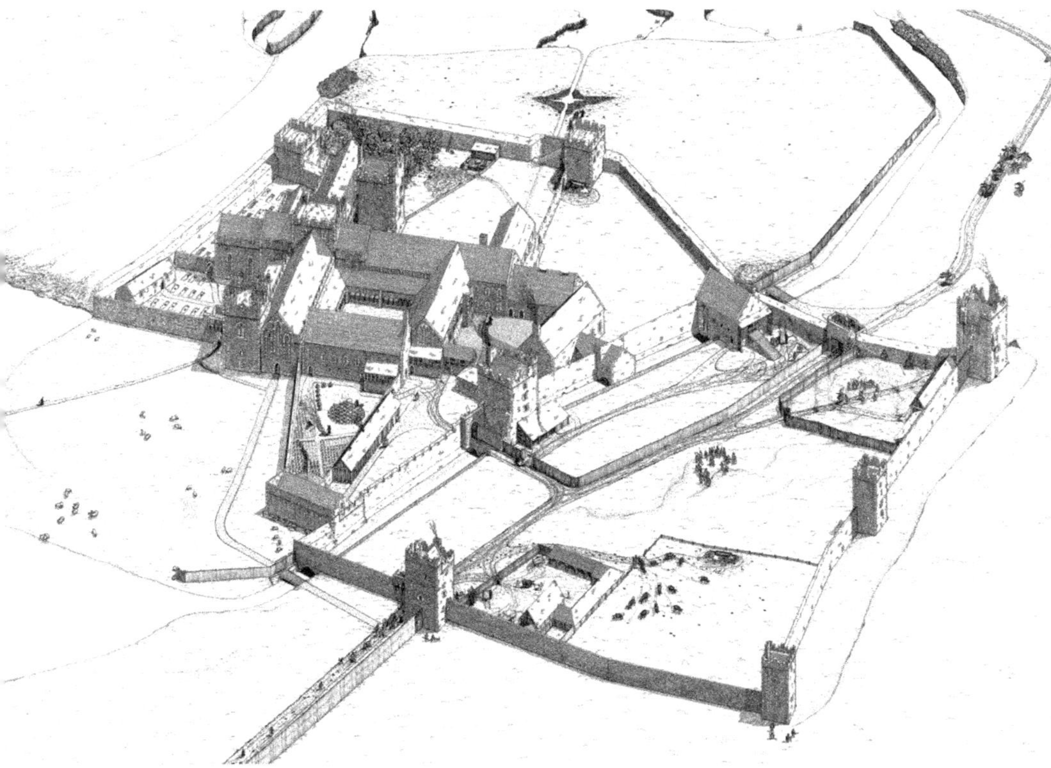

4.1 Kells Priory: the priory as it probably appeared towards the end of the fifteenth century. The priory can be divided diagonally, with the initial monastic precinct, much modified in the fifteenth century, occupying the upper-left half of the drawing and the fifteenth-century Burgess Court occupying the lower-right half of the drawing. North is to the left.

with the south transept of the early church, and ending with the west range. By that time, about the middle of the thirteenth century, the church had been enlarged to its present size with the chancel, nave, north transept and north transept chapel all being significantly lengthened and a belfry built at the north-west angle of the nave. An irregular second court was also built onto the south side of the cloister ranges to serve the priory kitchen and infirmary (figs 4.2 and 4.3a).

During the same period the priory was enclosed within a precinct wall. This wall was supplemented with towers toward the eastern end of the north wall alongside the King's River, midway along the east wall and midway along the south wall. The latter tower was also the first gateway into the monastic precinct, forming as it did a bridge of two spans over the millstream. The belfry at the north-west corner of the nave dominated the fourth side of the precinct, which was an area of open ground (fig. 4.2).

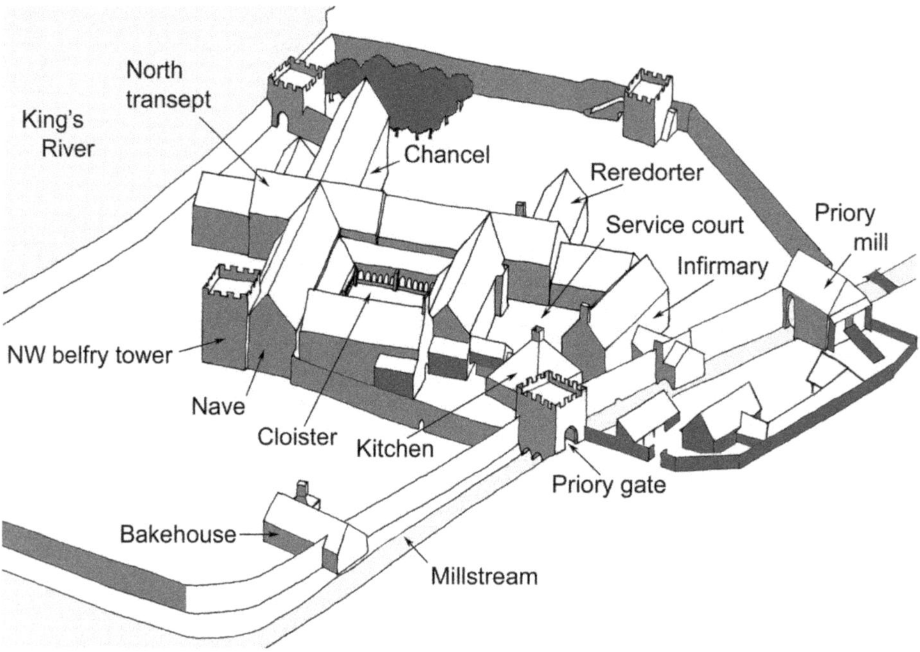

4.2 Kells Priory: annotated sketch of the priory as it probably appeared in the middle of the fourteenth century.

In the course of the century following the initial completion of the priory, it lost its close connection with the mother house in Cornwall and priors were elected from canons originating in the local community.[7] The violence of the later medieval period saw the priory assume the role of protector for the community from which its members came. With no town wall to defend the adjacent town, an extensive walled and towered enclosure, called Prior's Vill or Burgess Court, was built across the millstream from the monastic precinct and enclosing the road into Kells from Stonyford and the east (figs 4.1 and 4.3b).[8] Two of the Burgess Court towers, at the south-east corner and on the west side beside the gate into the town, are effectively small to medium-sized tower houses in their own right (fig. 4.4).

At the same time an apparent surplus of funds allowed for a major rebuilding programme within the precinct itself. That saw the church remodelled with the addition of a large new belfry over the crossing. A fine medium-sized tower house was built against the south wall of the chancel, presumably to accommodate the prior. The original gate-tower of the precinct was also rebuilt as a large tower house, perhaps to accommodate priory guests, and a thirteenth-century bakehouse a short distance to the west of the monastic ranges was

7 Empey, 'The sacred and the secular', pp 46–7. 8 Ibid., pp 149–50.

4.3 Kells Priory: two aerial views: (a) the inner precinct viewed from the west; (b) looking south-east across the inner monastic precinct towards Burgess Court (© National Monuments Service Photographic Unit).

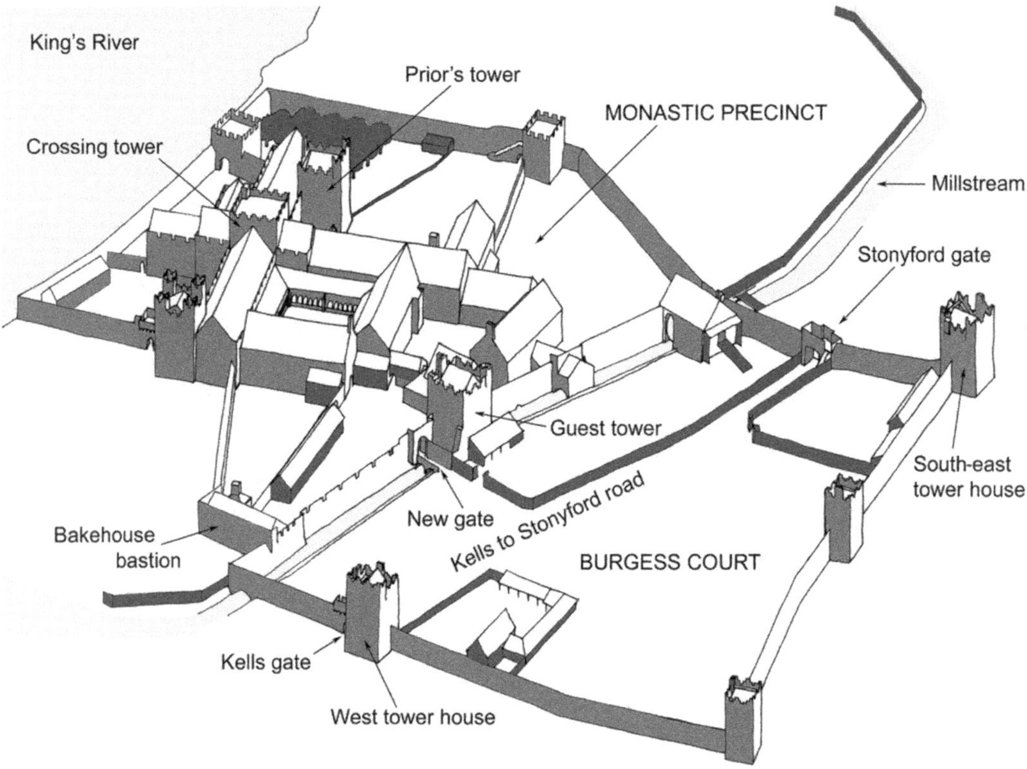

4.4 Kells Priory: annotated sketch of the priory as it probably appeared towards the end of the fifteenth century.

transformed into a fortified bastion overlooking the entry of the millstream into Burgess Court (fig. 4.4).

The priory continued in existence until it was dissolved in 1540. Prior Nicholas Tobin and the two remaining canons were pensioned off, but Tobin was subsequently re-employed as rector of Kells.[9] The road through Burgess Court was closed, a new road was constructed around its perimeter, and the priory buildings were transformed into a secular farm.

9 Ibid., p. 147.

William Marshal's great tower at Pembroke, Wales: a view from Ireland[1]

BEN MURTAGH

During a roughly thirty-year period (1189–1219) when William Marshal was active in construction works at his castles in south Wales,[2] largely on lands that he had gained through his wife, Countess Isabel de Clare, one of his most impressive structures was the circular great tower that he built during the early thirteenth century in conjunction with other works at his castle of Pembroke (fig. 5.1, pl. 8).[3] It is apparently the earliest[4] and probably the finest upstanding example of such towers to have been built by the Anglo-Normans or English in western Britain. It seems to have inspired and influenced the building of other such structures in Wales during the same century.[5] They were also built by the native Welsh princes and lords, who in addition developed a D-shaped or apsidal version.[6] The construction of circular great towers in the borderlands of north-east Wales continued late into the same century, and included, for example, the

1 The author thanks Patrick McInerney for his help with the figures, particularly the drawings. The photographs were taken by the author. 2 For works attributed to the Marshal at some of his other castles in south Wales, including Caerleon, Chepstow and Usk, see Richard Avent, 'William Marshal's building works at Chepstow Castle, Monmouthshire, 1189–1219' in J.R. Kenyon and Kieran O'Conor (eds), *The medieval castle in Ireland and Wales: essays in honour of Jeremy Knight* (Dublin, 2002), pp 50–71; Jeremy Knight, 'Welsh space and Norman invader: Usk Castle, 1136–1245' in J.K. Knight and Andy Johnson (eds), *Usk Castle, priory and town* (Logaston, 2008), pp 55–78; Rick Turner and Andy Johnson (eds), *Chepstow Castle: its history and buildings* (Logaston, 2006). 3 Today, the castle is owned and managed by the Pembroke Trust. 4 The base of a 9m-diameter small circular tower, apparently built by the native Welsh in the mid-/late twelfth century (i.e., pre-dating the Pembroke Tower) was discovered during recent excavations on the summit of the motte at Nevern Castle in north-east Pembrokeshire: see Chris Caple, 'News – Wales – Nevern Castle – Pembrokeshire', *CSGJ*, 23 (2009–10), pp 140–4; idem, 'Nevern Castle: searching for the first masonry castle in Wales', *Medieval Archaeology*, 55 (2011), pp 326–34 at p. 330. See also P.M. Remfry, 'The dating of medieval military architecture', *Castle Studies Group Newsletter*, 15 (2001–2), pp 86–94 at pp 88–94 for his early dating of 'round towers' in western Britain. 5 J.K. Knight, *The three castles: Grosmont Castle, Skenfrith Castle, White Castle. Hen Gwart moated site* (Cardiff, 1991), pp 34–5. For an outline and sequence of development of such towers in south-west Wales, starting at Pembroke, see Wiles, 'Marshal towers'. See also John Goodall, *The English castle* (New Haven and London, 2011), pp 162–4. 6 See Richard Avent, *Dolwyddelan Castle, Dolbadarn Castle, Castle y Bere* (Cardiff, 2010), pp 8–9, 11–13, 30–40. See also P.R. Davis, *Castles of the Welsh princes* (Ceredigon, 2011), pp 28, 30, 36–43, 53–7, 62–3, 71–3, 76, 87–8, 98–100; J.R. Kenyon, *The medieval castles of Wales* (Cardiff, 2010), p. 6.

5.1 South view of Inner Ward of Pembroke Castle from the Outer Ward.

5.2 West view of the great tower of Flint Castle, Flintshire, north-east Wales.

one at the royal castle of Flint, constructed in the period 1277–86 by the English king Edward I (fig. 5.2).[7] Viewed from Ireland, the context of the Marshal's great tower at Pembroke, together with his building of, for example, circular or rounded flanking towers at this site and at his other Welsh castles such as Chepstow (pl. 9) and Usk, as will be seen below, reflected rapid changes in military architecture and castle-building that were taking place in western Europe at that time. William Marshal was to the forefront of bringing these developments not only into Wales, but also into Ireland. In this regard, the great tower at Pembroke has been seen as an important influence or link in this chain. This, together with its architecture, development and context, will be examined below.

7 See R.A. Brown, *Castles from the air* (Cambridge, repr. 1992), pp 117–18; Goodall, *The English castle*, pp 213–14 and pl. 156; Vicky Perfect, *Flint Castle: the story of Edward I's first Welsh castle* (Mold, Flintshire, 2012), pp 40–5; A.J. Taylor, *The king's works in Wales, 1277–1330* (London, 1974), pp 313–18.

EVENTS AND DEVELOPMENTS IN FRANCE

At the time of the construction of the Pembroke great tower in the early thirteenth century, such towers had been and were being built at castles in France. The latter was an epicentre of new changes and developments in military architecture and castle-building, as exemplified by the appearance of the circular great tower or *la tour maîtraisse circulaire*.[8] Here the Angevin or Plantagenet kings of England, Henry II and his sons, John and Richard, the hereditary counts of Anjou in the Loire region, had been engaged in a protracted power struggle with the Capetian French king, Philip Augustus (r. 1180–1223).[9] William Marshal played an important role in these events that increased as he became a powerful Anglo-Norman magnate and senior baron of the English realm and Angevin empire, which were often as much about infighting within the Plantagenet family as they were about the French king extending his authority over the outer reaches of his kingdom.[10]

Philip Augustus was a great builder of circular great towers, particularly at castles he captured in lands conquered from the Angevins or English, such as in the war of 1202–6, and his towers were a type that became known as *la tour maîtresse philippienne*.[11] Examples of captured Plantagenet castles in the duchy of Normandy, where the French king constructed his circular great towers after 1204 as markers of his new-found authority there, include Gisors[12] and Falaise.[13] Located at an angle at the west end of their great castle of Chinon (Indre-et-Loire) in the county of Anjou, the Plantagenet kings (possibly Henry II) built in the second half of the twelfth century the Tour du Moulin or Mill Tower (fig. 5.3a). This is located a short distance south-west of Philip Augustus's later great tower, known as the Tour du Coudray (fig. 5.3b). The Tour du Moulin is an early example of a circular great tower with its deep plinth or spur base standing high above the River Vienne (a tributary of the Loire) and a marker of the kings' authority over the adjoining town and surrounding area (fig. 5.3a).[14] The castle was one of the strongest and most important in Anjou and it was here they had their treasury.[15] It was also here in his ancestral stronghold that Henry II met his ignominious end during 1189 in the presence of William Marshal and a handful

8 Mesqui, *Châteaux forts*, pp 290–1, 385. **9** See Jim Bradbury, *Philip Augustus, king of France, 1180–1223* (London and New York, 1998), pp 106–65, 287–95. **10** For the Marshal's role in events in France from 1188 to 1216, see David Crouch, *William Marshal: knight, war and chivalry, 1147–1219* (2nd ed., Harlow, 2002), pp 66–8, 82–6, 91–5, 122. **11** See Bradbury, *Philip Augustus*, pp 161, 163; Goodall, *The English castle*, p. 162; Mesqui, *Châteaux forts*, pp 290–1, 385. **12** Ibid., p. 187. **13** Ibid., pp 163–4; Goodall, *The English castle*, pl. 97; Panouillé, *Châteaux forts*, p. 31. **14** Ibid., p. 66; Goodall, *The English castle*, pl. 120; Hulme, 'Château Gaillard', pp 203–33 at p. 214 and figs 4–5: Mesqui, *Châteaux forts*, pp 125–6; Schweitz, *Châteaux et forteresses*, pp 12, 90, 98, 100, 107, 113, 136. **15** On the treasury of the early Plantagenet kings at Chinon, see John Gillingham, *The Angevin empire* (2nd ed., New York, 2001), pp 61, 69, 75, 87.

a b

5.3 Circular great towers at the castle of Chinon, Indre-et-Loire, France: a) Tour du Moulin; b) Tour du Coudray.

5.4 Interior view of abbey church at Fontevrault in the Loire Valley, western France, with the tombs of King Henry II and Eleanor of Aquitaine in the foreground.

of the king's remaining followers.[16] According to the *Histoire de Guillaume le Maréchal*, 'after that the Marshal and the barons carried his briar on their shoulders from Chinon to Fontevrault'.[17] After Henry was buried in the fine abbey church there (fig. 5.4) in the presence of his rebellious son and successor, King Richard I (d. 1199), William Marshal's star continued to rise.[18]

As for Chinon, it was to be lost after a protracted siege sixteen years later, along with Loches and the entire county of Anjou by Henry II's youngest son, King John (r. 1199–1216), to Philip Augustus.[19] The commander of the castle, who was also captured and held for ransom, was Hubert de Burgh (*c.*1175–1243).[20] Following in the steps of William Marshal and after the death of King John, he went on to become a great castle-builder, particularly in south-east Wales with circular towers, which included the free-standing great tower at Skenfrith.[21] After its capture in 1204, the French king set about refortifying the royal castle at Chinon, which included the Fort de Coudray and the construction of his own circular great tower (Tour du Coudray) that overlooks the nearby and earlier Tour du Moulin as a marker of his authority and permanent acquisition of this centre of Plantagenet power in western France (fig. 5.3b).[22] To add insult to injury, it was at this castle that an agreement was made with the French in 1214, whereby King John finally gave up trying to recover his lost territories in north-west France.[23]

Back in 1190, Phillip Augustus commenced the construction of his new geometric and revolutionary castle of the Louvre in his capital at Paris. This included probably his earliest *tour maîtresse philippienne*, a *c.*31m-high free-standing and circular great tower in the centre of a quadrangular curtain-wall enceinte, defended on the outside by projecting and circular towers that extended out into an enclosing moat.[24] This royal fortress of the Louvre represented a new type of castle, reflecting rapid changes taking place in military architecture during the second half of the twelfth century, such as in crossbow and stone-throwing technology, which emanated from the conflict in the Holy Land between the crusaders and the great Muslim leader, Saladin.[25] Such developments, derived to a great degree from advances in siege warfare, included the use of flanking rounded or circular towers along a curtain-wall enceinte. This

16 See Crouch, *William Marshal*, pp 65–6; John Gillingham, *Richard I* (New Haven and London, 1999), pp 99–100; *HWM*, i, lines 9039–46, 9079–220. **17** Ibid., lines 9220–3. **18** See Crouch, *William Marshal*, pp 66–9. **19** Bradbury, *Philip Augustus*, p. 153; Gillingham, *Angevin empire*, p. 94; W.L. Warren, *King John* (New Haven and London, 1997), p. 116. **20** Bradbury, *Philip Augustus*, p. 153; Warren, *King John*, p. 116. **21** Neil Guy et al., 'Castle Studies Group Conference – Abergavenny – April 2008', *CSGJ*, 22 (2008–9), pp 4–127 at pp 23–4; Kenyon, *Medieval castles of Wales*, pp 141–5; Knight, *The three castles*, esp. pp 26, 28–35. **22** Hulme, 'Château Gaillard', figs 11–12; Mesqui, *Châteaux forts*, pp 125–6; Schweitz, *Châteaux et forteresses*, pp 33, 98, 113–14, 118, 133. **23** Bradbury, *Philip Augustus*, p. 314. **24** Ibid., pp 238–9; Mesqui, *Châteaux forts*, pp 279–82, 290; idem, *Châteaux forts de la guerre à la paix* (Paris, 1995), pp 25–7. **25** Hulme, 'Château Gaillard', pp 207–17, 230–1.

5.5 View of the moat of the castle of King Philip Augustus of France, Louvre, Paris.

also included such towers forming parts of gateways or gatehouses that they would have helped to defend, usually on either side of the passageway. On the outside, the enceinte was often defended by a deep moat, which was sometimes stone-lined like that at the Louvre (fig. 5.5).[26] As in the case of the latter, the towers and linking curtain wall have a steep base batter or talus descending to the bottom of the moat, which helped to prevent undermining. As a further precaution, a stone-built counter-scarp was constructed along the outer edge of the moat. Another form of defence that was developed during this period was the arrow loop, particularly of the plunging variety, which worked in tandem with the developments in crossbow technology.[27]

Similarly, circular great towers displayed these new military architectural developments to varying degrees. For example, the one at the Louvre, only the base of which survives, has a steep batter, surrounded with its own circular moat and counterscarp.[28] Some were free-standing, but within the area of the curtain wall, as in the latter case, while others were located outside and separate from an angle of the enceinte, such as the French examples of Dourdan in Essonne, Île de France,[29] and Lillebonne in Seine-Maritime, Haute Normandy.[30]

Similarly, there is the late example of the great tower of Flint Castle in north-east Wales (fig. 5.2), referred to above, which was also located outside and separated from one corner of the curtain wall. In other cases, the great tower was attached to the curtain wall and projecting beyond the enceinte, such as the above examples at the castle of Chinon (figs 5.3a and b).[31]

Prior to the construction of the castle of the Louvre and its *grosse tour* by Philip Augustus, earlier versions of free-standing and circular great towers were

26 M. Fleury and V. Kruta, *The castle of the Louvre* (Dijon, 2000), p. 10 and figs 8–11, 24–5, 61. **27** See Hulme, 'Château Gaillard', pp 212–17; Mesqui, *Châteaux forts de la guerre à la paix*, p. 56; idem, *Châteaux forts*, pp 24–7. **28** Ibid., pp 279, 281; Fleury and Kruta, *The castle of the Louvre*, pp 16–17. **29** Mesqui, *Châteaux forts*, pp 148, 153, 290. **30** Ibid., p. 216. **31** Ibid., p. 125; Schweitz, *Châteaux et forteresses*, p. 98.

being built in the Paris region (Île de France) and adjoining areas loyal to the Capetian kings.[32] For example, such a tower was located in the Palais de la Cité at the west end of the Île de la Cité in the middle of the River Seine in Paris to the south-east of the Louvre, which is reputed to have been built by the French king Louis VI (r. 1108–37), grandfather of Philip Augustus.[33] Some earlier circular great towers, pre-dating the royal one at the Louvre, were built by French counts. These included the counts of Blois, long-time enemies of the counts of Anjou to the west, who built early examples of these towers during the twelfth century. They include the remains of the free-standing *tour maîtresse circulaire* at the castle of Fréteval, which is reputed to date to as early as *c.*1100.[34] To the north-east of this example, there is the enormous and fine one at Châteaudun (Eure-et-Loire), built between 1170 and 1190,[35] while to the east there is the one at Châtillon-Coligny (Loire), attributed to Count Étienne de Sancerre between 1180 and 1190.[36]

While developments continued apace in castle-building and military architecture in the lands of the French king, this was paralleled in the 'empire' of the Angevin or Plantagenet kings of England in relation to both royal and baronial castles. Not surprisingly this was quite pronounced in their lands in France at or near the sometimes shifting frontier with those of the French king. These included, for example, extensive works carried out before 1205 at the major Plantagenet castles in their county of Anjou, such as Chinon[37] and Loches, which in the case of the latter included large almond-shaped or 'beaked' (*en bec*) flanking towers with plunging arrow loops along the southern stretch of the curtain wall (figs 5.6a and b).[38] To the south-west of Anjou, in the neighbouring county of Poitou, there was the revolutionary Plantagenet geometrical castle of Le Coudray Salbart (pl. 10), built at the beginning of the thirteenth century, with its almond-shaped or 'beaked' flanking towers, including its great tower, which survives as an impressive ruin.[39]

Construction works and renovations were also conducted by Henry II at his castles at the north end of his lands in France, such as on the eastern frontier of

32 Steven Brindle, 'The keep at Conisbrough Castle, Yorkshire', *Château Gaillard*, 25 (2012), pp 61–74 at p. 65. 33 Ibid.; Mesqui, *Châteaux forts*, pp 282–3. 34 Ibid., pp 176–7; idem, *Châteaux forts de la guerre à la paix*, p. 24; O'Keeffe, 'Dublin Castle's donjon', p. 292 and n. 37. 35 See Richard Avent, 'William Marshal's castle at Chepstow and its place in military architecture' in Turner and Johnson (eds), *Chepstow Castle*, pp 81–90 at p. 89 and fig. 71; Pierre-Gilles Girault, *Loire Valley castles* (Paris, 2014), pp 27, 29; Mesqui, *Châteaux forts*, pp 113–14; Panouillé, *Châteaux forts*, p. 117; Schweitz, *Châteaux et forteresses*, p. 173. 36 Brindle, 'The keep at Conisbrough', p. 69; Mesqui, *Châteaux forts*, pp 115–16. 37 Ibid., pp 125–7. 38 Ibid., pp 217–18; Bernard Briais, *Loches through history* (Monts, 2012), pp 26–9; Hulme, 'Château Gaillard', p. 224 and fig. 9; Pamela Marshall, 'Making an appearance: some thoughts on the phenomenon of multiple doorways and large upper openings in Romanesque donjons in western France and Britain', *Château Gaillard*, 25 (2012), pp 233–42 at fig. 4; Schweitz, *Châteaux et forteresses*, pp 136–7. 39 Mesqui, *Châteaux forts*, pp 138–41; Panouillé, *Châteaux forts*, p. 77.

a

b

5.6 Loches, Indre-et-Loire, France: a) south-east view of the Plantagenet 'beaked' flanking towers on south curtain wall; b) internal view of one of the towers, showing Plantagenet-style arrow loop and inner embrasure.

his duchy of Normandy. Among these was the castle of Gisors (Eure), which included the heightening of the octagonal great tower on the motte and his outer curtain wall with flanking towers, such as the large circular tower of the 1180s,

5.7 View of great tower of King Richard the Lionheart's Château Gaillard, Eure, Haute-Normandie, France.

known as *la tour dite du Diable*, with its numerous arrow loops.[40] There were also Henry's works at the nearby Château-sur-Epte, which has a twelfth-century circular great tower that may also have been built by him.[41] These works were followed, as will be seen below, by the nearby revolutionary castle of Château Gaillard, with its 'beaked' great tower (fig. 5.7), built in the 1190s by Henry's successor, King Richard I (r. 1189–99), who had the Marshal with him on his French campaign. These developments in castle building in France not only made their appearance in England, but they soon extended to Wales and to Ireland. In this regard, William Marshal would have performed an important role, in which his great tower at Pembroke has been regarded as playing a significant part. This is not surprising, when considering the earl's high-level involvement in the Capetian–Plantagenet conflict in France, where he was in a position to view and inspect first-hand the ongoing architectural developments.

Meanwhile, developments in England had been taking place at both royal and baronial castles, no doubt reflecting events and the advances in siege warfare in the wars in France and the Holy Land. An early example of a round or polygonal baronial great tower in that country is the fine one at Conisborough Castle in Yorkshire, which was built by Earl Hamlin, brother of King Henry II, during the 1180s or 1190s, and it is adjoined by a perhaps slightly later curtain wall with

40 Christopher Gravett and Adam Hook, *Norman stone castles, 2: Europe, 950–1204* (Oxford, 2004), pp 30, 34; Mesqui, *Châteaux forts*, pp 186–9. 41 Ibid., pp 111–12; Gravett and Hook, *Norman stone castles, 2*, p. 38.

solid circular towers.[42] The great tower can be compared to other polygonal great towers in England of the second half the thirteenth century, such as Tickhill (also in Yorkshire), built 1179–82.[43] It also has affinities with some contemporary French towers, such as the two abovementioned examples at Châteaudun and Châtillon-Coligny, together with one at Mortemer in north-east Normandy.[44]

Although circular great towers, like polygonal or 'transitional' ones, were not widespread in England, those that were built include the very early example of New Buckingham, erected in the 1140s by William d'Albini.[45] Unlike in Wales and Ireland, by the late twelfth century a large number of masonry castles had already been constructed over the previous century throughout the English countryside, with more traditional oblong and rectangular keeps or donjons, so the need for a new type of great tower may not have been so acute. There is also Henry II's great tower at Dover, which guarded access to the south-east of England from France, with its more traditional style of great tower, surrounded by a curtain-wall enceinte with square or rectangular flanking towers.[46] These contrast with what he was building in France, as seen above, at Gisors or perhaps Chinon (fig. 5.3a), or the solid and rounded flanking towers on the south curtain wall at Loches (fig. 5.6a),[47] as well as the outer and later curtain wall at Dover with its rounded or D-shaped flanking towers.[48]

Contrasting with Henry II's work at Dover, there are the two great towers at the Tower of London, where Countess Isabel de Clare was in residence when William Marshal arrived in the city from France in 1189 to take her hand in marriage.[49] The first of these is the Bell Tower at an angle of the inner curtain wall (fig. 5.8a) and this was probably built by King Richard I (the Lionheart) in the 1190s; its polygonal lower part has early examples of plunging arrow loops, while the upper storey is circular.[50] Then there is the nearby larger and later circular Wakefield Tower (fig. 5.8b) that was commenced in the 1220s, during the minority of Henry III and soon after the regency (1216–19) and death of the Marshal, which became a residence of the king.[51]

42 See Brown, *Castles from the air*, pp 95–6; Goodall, *The English castle*, pp 149–51 and pl. 96; Mesqui, *Châteaux forts de la guerre à la paix*, p. 25; Brindle, 'The keep at Conisbrough', pp 63–4, 66–8 and figs 1–8. **43** See Avent, 'Chepstow's place', p. 83; Goodall, *The English castle*, p. 128 and fig. 25. **44** Brindle, 'The keep at Conisbrough', pp 66, 71; Mesqui, *Châteaux forts*, p. 458, no. 41. **45** Brown, *Castles from the air*, p. 129 and fig. 53. **46** See Goodall, *The English castle*, pls 54, 88–90. **47** Briais, *Loches*, pp 26–8; Marshall, 'Making appearances', fig. 4; Mesqui, *Châteaux forts*, p. 218. **48** See Brown, *Castles from the air*, p. 105; Goodall, *The English castle*, pls 54, 112, 119. **49** Crouch, *William Marshal*, p. 68; Sidney Painter, *William Marshal: knight-errant, baron and regent of England* (Toronto, repr., 2001), p. 76. **50** See R. Allen Brown and P.E. Curnow, *Tower of London* (London, 1984), pp 15–16, 44–6 and figs 7A and B, 16 and pl. xvii; Hulme, 'Château Gaillard', p. 220; Edward Impey and Geoffrey Parnell, *The Tower of London: the official illustrated history* (London, 2006), p. 22 and figs 17–19. **51** Ibid., p. 26 and figs 23, 25, 29, 36; Brown, *Castles from the air*, p. 116; Brown and Curnow, *Tower of London*, pp 17, 20, 55, 57, 59 and fig. 8A and B and pls xix–xx; Hulme, 'Château Gaillard', p. 229.

a  b

5.8 Circular great towers at the Tower of London: a) Bell Tower; b) Wakefield Tower.

5.9 External view of south section of Roman town wall of Caerwent, Monmouthshire, south-east Wales, with an added fourth-century flanking tower.

The appearance of circular and polygonal towers in Britain and France during the late twelfth and thirteenth centuries was in a sense a revival of the building of such defensive structures at angles and along the walls of forts and towns in these countries during the late Roman period. Substantial remains of many of these towers were still visible during the Middle Ages and some were reused, such as at the inner enceinte at Carcassonne (Aude) and at the enceinte of the royal palace at Senlis (Oise) to the north-east of Paris.[52] Similar examples in Britain[53] include the 'Multiangular Tower' at York[54] and the Roman town wall of Caerwent (*Venta Siluram*) in south-east Wales (fig. 5.9).[55] Then there are the examples of the Norman castles of Pevensey (Sussex) and Portchester (Hampshire), which were constructed within the well-preserved walls of late Roman forts with rounded or D-shaped flanking towers.[56] With the revival of the construction of polygonal and rounded flanking towers in the later twelfth century, the building of circular great towers was taking this a stage further to improve upon the defensive capabilities of earlier oblong or rectangular keeps or donjons of castles.

In his war against Philip Augustus, Richard I seemingly built his iconic and costly fortress of Château Gaillard, in an astonishingly short time (1196–8), so as to aid in recovering lost territory and to prevent the army of the French king from advancing further into Normandy.[57] This complex castle, which was faced with dressed ashlar masonry, utilised its cliff-top location to the utmost. It displayed many of the latest advances in castle-building and military architecture.[58] These included arrow loops, circular flanking towers on the curtain-wall enceintes, together with a fine great tower, which had machicolations as well as a pointed beak or prow, and occupied a commanding location high above the Seine at Les Andelys (fig. 5.7). The tower was not free-standing, however, but was attached to the castle's inner curtain-wall enceinte, the outer face of which was embossed in the form of corrugated or closely spaced, solid and rounded projections.[59] William Marshal, who had been on campaign with the English king in France, would have been familiar with this castle.[60] It was ironic that when Philip Augustus finally besieged it in 1203, Richard's brother and successor, the hapless King John (r. 1199–1216), sent the Marshal with a force in a futile attempt to relieve it.[61]

52 Mesqui, *Châteaux forts*, pp 91, 94, 354. 53 See Goodall, *The English castle*, p. 76. 54 D.B. Campbell and Brian Delf, *Roman legionary fortresses, 27BC–AD378* (Oxford, 2006), p. 57. 55 R.J. Brewer, *Caerwent Roman town* (Cardiff, 3rd ed., 2006), pp 24–6, 30–4. 56 See Goodall, *The English castle*, p. 148 and figs 26, 51, 94. 57 See Bradbury, *Philip Augustus*, p. 121; Gillingham, *Richard I*, pp 301–6. 58 Gravett and Hook, *Norman stone castles*, 2, pp 22–7; Hulme, 'Château Gaillard', pp 217, 220. 59 Ibid., pp 203, 206 and figs 3, 6–7; Brown, *Castles from the air*, p. 18; Gravett and Hook, *Norman stone castles*, 2, pp 22–7; Mesqui, *Châteaux forts*, pp 109–11; Panouillé, *Châteaux forts*, pp 51–3. 60 For William Marshal's role in King Richard's campaigning in the frontier region around Château Gaillard at the time of its construction, see *HWM*, ii, lines 10597–676. See also Crouch, *William Marshal*, pp 83–4; Hulme, 'Château Gaillard', pp 217, 225; Painter, *William Marshal*, pp 109–11. 61 Bradbury,

WILLIAM MARSHAL GOES TO WALES AND HIS WORKS AT CHEPSTOW CASTLE

After William Marshal had married Countess Isabel in 1189, it would appear that he quickly established himself at Chepstow and soon commenced building works at her ancestral castle there (fig. 5.10, pl. 9), the centre of her father's (Strongbow's) old lordship of Striguil in south-east Wales.[62] These were to span many years and display some of the latest developments in military architecture and castle-building.[63] They included, for example, the use of circular towers with arrow loops and thickened or battered bases (fig. 5.11). Initially, he seems to have concentrated on the lower ward in order to defend the eastern approach to the castle, which is located along a high cliff-top ridge. This involved the construction of a curtain wall with an adjoining east or main gatehouse defended on either side by circular towers with plunging arrow loops (fig. 5.10).[64] This revolutionary design in south-east Wales would have mirrored what Philip Augustus was building at the same time at the Louvre in far-off Paris in the early 1190s and its early date has been ascertained by the aid of dendrochronology.[65] It would indicate that the Marshal was not just a follower, but was to the forefront of these new developments.

There were also at least three other distinctive features of the Marshal's works at Chepstow, which are also to be found in his castles elsewhere: first, the extensive use of semi-circular or rounded arches (fig. 5.12);[66] second, the use of dressed Dundry stone in arrow loops, window and doorway surrounds, as well as arches;[67] and third, the construction of long, narrow and inward-splaying arrow loops through the thickness of the walls, without rear-arched embrasures for improved outward firing range for archers. As will be seen below, this is also a feature of the Marshal's works at his two other important castles of Pembroke (including the great tower) and Usk. These long splaying loops through the thickness of the walls are a feature of the circular towers of King Philip Augustus, such as the Tour du Coudray at Chinon and the one that he built at

Philip Augustus, p. 148; Crouch, *William Marshal*, pp 91–2; *HWM*, iii, p. 146, line 12705; Hulme, 'Château Gaillard', pp 224–5; Warren, *King John*, pp 86–7. **62** Avent, 'Gatehouse at Chepstow', p. 30; Avent, 'Marshal's Chepstow', pp 53–4; David Crouch, 'Chepstow under the Marshals' in Turner and Johnson, *Chepstow Castle*, pp 43–50 at pp 43–4; Hulme, 'Château Gaillard', p. 217; Turner and Johnson, *Chepstow Castle*, pl. 1. **63** For a general outline of the Marshal's works at Chepstow, see Avent, 'Marshal's Chepstow', pp 50–71. For an overview of same, see Avent, 'Chepstow's place'. Regarding the Marshal's early works at the castle, see also Richard Avent and Dan Miles, 'The main gatehouse' in Turner and Johnson, *Chepstow Castle*, pp 51–62. For the Marshal's later works at same, see Richard Avent and Rick Turner, 'The Middle Bailey' in Turner and Johnson, *Chepstow Castle*, pp 63–70. See also Rick Turner, 'The Upper Bailey' in ibid., pp 71–80. **64** Avent, 'Gatehouse at Chepstow', figs 5–7; Avent, 'Marshal's Chepstow', figs 3, 5; Avent and Miles, 'The main gatehouse', figs 42–4. **65** Ibid., pp 52–3; Avent, 'Gatehouse at Chepstow', pp 28–30. **66** Avent, 'Marshal's Chepstow', p. 55. **67** Ibid., p. 54.

5.10 South-east view of east end of Chepstow Castle, Monmouthshire, south-east Wales, with William Marshal's gatehouse on the right.

5.11 External view of circular south-east tower of William Marshal's Middle Bailey, Chepstow Castle.

Falaise in Normandy after the capture of the castle there in 1204. They contrast with those of the Plantagenets, which have rear-arched embrasures (figs 5.6b, 5.15).[68] All three distinctive features can be seen in the Marshal east or main gatehouse.

68 Hulme, 'Château Gaillard', fig. 11; Mesqui, *Châteaux forts de la guerre à la paix*, p. 56; idem, *Châteaux forts*, pp 25, 163–4.

5.12 Rear view of William Marshal's gatehouse in Lower Bailey, Chepstow Castle.

WILLIAM MARSHAL AND PEMBROKE

In his detailed study of Pembroke Castle, David Cathcart King was of the opinion that William Marshal commenced his construction works on the Inner Ward, including the great tower, soon after 1189 (fig. 5.1).[69] It is now clear that this was not the case. Unlike at Chepstow, the Marshal had to wait for over a decade before he could move west to Pembroke and the castle there remained in the hand of King Richard, and then John for a period when he was king.[70] Similarly, in Ireland he was unable to gain seisin of his wife's vast inheritance there for some years, as the king's brother Prince John, as lord of Ireland since 1185, had been making grants of Isabel's lands to his followers and he seemed determined to keep the Marshal out of the country.[71] Furthermore, a seneschal that the latter sent there was apparently completely ineffectual.[72] Finally, in 1199 with the accession of John to the throne, the new king made amends with the Marshal, probably for his support in the succession, by making him earl of Pembroke, a title that had been created for Isabel's grandfather, Gilbert de Clare, in the 1130s.[73] John was still reluctant to immediately hand over the lands that went with it, preferring to do so gradually. Finally, when he was still in high

69 Cathcart King and Cheshire, *Pembroke Castle*, pp 53–4. **70** Crouch, *William Marshal*, pp 69, 86–8. **71** See *HWM*, i, lines 9580–618; ibid., iii, p. 124, lines 9588, 9602. **72** See ibid., i, lines 9619–30; ibid., iii, p. 125, line 9625. **73** See ibid., p. 142, line 11982; Crouch, *William Marshal*, pp 69, 86; Painter, *William Marshal*, pp 122–4.

5.13 Map of Ireland and west Wales, showing location of circular great towers and castles mentioned in the text (Ben Murtagh and Patrick McInerney).

favour with the king, the earl arrived around September 1200 apparently to take seisin of the lands – at least those that had not been retaken by the Welsh.[74]

Furthermore, while in Wales, William Marshal apparently took the opportunity to take a ship to pay his first visit to Ireland along with Countess Isabel to inspect their lands there.[75] As in the case of Chepstow, once he had gained possession of Pembroke Castle it is likely that he would have turned his

74 See Crouch, *William Marshal*, pp 86–7; *HWM*, iii, p. 142, line 11982. Regarding recovery of lands by the Welsh of Deheubarth from the Anglo-Normans in Pembroke in the twelfth century, see J.B. Hilling, *Cilgerran Castle, St Dogmaels Abbey etc.* (Cardiff, rev. 2000), pp 6–7.
75 William Marshal's arrival in Ireland with Countess Isabel is indicated in his will, confirmed by King John on 3 December 1200, which includes the earl's charter granting lands for the founding of the abbey of Tintern *de Voto* in Wexford, following their narrow escape from shipwreck prior to their safe landing near there: see J.H. Bernard, 'The founding of Tintern

attention to refortifying the place, though this might have taken some time. He and the countess may have spent the years from 1189 making plans in the hope that the Marshal would eventually gain seisin of her ancestral lands in Pembroke. By 1200, he was in his 50s, an advanced age in an era when untimely death was an occupational hazard. His wife, therefore, must have been anxious after eleven years of marriage and with an ever-growing family that her husband would soon succeed in gaining full control of her inheritance, in relation to not just the earldom of Pembroke, but, more importantly, her late father's vast lordship of Leinster (fig. 5.13). In this regard, controlling Pembroke would have been of great strategic importance in maintaining direct contact with the Marshal lands across the sea, due to their proximity (being only about 100km from Milford Haven). It would therefore have been prudent and necessary for the earl to strengthen his newly acquired castle, which was nearby and had direct access to this major waterway that was a gateway to his Irish lordship (fig. 5.13). It was not a coincidence that the three English kings who visited Ireland during the Middle Ages used it to assemble the large fleets that transported their armies across the sea.[76]

WILLIAM MARSHAL'S PEMBROKE CASTLE AND ITS GREAT TOWER

The present castle, which is roughly oval in plan, has a commanding presence as it occupies a strategic cliff-top ridge, with the Inner Ward that is dominated by William Marshal's great tower being at the north end of the promontory, with the larger Outer Ward to the south (figs 5.1, 5.14). Beneath the rocky cliffs the site was further defended on two sides by a fork in the tidal Pembroke River, which once ebbed and flowed from Milford Haven to the north-west.[77] The adjoining medieval town, which is still largely walled, runs along a lower ridge to the south-east of the castle.[78] The strategic importance of the cliff-top

Abbey, Co. Wexford', *PRIA*, 33C (1917), pp 527–9; Crouch, *William Marshal*, pp 87–8 and n. 39; G.H. Orpen, *Ireland under the Normans, 1169–1333* (4 vols, Oxford, 1911–20), ii, pp 206–8. **76** The first of these expeditions to Ireland to have assembled and departed from Pembroke and Milford Haven was that of Henry II: see Cathcart King and Cheshire, *Pembroke Castle*, p. 7; G.H. Orpen (ed.), *The song of Dermot and the earl* (Oxford, 1892), lines 2497–527; Giraldus, *Expugnatio*, pp 88–93. For King John's expedition that assembled and departed from Milford Haven for Ireland in 1210, accompanied by William Marshal, see *HWM*, ii, lines 14240–54; ibid., iii, p. 158, line 14256; Crouch, *William Marshal*, p. 116; Painter, *William Marshal*, p. 169. In relation to the assemblage of Richard II's army and fleet, together with their departure from Milford Haven for Ireland in 1394, see J.F. Lydon, 'Richard II's expeditions to Ireland', *JRSAI*, 93 (1963), pp 135–49 at pp 139–40. Regarding the departure of the king's second expedition from Pembroke and Milford Haven, see Walter Harris (ed.), Item IV – 'The story of King Richard the Second; his last being in Ireland' in *Hibernica or, some ancient pieces relating to Ireland* – part 1 of 2 in vol. i, pp 49–58 at p. 50. **77** See Avent, 'Chepstow's place', fig. 70; Brown, *Castles from the air*, p. 178; Cathcart King and Cheshire, *Pembroke Castle*, pp 5–6; pls iv, vii; Ludlow, *Pembroke Castle*, p. 1. **78** Ibid., pp 9, 11;

5.14 North-west view of Pembroke Castle from across the Monkton Pill, showing dominating position of William Marshal's great tower.

promontory was recognised by the first Normans who invaded south-west Wales in the late eleventh century, under Roger of Montgomery.[79] The site was subsequently fortified or refortified, as in the case of the present Inner Ward, which may have been a defended Iron Age promontory fort and pre-Norman Welsh centre.[80] The initial Norman castle would appear to have been an earth-and-timber ringwork, roughly triangular in plan, with rounded corners, which is now defined by the Inner Ward. With cliffs on two sides, it is likely that its third side was crossed by an earthen rampart and timber palisade, which would have cut it off from the rest of the promontory to the south.[81] It is possible that the Outer Ward was defended by timber structures during this period prior to the construction works of William Marshal. Around the middle of the twelfth century, a fine hall with masonry walls was built, probably by Strongbow (d. 1176), in the eastern end of the northern fortified enclosure or Inner Ward, the remains of which survive within a complex of later buildings to the north-east of the great tower. This is apparently the earliest structure to survive on the site.[82]

The next identifiable phase of building on the site was the Marshal's refortifying of the early castle with masonry, which is likely to have initially involved the deepening of the existing moat at the south of the Inner Ward to provide building stone. The profile of this quarried ditch can be traced in the cliff face beneath the exterior of the present castle (fig. 5.14). The Marshal's building works included the great tower and enclosing inner curtain wall and its flanking towers (figs 5.1, 5.14). These were constructed of mainly locally quarried grey limestone bonded with lime mortar.[83] The lime is likely to have been produced on or near the site by burning the local limestone. Roughly dressed

Cathcart King and Cheshire, *Pembroke Castle*, pp 61–8 and fig. 1 and pl. iv; Wiles, 'Marshal towers', fig. 23. **79** Cathcart King and Cheshire, *Pembroke Castle*, pp 6–7; Ludlow, *Pembroke Castle*, pp 3–4. **80** Ibid., pp 2–3; Cathcart King and Cheshire, *Pembroke Castle*, p. 6. **81** Ludlow, *Pembroke Castle*, p. 4. **82** Ibid., pp 6–7, 24, 30, 32 and site plan; Cathcart King and Cheshire, *Pembroke Castle*, pp 51–3. **83** See ibid., p. 21.

a b c d

5.15 Rear views of plunging arrow loops: a) French-style south loop in Dungeon Tower, Pembroke Castle; b) French-style loops inside William Marshal's Garrison Tower at Usk Castle, south-east Wales; c) Plantagenet-style plunging arrow and embrasure at Chinon Castle, France; d) Plantagenet-style loop and embrasure in south tower of Kilkenny Castle.

5.16 View of south tower of William Marshal's Kilkenny Castle from moat in 1998 following excavation.

blocks of limestone were mostly used in the construction of the facings. These were laid in irregular courses, bonded with lime mortar, with smaller stone fragments used to underpin the larger ones. Rubble was used to infill the core of the walls. Well-dressed blocks of stone or ashlar, including mainly Dundry limestone and other light-coloured stone, were utilised in the construction of finer features, such as doorways, rear arches, arrow loops and larger window surrounds.

As noted above, a common feature of William Marshal's phase of the castle (fig. 5.15a), as can be seen for example at Chepstow and Usk (fig. 5.15b), was the use of the long inward-splaying arrow loop through the whole thickness of the wall, without having a rear-arched embrasure to improve the outward firing ranges of archers. The use of these French or *philippienne*-style arrow loops in the Marshal's construction works at Pembroke Castle, including the great tower and at his other Welsh castles, may seem odd for a loyal supporter of the early Plantagenet kings. It was in contrast to the style employed by these kings at their castles in western France, such as in the large-beaked flanking towers of the southern stretch of the curtain wall at the castle of Loches (fig. 5.6).[84] This style that was also used at their castle of Chinon (fig. 5.15c)[85] was in stark contrast to that later employed there by King Philip Augustus in his Tour du Coudray.[86] Interestingly, however, the Plantagenet style was employed at the Marshal's great castle at Kilkenny in the centre of his Irish lordship, in contrast to his Welsh castles (fig. 5.15d and below). As will be seen below, in contrast to the French-style arrow loops, the large twin-light windows, particularly those in the great tower, have parallel-sided embrasures on the inside, with overlying rounded or semi-circular barrel vaulting like those of the plunging arrow loops in Kilkenny Castle, which defended the stone-lined moat on the outside (fig. 5.16).

Construction work on the great tower would appear to have commenced prior to the south stretch of the curtain wall (see below). The latter was a substantial structure with three flanking towers along its length and a later hall-building at the west corner adjoining the castle's chapel (fig. 5.1).[87] The first of these towers was the Garderobe or Latrine Turret at the eastern corner of the enceinte.[88] To the south-west is the flanking and circular Dungeon Tower, which stands to the height of its rebuilt battlements.[89] It is to the east of and is dwarfed by the great tower (fig. 5.17). On first-floor level, it was defended by three plunging arrow loops, with basal oillets, which appear to be of carved Dundry limestone. The lower remains of the Inner or 'Horseshoe' Gate are located farther along the line of the curtain wall, to the south-west of the great tower. It was a flanking

84 See Hulme, 'Château Gaillard', fig. 10. 85 Ibid., fig. 6. 86 Ibid., fig. 11. 87 See Robert Innes-Smith, *Pembroke Castle: birthplace of the Tudor dynasty* (Derby, 1996), pp 12–13; Ludlow, *Pembroke Castle*, p. 33 and site plan. 88 Ibid., site plan; Cathcart King and Cheshire, *Pembroke Castle*, p. 50, fig. 5 and site plan. 89 Ibid., pp 39–40, fig. 5 and site plan; Ludlow, *Pembroke Castle*, p. 32.

5.17 South view from Outer Ward of Dungeon Tower on right and great tower in background, Pembroke Castle.

D-shaped tower that extended out into the now in-filled ditch or moat (fig. 5.18).[90] Only the lower courses survive above current ground level along with the curtain wall in that area. It had a doorway on one side giving access to the interior, from where another doorway opened into the courtyard or Inner Ward of the castle. The unusual design for this gate tower, which contrasted with his twin-towered structure at Chepstow (fig. 5.10), but can be compared to the Bohun Gate at nearby Caldicot Castle, appears to have derived from Crusader links in the eastern Mediterranean.[91]

The west end of the south stretch of the curtain wall terminates at the later hall at the western corner of the Inner Ward, at the north of which are the remains of the chapel (fig. 5.1).[92] The other two sides (north-west and north-east) of the enclosure or enceinte were defended by a low and insubstantial curtain wall above the cliff face (figs 5.14, 5.17). There is a small square turret with the nearby base of a larger one at the rounded north corner.[93] The north-east section of the curtain wall terminates at a substantial building adjoining the Garderobe or Latrine Turret at the east corner of the enceinte (fig. 5.19). This remarkable Marshal structure, known as the Wogan, is built into the underlying

90 Ibid., pp 28–9 and site plan. **91** Ibid., p. 41; Avent, 'Chepstow's place', pp 80–1 and fig. 72; Neil Guy et al., 'Castle Studies Group Conference', pp 83, 89–90; Kenyon, *The medieval castles of Wales*, pp 91, 109. **92** Ibid., p. 28 and site plan; Carthcart King and Cheshire, *Pembroke Castle*, pp 41–2 and site plan. **93** Ibid., p. 45 and site plan.

5.18 View of great tower at Pembroke Castle from west, with remains of Inner or Horseshoe Gate in foreground.

cliff face towards the eastern tidal tributary of the Pembroke River or Mill Pond. It formed a defensive facing to the entrance of a large cavern beneath the castle.[94] There is a large segmental archway at the bottom of the outer face, the dressed surround of which has been robbed out. This seems to have been a watergate, which would have enabled boats to be taken inside the Wogan like a boathouse from the adjoining river for their protection. Similarly, it would have enabled passengers to travel to and from the castle with the tide to and from seagoing

94 Ibid., pp 46–8; Ludlow, *Pembroke Castle*, p. 29.

5.19 North view of the Wogan at Pembroke Castle from across the Mill Pond.

vessels anchored in Milford Haven to the north-west. Plunging arrow loops in the exterior of the Wogan protected access to the archway. These have an inward splay through the thickness of the wall in the French *philippienne* style which, as seen above, is a typical feature of William Marshal's phases of works at his castles in south Wales.[95] The rear arches on the inside are round.[96]

Just above the level of the archway, to the south-east, there is a fine twin-light window in the north-east exterior of the Wogan facing the north branch or Mill Pond of the Pembroke River, which is constructed of finely or ashlar-dressed light-coloured stone in the Transitional style of the late twelfth and early thirteenth century (fig. 5.19). The two lights or lancets have Gothic heads, while the outer surround has a rounded or semi-circular head. As will be seen below, this closely resembles the two twin-light windows of the same style in the exterior of the Marshal's great tower up in the Inner Ward.

A spiral stairwell to the north-west of the archway, which is on the inside of a semi-circular projection or turret on the exterior of the Wogan, gives access to the castle above (fig. 5.19). It has a noticeable battered base on the outside. Higher up the stairway is lit by a fine arrow loop, which is constructed of ashlar-dressed blocks of light-coloured stone with a basal oillet (fig. 5.20a), like those in the Dungeon Tower (fig. 5.20b). As will be seen below, the same type of rectangular basal oillet on the Wogan loop can still be seen at the base of

95 Cathcart King and Cheshire, *Pembroke Castle*, fig. 4. **96** Innes-Smith, *Pembroke Castle*, pp 8–9; Ludlow, *Pembroke Castle*, p. 29.

5.20 Examples of William Marshal's plunging arrow loops with the same basal oillet type at his castles in south Wales: a) stair turret at the Wogan, Pembroke Castle; b) south-west arrow loop, Dungeon Tower, Pembroke Castle; c) Garrison Tower, Usk Castle; d) west arrow loop, Hanbury Arms Tower, Caerleon Castle.

surviving plunging arrow loops up on the battlement of the great tower, as well as in towers built by the Marshal at his other castles, such as the Garrison Tower of the Inner Ward at Usk (fig. 5.20c) and the Hanbury Arms Tower at Caerleon Castle (fig. 5.20d). The top of the Wogan was rebuilt and turned into a fine hall in the later thirteenth century by William de Valence, earl of Pembroke (d. 1296), who had inherited the castle through his marriage to Joan de Munchensy, a granddaughter of the Marshal.[97]

Apart from the Wogan, the most impressive of the Marshal's works at Pembroke Castle is of course his great tower (fig. 5.17). It is built on solid ground about midway along the inside of the curtain wall of the Inner Ward (figs 5.1, 5.18 and below). It is likely that this siting was deliberately chosen by the earl to command the end of the promontory and to provide added defence of the curtain wall and access from the Outer Ward to the south. In addition, the summit overlooks the surrounding countryside and underlying waterway (fig. 5.14), as well as providing a view of Milford Haven in the distance to the north-west. The Marshal's rebuilding of the early castle, together with the completed great tower, would have impressed anyone who saw it at the time. It would have also provided security and comfort to the local settler population in both the adjoining town and the nearby countryside. It would also have acted as a marker in demonstrating the aspiring power and wealth of the new earl of Pembroke.

The new castle is likely to have been a powerful statement of intent by William Marshal and Countess Isabel that their earldom of Pembroke had been re-established and was there to stay. They were not going to be driven out of the area by the native Welsh of Deheubarth, who no doubt wished and endeavoured to recover their lost ancestral lands in 'Little England beyond Wales'. Despite the best efforts of the Welsh, however, they never managed to capture the castle, so the earl's works must have been effective. Importantly, as noted above, it also helped in keeping open his direct link across St George's Channel to his lordship in Ireland (fig. 5.13).[98]

Although Cathcart King thought there was no reason that the Outer Ward, to the south of the inner one, had not been enclosed with the present curtain wall with its flanking towers by William Marshal (fig. 5.14),[99] this work would now seem to have post-dated his time. The architecture would appear largely to belong to a different style and later construction phase or phases than the earl's work in the Inner Ward. Although it has also been suggested that the building of the masonry defences of the Outer Ward were commenced by his sons,[100] the present architecture seems to point to a later date.

97 Ibid., p. 31; Cathcart King and Cheshire, *Pembroke Castle*, p. 46; Hamilton Hall, 'The Marshal pedigree', *JRSAI*, 43 (1913), pp 1–29 at pp 17–18. **98** Cathcart King and Cheshire, *Pembroke Castle*, p. 8. **99** Ibid., p. 54. **100** The postern beside the East Tower reputedly of the 1220s at Cilgerran Castle (fig. 5.21) has been compared with that beside the Monkton Tower to argue for a pre-1245 dating for the Outer Ward at Pembroke Castle: see Wiles, 'Marshal towers',

5.21 Outer view of the Marshal twin circular towers of the inner ward of Cilgerran Castle, Pembrokeshire, Wales.

For example, at Cilgerran in north-east Pembrokeshire (fig. 5.13), which was on the frontier with the Welsh of Deheubarth, the Marshal's eldest son and successor, William II, conducted rebuilding works to the castle during the 1220s. Furthermore, there is a view that they were continued after his death in 1231 by one or more of his younger brothers, which resulted in two nearby and flanking circular great towers along the curtain wall there (fig. 5.21).[101] The Marshal phase of work at Cilgerran, which might be seen as less refined than that of William I at the Inner Ward of Pembroke Castle, is still in the Transitional architectural style in the mixed use of, for example, the rounded and pointed or Gothic arches. As noted above, the building work on the Inner Ward at Pembroke would seem to be in an earlier architectural style than that used in the Outer Ward. Neil Ludlow contends that the latter is the work of William de Valence in the later thirteenth century.[102] John Goodall supports this view and points out that this successor to the Marshal earls of Pembroke, in wishing to bolster his prestige at his titular castle, conducted this major programme of work.[103] The general architectural uniformity and style, despite a lot of modern rebuilding, would tend to support this view in that it seems to be the product of a single and sustained large-scale building programme. This would have been more difficult to achieve under the relatively short and punctuated tenures of William Marshal's younger sons during the period 1231–45. It is possible, however, that the lower levels of the present enclosing wall of the Outer Ward incorporate earlier fabric.

p. 193. **101** Hilling, *Cilgerran Castle*, pp 12–15, 21; Kenyon, *Medieval castles of Wales*, pp 167–9. **102** See Ludlow, *Pembroke Castle*, pp 10, 27, 33. **103** Goodall, *The English castle*, p. 208.

Moreover, it is likely that in the time of the elder Marshal (d. 1219) and perhaps before, as noted above, the Outer Ward would have been enclosed and defended by at least timber defences, which were later replaced by the stone-built curtain wall and towers. The Inner Ward would have been rather small and confined to have accommodated all the buildings, such as barns and stables, that would have been necessary for the functioning of the Marshal's castle and adjoining lands. Parchmarks and wall foundations in the Outer Ward have been identified that would indicate the remains of buildings beneath the ground. A complex at the south end near the later main gate, which was excavated, appears to have been a large late medieval building that was aligned with a roadway running towards the Horseshoe Gate of the Inner Ward.[104] The dating of other buildings that are represented by parchmarks in the ground, however, is still unclear. The enclosure of the entire promontory, consisting of the Inner and Outer Wards during the Marshal period, would have made defensive sense, particularly in relation to the adjoining town. Perhaps future investigations and excavation will throw some light on this.

THE ARCHITECTURE OF THE GREAT TOWER

The present building stands on bedrock with a wide base batter to a height of about 24m and is solidly constructed, as noted above, with mainly locally quarried limestone masonry (fig. 5.17). It is midway along the inside of the south section of the curtain wall of the Inner Ward (figs 5.1, 5.18) instead of being built as a projecting flanking tower along its length, where it might have had a greater defensive effect. One reason for this may be that the builders opted to build on the surface of the solid bedrock, rather than out into the pre-existing moat or ditch, which is likely to have been deepened and used as a quarry for building stone. Furthermore, the inner face of the curtain wall seems to have partly overlain the base batter of the great tower, indicating that the lower storey of the latter at least was under construction first, perhaps truncating the inner slope of an earthen rampart of the older line of defence. The main body of the circular tower consists of four storeys beneath the two-tiered battlement with the remains of a central turret at the top (fig. 5.17 and below), consisting of ground-, first-, second- and third-floor levels (fig. 5.22). At first-floor level, above the underlying wide base batter on the ground or basement storey, the building is about 16.3m in diameter. Above this, the exterior of the tower narrows to the height of the ruined parapet enclosing the wall walk on the fourth-floor level (fig. 5.22). This is the result of two horizontal offsets of finely dressed stones, with a plain chamfer moulding. This feature can also be seen on towers of the period in

104 Cathcart King and Cheshire, *Pembroke Castle*, site plan; Neil Ludlow, 'Pembroke Castle: discoveries in the Outer Ward', *Castle Studies Group Bulletin*, 18 (Sept. 2014), pp 2–6.

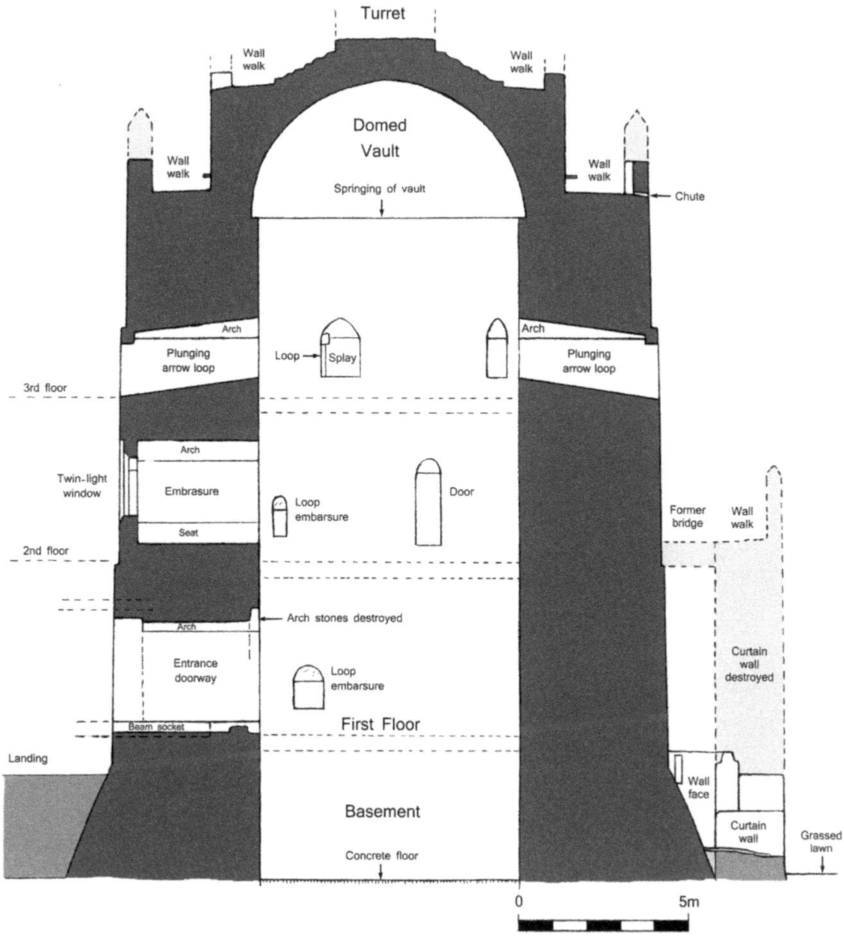

5.22 Cross-section looking east through the great tower at Pembroke Castle.

western France, such as Châteaudun,[105] Philip Augustus's Tour du Coudray at Chinon (fig. 5.3b) and the Plantagenet beaked tower at the south drawbridge gate at Loches (fig. 5.6a).[106] The first offset at the Pembroke tower is at second-floor level, while the second one is above the third floor (fig. 5.22).

The two offset courses subdivide the outer face of the main body of the tower above the battered base into three levels (figs 5.17–5.18). These are constructed of mainly roughly dressed blocks of locally quarried limestone, laid in irregular horizontal courses (as noted above) in the Marshal's other building works in the Inner Ward of the castle. This style of facing masonry differs from the finely

105 See Avent, 'William Marshal's castle at Chepstow and its place military architecture', fig. 71; Girault, *Loire Valley castles*, p. 29; Mesqui, *Châteaux forts*, p. 113. **106** Ibid., p. 218;

a b

5.23 External views of great tower at Pembroke Castle: a) from north-west; b) from north.

dressed ashlar of many castles in France, such as Chinon (fig. 5.3), Philip Augustus's Louvre (fig. 5.5) and King Richard's Château Gaillard (fig. 5.7).[107] Similarly, in England earlier great towers had been built of ashlar-dressed masonry, such as at Conisborough.[108] In the case of King Edward I's later great tower at Flint Castle in north-east Wales, for example, more irregular-shaped rectangular blocks of sandstone were used in the facing masonry (fig. 5.2). Although this was better dressed than the grey limestone masonry of the exterior of the Pembroke tower, the latter would not have been seen, as it was covered with lime render that is likely to have been lime washed (see below).

In addition to the irregular horizontal courses, the three levels of external limestone facing masonry of the main body of the tower above the battered base that are subdivided by the two offset courses (fig. 5.17) can be further subdivided by distinct construction levels, where building works would appear to have been temporarily or seasonally stopped (see below). Furthermore, the limestone facing masonry is punctuated inside and outside the tower by ashlar-dressed surrounds of doors, loops and windows, usually of lighter-coloured stone, including Dundry limestone. Some of these surrounds, particularly on the lower level, have been robbed out. Higher up, two particularly fine twin-light windows survive on the second and third storeys facing north and west (figs 5.23a and b).

Briais, *Loches*, pp 26–7. **107** This was often the result of abundant local supplies of quarried soft stone, which was easy to dress. **108** See Brindle, 'The keep at Conisbrough', fig. 3.

5.24 View of battlements and upper level of great tower at Pembroke Castle from south.

5.25 North-west view of upper exterior of main body of great tower at Pembroke Castle, showing twin-light window and two plunging arrow loops in the parapet and putlogs for timber hoarding.

These are constructed of ashlar-dressed, light-coloured (like Dundry limestone) and sculpted stonework, which belongs to the same school as the one down in the Wogan (fig. 5.19 and below).[109]

109 See Cathcart King and Cheshire, *Pembroke Castle*, pp 34–6 and pl. xi B–D; Ludlow, *Pembroke Castle*, pp 24, 29.

a  b

5.26 Early plunging arrow loops of 1190s on battlements of Framlingham Castle, Suffolk, England: a) external view of one of the towers; b) rear view of one of the loops.

5.27 View of wall walk of great tower at Pembroke Castle, showing the remains of plunging arrow loops in the enclosing parapet.

Around the top of the upper level of the outer facing of the main body of the tower is a ruined parapet that encloses the wall walk on the fourth-floor level, which is the lower one of the tiered battlement on the summit of the building (figs 5.22, 5.23, 5.24).[110] The parapet was crenellated with merlons pierced with plunging arrow loops. These had ashlar-dressed stone surrounds on the outside

110 See cut-away drawing by Ludlow in ibid., p. 27 and Innes-Smith, *Pembroke Castle*, p. 5. See also Cathcart King and Cheshire, *Pembroke Castle*, pp 36–8 and fig. 3 and pl. xiA.

of light-coloured stone (possibly Dundry) with basal oillets.[111] Two examples can be seen at the north-west of the tower (fig. 5.25).

These are of the same type as the one in the spiral stairwell turret of the Wogan (fig. 5.20a) and at the base of the south-west plunging arrow loop on the first floor of the Dungeon Tower (fig. 5.20b). The same style of basal oillets can be seen at William Marshal's other Welsh castles, such as the Garrison Tower of the Inner Ward at Usk (fig. 5.20c) and the Hanbury Arms Tower at Caerleon (fig. 5.20d). Similarly, this oillet-type can be seen at the base of a plunging arrow loop in the D-shaped tower of the earl's Middle Bailey at Chepstow (see below).[112]

The location of plunging arrow loops of the lower parapet of the great tower might be compared to those along the battlements of the curtain wall and towers at Framlingham Castle in Suffolk (figs 5.26a and b), dating to the construction works of Earl Roger Bigod II in the 1190s or so.[113] In the intervals or embrasures between the merlons containing the loops at Pembroke, the thickness of the parapet (*c.*0.75m) decreases noticeably (*c.*0.52m) and it becomes lower (figs 5.22, 5.27), which presumably would have facilitated archers shooting down from the battlements or soldiers throwing down missiles. Just beneath the level of the loops there are putlogs alternating with rainwater chutes around the exterior of the tower, apparently for timber hoarding (figs 5.24, 5.25).[114] Such a structure, if it was ever erected, might have obscured the arrow loops in the parapet.

Internally, each of the four storeys of the main body of the tower beneath the battlement had a single circular room or chamber, stacked one above the other (fig. 5.22). These had oak floors above the ground-storey basement,[115] which are now gone, resulting in a single high and vertical cylindrical space that is about 7.6m in diameter. The missing floors are now represented by large square or oblong beam or joist sockets in the surrounding wall face, resembling the putlogs for the hoarding high up in the exterior, with some having sawn-off ends of timber joists (fig. 5.28). The top of the high cylindrical space is covered by a fine domed vault with a slightly pointed profile (figs 5.22, 5.29). It supported the upper two tiers of the overlying battlement and is enclosed on the lower tier outside by the circular wall walk on the fourth-floor level on top of the main body of the building (figs 5.22, 5.24). The underside or soffit of the vault has impressions of small timber planks in the mortar,[116] which are the remains of the timber shuttering used in its construction (fig. 5.29). The impressions of this form of shuttering can be seen elsewhere within the tower, such as in the rear arches and vaulting, as well as in William Marshal's other works in the Inner Ward and the Wogan. During the course of this writer's recording work at the earl's Kilkenny Castle, the centre of his Irish lordship, it was found that small

111 Ibid., p. 37. **112** Avent and Turner, 'Middle Bailey', fig. 51:4. **113** See also Nicola Stacey, *Framlingham Castle* (London, 2009), pp 10–12. **114** See cut-away drawing in Ludlow, *Pembroke Castle*, p. 27 and Innes-Smith, *Pembroke Castle*, p. 5. **115** See ibid., pp 4–5. **116** Ibid.

5.28 Internal view of first-floor chamber of great tower at Pembroke Castle, showing fireplace in centre.

5.29 View from under domed vault of the Pembroke great tower.

planks like those employed at Pembroke were used in the timber shuttering for construction of, for example, barrel vaults and rear arches (fig. 5.15d and below).

There appears to have been a timber floor at fourth-floor level, the joist ends of which would have rested upon a wide offset that runs around the springing of the domed vault to form a loft at the top of the cylindrical inner face of the main body of the tower (fig. 5.22).[117] Access was gained at the north-west through an original doorway in the vault from the wall walk on the lower tier of the battlement outside (fig. 5.29). Light was provided through a window in the vault at the south. The floor may have initially supported the shuttering for construction of the overlying vault. This raises the issue of the arrangement of the large oak joists that supported the underlying timber floors. Tom McNeill has pointed out that they appear to have been arranged in a radial fashion, one solution for which he suggested would have required a central post rising from the ground floor.[118] It has also been suggested that this form of flooring existed at William Marshal's circular south or great tower at his castle in Kilkenny (fig. 5.16 and below). Meanwhile, at Pembroke the base or a socket in the underlying bedrock may still exist beneath the centre of the present floor of the circular basement room or cellar, which unfortunately consists of a concrete slab.

The basement or ground-floor room was unlit, being surrounded on the outside by the wide base batter of the tower (fig. 5.22). It is likely that it was used for storage. The face of the surrounding wall was not plastered, unlike the cylindrical chambers of the three overlying floors. A doorway at the north-west, which has had its dressed-stone surround robbed out, gives access to the bottom of an original spiral stairwell to the upper floors of the main body of the tower.[119] It is lit by four inward-splaying loops arranged in a vertical line on the exterior of the main body of the tower at the north-west. The externally dressed stone surrounds of all the loops have been robbed out (figs 5.23a and b). A caphouse at the top of the stairwell gives access onto the wall walk of the lower tier of the battlement on fourth-floor level. The original finely dressed newels of the stairwell were also robbed out and have been replaced in concrete. At the bottom, a later doorway into a building at the north-west was inserted through the base batter (figs 5.23a and b), which also gave access to the basement.

The original entrance to the tower was through a large doorway at the north above the base batter (figs 5.23b, 5.30a). There is an inward passageway (1.64m in width) under a segmental barrel vault, which runs through the thickness of the circular wall of the tower, giving access directly to the first-floor chamber (fig. 5.22). The ashlar-dressed stone surrounds at either end have been robbed out. A set of four large sockets or putlogs enclosing the entrance on the outer face of the building formerly contained large timbers for a form of drawbridge to a stairway that would have given access from the ground outside. This was

117 See ibid., cut-away drawing. 118 McNeill, 'Squaring circles', pp 104–5. 119 Cathcart King and Cheshire, *Pembroke Castle*, figs 2–3 and site plan.

a  b

5.30 Exterior views of the Pembroke great tower: a) remains of original first-floor north entrance to tower with overlying Gothic twin-light window on second floor; b) external doorway on second floor with ashlar-dressed surround and semi-circular head.

replaced with the present stone stairway (fig. 5.23). The circular first-floor chamber had a timber floor over the basement (fig. 5.22). Much of the lime plaster of the surrounding wall has fallen away. The chamber was poorly lit from the outside by two inward-splaying loops at the south-west (fig. 5.28) and the north-east.[120] These loops have round-headed surrounds on the inside, but the dressed ones on the outside have been robbed out. The impressions of plank centring can be seen in the soffit of the vaulting of the south-west loop. The most interesting feature is the fine original large fireplace at the west, which had an ashlar-dressed stone surround. Although the dressed stones on either side are gone, the overlying rounded arch is intact (fig. 5.28). At the north-west, between the fireplace and the main entrance passageway, are the remains of the round-headed doorway to the stairwell with the first of its two ashlar-dressed surrounds robbed out (fig. 5.28).

The overlying second-floor chamber would appear to have been the principal room of the tower.[121] It was entered through a doorway of two orders, as on the underlying floor. The remaining ashlar-dressed stones, which appear to be Dundry limestone, have evidence of diagonal tooling. The original wooden door

120 Ibid., fig. 2. **121** Ibid., p. 34 and fig. 2; Innes-Smith, *Pembroke Castle*, pp 4–5.

was secured from inside the chamber by wooden drawbars. The chamber, as in the case of the one below, has two *philippienne*-style or and inward-splaying plunging arrow loops opposite each other, at the north-east (fig. 5.22) and south-west.[122] Both have inner surrounds of ashlar-dressed stones that appear to be Dundry limestone and have rounded heads. There is also a fireplace at the west, directly above the one on the floor below. It too had a surround of ashlar-dressed stones, of which those on either side have been robbed out, but those of the overlying segmental arch are intact and appear to be Dundry limestone.

At the north, the chamber is lit by the fine twin-light window above the original entrance to the tower (figs 5.22, 5.23b, 5.30a).[123] Here it could have been used to defend access on the outside to the underlying doorway as well as providing a somewhat limited view out to the river. The two lights or lancets and outer surround, which are constructed of ashlar-dressed cream-coloured stone (like Dundry limestone), have pointed or Gothic heads. There is a weathered sculpted head in the tympanum between the window heads, while the chamfers on the outside of both lights are decorated. It is a fine example of pure Early English Gothic, which contrasts with much of the other ashlar-dressed features from William Marshal's phase of works on the castle, which have mostly semi-circular heads or are in the Transitional style. These include the two other similar-type twin-light windows from this phase, the first of which is the one in the Wogan with its Gothic-headed twin-lights or lancets, but round-headed outer surround (fig. 5.19), as well as the other window on the third floor of the great tower, the two lights of which have rounded heads, while the outer surround has a Gothic head (figs 5.23, 5.25). There is a rectangular embrasure on the inside of the second-floor window that runs south through the thickness of the wall of the tower (fig. 5.22). It has window seats on either side with an overlying rounded or semi-circular rather than pointed barrel vault. The ashlar-dressed (Dundry limestone?) surround at the south is intact.

Elevated perhaps 0.4m above the first-floor level at the south-east of this principal room or chamber is a doorway passage running through the thickness of the wall of the tower with a rounded or semi-circular barrel vault overhead. At the chamber end there is an ashlar-dressed surround of cream-coloured stone, like Dundry limestone. At the far end of the passageway there is a doorway surround of cream-coloured and ashlar-dressed stone blocks on the exterior. It has a rounded head and is rebated on the inside for a wooden door (figs 5.17, 5.22, 5.30b). There are two large beam sockets or putlogs on the outer face of the tower beneath the level of the threshold and the lower dressed-stone offset. Originally these would have supported a timber bridge giving access to the now-destroyed wall walk of the nearby south curtain wall of the Inner Ward.[124]

122 Cathcart King and Cheshire, *Pembroke Castle*, fig. 2. **123** Ibid., pp 34, 36 and fig. 2 and pl. ixB; Innes-Smith, *Pembroke Castle*, p. 4; Ludlow, *Pembroke Castle*, p. 24. **124** See ibid., cut-away drawing of tower; Cathcart King and Cheshire, *Pembroke Castle*, p. 36.

As the tower did not have garderobes or latrines of its own, it is likely that the doorway and bridge provided access to these facilities outside, either along the wall walk of the nearby curtain wall or in the Latrine Turret. This might be compared to the arrangement at Dundrum Castle, Co. Down, where a doorway on the first floor of the circular great tower originally gave access to a wooden bridge to the wall walk of the nearby curtain wall, which had latrines (fig. 5.31).[125] King John captured this castle with his army during his 1210 campaign against Hugh de Lacy II in Ulster, after he had set out from Pembroke and had advanced through south-east Ireland via Kilkenny, where he was apparently 'given a most lavish reception' by William Marshal at his castle.[126] Following its capture from de Lacy, Dundrum Castle remained in royal hands for seventeen years.[127] It is possible that John was responsible for the building of the great tower there. In 1211–12 it is recorded that construction works were being conducted on the castle, which included the great tower.[128]

The circular third-floor chamber of the Pembroke tower underlay the loft beneath the domed vault (figs 5.22, 5.32).[129] It differs from the two underlying chambers in that it does not have a fireplace, but it has lime plaster on the surrounding wall. A vertical chasing in the plaster at the south, which continues into the underlying chamber, indicates that they were later subdivided. As in the case of the underlying floor, access to the chamber was gained from the spiral stairwell through a doorway of two orders. Drawbar sockets on either side indicate that this door, like those on the two underlying floors, could be secured from within the chamber. Around the south-east half of the latter are four plunging arrow loops with Gothic rear arches in the French *philippienne* style (figs 5.22, 5.32), such as at King Philip Augustus's circular great tower at Falaise in Normandy.[130] The dressed jamb stones on the outside consist mainly of a weathered brown stone. Two of the loops directly overlooked the south curtain wall and the Outer Ward beyond (figs 5.17, 5.24), but their effectiveness for crossbowmen would have been somewhat limited. At the west of the chamber is the second of the tower's two fine twin-light windows (minus its mullion) (figs 5.23a, 5.25). On the inside is a rectangular embrasure running through the thickness of the wall. As in the case of the one on the underlying floor, it has window seats on either side with an overlying semi-circular barrel vault that has

125 Conleth Manning, 'Clogh Oughter Castle, Co. Cavan, and thirteenth-century circular towers in Ireland', *Château Gaillard*, 25 (2012), pp 223–32 at p. 230; H.G. Leask, 'Irish castles, 1180 to 1310', *Archaeological Journal*, 93 (1937), pp 143–99, fig. 8; T.E. McNeill, *Castles in Ireland: feudal power in a Gaelic world* (London, 2000), pp 27–8; Sweetman, *Medieval castles*, p. 87 and figs 67–8. **126** See Crouch, *William Marshal*, p. 116; *HWM*, ii, lines 14256–71; Orpen, *Normans*, ii, pp 143, 152–3; Painter, *William Marshal*, pp 163–5. **127** G.H. Orpen, 'Dundrum Castle, County Down, identified with the "Castrum de Rath"', *JRSAI*, 39 (1909), pp 23–9 at p. 24; idem, *Normans*, ii, p. 153. **128** McNeill, *Castles in Ireland*, p. 27. **129** See Cathcart King and Cheshire, *Pembroke Castle*, p. 36 and fig. 2; Innes-Smith, *Pembroke Castle*, pp 4–5; Ludlow, *Pembroke Castle*, p. 27, cut-away drawing. **130** Mesqui, *Les châteaux forts de la guerre à la paix*, p. 56; idem, *Châteaux forts*, p. 25.

5.31 View showing proximity of curtain wall to circular great tower at Dundrum Castle, Co. Down.

5.32 Rear view of Gothic French-style plunging arrow loops in third-floor chamber of Pembroke great tower.

impressions of plank centring in the soffit. On the outside, the window had a clear view of the Horseshoe Gate and anyone entering the Inner Ward (fig. 5.18) and the waterway beyond (fig. 5.14).

THE GREAT TOWER AS A LIGHTHOUSE

On the summit of the tower, in the centre of the upper battlement, is the surviving base of a cylindrical turret, about 3m in diameter (figs 5.22, 5.24, 5.33).[131] Cathcart King stated that this 'was clearly a watch-tower'.[132] It may have had another function however. John Wiles has compared the Pembroke tower, together with one at the nearby town of Tenby, with the medieval light-tower of Hook (fig. 5.34, pl. 12) in south-east Ireland, as William Marshal's sea marks at 'either end of the fraught Irish Sea passage' (fig. 5.13).[133] This stems from a belief that following the near-death experience on his apparent first visit to Ireland in 1200, the Marshal constructed the great free-standing circular tower at the treacherous Hook Head at the mouth of Waterford Harbour to aid trade and shipping travelling into the heart of his Irish lordship and his port of New Ross.[134] The abovementioned medieval royal expeditions, which sailed from Pembroke, entered Ireland through this harbour. The tower is a two-tiered structure, strongly built of locally quarried grey fossiliferous limestone. It is strengthened internally by three great ribbed vaults in the lower tier or main body of the building (fig. 5.34). The large upper vault supports the smaller upper tier of what was formerly known as 'the lighthouse'. It originally had ribbed vaulting inside and was enclosed on the outside by a battlement around the top of the main body of the building.

It is known that as far back as the seventeenth century at least, the exterior of Hook Tower was lime- or white-washed to act as a beacon for shipping entering Waterford Harbour by day near the low-lying and rocky Hook Head.[135] At night, however, an iron brazier or grate was lit at the top of the upper tier of the tower, which is now occupied by the nineteenth-century lantern (fig. 5.34). Similarly, the surviving traces of lime render on the exterior of the Pembroke great tower would suggest that the building was lime- or white-washed, which could have acted as a beacon by day for boats travelling along the tidal river from nearby Milford Haven to the castle or adjoining town. Furthermore, the turret at the top of the tower could have supported a brazier to provide a light at night, perhaps fuelled by timber, faggots or coals. The strongly built stone roof would have facilitated and supported such a feature, similar to the arrangement at Hook.

131 See ibid., Neil Ludlow's cut-away drawing. **132** Cathcart King and Cheshire, *Pembroke Castle*, p. 38 and fig. 3, no. 21 and pl. ixB. **133** Wiles, 'Marshal towers', p. 193. **134** Ibid.; Avent, 'Chepstow's place', p. 89; Billy Colfer, *The Hook Peninsula* (Cork, 2004), p. 84; Sweetman, *Medieval castles*, p. 88. **135** See Simon Loftus, *The invention of memory: an Irish family scrapbook, 1560–1934* (London, 2014), p. 161.

5.33 View of surviving base of circular turret at top of Pembroke great tower.

Despite the similarities between the two towers, work conducted by this writer on the Hook Tower since the 1990s has found some notable differences relating to both architectural detail and dating. First, the spiral stairwell in the main body of the Pembroke tower contrasts with the two intra-mural ones at Hook. Second, there is a lack of uniformity in the types of arches employed in the Pembroke tower. This would stem to some degree from the Transitional style that was employed in the castle architecture of both William Marshal and his son, William II. As the thirteenth century progressed, however, the Gothic arch became more pronounced, as it displaced the rounded or semi-circular variety in Wales and Ireland. In the case of the Pembroke tower, Gothic arches appear only on the second and third floors as one rises through the building, perhaps indicating a certain longevity or interruption in construction works (see below). On the other hand, this is not the case at the Hook Tower, where there is a general uniformity in the architecture and in the use of the Gothic arch throughout the building, such as in doorways and vaulting. It would seem that the whole structure was the product of a single and sustained building campaign. There is an absence of rounded or semi-circular arches, which has led this writer to form the view that the tower post-dated the lifetime of both William Marshal I and his son, with a construction date centring on the later Marshal period towards the middle of the century.

The above dating is supported by documentary evidence. A published abstract of a mandate of Henry III of 1247 relates to the existence of the tower at the end of the Marshal period in 1245. It states that Earl Walter (1241–5), the fourth and last of William I's sons to have had effective control of his lands, maintained a community of monks at Hook Head, who had built the tower there

5.34 Cut-away drawing of the Tower of Hook, Co. Wexford (by Phelim Manning and Ben Murtagh).

as a beacon for ships.[136] There is a more detailed and seemingly more accurate version of the same mandate from the patent rolls, when the Marshal lordship was in the king's hand following the end of the male line of that family.[137] It clearly states that in April 1247 the tower was under construction. Furthermore, the king ordered that those who were engaged in its erection were to continue to be supported out of the Marshal estate and that arrears owed to them since the death of Walter Marshal were to be paid out of the same. It would indicate that the building of the light-tower had commenced in the time of the same 'Earl Marshal', but that its completion was in the king's interests, as it would have directly aided shipping to his port city of Waterford (fig. 5.13).

Although there may have been a plan to construct a light-tower at Hook since the time of William Marshal I, to aid shipping to and from Wales and in particular Pembroke, it was not until Earl Walter's time that its construction began. Nevertheless, it is likely that his father's earlier structure at Pembroke provided an inspiration for a free-standing and circular great tower with an upper-tiered design, particularly if it also served as a beacon. It is interesting that the internal design was more in keeping with the style of the *tours philippiennes*, with their circular rib-vaulted rooms stacked one above the other, such as at Dourdan or Lillebonne.[138] In this regard, the contemporary Tour de Constance was built in the 1240s by the grandson of Philip Augustus, King Louis IX (r. 1226–70), at his strongly fortified new port city of Aigues-Mortes in the south of France on the Mediterranean.[139] This free-standing circular great tower also has internal ribbed vaulting, but interestingly it has a tall circular turret rising above the battlement, which was a beacon with a lantern at the top to guide shipping into the harbour.[140] It has the same diameter as the turret that stood on the summit of the Pembroke great tower, which supports the view that the latter served the same purpose.

THE DATING OF THE PEMBROKE GREAT TOWER

One handicap in dating construction works at baronial castles in Wales and in Ireland during the twelfth and thirteenth centuries is the lack of documentary evidence. This contrasts with royal castles, for which expenditure accounts were normally kept. Even in the case of a great baron like William Marshal, the

136 *CDI, 1171–1251*, no. 2872. **137** *CPR Henry III, AD1232–1247*, m.7 cont., pp 473–4, Feb. 15. Reading. This subject is addressed in more detail in Ben Murtagh, 'The medieval tower of Hook: a review of its dating and history' in Ian W. Doyle and Bernard Browne (eds), *Medieval Wexford: essays in memory of Billy Colfer* (Dublin, 2016), pp 124–80; idem, 'The medieval Tower of Hook, Co. Wexford: a beacon of commerce and symbol of Marshal power and wealth in Ireland', *Château Gaillard*, 27 (forthcoming, 2016), pp 223–36. **138** See Mesqui, *Châteaux forts*, pp 153, 216. **139** Ibid., pp 15–16; Patrick Florençon, *The city of Aigues-Mortes* (Paris, 2001), pp 2–3, 29–36. **140** Ibid., pp 31, 36.

remarkable and near contemporary history of his life is rather unhelpful as a record of his building works in either country. Pembroke, for example, gets only a single mention and that is in relation to the expedition of King John to Ireland in 1210.[141] In the absence of such records, one is left to rely upon the physical remains and architectural comparisons as well as sometimes peripheral historical sources dating the erection of the Pembroke great tower. Based on this, however, a great deal of information can be discerned regarding the construction of the building and a possible timeline for it.

Although it is generally accepted that William Marshal was responsible for building the tower, there seems to be less agreement as to when it was commenced and even less about when it may have been completed. As seen above, contrary to Cathcart King's view, the earl gained seisin of Pembroke only in 1200–1. Once he got possession of the castle, it is likely that he was anxious to commence rebuilding works so as to strengthen it. Some writers involved in castle studies in Wales are of the view that the Marshal did not commence these works until 1204, as he was busily employed since 1201 elsewhere with affairs on behalf of King John,[142] which largely involved the disastrous war in France.[143] Nonetheless, it is possible that he at least commenced preparations for works at the castle as early as 1200–1, leaving charge of them to his steward in his absence. He was certainly rich enough by this stage to afford them.

Following the loss of Normandy, in late 1204 the Marshal was back in west Wales, where he was engaged in a war with the Welsh of Deheubarth, capturing the strategic frontier castle of Cilgerran.[144] If he had not done so already, he must have taken the opportunity at that time to progress the rebuilding of his castle at Pembroke, prior to returning to France in the spring of 1205.[145] This would have included construction work on the tower, which seems to have taken some years to complete (see below).

The building of the lower part of the Pembroke great tower appears to have commenced prior to the south length of the curtain wall of the Inner Ward, which supports the view that it is the earliest of the Marshal's works here. Construction levels can be seen on the exterior of the tower, indicating separate seasons or stages of building works. These can be identified by a number of consistent courses of facing stonework – roughly dressed limestone – underlying a further phase of work. Works would not have been conducted during the winter, so a season would centre on the summer months, perhaps even commencing in the spring and continuing into the autumn, depending on the weather, available resources and manpower. In addition, each stage of

141 See *HWM*, ii, lines 14240–54; ibid., iii, p. 158, line 14256; Crouch, *William Marshal*, p. 116; Painter, *William Marshal*, p. 169. **142** Kenyon, *Medieval castles in Wales*, pp 89–90; Ludlow, *Pembroke Castle*, p. 8. **143** See Crouch, *William Marshal*, pp 90–3. **144** Ibid., pp 93–4. **145** William Marshal travelled to France to do homage to Philip Augustus for his lands in Normandy, which would eventually land him in trouble with King John: see ibid., pp 94–6.

construction could be built safely to a certain height only, in order to let the masonry settle before continuing. In this way, two stages and more might be built in one season. This would have been aided by the nearby supply of limestone and lime.

During intervening periods, the masons could move on to other building works elsewhere on the site. The ground storey, which includes the wide base batter, might have been built in a single season. The big oak joists for the first floor, possibly with a central post, were inserted before the construction of the next stage, consisting of inner and outer faces, with the space between them in-filled with core masonry.

At this rate, it could have taken five years to complete, without interruption. There is evidence that the construction of the tower was a more drawn out affair. Cathcart King contended that there was an interruption in works at the castle from 1207 to 1213, when William Marshal was mostly in Ireland, and while his castles in England and Wales were surrendered to the king with whom he was largely out of favour.[146] In 1210 the earl travelled from Ireland to Pembroke briefly to join John and his expedition against the de Lacys in Ulster. He returned during the following year after being summoned and somewhat coaxed by the king to support the war against Llywelyn ab Iorwerth, prince of Gwynedd in north Wales.[147] John, still apprehensive of the Marshal, particularly before allowing him to return to Ireland, held onto his son Richard as well as maintaining a hold over his castles in Britain.[148] If that was not enough, the earl's loyal knight and one-time seneschal in Leinster, Geoffrey fitz Robert, lord of Kells in Ossory, died around the same time, while a hostage in the king's custody.[149] In this unfavourable and uncertain situation, it is difficult to see the Marshal continuing to support building works at castles such as Pembroke.

Circumstances were to change two years later, for William Marshal at least, when the king summoned him permanently back to England and returned him to royal favour (which included the release of hostages) so as to aid John with his ever-growing difficulties with the English barons and renewed hostilities with the French king, Philip Augustus.[150] Furthermore, John not only restored the earl's position in south Wales, but enhanced it, giving him control of a series of castles in and near the Pembroke area.[151] During these remaining years of John's reign (1213–16), and even more so during the period of the Marshal's regency prior to his death in 1219, the latter would have been in a much stronger and more secure position to support construction works at his castles in Wales. In particular, these would seem to have included the continuation of works at Pembroke Castle, including the great tower.

146 Cathcart King and Cheshire, *Pembroke Castle*, p. 8. **147** See *HWM*, ii, lines 14473–80; ibid., iii, p. 159, line 14474; Orpen, *Normans*, ii, p. 218. **148** See painter, *William Marshal*, p. 170. **149** See *HWM*, ii, lines 14459–63, 14483–6. **150** See ibid., lines 14491–604. **151** Crouch, *William Marshal*, pp 118–19.

Of particular interest in relation to this are the plunging arrow loops with the distinctive rectangular basal oillets referred to above. These include those in the battlement of the great tower (fig. 5.25), the one in the stairway turret of the Wogan (fig. 5.20a) and one in the Dungeon Tower (fig. 5.20b). Each oillet is carved out of a single block of light-coloured stone, which looks like 'high-status' Dundry limestone. If these represent a contemporary phase of work in the Inner Ward of the castle, they would take on a particular significance when compared to the same loop-type found in the Marshal's building works at three of his castles in south-east Wales, as noted above. First there are the examples at the entrance to the primary phase of Garrison Tower at Usk (fig. 5.20c); second there are the three examples at the circular flanking tower known as the Hanbury Arms Tower, at the largely destroyed castle at Caerleon (fig. 5.20d), and third there is the example in the D-shaped tower of the Middle Ward at Chepstow Castle.[152]

Jeremy Knight, in his study of William Marshal's rebuilding of Usk Castle, has looked at these loops and their associated works at all three castles.[153] He has provided a date for their construction in the six-year period from the earl's return from Ireland in 1213 to his death in 1219. He has dated the building works at the Middle Bailey at Chepstow, including the D-shaped and south-east or corner towers (fig. 5.11), within this time bracket, while he has provided an even closer date for the works at Usk (1213–17) and for their commencement at Caerleon in 1218, which would have been completed after the Marshal's death the following year.[154] Knight's dating for these works and in particular the loops makes a strong case for a similar date range for those at Pembroke Castle (1213–19). This would support the view that there was a hiatus or perhaps significant slowing down in the Marshal's construction works at the Inner Ward, perhaps spanning the period 1207–13. As seen above, these were years during which he was mostly in Ireland, when he had to endure intermittent periods of royal displeasure or hostility and suspicion, while the 'tyrannical' English king continuously held family members and his key men as hostages, as well as maintaining a hold over his castles in Wales. Such an insecure environment would not have been conducive to continuing works at these castles. This situation was to change, of course, particularly from 1213 onwards, when the earl was in a more secure position to resume large-scale construction works at his Welsh castles.

In the case of the great tower, the above would point to a timescale spanning at least ten to fifteen years from the commencement of works by perhaps 1204 to the completion of the upper part of the building following the permanent return of the Marshal from Ireland in 1213. When considering the extent of the work involved in constructing the tower in conjunction with the other works in the Inner Ward, this would not have been an inordinate length of time. Such a slow

152 Avent and Turner, 'Middle Bailey', fig. 51:4; Knight, 'Usk Castle, 1136–1245', fig. 6:10. **153** See ibid., pp 59–68. **154** Ibid., p. 60.

pace of building might explain the initial and exclusive use of rounded or semi-circular arches in the lower storeys, contrasting with a Transitional architectural style on the second and third storeys with a mixture of the same type of arches with Gothic ones. If Knight's dating for the arrow loops – as identified with the Marshal's later building works at his castles in south-east Wales (figs 5.20c–d) – can be applied to the same type of loops at Pembroke (figs 5.20a–b, 5.25), it would infer that the upper part of the great tower, including the tiered battlement with the ashlar-dressed arrow loops, domed vault and turret at the summit, were not added until after 1213. Such a dating would also infer that the Wogan and the south curtain wall of the Inner Ward were not built until the same period (1213–*c*.1219).

THE PEMBROKE GREAT TOWER'S PARALLELS AND RELATIVES IN IRELAND

As seen above, the castle at Pembroke that William Marshal gained possession of in 1200–1 was strategically located near Milford Haven to control a vital link with his vast lordship of Leinster in the south-east of Ireland (fig. 5.13). His great tower there also symbolised and provided a marker of his authority in his Welsh earldom. Wiles has seen its erection as starting at the head of a diverse series of cylindrical towers in south-west Wales.[155] Meanwhile, across the sea, certain writers on Irish castles, such as Tom McNeill and Tadhg O'Keeffe, have attributed the origin of the cylindrical great towers in Ireland to the Marshal's remarkable one at Pembroke.[156]

It is not so evident, however, that the tower provided a prototype for the first of these structures in Ireland. For example, its construction would have only commenced after William Marshal had gained possession of the castle in 1200–1, or perhaps not until 1204, and its completion would seem not to have occurred until after 1213, when the Marshal had returned permanently from his Irish lordship. By that time the construction of such structures in conjunction with circular flanking towers had already occurred in the castles of the Anglo-Norman colony in Ireland. Instead, perhaps, these should be seen in a wider context as a more diverse and divergent development that came through both baronial and royal channels into the country, reflecting developments in military architecture in France particularly.

Rather than looking to Pembroke, it might be more appropriate to look to King John's mandate of 1204 to his justiciar, Meiler fitz Henry, for the building of possibly the first or at least one of the earliest circular great towers in Ireland at Dublin Castle to house the royal treasury.[157] Also to ingratiate himself with,

155 Wiles, 'Marshal towers', p. 199. 156 See McNeill, *Castles in Ireland*, pp 52–3; idem, 'Squaring circles', p. 96; O'Keeffe, 'Dublin Castle's donjon', pp 283–4, 291–2. 157 See J.T.

and not to incur the displeasure of, such an unpredictable, often cruel and vindictive monarch, it is likely that fitz Henry quickly moved on putting such an order into effect by at least commencing the work. It is interesting that he was ordered to raise at least some of the funding by calling in a debt of three hundred marks from William Marshal's trusty lieutenant in Leinster, Geoffrey fitz Robert, lord of Kells in Ossory. When the money had apparently not arrived by March 1206, a by now impatient king instructed his justiciar to seize it out of his lands and chattels.[158] Geoffrey died in 1211 while being held hostage in a royal prison to ensure the Marshal's good behaviour.

The rebuilding of Dublin Castle, commencing in the reign of King John, was apparently a long and drawn-out affair. Nonetheless, beginning with the construction of what appears to have been a circular great tower at the chief royal castle and residence of the governor of the English lordship in Ireland, as Con Manning has pointed out, could have been an inspiration for the building of other such structures in the country during the early thirteenth century, whereby 'as a symbol of royal authority it was likely to be copied, at least in its general form, in other royal works and by some of the Anglo-Norman lords'.[159] The order to build the tower would appear to have been carried out. There has been a problem, however, in identifying which one it would have been of the four circular towers of the completed thirteenth-century castle (fig. 5.35). This may stem in part from an apparent change from what was envisaged in the original mandate to what was actually built. When King John ordered his justiciar in 1204 to erect a strong castle with good ditches and strong walls,[160] it would appear to have involved the rebuilding of the existing one. The latter along with *le donjun* are attested as far back as 1172, when their custody along with the city was given to Hugh de Lacy I by King Henry II at the end of his royal visit to Dublin.[161] Furthermore, it is reported that during Easter of 1200, one William le Brun fell into the ditch of the castle after being struck with a hatchet in an altercation on the bridge above.[162] These references provide a picture of a substantial pre-1204 fortress, though seemingly smaller than the later one (see below).

Following the erection of the tower, the 1204 mandate apparently envisaged the building, or perhaps rebuilding, of the bailey.[163] Prior to his death in 1216, King John had to provide compensation for damage incurred upon adjoining church property and land 'lost by the fortification of the castle of Dublin'.[164]

Gilbert (ed.), *Historic and municipal documents of Ireland, AD1170–1320* (Dublin, 1870), p. 61; *CDI, 1171–1251*, no. 226. Also Ann Lynch and Conleth Manning, 'Excavations at Dublin Castle, 1985–7' in Seán Duffy (ed.), *Medieval Dublin II* (Dublin, 2001), pp 169–204 at pp 172, 174; Conleth Manning, 'Dublin Castle: the building of a royal castle in Ireland', *Château Gaillard*, 18 (1996), pp 119–22 at p. 119; O'Keeffe, 'Dublin Castle's donjon', p. 279; Orpen, *Normans*, ii, p. 273. **158** *CDI, 1171–1251*, no. 287. **159** Manning, 'Clogh Oughter Castle', p. 227. **160** Gilbert, *Historic and municipal documents*, p. 61. **161** Orpen, *Song of Dermot and the earl*, lines 2713–16. **162** See *CDI, 1171–1251*, no. 116. **163** See Gilbert, *Historic and municipal documents*, p. 61. **164** *CDI, 1171–1251*, nos 805, 848, 1790, 1803.

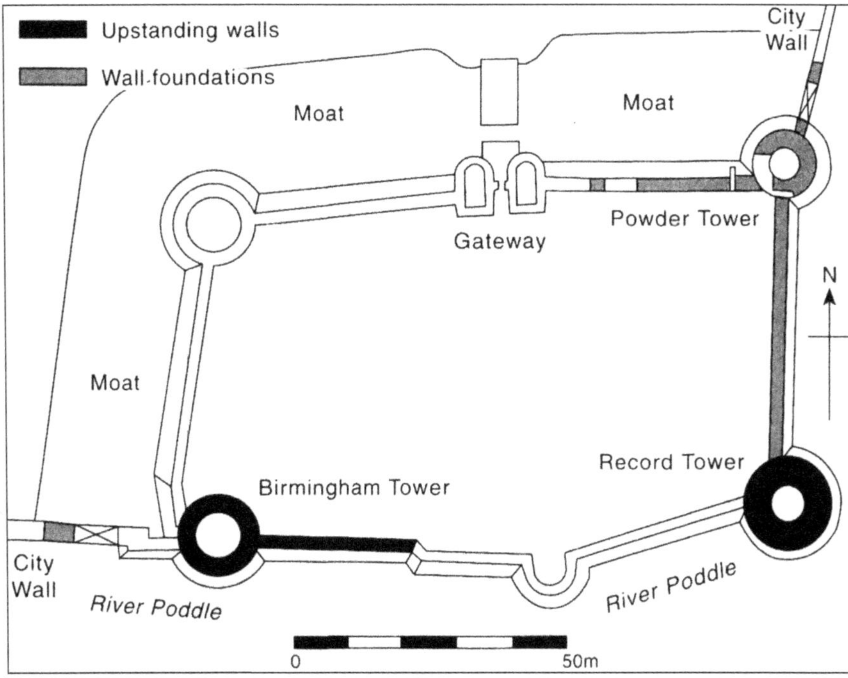

5.35 Plan of enlarged thirteenth-century Dublin Castle (after Sweetman, *Medieval castles*, fig. 36).

This would indicate that the castle was expanded, which would appear to have included the digging of a wider enclosing ditch or moat. A quarter of a century after the original mandate, works on the completion of the towers were ongoing, being completed by 1243.[165] During this period the castle acquired its quadrangular plan with large circular flanking towers (fig. 5.35).[166] There was, however, a noticeable anomaly at the south-west corner of the curtain-wall enceinte. Here, excavations in the 1980s found that the circular south-west or Birmingham Tower had been built into the curving south end of the earlier western stretch of curtain wall that would appear to have been part of the pre-1204 castle (fig. 5.35).[167] Only the battered base of the original tower survives, but the overlying circular structure, which was completely rebuilt in the eighteenth century, was apparently 15m in diameter,[168] being smaller than the Pembroke great tower.[169] Manning has convincingly made the case that this was the one that was ordered to be built in the mandate of 1204.

O'Keeffe has challenged the view that the Bermingham Tower was the result of the royal mandate, however, in favour of the flanking and slightly larger

165 Manning, 'Dublin Castle', p. 119. **166** Ibid., fig. 1. **167** Lynch and Manning, 'Dublin Castle', p. 183. **168** Ibid. **169** The Pembroke tower is about 16.3m in diameter.

Record Tower, which was located at the south-east corner of the completed thirteenth-century enceinte (fig. 5.35).[170] This circular tower, unlike the former, survives to three storeys above its battered base, its present upper storey and battlement being added in the early nineteenth century.[171] O'Keeffe has contended that the diameter of the Pembroke great tower (*c*.16.3m) was more or less the same as that of the Record Tower (15.4m). This, together with a first-floor entry, has led him to argue for the latter being the primary tower at Dublin Castle, on the basis that the 'ancestry for the Irish series' of circular great towers or donjons is in south Wales, where William Marshal I built 'Pembroke Castle's donjon'.[172] As has been outlined above, this 'ancestry' now appears unlikely from the point of view of dating.

There are also notable architectural differences between the Pembroke and Record towers. First, for example, the latter was a flanking corner tower built with the adjoining stretches of curtain wall out into the River Poddle at the south-east corner of the walled city (fig. 5.35),[173] in contrast to the free-standing Pembroke tower (fig. 5.18). Second, Pembroke has a circular basement (fig. 5.22), which the other tower lacks. Third, the Record Tower does not have horizontal offsets on the exterior, as can be seen on the main body of the Pembroke tower (figs 5.17, 5.18, 5.22–5.24, 5.30), a feature that can also be seen on William Marshal's circular towers in the Middle Bailey of Chepstow Castle (fig. 5.11).[174] This feature can also be seen on circular great towers in France, such as the twelfth-century Châteaudun[175] and Chatillon-Coligny[176] or the later *philippienne* examples built on conquered Plantagenet lands, such as Chinon (fig. 5.3b) and Lillebonne.[177] There is also the example of one of the Plantagenet beaked flanking towers at Loches (fig. 5.6). These horizontal offsets are not a feature of thirteenth-century circular towers in Ireland, however; not just the Record Tower, but also, for example, the three surviving towers of William Marshal's Kilkenny Castle.

There is a fourth important difference between the Record and Pembroke towers. This relates to plunging arrow loops having parallel-sided embrasures with an overlying barrel vault running through the thickness of the circular wall of the Record Tower.[178] The arrangement of an arched or vaulted embrasure giving access to a plunging arrow loop was the norm in the 'Irish series' of these circular towers (see below), which included the south tower of the Marshal's Kilkenny Castle (fig. 5.15d).[179] As seen above, this arrangement was also a feature

170 See O'Keeffe, 'Dublin Castle's donjon'. **171** See Conleth Manning, 'The Record Tower, Dublin Castle' in Kenyon and O'Conor, *The medieval castle in Ireland and Wales*, pp 72–95. **172** See O'Keeffe, 'Dublin Castle's donjon', pp 283–4. **173** See Lynch and Manning, 'Dublin Castle', figs 1–2; Manning, 'The Record Tower', figs 1, 9–11. **174** Avent and Turner, 'Middle Bailey', fig. 50. **175** Avent, 'Chepstow's place', fig. 71; Mesqui, *Châteaux forts*, p. 113. **176** Ibid., p. 116. **177** Knight, 'Usk Castle, 1136–1245', fig. 6.13c. **178** See ibid., figs 5, 12, 14–15, 17. **179** Ben Murtagh, 'Kilkenny Castle, the Parade, Kilkenny', *Excavations 1997* (Bray, 1998), pp 102–4, no. 304 at p. 103.

1 Duiske Abbey, Graiguenamanagh, Co. Kilkenny: interior of nave (courtesy of Neil Jackman/Abarta Heritage).

2 Tintern Abbey, Co. Wexford (courtesy of Neil Jackman/Abarta Heritage).

3 Kildare Cathedral (courtesy of Neil Jackman/Abarta Heritage).

4 Ferns Castle, Co. Wexford (courtesy of Neil Jackman/Abarta Heritage).

5 Carlow Castle (courtesy of Neil Jackman/Abarta Heritage).

6 Kells Priory, Co. Kilkenny: aerial view (courtesy of Neil Jackman/Abarta Heritage).

7 Kells Priory, Co. Kilkenny (courtesy of Neil Jackman/Abarta Heritage).

8 Pembroke Castle, Wales (courtesy of Wikimedia Commons).

9 Chepstow Castle, Wales (courtesy of Wikimedia Commons).

10 Coudray Salbart Castle, France (courtesy of Wikimedia Commons).

11 Kilkenny Castle (courtesy of Neil Jackman/Abarta Heritage).

12 Hook Lighthouse, Co. Wexford (courtesy of Neil Jackman/Abarta Heritage).

13 Clogh Oughter, Co. Cavan (courtesy of Neil Jackman/Abarta Heritage).

14 Talbot's Tower and Kilkenny Castle (courtesy of Airshots and Kilkenny County Council).

15 St Canice's Cathedral, Kilkenny (courtesy of Airshots).

16 St Canice's Cathedral, Kilkenny (photograph: Cóilín Ó Drisceoil).

17 St Canice's Cathedral, Kilkenny: interior of nave (courtesy of Neil Jackman/Abarta Heritage).

18 St Canice's Cathedral, Kilkenny: interior of nave (courtesy of Neil Jackman/Abarta Heritage).

19 Newtown Jerpoint, Co. Kilkenny (photograph: Cóilín Ó Drisceoil).

20 Newtown Jerpoint, Co. Kilkenny: graveslab (photograph: Cóilín Ó Drisceoil).

21 Black Abbey Dominican friary, Kilkenny (courtesy of Airshots).

22 St Mary's Church, Kilkenny: aerial view (courtesy of Kilkenny County Council).

23 Aghaboe, Co. Laois: aerial view (courtesy of Neil Jackman/Abarta Heritage).

24 Inistioge, Co. Kilkenny: aerial view (photograph: Cóilín Ó Drisceoil and Pat Nolan).

25 Grenan Castle, Co. Kilkenny (photograph: Cóilín Ó Drisceoil).

26 Clonmines, Co. Wexford (courtesy of Niall Colfer).

27 St Mary's Church, New Ross, Co. Wexford (courtesy of Neil Jackman/Abarta Heritage).

28 Temple Church, London: tomb of William Marshal (courtesy of Neil Jackman/Abarta Heritage).

of the works of the early Plantagenet kings at their castles in western France, such as at Chinon (fig. 5.15c) and Loches (fig. 5.6b). This is in sharp contrast to the French or *philippienne* plunging arrow loops of the Marshal's works at his castles in south Wales, ranging from the Main Gate and the towers of the Middle Bailey at Chepstow[180] and the Garrison Tower at Usk (fig. 5.15b) to Pembroke Castle, including the Dungeon Tower (fig. 5.15a) and the great tower itself (figs 5.22, 5.32). Also in the case of the latter, the parallel-sided embrasures are confined to the two large twin-light windows.

There is what might be regarded an exception in the 'Irish series' of towers in the case of the free-standing and isolated tower at Inchiquin, Co. Cork (fig. 5.13), which may have been built by the Anglo-Norman baron Maurice fitz Gerald after 1215.[181] Here there are simple and inward-splaying loops in the basement that run through the thickness of the wall of the building, in contrast to the parallel-sided embrasures of the windows on the first floor and this compares to the Dundrum great tower, Co. Down.[182] The walls of both towers, however, are rather thin when compared to, for example, the Record Tower or Kilkenny and Pembroke great towers, all of which have long Plantagenet-style arrow-loop embrasures.[183]

G.H. Orpen was of the opinion that John de Gray, bishop of Norwich, justiciar (1209–13) and Meiler fitz Henry's successor, continued work on Dublin Castle, as he was an 'energetic castle-builder' and at the end of his term, King John ordered him to hand custody of it over to his successor, Henry of London, archbishop of Dublin.[184] Orpen further thought that as the new justiciar was credited with the actual building of the castle, he might have merely completed the works.[185] Manning credits the archbishop with remodelling the castle during his two terms as justiciar (1213–15; 1221–4), however, transforming it into a roughly quadrangular enclosure with circular angle towers and incorporating earlier works, such as those carried out as a result of the 1204 mandate, including the Bermingham Tower.[186] This may have involved extending the castle enclosure south-eastwards into the tidal river with the construction of the flanking and thick-walled Record Tower, forming a corner with two new stretches of curtain wall (fig. 5.35). It is tempting to view the early defences that were exposed under the north-east Powder Tower[187] as continuing south-westwards towards the middle tower along the south side of the later enceinte.

180 Avent, 'Gatehouse at Chepstow', figs 7, 9–10; idem and Miles, 'The main gatehouse', figs 43–4; Avent and Turner, 'Middle Bailey', figs 46, 48. **181** See Manning, 'Clogh Oughter Castle', p. 229. **182** See ibid., fig. 7; Sweetman, *Medieval castles*, figs 67–8. **183** See Manning, 'Clogh Oughter Castle', p. 229 and table 1. The 4m given in the latter for Kilkenny is a median measurement that increases to 4.2m outside the curtain-wall enceinte, while that for Pembroke is about 4.35m. **184** Orpen, *Normans*, ii, p. 273. **185** Ibid. **186** See Lynch and Manning, 'Dublin Castle', p. 174; Manning, 'Dublin Castle', pp 119–22; idem, 'The Record Tower', p. 92. **187** See Lynch and Manning, 'Dublin Castle', p. 182 and figs 8–9 and pl. 2.

If Manning's view of the development and dating of the thirteenth-century Dublin Castle is correct, it suggests that construction of the Record Tower and adjoining stretches of curtain wall had commenced perhaps by the middle of the 1210s. The consistent style of architecture and masonry of the tower, unlike perhaps the Pembroke great tower, suggests a continuous building campaign. This might be explained by it being strategically located at the south-east corner of the walled city, whereby work may have concentrated on its early completion, as opposed to works in other parts of the castle. The visible arches and vaulting in the original structure consist of a mixture of semi-circular and segmental ones, rather than Gothic or pointed ones.[188] On the exterior of the tower, the remains of some plunging arrow loops can still be seen and these are constructed of the same roughly dressed and locally quarried calp limestone.[189] For a premier royal castle, these contrast with the high-quality ashlar-dressed surrounds of the plunging arrow loops of William Marshal's works at his castles of Caerleon, Kilkenny and Pembroke, including the great towers (figs 5.16, 5.20a and d, 5.25).

Manning is also of the view that the quadrangular castle that developed at Dublin by the 1220s (fig. 5.35) was a forerunner of the Edwardian castles of the latter part of the century, whereby the idea of any of the circular towers of the enceinte being the dominant one as a 'keep or donjon' had become anachronistic and he would include the royal castle of Limerick together with William Marshal's Kilkenny Castle in this category.[190] This writer is not of that view in relation to Kilkenny (see below). These three urban fortresses were first categorised by Harold Leask as 'keepless castles' in the 1930s.[191] Manning would see these castles as a move away from plans with a free-standing donjon and concentrating the defence on the perimeter with strong projecting towers giving flanking fire along the curtain walls, emanating from such castles in France as the early Plantagenet Le Coudray Salbart (pl. 10).[192] Furthermore, he has even regarded the concept of ordering the building of a great tower at Dublin Castle in a mandate of 1204 as outdated by that time.[193]

Based on this view, William Marshal's free-standing great tower of Pembroke would be seen as outmoded, which was not the case. Instead, this structure was part of a trend that appeared in Wales and Ireland in the early thirteenth century, emanating from France, where such towers continued to be built by the French king, for example, either in captured Plantagenet castles (fig. 5.3b) or in new geometrical ones with lesser circular flanking towers (see also below). Therefore, the appearance of these great towers in the colonial lands of the English crown or Anglo-Normans in Ireland and Wales should not be seen as surprising,

188 See Manning, 'The Record Tower', pp 84–7. **189** See ibid., p. 84 and fig. 13. **190** Ibid., p. 72; Manning, 'Dublin Castle: the building of a royal castle in Ireland', p. 121; idem, 'Clogh Oughter Castle', p. 230; Lynch and Manning, 'Dublin Castle', pp 200–1. **191** Leask, 'Irish castles, 1180 to 1310', pp 145, 176–80. **192** Manning, 'Dublin Castle', p. 121. **193** Ibid.; Lynch and Manning, 'Dublin Castle', p. 174.

particularly when great barons like William Marshal and Hubert de Burgh, who were responsible for building some of them, were veterans of the wars in France. Moreover, it may have been King John and his justiciar who started the trend in Ireland at Dublin Castle, where the base may be all that remains of the prototype. Fortunately, the upstanding remains of a good selection of these towers survive in Ireland for study.

Outside Dublin, there is a good surviving example of a royal circular great tower in the form of Reginald's Tower, which was located at the eastern apex of the medieval port city of Waterford (fig. 5.13). Although the original structure was not as large as the Pembroke tower, it is roughly contemporary with it. This was strategically located at the confluence of the tidal River Suir and its tributary, John's River. The writer conducted a detailed survey and study of the fabric to facilitate restoration of the tower by the local authority and the National Monuments Service, which was completed in 2003. The original building, which is constructed mainly of locally quarried stone, consists of ground and first storeys that are 13.5m in diameter, with a large circular chamber on each with an adjoining garderobe.

The base of the tower, which was washed by the tidal water, is now concealed by the present street level on the Quay. The building was heightened in the later Middle Ages, preserving the original crenellations. In 1997, this writer conducted an excavation within the ground-storey interior, revealing the original floor level within the circular chamber, which is 7.13m in diameter.[194] Four embrasures with overlying semi-circular vaults gave access to loops facing the river. A doorway passage at the north leads to the original entrance to the building and spiral stairwell to the upper floors. Original stairwell newels, which survive at the bottom, are of Dundry limestone from Somerset.

The circular first-floor chamber was the principal room of the original building, which was entered from the stairwell through a doorway with a semi-circular head. Beside this to the west of the chamber, a passageway with an overlying semi-circular vault leads to a doorway that gave access to the wall walk of an adjoining stretch of defensive wall outside (fig. 5.36a). In contrast to the ground floor, the four window embrasures around the south-east half of the main chamber have overlying Gothic vaults (fig. 5.36b), demonstrating the Transitional style of the building, which was constructed in a sustained campaign in the early thirteenth century, centring on the reign of King John. He took a particular interest in the city, as it was his personal possession, which he visited twice, as well as granting it a charter in 1215.[195] In 1207, as well as granting murage to the city he established a mint there.[196] This would have required a strong and secure royal building, like Reginald's Tower. If work had not

194 Ben Murtagh, 'Reginald's Tower, the Quay, Waterford', *Excavations 1997* (Bray, 1998), pp 186–7, no. 580. **195** Julian Walton, *The royal charters of Waterford* (Waterford, 1992), pp 17–18. **196** Ibid., p. 16.

a

b

5.36 Interior views of first-floor chamber of thirteenth-century phase of Reginald's Tower, Waterford: a) doorways at south-west; b) Gothic-headed embrasures of windows.

commenced by then, it is likely that it would have been made a priority as part of refortification of the city (see below), the ultimate responsibility for the progress of which would have fallen to the then justiciar, Meiler fitz Henry. If the work had not been completed or even started by the end of his tenure by early 1209 it is likely to have been progressed by his successor, Bishop John de Gray, the 'energetic castle-builder'. In June 1210 he met the king near Waterford, after his arrival from Pembroke.[197] The king appears to have made a brief visit into his city, where he would have viewed the work on the defences. It is probable that this included the tower, work on which must have at least commenced by that time.

Interestingly, the castle of Waterford is referred to in conjunction with that of Dungarvan, when custody of both was granted in 1215 along with the county to Thomas fitz Anthony, loyal baron and one-time seneschal of William Marshal.[198] This castle at Waterford must have been the tower and the adjoining stretch of contemporary defensive wall running to the south-west, which was part of the refortification of an earlier fortress known as the Dundory. Triangular in plan, it apparently functioned as a type of castle or citadel of the late Hiberno-Scandinavian or Ostman walled town.[199] When the Marshal's father-in-law, Strongbow, attacked and seized Waterford with his followers in 1170, according to Giraldus Cambrensis, the local leaders took refuge in *turre Raghenaldi* (Raghnall's tower), which was later used as a prison and stronghold by the Anglo-Normans.[200] This would appear to have been located in the Dundory and was replaced by King John's tower. It may have been planned that this would be the great tower of a new stone castle, similar to what was envisaged in the 1204 mandate for Dublin. Like the latter, however, it apparently morphed into something else, but with different results. While the one in Dublin was transformed into a quadrangular enceinte, that at Waterford would seem to have become defunct or redundant in the reign of Henry III.

The land occupied by the Dundory was largely redeveloped by being given to the newly arrived Franciscans, who founded a friary there before 1245.[201] It is not clear if this apparent new castle would have got beyond building the tower and the adjoining stretch of new wall, both of which would have then become part of the south-eastern stretch of the defensive wall of the older part of the city. In 1463, the Irish parliament ordered that coins would be minted 'at a place called Dondory otherwise Raynoldis tour',[202] now known as Reginald's Tower, which in 1528 was called 'the great towre of Dondoree'.[203]

197 Orpen, *Normans*, ii, p. 248; *CDI, 1171–1251*, i, no. 401 (20 June). **198** See ibid., nos 576, 580. **199** John Bradley and Andrew Halpin, 'The topographical development of Scandinavian and Anglo-Norman Waterford' in William Nolan and T.P. Power (eds), *Waterford: history and society* (Dublin, 1992), pp 105–29 at pp 107–8. **200** Giraldus, *Expugnatio*, pp 66–7, 92–3, 140–1, 301, nn 83–4. **201** See Bradley and Halpin, 'Scandinavian and Anglo-Norman Waterford', pp 121–2 and figs 5.1, no. 6, 5.4–5.5; *CDI, 1171–1251*, no. 2776. **202** H.F. Berry (ed.), *Statute rolls of the parliament of Ireland, 1–12 Edward IV* (Dublin, 1914), p. 131. **203** N.J. Byrne (ed.), *The Great Parchment Book of Waterford*

To the south-west of the city in the same county was the medieval and strategic port town of Dungarvan with its royal castle (fig. 5.13).[204] The custody of the castle was granted along with that of the castle and county of Waterford to Thomas fitz Anthony. Initially it consisted of a shell keep to which was added an irregular-shaped ward, enclosed by a curtain wall with a gatehouse with D-shaped towers at the south-east angle and a large circular tower at the south-west angle, which consisted of three storeys and was 10.7m in diameter (fig. 5.37).[205] According to O'Keeffe, the latter is a circular great tower.[206] It has a projecting spiral stairwell which was built onto the end of the southern curtain wall of the castle, according to Dave Pollock, who conducted extensive excavations on the site. He suggested also that the space between the tower and the shell keep was deliberately left open for a period to accommodate a ditch until the gap was closed by a stretch of curtain wall.[207]

O'Keeffe has pointed to a concentration of circular and polygonal great towers in Munster, which were mostly baronial. In the case of one at least – the circular tower in Dunmore East at Waterford Harbour – it is more likely to be the remains of a later medieval tower house.[208] In the case of another, however, at the west end of Co. Waterford, the one at Mocollop (fig. 5.13) is an example of a free-standing, thirteenth-century baronial great tower, 12.5m in diameter, within a tight curtain-wall enceinte occupying a commanding location.[209]

Moving to north Munster, the rebuilding of the royal castle in Limerick city on the River Shannon (fig. 5.13), which was underway by 1211–12,[210] apparently like Dublin Castle, became a long and drawn-out process that continued after the death of King John in 1216.[211] Leask saw the present thirteenth-century five-sided structure, with its three circular corner towers and gatehouse, as an early example of his 'keepless castles' along with Dublin and Kilkenny.[212] He was also of the view that the north-west tower was 'the highest and most important' one in the castle.[213] Oddly, he saw the latter along with the south-west tower and the long western stretch of curtain wall linking the two and facing the river as the earliest part of the thirteenth-century castle.[214]

Resulting from his archaeological investigations of the 1990s in the east of the castle, Kenneth Wiggins revealed a rather different picture. It showed that the initial works of King John apparently involved a partial refortification of an

(Dublin, 2007), p. 252. **204** Moore, *AI Waterford*, p. 204, no. 1536 and map on p. 315. **205** Ibid., pp 213–14 and fig. 52; Sweetman, *Medieval castles*, fig. 43. **206** O'Keeffe, 'Dublin Castle's donjon', p. 288. **207** Dave Pollock, 'Dungarvan Castle', *Excavations 1995* (Bray, 1996), pp 84–5, no. 265; idem, 'Dungarvan Castle', *Excavations 1998* (Bray, 2000), pp 206–7, no. 635, plan of castle. **208** See Moore, *AI Waterford*, pp 214, 215, no. 1563. **209** See ibid., no. 1565; O'Keeffe, 'Dublin Castle's donjon', pp 289–90 and fig. 17.8. **210** See McNeill, *Castles in Ireland*, p. 46. **211** Kenneth Wiggins, *Anatomy of a siege: King John's Castle, Limerick, 1642* (Bray, 2000), p. 18. **212** See Leask, 'Irish castles, 1180–1310', pp 178–80; idem, *Irish castles and castellated houses* (Dundalk, repr. 1964), pp 53, 55–7. **213** Ibid., p. 55. **214** Leask, 'Irish castles, 1180–1310', p. 179.

5.37 External view of Dungarvan Castle, Co. Waterford, showing thirteenth-century south-west circular tower.

5.38 North-east view of Limerick Castle, showing circular north-east tower on left with twin-towered gatehouse on right.

earlier 'ringwork' that occupied an elevated bedrock shelf, which included the twin-towered gatehouse at the north and the north-east circular tower with the short stretch of curving curtain wall linking the two (fig. 5.38), together with a short stretch of eastern curtain wall and a short stretch at the north-west.[215] This

215 Wiggins, *Anatomy of a siege*, pp 13, 16, 18.

would have involved the older defences on the west and south remaining in use for a period, perhaps after the death of King John. These included a twelfth-century stone-faced rampart with an outer ditch, some of the southern stretch of which was exposed in the excavations.[216] In this form, the circular north-east tower would have functioned as the great tower of the castle for a period (fig. 5.38) before the westward and southward expansion, which may not have been completed as envisaged.[217] This initial phase of rebuilding might be compared to that at Dublin Castle, following the 1204 mandate with its single circular great tower. The top of the original north-east tower was reduced in height and rebuilt in the seventeenth century to accommodate artillery (fig. 5.38).[218] At 14.5m in diameter, it is the largest in girth of the three main flanking towers of the present castle.[219]

Moving upriver on the Shannon to Athlone (fig. 5.13), in the reign of King John the royal castle commanded a bridge-head on the frontier with the kingdom of Connacht. Justiciar de Gray rebuilt it with masonry after its predecessor had been burnt by the king of Connacht, resulting in the construction of a curtain wall enclosing and revetting the base of an earthwork or motte, with what appears to have been a free-standing tower within the elevated ground of the enclosure, which collapsed in 1211, killing nine Englishmen.[220] Its replacement soon afterwards was a roughly centrally placed, free-standing and polygonal great tower, which was greatly modernised in the early nineteenth century.[221] This shows that in the second decade of the thirteenth century such a free-standing great tower was being constructed at a royal castle in Ireland, which may have coincided with the completion of William Marshal's Pembroke tower. At Dundrum Castle in east Ulster (fig. 5.13), following its capture by King John in 1210, the free-standing and circular great tower was either built or completed with royal funding (fig. 5.31), around the same time as the new one at the royal castle of Athlone was constructed. In south Ulster (fig. 5.13), the construction of the primary phase of the free-standing and island great tower of Clogh Oughter (pl. 13), consisting of the ground and first storeys, has been attributed to William Gorm de Lacy and dated to the years 1221–4 by Manning, who excavated it.[222] As seen above, the free-standing great tower of Hook (pl. 12), at the southern tip of Leinster, was under construction at the end of the Marshal period and funded out of the lordship.

Apart from the above, what has often been considered to be the finest and even the earliest example of a baronial circular great tower in Ireland is at

216 Ibid., figs 4, 12; idem, 'King John's Castle, St Mary's parish', *Excavations 1990* (Bray, 1991), pp 43–4, no. 44 and cover. **217** Idem, *Anatomy of a siege*, p. 34; McNeill, *Castles in Ireland*, p. 46. **218** See Wiggins, *Anatomy of a siege*, pp 15, 27. **219** See Manning, 'Clogh Oughter Castle', table 1. **220** See Leask, 'Irish castles, 1180 to 1310', pp 167–8; idem, *Irish castles*, p. 42; Orpen, *Normans*, ii, pp 186, 281–2. **221** See D.N. Johnson, *The Irish castle* (Dublin, 1985), fig. 6; P.M. Kerrigan, *Castles and fortifications, 1485–1945* (Cork, 1995), p. 228; McNeill, *Castles in Ireland*, fig. 82. **222** Manning, 'Clogh Oughter Castle', pp 224–6.

Nenagh in north Co. Tipperary (fig. 5.13).[223] It was heightened in the nineteenth century with an extra storey and battlement,[224] but an earlier drawing of 1833 shows the thirteenth-century tower without its crenellations, together with the rest of the then ruined castle (fig. 5.39).[225] A drawing of about fifty years earlier by Austin Cooper provides a similar picture of the place some years after an unsuccessful attempt had been made to demolish the tower but, like the later drawing, it also shows the then upstanding remains of the now destroyed western side of the curtain-wall enceinte.[226] The Nenagh great tower, unlike Pembroke, was not a free-standing structure (fig. 5.39). Originally consisting of three storeys, it was located at the northern apex of a small pentagonal enclosure or ward with small circular towers at the east and west apexes, together with a gatehouse at the south with circular towers at either side of the passageway.[227] The latter in its original form closely resembled, for example, the gatehouses of William Marshal at Chepstow (fig. 5.10) and Kilkenny (fig. 5.40), as well as King John's Limerick Castle (fig. 5.38)[228] and Philip Augustus's castle at the Louvre (fig. 5.5).[229] The towers at Nenagh were linked by a curtain wall, which apparently had an outer base batter and ditch that may have followed the plan of an earlier ringwork.[230]

The original great tower consists of a basement with a base batter on the outside like the one at Pembroke (figs 5.22, 5.39).[231] Access was gained on the first storey from the adjoining ward to the south.[232] The circular chamber inside has two adjoining and parallel-sided embrasures running lengthways through the thickness of the enclosing wall, each of which has a rounded barrel-vault with a plunging arrow loop at the end that overlooks the ground outside the curtain-wall enceinte.[233] On the second floor there are four parallel-sided embrasures around the circular chamber with loops.[234] A short original passageway leading from the north-east embrasure gave access to the wall walk of the adjoining curtain wall.[235] In a second phase of work later in the thirteenth century, another storey was added to the tower, bringing it to four storeys beneath the roof and battlement level, like the Pembroke great tower (figs 5.22, 5.39).[236] It would

223 See Leask, *Irish castles*, pp 43, 46; Manning, 'Clogh Oughter Castle', p. 227; McNeill, *Castles in Ireland*, pp 28, 31; O'Keeffe, 'Dublin Castle's donjon', p. 287. **224** Gleeson and Leask, 'Nenagh', pp 259–60; Leask, *Irish castles*, pp 43, 45; Neil Guy et al., 'Castles of north Munster', *CSGJ*, 23 (2009–10), pp 4–116 at pp 28 (Section A–A), 32; McNeill, *Castles in Ireland*, fig. 16; Sweetman, *Medieval castles*, fig. 65. **225** Anon., *Dublin Penny Journal*, 1:38 (16 Mar. 1833), p. 1. **226** Peter Harbison, *Cooper's Ireland: drawings and notes from an eighteenth-century gentleman* (Dublin, 2000), pp 144–5. **227** Guy et al., 'Castles of north Munster', p. 28; Leask, 'Irish castles, 1180 to 1310', figs 9–10; idem, *Irish castles*, figs 27–8; Hodkinson, 'Nenagh', figs 1–2. **228** Guy et al., 'Castles of north Munster', p. 15; McNeill, *Castles in Ireland*, fig. 32. **229** Fleury and Kruta, *The castle of the Louvre*, figs 9–10, 53–4, 61, 63–4, 71, 74, 114. **230** Brenda O'Meara, 'Nenagh Castle, Nenagh', *Excavations 2006*, p. 509, no. 1903. **231** Guy et al., 'Castles of north Munster', p. 28. **232** Ibid. **233** Ibid.; Leask, 'Irish castles, 1180 to 1310', p. 166 and fig. 10. **234** Ibid. **235** Ibid.; idem, *Irish castles*, figs 27, 29. **236** Ibid., fig. 27; idem, 'Irish castles, 1180 to 1310', p. 166 and fig. 10; Gleeson and Leask, 'Nenagh', p. 267; Guy et al., 'Castles of north Munster', p. 28.

5.39 West view of ruins of thirteenth-century Nenagh Castle from *Dublin Penny Journal* of 16 March 1833, prior to heightening of the tower around 1860.

appear that this second phase of work included the addition of a rectangular block to the rear of the gatehouse with a first-floor hall.[237]

Back in the 1930s Harold Leask and Dermot Gleeson suggested – not unreasonably at the time – that the primary phase of the great tower and stone castle dated to the time of Theobald Walter I in the period 1200–5.[238] This dating has been followed by more recent writers and McNeill, for example, suggested that the second phase of work dated to the time of Theobald II in the 1220s.[239] The latter's father, Theobald I (d. 1205), was the founder of the famous Butler family in Ireland – the future earls, marquises and dukes of Ormond with their seat at William Marshal's Kilkenny Castle from the 1390s to the twentieth century – and he was the younger brother of Hubert, archbishop of Canterbury (1193–1205), and King John, who had earlier created him his chief butler, also made large land grants to him, including in the area of north Tipperary where this aspiring Anglo-Norman magnate created Nenagh as his chief centre.[240]

237 Ibid.; Hodkinson, 'Nenagh', pp 164–6 and fig. 1. **238** Gleeson and Leask, 'Nenagh', pp 248, 269. **239** McNeill, *Castles in Ireland*, p. 31; O'Keeffe, 'Dublin Castle's donjon', p. 287. **240** See Gleeson and Leask, 'Nenagh', pp 248–9, 253; Lord Dunboyne, *Butler family history*

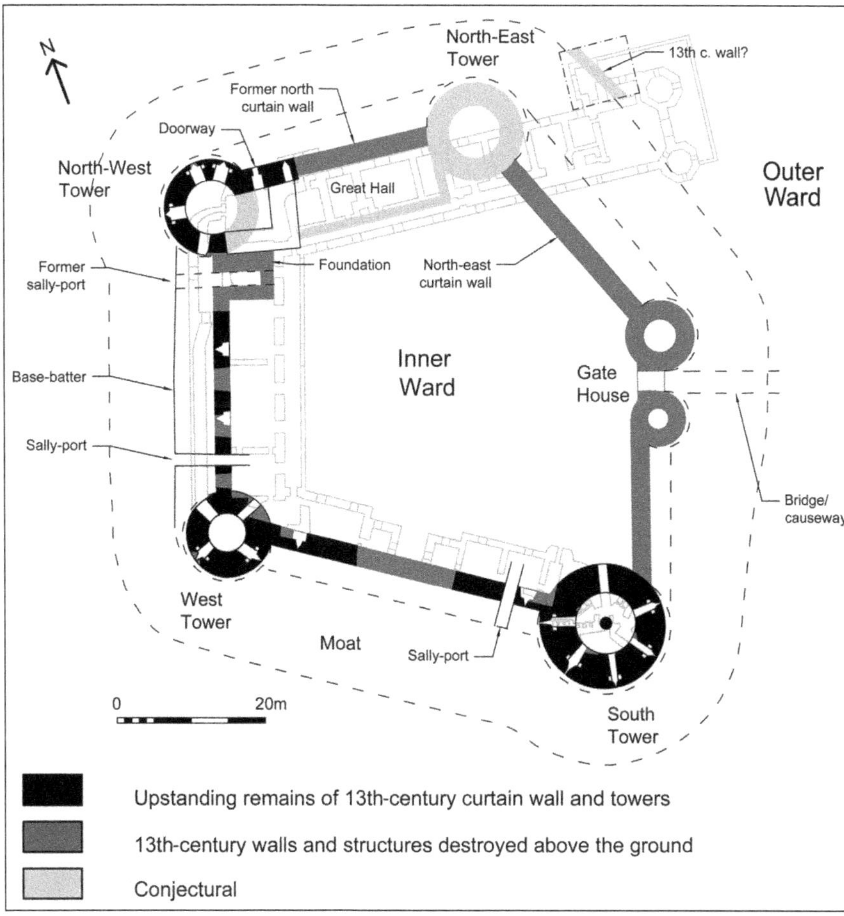

5.40 Plan of William Marshal's stone-built Kilkenny Castle (Ben Murtagh and Patrick McInerney).

Leask also drew attention to a finely decorated late Romanesque rear arch in the principal chamber of the tower (before it was heightened) to confirm his dating of the first phase of the stone castle.[241]

This early dating has been challenged from a historical point of view, however, and more recently by the finding of a 'slightly worn' English silver short-cross penny of 1205–*c*.1218 in a sealed context in the foundation trench of the original gatehouse during excavations by Brian Hodkinson in 1996–7.[242] This would indicate that the construction of the first phase of the stone castle post-dated the

(7th ed., Kilkenny, 1991), pp 4–8, 11, 18–19; Orpen, *Normans*, ii, p. 188. **241** Gleeson and Leask, 'Nenagh', pp 267, 269; Leask, 'Irish castles, 1180–1310', p. 166; idem, *Irish castles*, p. 46. See also Guy et al., 'Castles of north Munster', p. 31; McNeill, *Castles in Ireland*, fig. 17. **242** See Hodkinson, 'Nenagh', pp 166, 178–9.

time of Theobald I and is more likely to date to either the minority of his son, Theobald II, or, more likely again, his majority in the 1220s. Therefore McNeill's contention that the idea for the Nenagh great tower derived from William Marshal's one at Pembroke is less probable, particularly when there would have been royal examples in Ireland to have inspired such a structure as a marker of authority, such as at Dublin Castle, as well as perhaps the early phases of Limerick (fig. 5.38) or Waterford. Moreover, as will be seen below, the inspiration for the phase-1 stone castle at Nenagh is more likely to have derived from the Marshal's masonry castle at Kilkenny of *c*.1207–13 (fig. 5.40) than Pembroke. Though there is a difference in scale, these two castles in Ireland have a similar pentagonal plan with circular flanking towers at the angles, including a circular great tower and a similar type of twin-towered gatehouse.

Theobald I held three substantial fiefs in the lordship of Leinster from William Marshal, including Oskelan (Gowran), Tullow and Arklow.[243] It is interesting that following the death of the former, custody of his lands in Leinster was granted to the Marshal by King John.[244] It may have been the case that when Theobald II reached his majority in the 1220s he wished to rebuild his castle in masonry at his caput at Nenagh to emulate the great masonry castle of the late 'Earl Marshal' at Kilkenny, which was in the possession of his then overlord in Leinster, Earl William II (r. 1219–31). Interestingly, the medieval stone castle at Arklow, Co. Wicklow, on the east coast (fig. 5.13), had what appears to have been a circular great tower at an angle of the curtain-wall enceinte like Nenagh Castle, which is depicted in an eighteenth-century view.[245] Although he had been granted this strategic manorial castle along with the adjoining port town by the then Prince John back in the 1180s, following the intervention of King Richard I (r. 1189–99), Theobald Walter I held Arklow from his overlord in Leinster, William Marshal I.[246] While little can now be seen of it, it is to be hoped that future investigations will reveal more of this once-important castle, including the apparent circular great tower.

O'Keeffe has contended that Earl William I's masonry castle at Kilkenny was regularly planned and that its 'overall layout can be explained by looking to France', such as to Saumur (Maine-et-Loire) with its trapezoidal plan and circular corner towers.[247] There are two problems with this. First, the latter in its thirteenth-century form differs from the pentagonal plan of Kilkenny (fig. 5.40) and, second, the Marshal's work there would substantially pre-date that at

243 C.A. Empey, 'County Kilkenny in the Anglo-Norman period' in William Nolan and Kevin Whelan (eds), *Kilkenny: history and society* (Dublin, 1990), pp 75–95 at p. 88; *HWM*, i, lines 9612–15; Painter, *William Marshal*, pp 80, 151. **244** *CDI, 1171–1251*, i, no. 296. **245** See Francis Grose, *Antiquities of Ireland* (2 vols, London, 1791–5), ii, p. 62 and pl. 116; Peter Harbison, 'Barralet and Beranger's antiquarian sketching tour through Wicklow and Wexford', *PRIA*, 104C (2004), pp 184–5. **246** See *Ormond deeds*, 1172–1350, nos 17, 31; *HWM*, i, lines 9605–19; Orpen, *Normans*, i, p. 371; ibid., p. 203; ibid., iv, p. 13. **247** O'Keeffe, 'Dublin Castle's donjon', p. 287 and n. 37.

Saumur, which was conducted around the late 1220s.[248] Con Manning and David Sweetman, for example, view Kilkenny Castle as having a sub-rectangular or geometric plan similar to Dublin Castle after 1210 or to William Marshal's Usk Castle, which Knight saw as deriving from castles in France like the Plantagenet Le Coudray Salbart (pl. 10).[249] The investigations conducted by this writer during the 1990s found that the outline of William Marshal's masonry castle at Kilkenny was determined primarily by the local topography and the earlier earthwork castle over which it was built, rather than some blueprint emanating from France (fig. 5.40). Instead, it incorporated many of the latest advances and developments in military architecture that had appeared in the castles and defences in that country. These included, for example, plunging arrow loops, circular flanking towers, substantial base batters and sally ports, together with a stone-lined moat and gatehouse like those at Philip Augustus's castle at the Louvre (figs 5.5, 5.16, 5.40). The investigations, which were conducted above and beneath the ground,[250] also indicated that the Marshal's masonry fortress was constructed on an enormous scale in a sustained building campaign, centring on the period 1207–13, when he was mostly 'in exile' in Ireland and based at Kilkenny in what was his chief castle in his lordship. As seen above, it was here that he entertained King John and his entourage for two days in June 1210 with apparently 'a most lavish reception', when they were on their way to Ulster.[251]

Although the upper part of the Marshal's masonry castle underwent extensive renovations and large-scale demolition in later centuries, particularly along its north and east sides (fig. 5.40), the investigations have revealed that extensive remains survive both beneath and above the ground. Like Nenagh and Pembroke castles, for example, it is constructed mainly of grey and locally quarried Carboniferous limestone, bonded with lime mortar. The roughly dressed facing stones were laid in irregular courses. Lighter-coloured ashlar masonry was used in the construction of features like loops and doorways. One noticeable feature of the building works from this period is the almost exclusive use of the rounded or semi-circular arch in doorways, rear arches and vaulting. Although it is possible that they existed in the destroyed upper part of the castle, no Gothic arches have been encountered in the Marshal's phase of work. Among other noticeable features, apart from the large stone-lined and now in-filled moat, are

248 See Mesqui, *Châteaux forts*, p. 348; Emmanuel Litoux, 'La construction de la forteresse du XIIIe siècle: un château Philippien' in Société Française d'Archéologie, *Le château et la citadelle de Saumur: architectures du pouvoir* (2010), pp 39–48. **249** See Manning, 'Dublin Castle', p. 121; Knight, 'Usk Castle, 1136–1245', pp 65–7; Sweetman, *Medieval castles*, p. 50. **250** For summaries of the findings of the excavations, see Ben Murtagh, 'Kilkenny Castle, Kilkenny', *Excavations 1991* (Bray, 1992), pp 29–30, no. 81; idem, 'Kilkenny Castle Archaeological Project, 1990–1993: interim report', *OKR*, 45 (1993), pp 1101–17; idem, 'Kilkenny Castle, Kilkenny', *Excavations 1992* (Bray, 1993), pp 39–40, no. 115; idem, 'Kilkenny Castle', pp 102–4, no. 304; idem, 'Kilkenny Castle, the Parade, Kilkenny', *Excavations 1999* (Bray, 2000), pp 146–7, no. 449. **251** See n. 126 above.

the remains above ground of the three large circular flanking towers at the north, west and south angles, linked by the remains of two long sections of curtain wall (fig. 5.40), all of which are now incorporated into the present castle and, together with its adjoining grounds, form a historic property in state care.[252]

The smallest of the three towers is the middle one at the west angle, which has an external diameter of 10.85m on the ground. It has three parallel-sided embrasures around the circular chamber inside at the end of which are plunging arrow loops that overlooked the moat outside (fig. 5.40). There was no direct access between the ground storey and the one above, as each had a separate entrance. The first-floor one had a round-headed doorway and inner passageway through the thickness of the wall, similar to that on the second storey of the Pembroke great tower (fig. 5.30b). The present vaulting over the ground- and first-floor chambers was inserted by the Butlers in the late medieval period. A spiral stairwell gave access from the first floor to the upper part of the tower. The north-west tower, which has an external diameter of about 13.1m on the ground storey, has four parallel-sided embrasures around the chamber inside, at the end of each one of which was a plunging arrow loop viewing out beyond the curtain-wall enceinte (fig. 5.40).

The largest of the three towers was at the south angle of the curtain-wall enceinte (fig. 5.40). It stands to four storeys beneath the roof and above the battered base, some of which was partially exposed in excavations of the moat by this writer (fig. 5.16). The inner face of the tower above the ground storey was removed by the first duke of Ormonde around the late 1670s for the creation of larger space on the upper floors and the insertion of large windows. The removed masonry was used to fill the moat on the outside. The original thickness of the circular wall of the tower that survives on the ground storey on the outside of the curtain-wall enceinte is up to 4.2m, which is near the wall thickness above the base batter at Pembroke tower (*c*.4.35m). These are among the greatest wall thicknesses of any such towers in either Britain or Ireland; among the few to exceed this thickness are the later thirteenth-century examples at Flint and Hawarden in north-east Wales.[253] There are five large and parallel-sided embrasures around the circular ground chamber (fig. 5.40), with overlying semi-circular barrel-vaulting, at the end of which is a plunging arrow loop (figs 5.15d, 5.16). These would have provided a formidable firing range for bowmen down into and beyond the moat, projecting outside the south angle of the curtain-wall enceinte (fig. 5.16). While there was nothing to match this at the lower part of the Pembroke great tower, for example, there would have been a formidable firing

252 For an introduction and guide to the history, architecture and contents of the present castle, see John Bradley, *Discover Kilkenny* (Dublin, 2000), pp 67–93. See also Jane Fenlon, *Kilkenny Castle: visitor's guide* (Dublin, 2007). **253** The wall thickness for Flint is about 7m: see Perfect, *Flint Castle*, p. 40; while that for Hawarden is about 4.6m: see E.W. Gladstone, *Hawarden old castle* (privately published, 2003), p. 5.

range from the plunging arrow loops around the top (fig. 5.25), which would have overlooked the south curtain wall of the Inner Ward into the Outer Ward (figs 5.1, 5.17, 5.18). Apart from these, the Plantagenet-style plunging arrow loops at Kilkenny Castle provided a superior firing range for bowmen than the long splaying French-style ones constructed in the Marshal's castles in south Wales, including Pembroke.

Another example of diversity between the circular towers of the Marshal's Kilkenny Castle and those that he built at his castles in south Wales, are the horizontal offsets that can be seen on the exterior of some of the latter, including those of the Middle Bailey at Chepstow (fig. 5.11), the Garrison Tower at Usk and the Pembroke great tower (figs 5.17, 5.18, 5.22–5.25). These offsets were also a feature of French circular great towers, including those of Philip Augustus, such as his Tour du Coudray at Chinon (fig. 5.3b) that contrasts with the nearby, earlier and vertically faced Plantagenet Tour du Moulin (fig. 5.3a). These external offsets, the 'Frenchness' of which has previously been referred to by O'Keeffe in regard to the Pembroke tower,[254] are not a feature of thirteenth-century circular towers in Ireland (as noted above). Its appearance, together with the long splayed plunging arrow loops in the Marshal's building works at his castles in south Wales, might suggest that he engaged the services of at least one person to direct the works, such as a master mason or engineer, who had previously worked for the French king or one of his vassals like the count of Blois, but he did not make it to Ireland.

Excavations by this writer inside the south tower at Kilkenny Castle revealed that the southern part of the tower had been constructed down into the fosse of the earlier castle in the form of a base batter on the outside of the curtain-wall enceinte (figs 5.16, 5.40).[255] It was also revealed that the circular ground-storey chamber had a central stone pillar, which may have supported an overlying vault. Manning has suggested that it supported radial beams like the method of flooring that has been suggested by McNeill for the Pembroke great tower.[256] As noted above, Manning is of the view that referring to any of the towers of Kilkenny Castle, like those of Dublin and Limerick Castles, 'as a keep or donjon is probably incorrect and anachronistic … in this new type of castle where having a single dominant tower was no longer a design imperative'.[257] In the cases of the latter two castles, he is obviously referring to them in their extended forms. Kilkenny was a different situation, however, with its south tower. The latter is noticeably larger than the other two surviving flanking towers. Moreover, at a maximum diameter of around 16.4m on the ground storey above the battered base, it would appear to be the largest thirteenth-century circular great tower in Ireland. It is exceeded in diameter in Britain perhaps only by Flint (over

254 O'Keeffe, 'Dublin Castle's donjon', n. 37. 255 Murtagh, 'Kilkenny Castle', p. 14. 256 See Manning, 'Clogh Oughter Castle', p. 230. 257 Ibid., table 1.

20m) and Harwarden (*c.*19m) in north-east Wales (fig. 5.2), but equates closely with, and is only slightly larger than, Pembroke, which is around 16.3m.[258]

O'Keeffe has also noted the large size of the south tower of Kilkenny Castle, but he has pointed to what he argues to have been an even larger one at the north-east angle of the curtain-wall enceinte.[259] This is based on a 1767 plan of the castle, which depicts a large circular feature that has the appearance of a very large flanking tower.[260] It does not seem to represent a standing building as such, however, rather a semi- or partially circular low-lying wall, which the draughtsman or surveyor at the time would appear to have interpreted as the remains of a large tower. This 'tower' interestingly is not shown on the earlier Rocque map of the city (1758), which includes a detailed plan of the castle and its grounds.[261] Instead, it shows a curving indentation in the enclosing wall of the bowling green to the east of the castle. This indentation is replicated on the 1767 plan as part of the 'tower'. To judge from the scale of the curve on Rocque, such a circular feature would have been nearly double the size of the south tower, which would have been more like a shell keep than a great tower.

The indentation on Rocque might be explained by some of the bowling green wall having been built on top of the curve of the counterscarp of the in-filled moat in that area and the draughtsman of the later map converting it into a circle to fit in with the other flanking towers. The 1767 map does depict the two circular towers of William Marshal's gatehouse, which was demolished some years later, and it indicates the alignment of the north-east or fifth side of the pentagonal enceinte of the earl's castle. This appears to be confirmed by a recent geophysical survey, which has located what look like the remains of the curtain wall and the adjoining gatehouse beneath the ground.[262] If the curving indentation in the Bowling Green wall, as depicted on the Rocque map, represents the counterscarp of the moat, the enclosing tower might be similar to the north-west tower and noticeably smaller than the south one (fig. 5.40). This would support the view that the latter was the great tower of the Marshal's masonry castle.

The Cromwellian Civil Survey of the 1650s noted that, apart from various other building and structures, the 'Castle of Kilkennis In wch said Castle are 3 Towers ye walls Stone and Lime and theire Roofes slated' and that these were apart from 'ye gate'.[263] This would indicate that there was no north-east tower at

258 The diameter given in Manning, 'Clogh Oughter Castle', table 1 for the Pembroke great tower seems to be a bit short, while Flint and Hawarden are not included. **259** O'Keeffe, 'Dublin Castle's donjon', p. 287. **260** O'Keeffe refers to a version of the 1767 Steele plan that was published by Mary Kenealy, 'Plan of Kilkenny Castle, 1767', *OKR*, 2:4 (1982), pp 343–6 at p. 344. **261** See Bradley, *Kilkenny*, map 5. **262** See Earthsound Archaeological Geophysics, 'Kilkenny Castle grounds, Kilkenny: archaeological geophysical survey' (unpublished report for Kilkenny Archaeology, 7 Nov. 2010), esp. figs 14–15. The writer is grateful to Cóilín Ó Drisceoil for making the findings of the report available to him. **263** R.C. Simington, *Civil Survey, AD1654–1656, vi: County Waterford, with appendices: Appendix F: Kilkenny City and Liberties* (Dublin, 1942), p. 534.

that time, suggesting that it had disappeared by then. The south tower might provide an explanation for this. As noted above, the battered base was built out into the moat or earlier fosse, while the remainder of the circumference of the tower was supported by the underlying and older earthen rampart, which was also the case with the other two towers. This resulted in eventual movement in the outer base of the south tower that caused cracking up through the overlying structure, but apparently this stabilised, perhaps due to the enormous size of the building.

Something similar may have happened in relation to the smaller north-east tower, but with more serious consequences and perhaps leading to the collapse of the front half of the building out into the moat. In such a situation, rather than rebuilding the tower, it might have been more expedient to simply rebuild the exposed angle as a corner to the curtain wall. Unfortunately, any remains of this angle or tower of the medieval masonry castle that may have survived beneath the ground would have been truncated or destroyed by the extensive foundations and basement of the modern north or river wing.

As noted above, the pentagonal plan of the Marshal's Kilkenny Castle (fig. 5.40), with its circular flanking towers, including a great tower at one angle and a Chepstow-style gatehouse at another, closely resembles the original masonry castle at Nenagh. O'Keeffe contends that 'One can certainly accept that there is a line of influence from Pembroke to Nenagh to Kilkenny'.[264] In view of what has been outlined above, this is difficult to accept. Although the work on the Marshal's great tower at Pembroke may have commenced prior to that on his masonry castle at Kilkenny, it would seem that the latter may have been completed first. As seen above, the former would appear not to have been completed until after he had permanently returned from Ireland in 1213, by which time the work on his premier Irish castle may have been more or less completed, as the extensive surviving architecture is rather uniform. It would seem to have been the product of a sustained building campaign at a time when the earl would have been in a position to personally oversee it and devote the vast resources in his Irish lordship to its completion, in contrast to Pembroke. Kilkenny Castle would seem to have been a more advanced fortress, with influences emanating directly from developments in France, rather than coming through Pembroke, for example. As for the primary phase of the masonry castle at Nenagh of around the 1220s, as seen above, it is more likely to have been influenced by the completed great masonry castle of the Marshal in neighbouring Co. Kilkenny with its similar pentagonal-type plan with circular flanking towers, including a circular great tower and its twin-towered gatehouse (fig. 5.40), rather than by his work at Pembroke, including his great tower there (see below).

264 O'Keeffe, 'Dublin Castle's donjon', p. 291.

CONCLUSION

William Marshal's great tower at Pembroke is probably the most impressive single structure to survive from his extensive building works at his castles in south Wales. It was not just a donjon or keep of last retreat within the Inner Ward of the castle; it was a dwelling perhaps normally used by the constable or the earl's seneschal. It was also a symbol of the Marshal's authority as well as a marker of his control over his earldom, which was somewhat isolated and threatened by the native Welsh of Deheubarth in the south-west corner of Wales. For the earl, controlling Pembroke was also important in providing him with direct access across the sea to his Irish lordship (fig. 5.13). In this regard, in addition to the tiered battlement providing a valuable lookout over the adjoining waterway, it is likely that a fire, perhaps supported by an iron brazier or grate mounted on the turret on the summit, enabled the tower to be used as a beacon for the aid of approaching boats and small ships travelling from nearby Milford Haven at night and in foggy conditions (figs 5.14, 5.17, 5.22, 5.24, 5.33).

Although its construction may have been lengthy and intermittent, far from being something anachronistic or outmoded, in its completed form, the great tower with its thick circular wall over the battered base and circuit of plunging arrow loops around the tiered battlement and vaulted stone roof, would have provided a formidable defence of the Inner Ward at the end of the cliff-top promontory in the event of the Outer Ward being overrun in a siege. Furthermore, the wide and battered base overlying bedrock would have made undermining by besiegers difficult, if not impossible (fig. 5.22). The completed tower was the product of tried and tested developments in military architecture that had taken place by the early thirteenth century, especially in France, such as in the building of circular towers, particularly great towers or *tours maîtresses*, both of the free-standing and the flanking types.

As seen above, some polygonal great towers were built in England in the latter half of the twelfth century, such as Conisborough and the Bell Tower in the Tower of London (fig. 5.8a), followed by the Plantagenet 'beaked' variety in France, such as at Château Gaillard (fig. 5.7), which ironically did not find favour in Britain or Ireland. Some polygonal great towers were built in Ireland during the first half of the thirteenth century, such as at the royal castle at Athlone, together with another free-standing example at Shanid, Co. Limerick, and the flanking one at Castleknock, near Dublin.[265] Apart from these, the circular variety became the norm, promoted by the French king Philip Augustus. The curving face of such towers was ideally suited to deflecting stone-throwing weapons like the mangon and the trebuchet. Interestingly, in the case of the Pembroke great tower, the entrance and the two large windows faced away from the landward

265 For Castleknock, see Leask, *Irish castles*, p. 43 and fig. 26. For Shanid, see ibid., pp 41–2 and fig. 2 and pl. 11; Sweetman, *Medieval castles*, p. 85 and figs 16, 66.

side, thus reducing the possibility of any exposure to such weapons in the event of the Outer Ward being overrun or captured in a siege (fig. 5.23).

The construction of circular great towers remained a feature of the castles of Philip Augustus until his death in 1223. They were built in Angevin or Plantagenet castles and lands captured from King John in 1204–5 by the French king as a symbol of his new-found authority in that part of France, examples of which include Chinon (fig. 5.3b), Falaise and Lillebonne. Even in the case of the Plantagenet castle of Le Coudray Salbart (pl. 10) in Poitou, with its beaked flanking towers and quadrangular or geometrical design dating to *c.*1200, which has been seen by Knight as inspiring William Marshal's Usk and the later redesign for Dublin,[266] the south-west tower is classified by Jean Mesqui as the *Grosse Tour*.[267] At Usk in south-east Wales, the Marshal's flanking Garrison Tower is regarded by Knight as a great tower (fig. 5.15b).[268] In the case of Philip Augustus's late castle of Dourdan, the circular great tower is a free-standing structure at the north corner of the geometrical enceinte.[269] The same plan was followed later in the same century in the early Edwardian castle at Flint in north Wales (fig. 5.2). The same plan had been employed by Louis IX in the 1240s at Aigues-Mortes in the south of France, where the free-standing and circular Tour de Constance stands detached and strategically located at the north-west corner of the geometrically planned and walled port city.[270]

Flint is a late and very large-girthed example of a circular great tower being built by the English crown on its colonial frontier (fig. 5.2), along with the near-contemporary and nearby Hawarden, which was built on a motte like other circular great towers on either side of the Anglo-Welsh border, such as Bronllys (Breconshire), Caldicot (Monmouthshire) and Longtown (Herefordshire).[271] Even in the centre of English royal power, the Wakefield Tower (fig. 5.8b) at the Tower of London apparently has the same diameter as Dublin's Record Tower[272] but is somewhat smaller than the tower at Pembroke and the south tower of Kilkenny Castle. The Wakefield Tower was commenced in the 1220s, apparently under the direction of then justiciar, Hubert de Burgh, and was used as a residence by Henry III (r. 1216–72).[273] It is an example of a flanking type located at an angle in the curtain wall, similar to the nearby and earlier Bell Tower (fig. 5.8b). In contrast, there is de Burgh's free-standing and circular great tower at Skenfrith Castle in south-east Wales (1219–32), which is located within the curtain-wall enceinte.[274]

266 Knight, 'Usk Castle, 1136–1245', p. 65 and fig. 6.14. **267** Mesqui, *Châteaux forts*, pp 138–9. **268** Knight, 'Usk Castle, 1136–1245', p. 61 and figs 6.6, 6.8, 6.11. **269** Mesqui, *Châteaux forts*, pp 148, 153–4, 290. **270** Florençon, *The city of Aigues-Mortes*, pp 2–3 and plan of walled city. **271** See Gladstone, *Hawarden old castle*, pp 4–6 and site plan; Goodall, *The English castle*, p. 222 and pl. 157 for Hawarden; Paul Remfry, *The castles of Breconshire* (Logaston, 1999), pp 135–9, Bronllys; Guy et al., 'Castle Studies Group Conference', pp 99, 101, Caldicot; Ron Shoesmith, *Castles and moated sites of Herefordshire* (Logaston, 2009), pp 207–17, Longtown. **272** See Manning, 'Clogh Oughter Castle', table 1. **273** See Hulme, 'Château Gaillard', pp 288–9. **274** See Guy et al.,

The building of circular great towers was mirrored by and extended to the castles of the Welsh princes and lords during the course of the thirteenth century, from which they apparently developed their own D-shaped variety.[275] It is likely that they were reflecting or were inspired by circular great towers of Anglo-Norman barons in nearby or bordering lands, like those of de Burgh and the 'Earls Marshal', in particular William I's tower at Pembroke, being probably the earliest and finest Anglo-Norman examples in Wales. Diversification from the latter seemingly morphed into a development that was more local. This involved a small number of masonry castles with twin flanking circular towers in the curtain-wall enceinte.[276] The first was Cilgerran in the north-east of Pembrokeshire (figs 5.13, 5.21), apparently commenced by William Marshal II in the 1220s, followed by the mid-thirteenth-century inner ward at Laugharne[277] and the small castle of Benton.[278]

While Wiles would see William Marshal I's great tower at Pembroke as being at the head of a diverse series of cylindrical towers built in the first half of the thirteenth century, with an irregular descent in south-west Wales,[279] others have viewed it as the inspiration for the building of circular great towers in Ireland (as seen above). It is the view of this writer that such an assumption seems unlikely. First, although construction of the tower had probably commenced by 1204, when the Marshal was personally active in strengthening his hold in south-west Wales, its completion along with his other building works in the Inner Ward may not have occurred until at least a decade later. This is supported by the style of basal oillets in the battlement of the tower, as well as in the Dungeon Tower (fig. 5.20b) and the Wogan (fig. 5.20a). These are of the same distinctive form seen in other works of William Marshal in south Wales. Knight has dated those at Usk (fig. 5.20c) to 1213–17 and Caerleon (fig. 5.20d) to 1218–19 at the earliest, while he has proposed a date of 1214–18 for that in the D-shaped tower of the Middle Bailey at Chepstow.[280]

Such a late date for the completion of the Pembroke great tower would make it less likely as the inspiration for the building of such towers in Ireland. Instead, a more likely candidate might be a circular great tower at Dublin Castle, the centre of English royal power in Ireland, which was ordered by King John in 1204. He went on to build other such towers, both free-standing and flanking, at castles around his Irish lordship. In the cases of Dublin and Limerick (fig. 5.38), these were later incorporated into the subsequent redesign and enlargement of these castles, apparently becoming just one of a number of large circular flanking towers. John is widely regarded in England as having been a tyrant, while in

'Castle Studies Group Conference', pp 21, 23–4; Knight, *The three castles*, p. 26. **275** See Kenyon, *Medieval castles of Wales*, fig. 1. **276** See Wiles, 'Marshal towers', fig. 3. See also n. 5 above. **277** Richard Avent, *Laugharne Castle* (Cardiff, 1995), p. 10 and ground plan. **278** Mike Salter, *The castles of south-west Wales* (Malvern, 1996), p. 49; Wiles, 'Marshal towers', p. 191. **279** Ibid., p. 199. **280** Knight, 'Usk Castle, 1136–1245', pp 60, 65. See also for Caerleon, Avent and Turner, 'Middle Bailey', p. 69 and fig. 51.4.

Ireland he is remembered as a great castle-builder. Of course, the works on his Irish castles were conducted and overseen on his behalf by his agents and justiciars, like Bishop John de Gray.

With regard to the building of the first circular great towers in Ireland by the Anglo-Norman barons, William Marshal may well have been to the forefront; for example, with his tower at the southern apex of his pentagonal masonry castle of *c.*1207–13 at Kilkenny (figs 5.16, 5.40), apparently later followed along a similar plan by Theobald Walter II at Nenagh (fig. 5.39). It is also possible that the construction of the great tower at Dundrum Castle in Co. Down (fig. 5.32) was commenced by Hugh de Lacy II prior to its capture in 1210 by King John, who would appear to have at least finished the job. The building of baronial circular great towers in Ireland continued throughout the first half of the thirteenth century, including the free-standing and isolated examples of Clogh Oughter (fig. 5.13, pl. 13) and Hook Tower (figs 5.13, 5.34, pl. 12), the construction of which was underway in 1247. The latter may have been inspired by the Pembroke great tower.

Although there are similarities and comparisons to be made between William Marshal's construction works at his castles in south Wales and contemporary castles in Ireland, including his own Kilkenny Castle, there are also important differences, including in the architecture of circular great towers. One common feature is the continued late use of round-headed doorways and windows, as well as semi-circular arches and barrel vaults in the castle and ecclesiastical construction works of both the Marshal and at least his older sons in both Leinster and Wales. One noticeable difference is in the form of plunging arrow loops. The Pembroke great tower has the French *philippienne* loops (fig. 5.32), which continue splaying inwards through the entire thickness of the cylindrical wall. These are replicated, not only in his other works in the Inner Ward of the castle, but also at his other castles in south Wales (figs 5.15a–b). This style of loop apparently had a long lifespan in building works of the earl and his sons from the east gatehouse at Chepstow in the 1190s (fig. 5.10) to Cilgerran of the 1220s–30s (fig. 5.21), to the work in the work in the Upper Barbican at Chepstow of around the mid- to late 1230s.[281]

The same style, as noted above, contrasts with the Plantagenet-style plunging arrow loops found in masonry castles in Ireland dating to the first half of the thirteenth century, as exemplified by Kilkenny Castle. Here the numerous arrow loops had parallel-sided embrasures on the inside running through the thickness of the castle walls, including in the enormous south tower (figs 5.15d, 5.40). These were also a feature of Plantagenet castles in western France, such Chinon (fig. 5.15c) and Loches (fig. 5.6b), both of which were familiar to William Marshal. It is easy then to understand why they would occur in his chief castle and caput in Ireland, but less so perhaps in relation to the different style

281 See Rick Turner, 'The Upper Barbican' in Turner and Johnson, *Chepstow Castle*, pp 113–18.

employed in his Welsh castles, such as that found in the castles of the French king. Another French-style feature of the Pembroke great tower are the horizontal offsets on its exterior (figs 5.17–5.18, 5.22–5.25), which can also be seen on two of the towers of his Middle Bailey at Chepstow (fig. 5.11), as well as the Garrison Tower at Usk, but not on thirteenth-century circular towers in Ireland, including those of Kilkenny Castle.

Another example of divergence in the construction works between the Marshal castles in Ireland and Wales was the building of what Leask termed 'towered keeps' at some important and strategic castles and settlements in Leinster.[282] These rectangular donjons with circular corner towers were apparently not built by William Marshal and his sons at their Welsh castles. They include the now-destroyed Wexford Castle (fig. 5.13),[283] the ruined castles at Carlow and Lea on the River Barrow with Plantagenet-style loops,[284] and the later example at Ferns Castle, Co. Wexford.[285]

William Marshal's completed great tower at Pembroke would have been a remarkable building in its own right, a notable symbol of his and his sons' authority in south-west Wales. It would not seem, however, to have been the inspiration for or origin of the building of such towers in Ireland. New developments and ideas in military architecture were able to come directly into Ireland from France through royal and baronial channels, without having to appear beforehand in Wales, for example. While the Marshal's gatehouse at Kilkenny Castle could be seen as a descendent of his early one at Chepstow Castle, his use of Plantagenet-style plunging arrow loops is an example of ideas coming separately into Ireland from France. The same might be said about circular great towers.

Perhaps the best way to interpret the differences and divergences between the building works of William Marshal in Ireland and Wales would be to view them as separate branches of the same tree. The building of his largest masonry castle in Ireland at Kilkenny, with its own enormous great tower, before the completion of his works at the Inner Ward of Pembroke Castle, with its great tower, would have been a major achievement in its own right. Nevertheless, if one views the extent of his combined building works at his castles in the two countries as exemplified by his great tower at Pembroke, together with his abbeys, churches and other projects, they are a testament to the scale of his many achievements with the support and, it would seem, guidance of his wife, Countess Isabel de Clare, in lands that were largely derived from her inheritance.

282 See Leask, *Irish castles*, pp 47–51; Ben Murtagh, 'Enniscorthy Castle, Co. Wexford: an Elizabethan castle on the borderland with Gaelic Ireland', *Château Gaillard*, 26 (Caen, 2014), pp 271–82 at pp 271, 281. **283** See Billy Colfer, *Wexford: a town and its landscape* (Cork, 2008), pp 75–8. **284** See Leask, 'Irish castles, 1180 to 1310', pp 168–70, 173–5; McNeill, *Castles in Ireland*, pp 118–22; Kieran O'Conor, 'The origins of Carlow Castle', *Archaeology Ireland*, 11 (1997), pp 13–16. **285** Leask, 'Irish castles, 1180–1310', pp 170–3; McNeill, *Castles in Ireland*, pp 123–4 and figs 74–5; Tadhg O'Keeffe and Margaret Coughlan, 'The chronology and formal affinities of the Ferns donjon, Co. Wexford' in Kenyon and O'Conor, *The medieval castle in Ireland and Wales*, pp 133–48; P.D. Sweetman, 'Archaeological excavations at Ferns Castle, Co. Wexford', *PRIA*, 79C (1979), pp 217–45.

William Marshal's castle at Kilkenny in about 1395: a new reconstruction

DANIEL TIETZSCH-TYLER

During a long visit to Ireland in 1394–5, Richard II spent the month of April 1395 in the earl of Ormond's great castle at Kilkenny. As part of the process of producing a new guidebook to Kilkenny Castle by Jane Fenlon, a new reconstruction of the castle was commissioned.[1] A series of earlier reconstructions of the castle by Jenny Baker showed what the castle might have looked like in the early thirteenth century, shortly after it was first completed in stone by William Marshal and again in the late seventeenth century and the late nineteenth century.[2] The new reconstruction drawing discussed here, modified slightly for this essay from the version that appeared in the recently published guidebook, attempts to show what the castle might have looked like at the height of its medieval development, around the time of Richard's visit (fig. 6.1). Those with keen eyesight will find Richard II standing in the inner ward of the castle, just beyond William Marshal's twin-towered gatehouse, being received by James Butler, third earl of Ormond, kneeling in homage. Less than two centuries after this date, one of Ireland's greatest castles underwent the first of a series of conversions, to become first a Renaissance mansion for Thomas Butler, tenth earl of Ormond, then a magnificent Restoration château-palace for James Butler, the twelfth earl, and finally the Georgian-Victorian mansion that remains to this day (fig. 6.2).

The Kilkenny Castle we see today represents only a small proportion of the castle at its fullest development. It represents the inner ward of the late medieval castle, and only half of the original inner ward's enclosing curtain walls and three of its four corner towers survive. John Bradley pointed out that a towered outer wall, probably with an outer ditch, once surrounded this inner ward of the castle, making the castle at least twice the size we see today.[3] More specifically, the earl of Ormond made a grant to a Robert Chamberlyn in 1434 of 'a vacant piece of land [lying] between the inner and outer walls of his castle of Kilkenny'.[4]

1 Jane Fenlon, *Kilkenny Castle: a visitor's guide* (Dublin, 2007). 2 Paddy Friel, *Kilkenny Castle* (Dublin, 1989), pp 4–5, 12–13, 18–19; Sweetman, *Medieval castles*, fig. 41. 3 John Bradley, 'The early development of the medieval town of Kilkenny' in William Nolan and Kevin Whelan (eds), *Kilkenny: history and society* (Dublin, 1990), pp 63–73 at p. 68; idem, *Kilkenny*, p. 2. 4 *Ormond deeds, 1413–1509*, p. 106, no. 115.

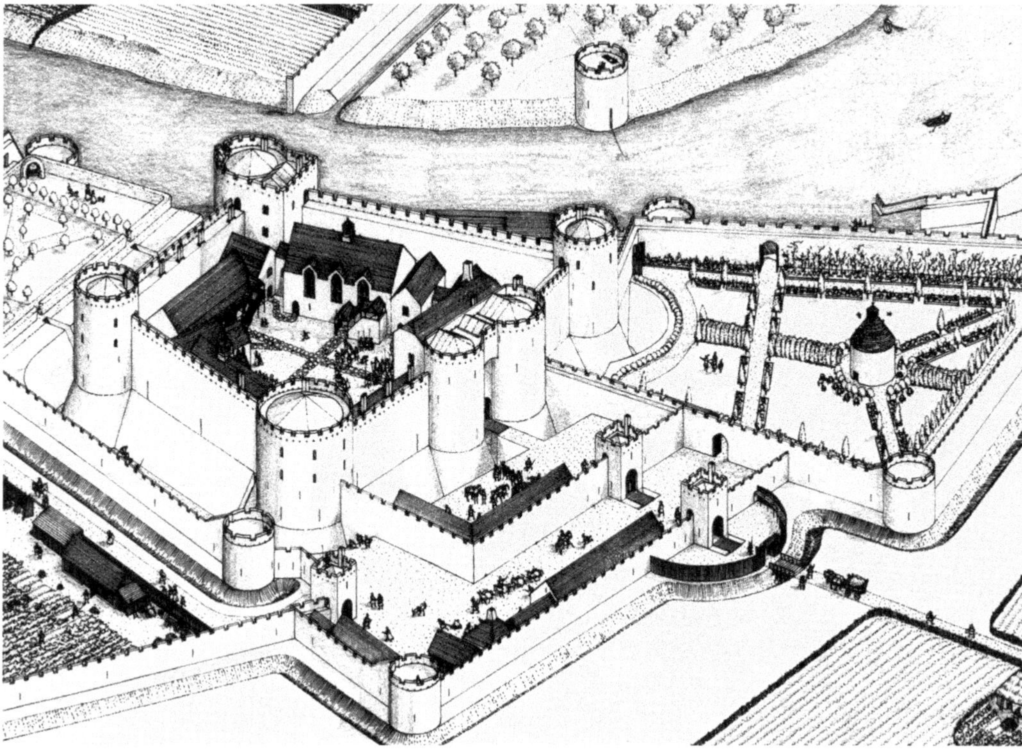

6.1 Kilkenny Castle reconstructed as it might have appeared for the visit of King Richard II during April 1395.

6.2 Kilkenny Castle as it is today, viewed through the site of William Marshal's great gatehouse towards the accommodation block against the north-west curtain. The White Tower terminates the left-hand wing. The right-hand wing, of nineteenth-century date, was built on medieval foundations and houses the Picture Gallery.

Chamberlyn was permitted to build thatched houses on this land for rent-paying tenants who would have 'free entry and exit by the outer gate of the castle'. Thus it would seem that Kilkenny Castle at the height of its medieval development was a concentric fortress of considerable extent.

THE INNER WARD: THE CASTLE WE SEE TODAY RESTORED

Kilkenny Castle began as a great ringwork castle in the late twelfth century. The trapezium-shaped earthwork castle most probably comprised a single enclosure surrounded by a man-made embankment over 3m high that survives in the foundations of the later stone walls of the castle.[5] The embankment would have been surmounted by a timber palisade and surrounded by a deep ditch, and a variety of thatched timber buildings within the enclosure would have accommodated the occupiers and activities of this early Anglo-Norman fortification. A fortification destroyed by Irish forces in 1173, to the 'grief [of] the foreigners of Ireland' who fled to Waterford,[6] may have been this ringwork, though it may have been incomplete at that date.[7] Alternatively, this major timber and earthwork castle may have been the one recorded as built for William Marshal in 1192, after the Marshal had finally been granted the lordship of Leinster.[8]

After a brief first visit in 1200, during which he founded the Cistercian monasteries of Tintern *de voto* (pl. 2) and Duiske (pl. 1), William Marshal returned to Ireland in 1207 and stayed until 1213 in order to pacify his lordship of Leinster and to put in place an effective administration.[9] One of the Marshal's first tasks during his six-year sojourn in Ireland was to replace the earlier ringwork castle with a major stone castle. The design the Marshal chose bears comparison with two royal castles built at the command of King John at about the same time: Dublin Castle, begun after 1204; and Limerick Castle, begun in 1211–12,[10] but with the castle in Dublin planned on a much larger scale than either of the other two (fig. 6.3). Each of these castles was presumably intended to define an irregular quadrilateral with a round tower at each corner and a twin-towered gatehouse near the midpoint of one side, though Limerick was never actually completed to this plan.[11] The high curtain walls of the Marshal's castle retained the trapezium shape of the earlier earthwork. Ben Murtagh's excavations in the 1990s showed that the steep stone talus or batter at the exterior base of the walls (figs 6.5c and d), carrying them down into a deep moat, simply

5 Ben Murtagh, 'The Kilkenny Castle Archaeological Project, 1990–1993: interim report', *OKR*, new ser., 4:3 (1993), pp 1101–17 at pp 1108–10. See also Murtagh, this volume. 6 Orpen, 'Castles in Ossory', p. 316; idem, *Normans*, i, p. 332. 7 Murtagh, 'Kilkenny Castle Archaeological Project', p. 1103. 8 Ibid., p. 1104. 9 Crouch, *William Marshal*, p. 101. 10 T.E. McNeill, *Castles in Ireland: feudal power in a Gaelic world* (London, 1997), pp 45–7. See also Murtagh, this volume. 11 Kenneth Wiggins, *Anatomy of a siege: King John's Castle, Limerick, 1642* (Bray, 2000), p. 34.

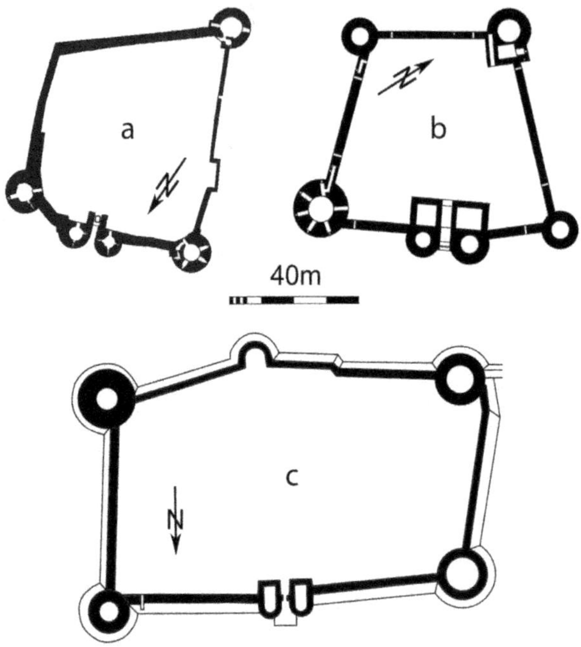

6.3 Comparative simplified plans of: a) King John's Castle, Limerick; b) Kilkenny Castle's inner ward; and c) Dublin Castle.

encases the outer face of the earlier ringwork embankment, with the curtain walls founded on the truncated crest of the embankment.[12]

Of the four corner towers, the south tower, or White Tower (fig. 6.5a), is significantly larger than the other three and dominates the castle ward (fig. 6.4). This compares with Dublin Castle, where the south-east or Record Tower also dominated the castle ward. Though there is no obvious dominant tower at Limerick – the castle there was built in several stages, probably with pragmatic modifications to the original design at each stage – the early north-east tower has a certain majesty about it. It is also possible that a dominant tower was originally intended for the south-east angle, where no tower was ever built. These dominant towers may have taken the place of the great circular keeps being built elsewhere at this time, such as at Pembroke Castle in south-west Wales, again by William Marshal, and at Dundrum and Nenagh in Ireland.[13] Presumably the White Tower was the administrative and judicial hub of the castle, essentially a public space. The next largest tower at Kilkenny is the north tower, which overlooks the river (fig. 6.5b). At some date in the late fourteenth or early fifteenth century a trapezium-shaped extension was added to this tower, giving it a keyhole-shaped plan. This extension is depicted in the reconstruction drawing even though it is not certain if it was built prior to 1395 (fig. 6.4). The north tower probably

12 Murtagh, 'Kilkenny Castle Archaeological Project', pp 1108–11 and fig. 3. See fig. 5.40, above, for an alternative plan of Kilkenny Castle. **13** Richard Avent, 'William Marshal's castle at Chepstow and its place in military architecture' in Turner and Johnson, *Chepstow Castle*, p. 87.

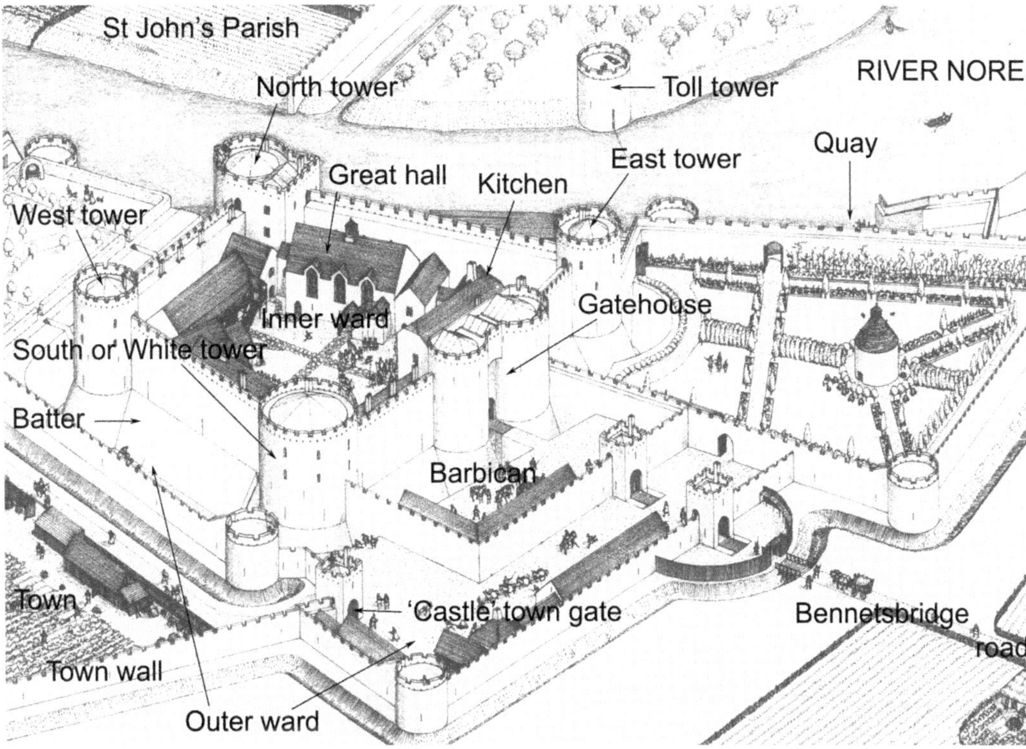

6.4 The reconstruction of Kilkenny Castle in fig. 6.1 with annotations identifying the main features of the castle.

housed the private accommodation of the lords of Leinster from the beginning. The later extension may have housed a solar and private chapel, and was probably connected by at least a covered walkway to the free-standing hall nearby. The west tower and probably the east tower, the latter demolished in the seventeenth century, were smaller than the other two towers (figs 6.3 and 6.4). For the purposes of the reconstruction, the east tower is assumed to be about the same size as the west tower.

The Marshal's twin-towered gatehouse was built near the midpoint of the south-east curtain of the castle, between the White Tower and the east tower (figs 6.3–6.4), providing entry into the castle only from outside the walled town. Though this gatehouse was demolished in the later eighteenth century, it is still to be seen in Francis Place's drawings of the castle made in 1698 (fig. 6.6). It is also clearly present on plans drawn in 1758 by John Rocque, and again for Walter Butler of Garryricken, sixteenth earl of Ormonde, in 1767 (fig. 6.7).[14] Both eighteenth-century plans indicate this to have been an asymmetrical structure,

14 Mary Kenealy, 'Plan of Kilkenny Castle, 1767', *OKR*, new ser., 2:4 (1982), pp 343–6 at p. 344.

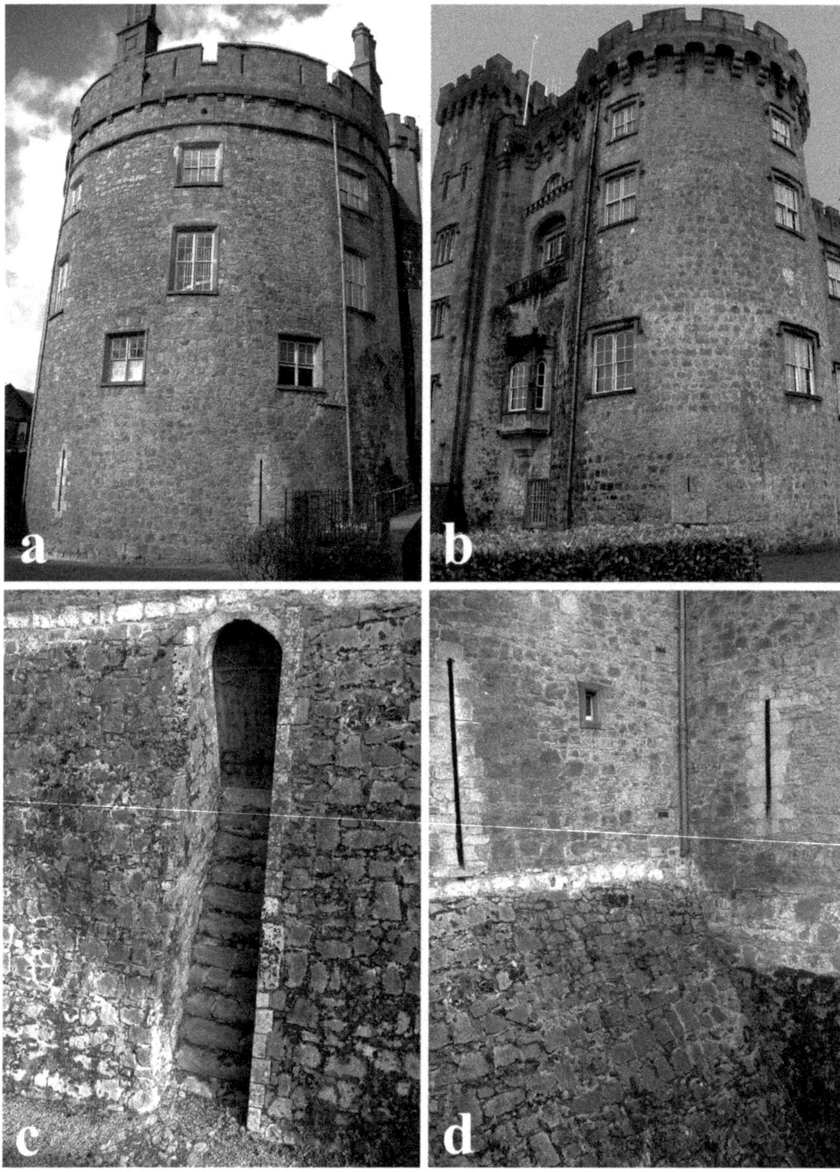

6.5 Details of the medieval inner ward of Kilkenny Castle: (a) the White Tower is the most substantial and best preserved of the medieval towers and retains its original height; (b) the north tower with the late fourteenth- or early fifteenth-century addition at the rear that gives it its keyhole shape. This tower and west tower both had an extra storey added in the nineteenth century. The tall flag tower behind the north tower is entirely a nineteenth-century confection; (c) the postern gate and steps down into the moat beside the White Tower; (d) the junction between the south-west curtain and the White Tower illustrating the steep talus or base batter of the inner ward curtain, which faces the original earthen ringwork embankment. Note also the long plunging arrow loops of the early thirteenth century.

a

b

6.6 Details from two views of Kilkenny Castle by Francis Place dating from 1698: (a) as viewed from the south-east, with the crenellated gatehouse in the centre of the drawing; and (b) as viewed from the east, with the gatehouse just overlapping the conically capped White Tower on the extreme left of the drawing (National Gallery of Ireland).

with one large and one small round tower on either side of the gate passage, though they differ in the sense of asymmetry. Rocque's map shows the north-eastern tower to be the larger of the two (fig. 6.7a), whereas the 1767 map shows the south-western tower to be the larger (fig. 6.7b). In both cases, the gatehouse appears to have been subsumed into a later range of buildings. The gatehouse appears in two of Place's drawings of the castle, viewed from the south-east (fig. 6.6a) and at some distance from the east (fig. 6.6b). The former is just a rough sketch and appears to show the south-western tower as square in plan, but the more finished drawing viewed from the east clearly depicts two round towers of which the north-eastern is the larger. Both drawings also depict a roofed, rectangular structure projecting back into the castle from the towers.

These depictions of the Kilkenny Castle gatehouse bear close comparison with the roughly contemporary gatehouse built by the Marshal at Chepstow

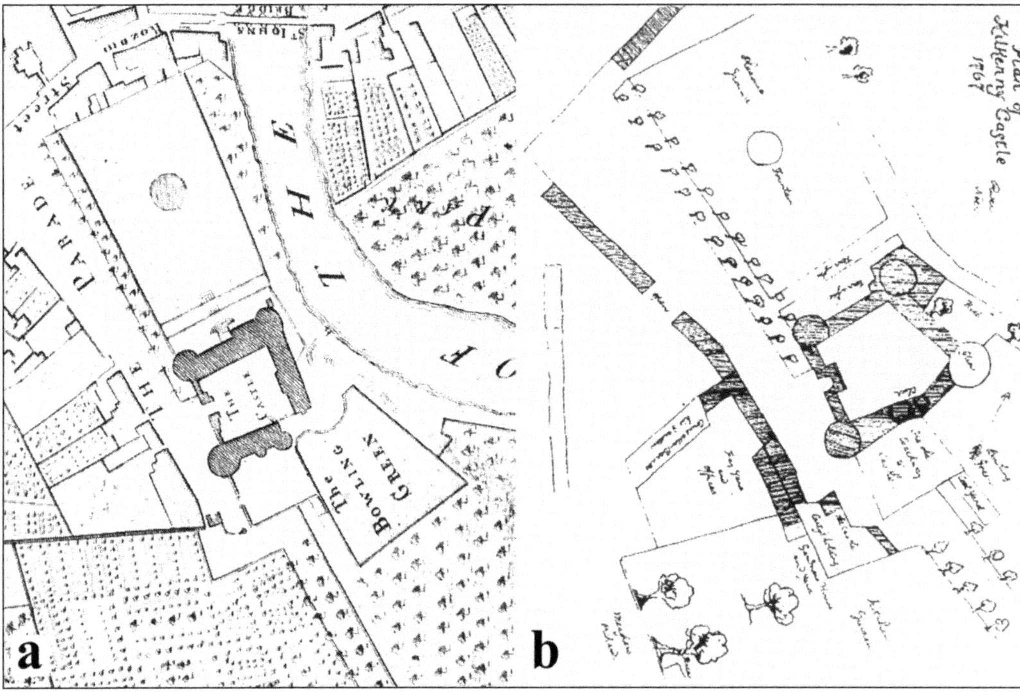

6.7 Two eighteenth-century maps of Kilkenny Castle: (a) from 1758 by John Rocque (reproduced courtesy of Trinity College Dublin); and (b) from 1767. The maps have been rotated for comparison with fig. 6.9 and north is approximately towards the top in both.

Castle in his lordship of Striguil in south-east Wales, soon after he acquired the castle in the late 1180s (see Murtagh, above).[15] Chepstow's great twin-towered gatehouse, one of the earliest of its kind, has one larger and one smaller round tower closely spaced on either side of a gate passage (fig. 6.8), which continued through a narrow accommodation block, now gone, built across the rear of both towers. Richard Avent suggested that this block would have had a pitched roof, either gabled or hipped.[16] The gatehouse at Chepstow is used as the model for the Marshal's gatehouse at Kilkenny in the new reconstruction, but with two differently sized towers reversed to reflect its appearance in Place's drawing (figs 6.6b and 6.8) and on Rocque's 1758 map (fig. 6.7a). A half-hipped roof is depicted in fig. 6.1, but without the battlemented parapet that is commonly depicted in reconstructions of Chepstow's gatehouse.[17] Taking the analogy with Chepstow just a little further, we can suppose that the outer end of the gate

15 Richard Avent, 'William Marshal's building works at Chepstow Castle, Monmouthshire, 1189–1219' in Kenyon and O'Conor, *The medieval castle in Ireland and Wales*, pp 50–71 at pp 53–4. **16** Ibid., p. 59. **17** For example, Rick Turner, *Chepstow Castle* (2nd ed., Cardiff, 2006), p. 13.

6.8 William Marshal's great gatehouse at Chepstow Castle (Cadw, Crown copyright). The gatehouse at Kilkenny Castle was probably very similar, but with the larger tower on the right-hand side. Left-hand inset: Chepstow's gatehouse reversed and with the later windows restored to earlier forms. Right-hand inset: the gatehouse of Kilkenny Castle (centre) in Francis Place's 1698 drawing (courtesy of National Gallery of Ireland).

passage was defended in succession by a murder slot extending up to the wall walk behind the arch-supported parapet, an outer portcullis, two great iron-shod oak doors secured by drawbars, and finally a second inner portcullis which, when lowered, further impeded the opening of the oak doors.[18]

18 Avent, 'Marshal's Chepstow', p. 57.

ACCOMMODATION, ADMINISTRATION AND SERVICE BUILDINGS IN THE INNER WARD

Though nothing remains, there is documentary evidence that numerous buildings were ranged about the inner ward of Kilkenny Castle during the medieval period. The earliest reference to the castle in 1307 describes it as containing 'a hall, four towers, a chapel, a moat and other divers houses necessary to the castle'.[19] The description of the castle in the Civil Survey, completed between 1654 and 1656, includes a hall 64 feet (19.5m) long by 36 feet (11m) wide, a slate-roofed stone kitchen 'neere ye walls', another stone building on the east side of the courtyard and a brick-built block of soldiers' accommodation.[20] Also described is 'the main building', 132 feet (40m) long by 20 feet (6m) wide with 25 rooms. The latter building was the great Renaissance mansion built in the late sixteenth century against the north-west curtain of the castle, on the site of the main residential block today, by Thomas Butler, the tenth earl of Ormond.[21] A medieval precursor was identified beneath the north-east end of Thomas Butler's house during the last great conversion of the castle in the nineteenth century.[22]

The hall, referred to as 'a building on ye east side, formerly ye hall' with walls of stone and a slate roof, is probably that described already as far back as 1307.[23] It is almost certainly the two-storey building with pitched roof and dormer gables over the windows that appears in front of the main residential block of the castle in Place's finished drawing (fig. 6.6b). The hall is depicted in the reconstruction with three large windows extending up to dormer gables (fig. 6.4) and positioned where it appears in Place's drawing. The slate-roofed stone kitchen, described as 'neere ye walls' in 1307, is depicted with a central chimney and is just visible behind the Marshal's gatehouse in the reconstruction, situated between the hall and the east tower (fig. 6.4). The chapel of 1307 is shown beside the west tower, with a smaller chancel at its east end lit by south-facing lancet windows.

The other buildings in the reconstruction are representative of the 'other divers houses necessary to the castle' recorded in the 1307 inquisition, all of them presumably accommodation and service buildings. In his 1995 and 1998–9 excavations, Ben Murtagh identified the demolished south-east curtain of the inner ward and, with it, the remains of the seventeenth-century block that subsumes the Marshal's gatehouse in the two eighteenth-century plans of the castle (fig. 6.7).[24] Against the south-west curtain, Murtagh also recovered a large quantity of bricks from the seventeenth-century block of soldiers'

19 *CDI, 1302–7*, p. 186; Murtagh, 'Kilkenny Castle Archaeological Project', p. 1106. **20** *Civil Survey*, vi, p. 534. **21** Murtagh, 'Kilkenny Castle Archaeological Project', p. 1112; Fenlon, *Kilkenny Castle*, p. 27. **22** J.G. Robertson, 'Architectural notes on Kilkenny Castle', *JRSAI*, 2 (1852–3), pp 115–18 at p. 116. **23** *Civil Survey*, vi, p. 534. **24** Ben Murtagh, 'Kilkenny Castle, the Parade, Kilkenny', *Excavations 1999*, pp 146–7 at p. 146.

accommodation.[25] The demolition of these two blocks, in the later eighteenth century and the late seventeenth century respectively, probably represented the end of a much longer history of building on these two sides of the inner ward. Reflecting all this evidence, the reconstruction shows buildings ranged along all four sides of the inner ward of Kilkenny Castle, as would be expected for the administrative centre of an important earldom, such as Ormond, in the later Middle Ages.

THE OUTER DEFENCES: VISUALISING THE CONCENTRIC FORTRESS

Until the seventeenth century, the inner ward of the castle was surrounded by a wide stone-lined moat up to 8.5m deep, the steeply inclined inner wall of which corresponded to the outer face of the original ringwork bank.[26] Flights of steps descend into the moat from several postern gates in the inner ward. One flight, exposed now to public view (fig. 6.5c), descends from a door towards the top of the batter at the base of the south-west curtain near the White Tower. The arched opening from a garderobe chute occurs midway between the base of these steps and the White Tower.[27] A second sally port exiting from the batter at the base of the north-west curtain beside the west tower was found in excavation,[28] and a third, at the opposite end of the north-west curtain beside the north tower, came to light during nineteenth-century renovations.[29] In each case, a flight of steps led down from courtyard level within the inner ward to a small lobby just inside the postern gate. The slightly recessed steps from the postern beside the White Tower are just visible in the reconstruction. Two flights of recessed steps are also shown climbing back out of the north-western moat to give access to the garden beyond, but these are purely speculative. It is possible that the posterns only provided access to the bottom of the moat so that garderobe chutes could be cleared of waste accumulating there.

The difficulty when attempting to visualise the outer defences of Kilkenny Castle lies in their complete absence, both from the ground today and, at least in any obvious way, from the earliest maps and plans of the castle. That they existed seems clear from the reference in 1434 to land lying between 'the inner and outer walls of his castle'. Other evidence comes from the description of structures associated with the castle in the 1654–6 Civil Survey.[30] Reference to a 'small castle between the outer gate and the greate castle' again suggests at least two lines of defence outside the inner ward, as does mention of two stables described in association with the small castle noted above, one in a yard between the 'small

25 Ben Murtagh, pers. comm., 2007. 26 Murtagh, 'Kilkenny Castle Archaeological Project', pp 1108–11 and fig. 3. 27 Murtagh, 'Kilkenny Castle, the Parade, Kilkenny', p. 102. 28 Murtagh, 'Kilkenny Castle Archaeological Project', p. 1111 and fig. 2. 29 Robertson, 'Architectural notes on Kilkenny Castle', p. 117. 30 *Civil Survey*, vi, p. 534.

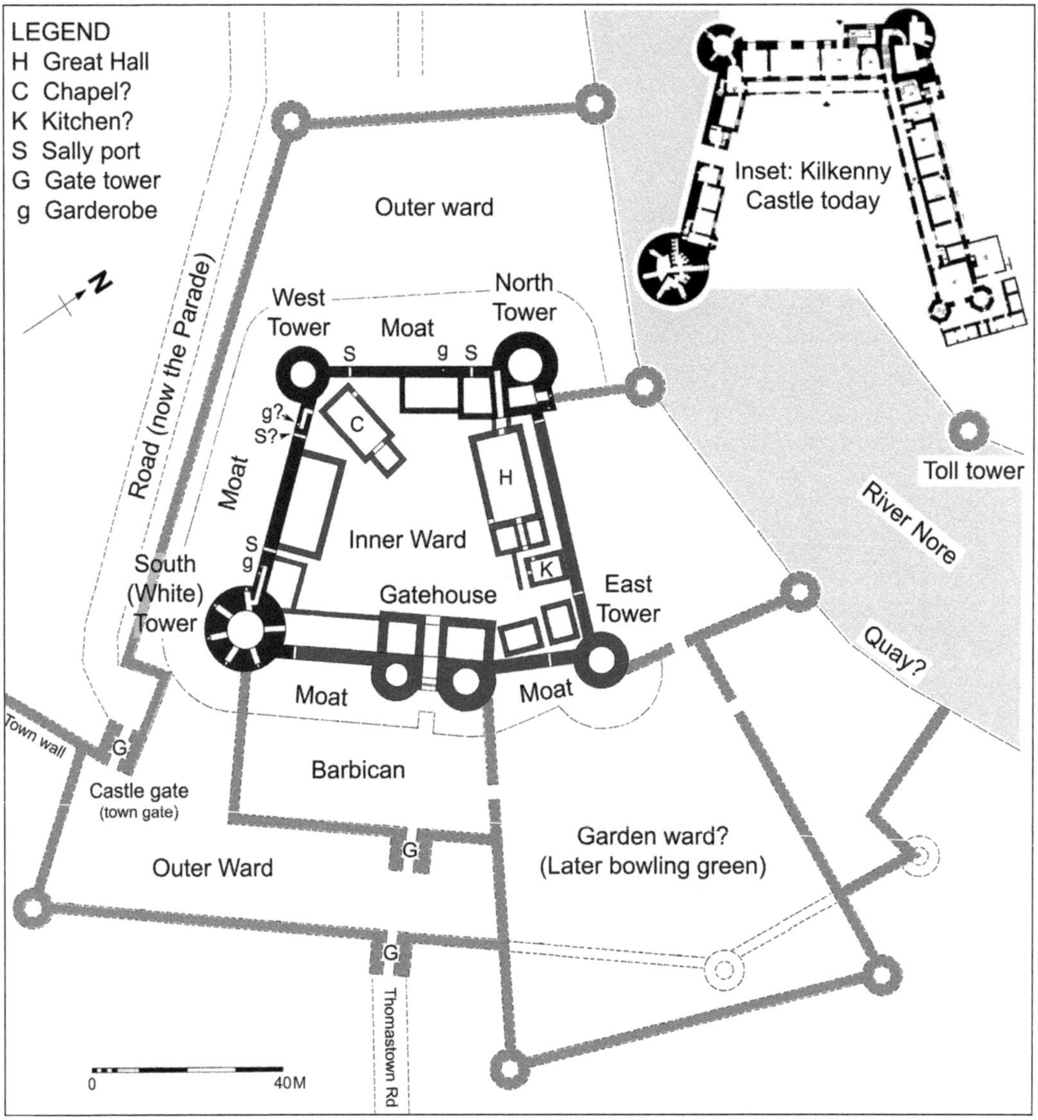

6.9 A hypothetical working plan of the greater Kilkenny Castle compiled during the reconstruction project. Inset, top right, is a plan of Kilkenny Castle today at the same scale. Recent public works on the Parade exposed the outer edge of the moat around the White Tower, demonstrating that it followed the curve of the tower more closely, as shown around the east tower on this plan.

castle' and the main castle, and another between the small castle and the 'mount'. The stone-built 'mount' described as being outside the gate of the castle probably refers to a bastion erected in response to the seventeenth-century confederate and civil wars. What might have been the configuration of these

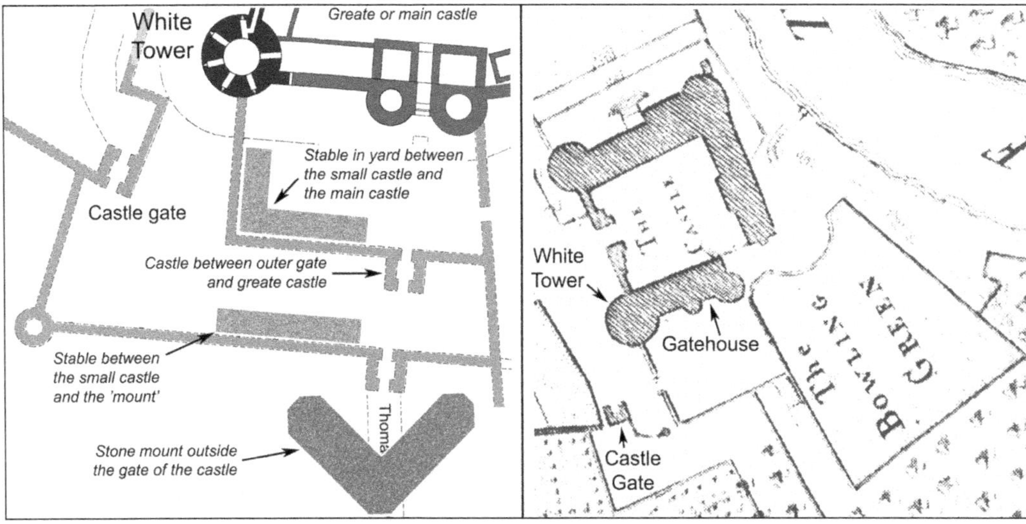

6.10 The outer walls of Kilkenny Castle south-east of the inner ward: (a) detail of fig. 6.9 showing suggested approximate locations for features listed in the 1654–6 Civil Survey; (b) detail of John Rocque's 1758 map showing boundaries that might have been inherited from the outer walls of the medieval castle (reproduced courtesy of Trinity College Dublin).

outer walls, 'castles' and yards? Since many of the buildings of the castle's inner ward were still standing in 1654 together with at least some of the outer walls and towers, it is at least possible that the latter persisted in some form beyond that date or were inherited by later boundaries. Perhaps the earliest post-medieval maps of the castle area together with drawings of the castle that pre-date its nineteenth-century conversion can provide some evidence, albeit circumstantial, for the configuration of these walls.

The outer walls must have stood outside the stone-lined moat that surrounds the inner ward on at least three sides. Infilling of the moat and construction of the Parade outside the south-west curtain of the inner ward by the twelfth earl and first duke of Ormonde in the later seventeenth century necessitated the removal of the outer wall on this side of the castle and there is no evidence for it on the earliest maps.[31] Whatever its location, this wall had to accommodate Castle Gate (fig. 6.9), the town gate that gave access from the town into the castle and from there on to the Thomastown road. This gate stood just 20m south of the White Tower. In the reconstruction, the wall is shown standing just outside the moat around the inner ward, with an angular embayment accommodating access to and from Castle Gate (fig. 6.4). This wall is projected some distance north of the west tower before it turns north-east to enclose a garden, perhaps

31 Murtagh, 'Kilkenny Castle Archaeological Project'; John Bradley, 'The creation of the Parade: Ormond's deal with Kilkenny Corporation, 1677', *OKR*, 58 (2006), pp 77–116.

6.11 'Talbot's Bastion', a thirteenth-century mural tower on Kilkenny's town wall. Note the parapet that protects a stairway to the tower roof from the town wall below (courtesy of Ian Doyle, Heritage Council).

corresponding to the Shirehall Garden recorded in 1435.[32] Perhaps the Shire Hall, associated with a garden and a tower,[33] was located in this western corner of the castle's outer ward. The outer wall is continued parallel to the north-west curtain of the inner ward before dropping down the steep slope to the River Nore (fig. 6.1).

A more complex configuration of the outer walls is interpreted for the south-east side of the castle. The Civil Survey identification of a 'small castle between the outer gate and the greate castle' suggests the presence of three gates: the Marshal's great gatehouse, an outer gate and an intermediate gate-tower between them (fig. 6.10a). The simplest explanation for this is the existence of a barbican across the moat from the great gatehouse (figs 6.4 and 6.9). The stable identified in a yard between the 'small castle' and the 'main castle' would then be within this barbican, and the other would be outside it in the outer ward. Rocque's map still shows a concentric arrangement of walls defining two rectangular yards in 1758 (fig. 6.10b). The inner yard encloses the great gatehouse before abutting the wall of a larger trapezium-shaped enclosure surrounding the demolished east tower and identified as a bowling green. The second yard encloses the inner yard and Castle Gate before also abutting the wall of the bowling green, but has been opened up to allow free access from the town onto the Thomastown road. It does not seem unreasonable to suppose that these walls reflect a pre-existing arrangement and as such they have been used in the reconstruction as the basis for a series of walls defending the entrance to the inner ward.

The reconstruction extends this argument to include the 1758 boundaries of the bowling green in the arrangement of wards associated with the medieval

32 *Ormond deeds, 1413–1509*, p. 114, no. 124; Bradley, *Kilkenny*, p. 14 and John Bradley, pers. comm., 2007. 33 Bradley, *Kilkenny*, p. 14.

a

b

6.12 Details from two further views of Kilkenny Castle: (a) the main accommodation block of the castle by Francis Place in 1698 viewed from the north-west, with a tower from the outer walls in the bottom left-hand corner of the drawing (National Gallery of Ireland); (b) the same tower at the end of a stretch of low wall as viewed from across the River Nore in 1814. Note the wall climbing to the tower parapet, presumably to protect a stairway (courtesy of Royal Society of Antiquaries of Ireland).

castle. Interestingly, the curved embayment into the bowling green close to where the east tower once stood suggests that although the tower had gone by this date – perhaps demolished following damage inflicted during Cromwell's week-long siege in March 1650 – the moat may still have existed there. Adopting the outline of the 1758 bowling green into the medieval outer ward, however, may be a step too far and the working plan in fig. 6.9 also offers an alternative solution wherein the south-east curtain of the outer ward continues across the later bowling green to link up with a wall that zigzags down to the River Nore (fig. 6.9, dashed lines).

The height and thickness of the outer walls of the castle are based on those of the surviving town wall. Six mural towers augmented the town wall encompassing Kilkenny's Hightown, four of which appear on Rocque's 1758 map where they are depicted as round towers.[34] The Civil Survey refers to a 'stone wall upon which are three flankers', presumably small towers, associated with the castle.[35] In the reconstruction these are taken to be small round towers on the outer walls, each based upon 'Talbot's Bastion' (known in the Middle Ages as St Patrick's Tower), the most intact of the towers on the town wall. 'Talbot's Bastion' is a round tower with a diameter of 8.8m and a maximum height today of 9.7m (fig. 6.11, pl. 14). The tower's parapet is carried on a thin flagstone course that projects slightly from the tower's outer face and has closely spaced drainage holes around the base. The top of 'Talbot's Bastion' is reached from the wall walk below by a stairway, which is protected by a climbing parapet wall. Another drawing by Francis Place of the castle in 1698 depicts what appears to be a tower very similar to Talbot's Castle, with a flagstone course and drainage holes at the foot of the parapet, beside the River Nore below the north tower of the inner ward (fig. 6.12a). A drawing from 1814 by another artist appears to show the same tower and a stretch of low curtain wall from across the river, in this case with a climbing parapet wall protecting a stairway from the curtain wall walk to the top of the tower (fig. 6.12b). An isolated round tower with the same diameter as 'Talbot's Bastion' was recently excavated on the east bank of the River Nore (fig. 6.9). This tower probably housed one end of a chain across the river that was used to enforce the payment of tolls by boats entering the city.[36] It almost certainly had a twin on the opposite riverbank, below the castle, to house the other end of the chain. These separate pieces of circumstantial evidence all suggest that round towers closely comparable with those on the town wall also augmented the outer walls of the Kilkenny Castle.

In the reconstruction, the gateways into the different castle yards are modelled on the extant remains and on old views of Kilkenny's town gates, such as Black Friars' Gate, St James's Gate (demolished in 1860), St Patrick's Gate (demolished in about 1895) and Castle Gate (beside the White Tower) (demolished in 1769).[37] Like so many town gates in Ireland, the gate passages passed through simple square towers. To complete the reconstruction, the area of the later bowling green (or the slightly smaller area in the alternative solution for this area) has been interpreted as a garden ward, its walls enclosing lawns, trees, raised beds, beehives and a dovecote. This represents the gardens

34 Julian Munby and Ric Tyler, *Kilkenny city walls conservation plan* (Kilkenny, 2005), pp 49–133. 35 *Civil Survey*, vi, p. 534. 36 I.W. Doyle, 'Excavation of a riverside circular tower in College Park, Kilkenny City', *OKR*, 57 (2005), pp 32–42. 37 Bradley, *Kilkenny*, p. 14; Munby and Tyler, *Kilkenny city walls conservation plan*, pp 49–133.

described in 1375 'opposite the gate of the castle'.[38] Finally, the small irregular wall that zigzags from the later bowling green down towards the River Nore on Rocque's map has been interpreted in the reconstruction to extend down to the river to enclose and protect a small riverside quay.

CONCLUSION

The creation of a reconstruction drawing for an archaeological site or a partially preserved ancient monument, if it is to be as accurate as possible, requires careful and integrated analysis of all evidence available for the site. Such analysis can introduce new and valuable insights into the discussion about the site. In this case, the evidence included the relict medieval architecture of the castle, the results of architectural and archaeological investigations going back nearly two centuries, early post-medieval maps of the castle and its surroundings, and pictorial representations of the castle from the seventeenth and early nineteenth centuries. The resulting reconstruction discussed here attempts to show Kilkenny Castle as it might have looked at the height of its development during the later Middle Ages. The date of 1395 is, to some extent, arbitrary and introduced simply to reflect an auspicious occasion in the castle's history. The achievement of this final form may have occurred a little later, perhaps in the early decades of the fifteenth century.

All the evidence points to Kilkenny Castle developing from an earth-and-timber ringwork in the late twelfth century into a vast concentric stone fortress of quite formidable design. Castles designed from the beginning for concentric defence did not generally appear in Britain and Ireland until the second half of the thirteenth century, with the castles of Caerphilly (1268–71), Roscommon (1269–70 and 1275–8), Aberystwyth (1277–9), Rhuddlan (1277–80), Harlech (1285–90) and Beaumaris (1295–1326) principal among them.[39] Earlier concentric castles, such as the Tower of London and Dover Castle, became concentric through the incremental addition of new surrounding walls over a long period. Dates for the substantial completion of Edward I's castles in north Wales and Roscommon Castle in Ireland (above) suggest that the inner ward of Kilkenny Castle, if begun in 1207, is likely to have been substantially complete before the Marshal left Ireland in 1213. By analogy with the surviving towers of Kilkenny Castle, Bradley placed the construction of 'Talbot's Bastion' at *c.*1230[40] but this was before the recent investigations by Cóilín Ó Drisceoil and Ben

38 *Ormond deeds, 1350–1413*, p. 141, no. 201. 39 Main building periods after C.N. Johns, *Caerphilly Castle, Mid Glamorgan* (Cardiff, 1978); Derek Renn, *Caerphilly Castle* (2nd ed., Cardiff, 1997); Daniel Tietzsch-Tyler, 'Roscommon Castle: staged construction, unrealised vision' in John Bradley and Ben Murtagh (eds), *Castles and defences in Ireland and beyond: essays in honour of David Newman Johnson* (Dublin, forthcoming); A.J. Taylor, *The king's works in Wales, 1277–1330* (London, 1974). 40 John Bradley, 'The town wall of Kilkenny revisited:

Murtagh, which indicate that a date in the third quarter of the century is more likely.[41] The similarity between 'Talbot's Bastion' and, from the little evidence that is available, the towers on the outer walls of the Kilkenny Castle suggests that they may be contemporary and thus that the outer walls of the castle were completed within fifty years of the Marshal's departure.

It seems likely that Kilkenny Castle was the most formidable castle in Ireland by the middle of the fourteenth century, easily comparable with the great castles of Dover, the Tower of London and Kenilworth in England, perhaps pre-dating the designer concentric castles of Caerphilly in Wales and Roscommon in Ireland. It easily surpassed in terms of military engineering the great royal castle of Dublin and the greater baronial castles of Trim, Dunamase and Carrickfergus. As such it probably accurately reflects the power wielded by its medieval lords, first William Marshal and his heirs up to 1391 and then the Butler earls of Ormond. This is worth remembering when we look at the castle today following its post-medieval transformation into a fanciful, rather benign and purely residential mansion.

a review article', *OKR*, 58 (2006), pp 185–95 at p. 187; but see idem, 'The town wall of Kilkenny', *OKR*, new ser., 1:2 (1975), pp 85–103; 1:3 (1976), pp 209–18 at p. 213; and idem, *Kilkenny*, p. 14, where he favoured a late thirteenth-century date. **41** Coilín Ó Drisceoil, pers. comm., 2007.

William Marshal's charter to Kilkenny, 1207: background, dating and witnesses

JOHN BRADLEY† AND BEN MURTAGH[1]

William Marshal's charter to Kilkenny is conventionally dated to between 1207 and 1211. The date is based upon what is known about three individuals mentioned in the grant: the Marshal himself; Hugh le Rous, bishop of Ossory; and Geoffrey fitz Robert. The earl was in Ireland briefly in 1200 and for longer periods between 1207 and 1213; le Rous, however, became bishop of Ossory in 1202, so the date can be narrowed to the second of the Marshal's visits, while fitz Robert died in 1211.[2] More recently David Crouch has placed the charter in the period 1208–11, but here it will be argued that a closer analysis of it, particularly the witness list, shows that it belongs to the time that the Marshal spent in Ireland during 1207.[3]

This essay outlines the background to the arrival in 1169 of the Anglo-Normans in the kingdom of Osraige, centring largely in modern Co. Kilkenny (sect. I). This is followed by an account of their presence in the region during the years 1169–89 (sect. II) and the extent of William Marshal's early involvement there in the period 1189–1207 (sect. III), from the initial opposition to his gaining seisin of the lordship of Leinster from his overlord in Ireland, Prince John, count of Mortain, who settled some of his followers such as Theobald Walter I, ancestor of the Butler clan, in Osraige, to the Marshal's own attempts and successes at settlement and making land grants to his knights in the same region, leading to his first visit to Kilkenny in 1200. This is followed (sect. IV) by

1 This essay was completed by Ben Murtagh from a draft written by and from discussions with the late John Bradley before his death in November 2014. 2 See, for instance, Eric St J. Brooks (ed.), *Knights' fees in Counties Wexford, Carlow and Kilkenny (13th–15th century)* (Dublin, 1950), pp 183, 211, 215 (although elsewhere he dates it more exactly to *c.*1208: ibid., p. 177); Mac Niocaill, *Na buirgéisí*, p. 135; James Graves and J.G.A. Prim placed it in the episcopate of Hugh le Rous (1202–18): *The history, architecture and antiquities of the cathedral church of St Canice, Kilkenny* (Dublin, 1857), p. 29n. Mary Bateson dated the charter to 1202–10 in her *Borough customs* (2 vols, London, 1904–6), i, p. xxxv, which was followed by Adolphus Ballard, *British borough charters, 1042–1216* (Cambridge, 1913), pp xxxiii, xxxv. Elsewhere in the same volume, Bateson (p. 109n.) dated it to *c.*1202, but this may have been a slip for *c.*1202–10. See also sect. V, no. 1 below for Hugh le Rous and sect. V, no. 6 for Geoffrey fitz Robert. 3 David Crouch, *William Marshal: knighthood, war and chivalry, 1147–1219* (London, 2002), p. 171, a dating followed by Ronan Mackay and David Beresford, 'Marshal, William (I)' in *DIB*, vi, pp 372–6 at p. 373.

an outline of his second visit in 1207 and his granting of the charter to his new town at Kilkenny. The new town also became known as Hightown, distinguishing it from the older adjoining and pre-Anglo-Norman Irishtown. The same section addresses the dating of the charter and includes a brief outline of its contents, which is followed by profiles of fourteen charter witnesses (sect. V), followed by a conclusion (sect. VI). An English translation of the charter is provided in the Appendix.

I

The diocese of Ossory, with its cathedral at Kilkenny (fig. 7.1), was established in 1111 at the synod of Ráith Bressail.[4] A little over forty years later, in March 1152, this arrangement was confirmed at the synod of Kells in Meath.[5] At Ráith Bressail, the diocese (then known as Kilkenny) was described as extending from the Slieve Bloom Mountains in the north (border of modern Cos Laois and Offaly) to Mileadhach, the junction of the three sisters – the rivers Barrow, Nore and Suir – in the south, and from Grian Airbh (Greenhill, near Urlingford, Co. Kilkenny, part of the Slieveardagh range) on the west to Slieve Mairge (the hills running north from Gowran to the Castlecomer plateau) on the east. It was a sizeable area, spread across three modern counties, and it reflected the extent of Osraige's political power at the time.[6] In common with other dioceses established at the synod, the cathedral was located at the political capital of the kingdom, in this instance Kilkenny, situated just to the north of centre within the fertile plain of Mag Roigne ('the settled area of Rogen', a mythical ancestor of the Osraige). Here, during the fifth century, one of the first Christian churches in the south-east of Ireland was established, while from at least the seventh century there was a second ecclesiastical foundation, 'the church of Cainnech (Canice)', which, in due course, gave the town its name.[7]

The central lowlands of Co. Kilkenny had been important since the Bronze Age. Their fertility provided the wealth that supported ambitious rulers and gave them the patronage to retain clients and allies. The rich land of Mag Roigne became synonymous with the kingship of Osraige. In 861 when Cerball mac

4 Geoffrey Keating, *Foras feasa ar Éirinn: the history of Ireland*, ed. David Comyn and P.S. Dinneen (4 vols, London, 1902–14), iii, pp 304–5. Keating transcribed his information on the synod from the lost Book of Clonenagh. See John Mac Erlean, 'Synod of Ráith Bressail: boundaries of the dioceses of Ireland', *Archivium Hibernicum*, 3 (1914), pp 1–33 at p. 10; T.W. Moody, F.X. Martin and F.J. Byrne (eds), *NHI*, ix: *maps, genealogies, lists: a companion to Irish history, part ii* (Oxford, 2011), map 24 and pp 101, 313n.12. 5 Keating, *Foras feasa*, iii, pp 312–17; Brendan Ó Ciobháin, 'Deoisí na hÉireann i ndiaidh Shionaid Cheanannas, 1152 – teacsanna [text]', *Dinnseanchas*, 5:2 (1972), pp 52–6; 'Foinsí éagsúla [various sources]', ibid., 5:3 (1973), pp 71–85; 'Nótaí téacsa [textual notes]', ibid., 5:4 (1973), pp 119–28; *NHI*, ix, map 25 and p. 101. 6 We shall refer to the diocese as Ossory and the population group/kingdom as Osraige. 7 Bradley, *Kilkenny*, p. 1.

7.1 View of the thirteenth-century St Canice's Cathedral, Kilkenny, refurbished in the nineteenth century, with nearby pre-Anglo-Norman round tower (photograph: Cóilín Ó Drisceoil).

Dúnlainge (king of Osraige, 842–88) celebrated his sovereignty over the kingdom it was by hosting the 'Oenach Roigne'.[8] In later times, a poet commemorating the death of Donnchad mac Cellaig (king of Osraige, 934–76) used Osraige and Roigne interchangeably.[9] When enemies wished to punish Osraige, it was Mag Roigne that they attacked. So, in 930, when the Scandinavians of Limerick attempted to establish a long-term base in Osraige, it was at Loch mBeathrach in Mag Roigne (Loughmerans, just north of Kilkenny city).[10] In 967, when Osraige was invaded by Murchad mac Finn, king of Leinster, it was Mag Roigne that he plundered.[11] Similarly, in 1026, when the Uí Muiredaig, who held the kingship of Leinster under their leader Donnchad mac Dúnlainge, raided Osraige they plundered as far as Tullamaine (in west modern Co. Kilkenny), at the western edge of Mag Roigne.[12]

The rise of Kilkenny and its selection as the diocesan see was a natural result of its location. It was the major central place within Mag Roigne and an important crossing point of the River Nore but there were also political factors. In the mid-ninth century, Osraige produced a powerful and ambitious king, Cerball mac Dúnlainge who, as *Kjarvalr Irakonungr* (Kjarval the Irish king), was subsequently remembered in the genealogies of some of the leading Icelandic

8 *AFM*, 859; *FAI*, 861. 9 Keating, *Foras feasa*, ii, pp 218–19. 10 *AFM*, 928, 929; *CS*, 931; *AI*, 930; the identification with Loughmerans has been made by Raghnall Ó Floinn (pers. comm.). 11 *AFM*, 965. 12 *AFM*; *ATig*.

families.[13] The Viking presence brought a new dimension to Irish waterways, so that the Nore and the Barrow, reaching over 100km into the interior of Ireland, became major arteries of communication. Cerball's success was founded on his domination of the river valleys and during the 870s and 880s this made him the most powerful king in Leinster. The relevance of Cerball mac Dúnlainge's rise to prominence, and that of his Mac Gilla Pátraic successors, lies in the fact that their lands – the fertile plain of central modern Co. Kilkenny – became one of the major power centres in south-eastern Ireland. This growth in power, which commenced in the late ninth century and was consolidated in the tenth and eleventh centuries, effectively marks Kilkenny's beginnings as a town.

Given Kilkenny's centrality it is not at all clear how or when the myth of the transfer of the cathedral of Ossory from Aghaboe (Achad Bó) in modern Co. Laois (fig. 7.2) to Kilkenny originated.[14] It is first documented in the sixteenth century as an aside in a rather error-prone list of the bishops of Ossory known as *Nomina reverendorum patrum episcoporum Ossoriensium* ('the names of the reverend fathers bishops of Ossory'). This catalogue originally formed part of the (now lost) White Book of Ossory. The compiler placed the move from Aghaboe to Kilkenny within the episcopate of Felix (O'Dullany) Ua Duib Shláine (*c.*1179–1202) (fig. 7.3).[15] In the nineteenth century, however, the narrative took on a new twist when James Graves (1816–86) invented the theory that the 'move' had occurred not during Felix's episcopate, but in the time of his successor, the first English bishop of the diocese, Hugh le Rous (1202–18).[16] In coming to this conclusion, Graves simply reflected the mindset of the Victorian era. In a world dominated by the industrial production, economic wealth and political power of England, it made sense to believe that medieval English ancestors were the ones with the insight to reorganise a diocese. So, for Graves (and the italics are his): 'there was little to induce the *Irishman* O'Dullany to remove the see from the centre of an unconquered district to the heart of the *English* settlement at Kilkenny', but it was understandable that le Rous would wish to relocate from 'neighbours little suited to his taste among the O'Mores and Mac Gilla Pátraics of Leix and Upper Ossory'.[17] William Carrigan

13 F.J. Byrne, *Irish kings and high-kings* (London, 1973), p. 162; Clare Downham, 'The career of Cearbhall of Osraighe', *OLL*, 1 (2004), pp 1–18. 14 John Bradley, 'Pulp facts and core fictions: translating a cathedral from Aghaboe to Kilkenny' in Emer Purcell, Paul MacCotter, Julianne Nyhan and John Sheehan (eds), *Clerics, kings and Vikings: essays on medieval Ireland in honour of Donnchadh Ó Corráin* (Dublin, 2015), pp 169–84. 15 Carrigan, *Ossory*, i, p. 279. 16 Graves and Prim, *St Canice's*, pp 29–32. See also sect. V, no. 1, below. 17 Graves and Prim, *St Canice's*, p. 30; Graves makes the assumption that the area around Aghaboe was unconquered, whereas the 'half-cantred of Aghaboe' had been granted to Adam de Hereford before Strongbow's death in 1176 and was in the second generation of colonisation during the episcopate of Hugh le Rous (1202–18). There was probably a Mac Gilla Pátraic presence in Upper Ossory from early times, but it was not until the thirteenth century that it became their heartland, as is indicated by the soubriquets of Domnall Clannach Mac Gilla Pátraic (d. 1229), his son Domnall Mór Magh Laoighse, Domnall's Mór's son Uilliam Clannaigh, and in the death notice of Seffraidh (d. 1269), another son of Domnall Clannach, who is described as

7.2 South-east view of St Canice's Church, Aghaboe, Co. Laois, in 1792 by Daniel Grose. This is the reputed site of the pre-Anglo-Norman cathedral of Ossory prior to the 'move' or 'transfer' to Kilkenny, with the ruined Dominican friary in the background (Grose's *Antiquities*, 2, pl. 77).

demonstrated that Graves's theory could not be sustained because there is clear evidence for a functioning diocesan chapter at Kilkenny in the 1190s.[18] Nonetheless, Graves has led many subsequent scholars astray.[19] The story of the 'move' may have had an origin simply in the memory that once upon a time Aghaboe had been the mother church of Kilkenny. On the other hand, the

king of Sliabh Bladhma (Slieve Bloom): see *Leabhar mór na ngenealach, The great book of Irish genealogies compiled (1645–66) by Dubhaltach Mac Fhirbhisigh*, ed. and trans. Nollaig Ó Muraíle (5 vols, Dublin, 2003), ii, pp 295–7, 480.2 and 480.4; ibid., iii, pp 576–7, 1244; 'O'Clery book of genealogies', ed. Seamus Pender, *Analecta Hibernica*, 18 (1951), pp 1–198 at p. 134, nos 1783, 1785; 'Short annals of Leinster', ed. Pól Breatnach, *Irish Book Lover*, 24 (1936), pp 58–60, under the year 1229; *ALC*, 1269. **18** Carrigan, *Ossory*, i, pp 24–6. **19** Among them, G.H. Orpen, *Ireland under the Normans* (4 vols, Oxford, 1911–20), ii, p. 227; W.G. Neely, *Kilkenny: an urban history, 1391–1843* (Belfast, 1989), p. 9; Crouch, *William Marshal*, p. 152.

7.3 View of the effigial tomb of Felix O'Dullany (Ua Duib Shláine), bishop of Ossory 1179–1202, in the church of the former Cistercian abbey of Jerpoint, Co. Kilkenny (Edwin Rae Collection © TRIARC, Trinity Irish Art Research Centre).

account of the 'transfer' may have been devised as part of an attempt to validate church claims to lands and estates in northern Osraige after the shiring of Laois (Queen's County) and Offaly (King's County) in 1556.[20] In any event, the tale clearly originated within a community that had lost access to the Gaelic-Irish sources.

Even in 1111, however, Osraige's heyday as a regional power was waning. Like all Irish kingdoms, it was a federation of dynastic groups, bound together by intermarriage, a belief in a common ancestry, and participation in shared activities such as warfare. Each dynasty had the fundamental task of perpetuating its lineage, preserving (and, if possible, extending) its hereditary estates and competing for political power. Power could be achieved by diplomacy, bribery or battle, but it was essential because it brought patronage. Without patronage, kings could not retain their clients; without clients, kings were powerless, and powerlessness tended to have fatal consequences. Kings and peoples did not have friends in twelfth-century Ireland, they had interests; allies were fickle because

20 It seems likely that Bishop Tonery's interest in transcribing and preserving the ancient charters of the diocese, like that of Archbishop Alen in Dublin, was motivated by practical reasons of economic necessity and the desire to claim estates lost since the fourteenth century, rather than the historical interest assumed by Carrigan, *Ossory*, i, pp 70–1.

they had interests too. Kings had to be vigilant, warlike and aggressive because, to use a phrase applied to the modern warlords of central Asia, if they were not seen to be at the table then they and their kingdoms were on the menu.

There were eight or nine major dynastic groups within the Osraige. One in particular – the descendants of Cerball mac Dúnlainge, otherwise the Mac Gilla Pátraics – had provided the kings of Osraige for over two hundred years. In the course of the twelfth century, however, the kingdom fragmented as new dynasties emerged and challenged for power. Old allegiances dissolved and family bonds broke down when confronted by new and mightier forces. Osraige was not alone in its fate. The kingdom of Mide also fell apart in the course of the twelfth century. In large measure, this can be attributed to the rise of powerful neighbours, Uí Briain and Uí Conchobair in the case of Mide, and Toirdelbach Ua Conchobair (d. 1156) and the Mac Murchadas of Uí Chennselaig in the case of Osraige. It is not fully clear why the Mac Murchadas became so over-mighty in the twelfth century but one factor is the wealth generated by the Hiberno-Scandinavian port towns. By 1050, if not before, it no longer mattered if an aspirant high-king controlled Tara for he now had to control Dublin. The tax revenue from a town could bankroll a campaign, reward supporters, win favour with the clergy by the foundation of an abbey, or impress the populace with the construction of a new stone church or fortress. The revenue derived by the Mac Murchadas from the town of Wexford alone was perhaps sufficient to make them serious contenders for the kingship of Leinster, but at times they also extended their power into Dublin and Waterford.

By contrast, the resources of Osraige in the twelfth century were exactly what they had been one hundred years before. The wealth of the Uí Chennselaig kings expanded while that of their Osraige counterparts stagnated. In the first sixty years of the twelfth century, Osraige was partitioned on at least five occasions, its kings were regularly assassinated or deposed – those who survived were occasionally reinstated with humiliatingly diminished power – new families, who were allies of the Mac Murchadas, were intruded into the kingship, and for a period of two or three years, a member of the Mac Murchada family actually ruled as a king in Osraige. However, the Mac Murchadas were not the only threat. To the north the Loígis, to the south the Déisí and men of Waterford, to the east the Uí Bairrche, and to the west the Uí Briain were all long-time rivals. The rapid turnover of kings in Osraige also created instability. Between 1103 and 1169 there were eighteen different kings. One of these ruled for twenty years, meaning that the other seventeen had very short reigns, although sometimes up to three kings might rule simultaneously. Of the six kings whose death circumstances are recorded, three were assassinated, two died in battle and one died as the result of an accident. In the twelfth century, the problem for an Osraige dynast was not to challenge for the kingship of Leinster, as his ancestors had done, it was simply to survive.

Carrigan attributed the collapse of Osraige to the power vacuum that occurred after the Battle of Mag Coba in 1103, but Donnchadh Ó Corráin has pointed out that there are indications of decline already in the eleventh century.[21] At Mag Coba, which was fought near Dromore, Co. Down, the king of Osraige, Gilla Pátraic Ruaid, was killed and the 'royal family' (*rigraidh*) was wiped out.[22] Cerball mac Domnaill mac Gilla Pátraic succeeded. Dynastically, he had all of the right connections. One of his brothers, Donnchad (d. 1090), had been king of Osraige while another, Muirchertach (d. 1095), had been heir presumptive to Gilla Pátraic Ruaid. Cerball was probably meant to be nothing more than a stopgap but it quickly became apparent that he was ineffectual. Within a year the kingdom dissolved and he had to accept other kings in the form of his nephew, Domnall mac Donnchada ua Gilla Pátraic, and a distant relation, Finn Ua Cáellaide (O'Kealy).[23] The term *leth-rí*, 'half king', was used to describe these rulers, but it should not be confused with the concept of 'joint-kingship' or power sharing. In fact, *leth-rí* meant exactly the opposite and, as Marie Therese Flanagan has pointed out, it would be better translated as 'part king', 'anti-king' or 'rival king'.[24]

Of the three kings, Finn Ua Cáellaide (O'Kealy) is the most interesting, if only because he was the first of a new ruling dynasty. He was a member of a family closely associated with the Mac Murchadas that is first documented in 1041 when Muirchertach mac Gilla Pátraic, lord of half-Osraige (*tigerna leithe Ossraighe*) was killed treacherously by Ua Cáellaide, who is described as 'one of his own people (*muinter*)'.[25] According to the fourteenth-century topographical poems of Ó Dubhganáin and Ó hUidhrín, the Uí Cáellaide were the lords of Uí Berchon.[26] This was an extensive area of south-east modern Co. Kilkenny beginning just south of Graiguenamanagh, incorporating the triangle of land between the Barrow and the Nore (including the Rower, Clonamery and Inistioge), and then running southwards along the west side of the River Barrow from Rosbercon through Glenmore and Slieverue, to the River Suir opposite the Hiberno-Scandinavian town of Waterford.[27] Unfortunately, the old Uí Berchon genealogies fade out in the ninth century and the Uí Cáellaide of the eleventh

21 Carrigan, *Ossory*, i, intr., p. 52; Donnchadh Ó Corráin, 'The education of Diarmait Mac Murchada', *Ériu*, 28 (1977), pp 71–81 at p. 77. 22 *AU*; *ALC* '*rigraidh*'; *AI*, *ATig.* and *CS* also give the title '*rí*' without mentioning the supporters, while *AFM* uses the words *tigerna*, 'lord', and *maithaib*, 'nobles'. 23 The following is based on a reading of the king-list in the Book of Leinster supplemented by the annals: see *Bk Leinster*, i, p. 190. 24 M.T. Flanagan, 'Strategies of lordship in pre-Norman and post-Norman Leinster', *Anglo-Norman Studies*, 20 (1998), pp 107–26 at p. 121. 25 *AFM*. The entry is repeated under 1036, but since Donnchad mac Gilla Pátraic was sole king of Osraige at that time, the date of 1041, which is the date given in *ALC*, *ATig.* and *AU*, is preferable. 26 *The topographical poems of John O'Dubhagain and Gilla na Naomh O'Huidhrin*, ed. John O'Donovan (Dublin, 1862), p. 97; *Topographical poems by Seán Mór Ó Dubhagáin and Giolla-na-naomh Ó hUidhrín*, ed. James Carney (Dublin, 1943), p. 44, lines 1165–8; *Leabhar mór na ngenealach*, iii, p. 291, 950.19. 27 Carrigan, *Ossory*, i, intr., pp 19–20; MacCotter, *Medieval Ire.*, p. 183.

and twelfth centuries cannot be connected with them. However, the annalistic entry of 1041 suggests that they were related to the Mac Gilla Pátraics and were part of the Osraige, so it seems reasonable to infer that they were descended from the Uí Berchon.

The Uí Cáellaide also had a separate block of land in northern Osraige, part of the territory known as na Clandaibh, which, as the 'half cantred of Aghaboe', was granted in 1172 or shortly thereafter to Adam de Hereford as 'Ochelli Deremod [Diarmait Ua Cáellaide] held it'.[28] The family had a further lordship in Uí Buide (in modern Co. Laois), outside the boundary of Osraige.[29] The connection with the Mac Murchadas is first evidenced in 1103, when a member of the Uí Cáellaide blinded the last major rival to Mac Murchada control of the kingship of Leinster. About a decade later, as a reward and, doubtless, as a reflection of the closeness of the bond between the two families, the young Diarmait Mac Murchada was fostered among the Uí Cáellaide.[30] Diarmait remained a loyal friend of the Uí Cáellaide and imposed two of them as *leth-rí* of Osraige, his foster-brother Murchad (*c.*1152–*c.*1160) and Diarmait Ua Cháellaide (*c.*1170–2), who may have been the latter's son.[31] The connection between Mac Murchada and Ua Cáellaide was perceived to be so close that in 1167 Ruaidhrí Ua Conchobair took a son of Murchad Ua Cáellaide as a hostage for Mac Murchada's good behaviour. The son, whose name is not preserved, was executed three years later. Diarmait Mac Murchada also promoted the ecclesiastical career of two members of the Uí Cáellaide, Áed, referred to by Mac Murchada as 'his spiritual father and confessor', who became bishop of Louth (Clogher, 1138–78, d. 24 August 1182), and Dúngal, who became bishop of Leighlin (*c.*1152–81).[32] Further evidence of the close relationship with Uí Cáellaide was Mac Murchada's foundation of a nunnery at Kilculliheen, opposite the Hiberno-Scandinavian town of Waterford, within Uí Berchon.[33]

When Cerball mac Domnaill mac Gilla Pátraic died in 1105, he was described as king of southern (*desceart*) Osraige, implying that his nephew ruled northern Osraige while Ua Cáellaide controlled a disconnected strip along the east of the kingdom from the River Suir to Aghaboe.[34] This threefold division reflects the

28 Carrigan, *Ossory*, ii, p. 40; *Ormond deeds, 1171–1350*, p. 1, no. 1. 29 *Topographical poems*, ed. O'Donovan, pp 86–7; *Topographical poems*, ed. Carney, p. 39, lines 1025–8; *Leabhar mór na ngenealach*, iii, pp 282–3.949.10. 30 Ó Corráin, 'Education of Diarmait Mac Murchada', p. 78. 31 *Bk Leinster*, i, p. 190; *AFM*. 32 Flanagan, 'Strategies of lordship in pre-Norman and post-Norman Leinster', pp 121–2; eadem, 'Irish church reform in the twelfth century and Áed Ua Cáellaide, bishop of Louth: an Italian document' in Michael Richter and J.M. Picard (eds), *Ogma: essays in Celtic studies in honour of Próinséas Ní Chatháin* (Dublin, 2002), pp 94–104; eadem (ed.), *Irish royal charters: texts and contexts* (Oxford, 2006), p. 73. 33 Flanagan, *Irish royal charters*, p. 384. 34 *AI*. From the obit it is clear that Cerball was a brother of Donnchad (d. 1090) and Muirchertach, the *rídamna Osrige* who died of plague in 1095 (*AI*) and so he can be linked in to the main line of the genealogical chart given in *NHI*, ix, p. 135, while the date of his death should read 1105 rather than *c.*1113: ibid., p. 202. Our order of succession to Cerball differs from that in *NHI*, ix, pp 135, 202 and instead reads: Domnall

political fault lines that characterised Osraige throughout the twelfth century. Indeed, the understanding of these divisions is the key to comprehending the subsequent Anglo-Norman settlement of Osraige.

Politically, there was a new development in 1118 that was to become a regular occurrence. Toirdelbach Ua Conchobair (d. 1156), king of Connacht and claimant to the high-kingship, invaded, obtained the submission and hostages of Osraige, deposed the existing king and nominated a king of his own, Donnchad Bacach mac Gilla Pátraic Ruaid.[35] Donnchad proved his loyalty by campaigning with Toirdelbach in Munster the following year, but his reign was short.[36] In 1123, while Toirdelbach was distracted elsewhere, Donnchad was assassinated 'by his own immediate family' and the Mac Murchadas, who were probably behind the killing, imposed Murchad Mac Murchada as a *leth-rí*. Toirdelbach returned in 1125 and 1126, however, deposed the Mac Murchada candidate and put his support behind Gilla Pátraic mac Domnaill Mac Gilla Pátraic. He was clearly a good choice. He ruled for twenty years until 1146, when he too was assassinated in his residence (*tech*) 'in the middle of Kilkenny' by the sons of Congalach Ua Braenáin of Uí Duach.[37] Subsequent rulers were not able to withstand the concentrated power of the Uí Chennselaig kings of Leinster and during the 1150s King Diarmait Mac Murchada (r. *c*.1132–71) intervened in Osraige on at least five occasions. In 1151 he captured Cerball, the king of Osraige, 'through treachery and guile', deposed him and divided the kingdom between two of his nominees, Murchad Ua Cáellaide and Donnchad mac Gilla Pátraic Mac Gilla Pátraic, the son of the assassinated king.[38] When this arrangement did not work, he restored Cerball, but only as a *leth-rí* and ruling with the others. Subsequently Mac Murchada deposed Donnchad and imprisoned him, then changed his mind and restored him as *leth-rí*. Finally, he deposed Cerball (d. 1163) and permitted Donnchad (d. 1162) to rule alone.[39]

In 1166 there was a momentary respite when Tigernán Ua Ruairc, king of Bréifne (d. 1172), marched on the Uí Chennselaig capital of Ferns (Co. Wexford), destroyed its 'castle' and, with the blessing of the then high-king of Ireland, Ruaidhrí Ua Conchobair, deposed Diarmait Mac Murchada and sent him into exile.[40] To add insult to injury, Diarmait's ancestral kingdom of Uí Chennselaig was itself partitioned between two *leth-rí*, his brother Murchad and his enemy, Donnchad Mac Gilla Pátraic, king of Osraige.[41] The arrangement did not last for

Ruadh mac [Domnall] mac Gilla Pátraic (d. 1109: *AFM*, *ALC*, *AU*); Domnall mac Donnchada Mac Gilla Pátraic (d. 1113, killed by his first cousin Goll Gabhráin: *AI*, *AU*); Donnchad Balc Mac Gilla Pátraic (=Ua Gilla Pátraic, d. 1115: *AI*); Donnchad Dub (antecedents unknown, deposed *c*.1118); Donnchad Bacach mac Gilla Pátraic Ruaid (d. 1123: *AFM*, *AI*, *ALC*, *ATig.*, *AU*, *CS*). **35** *AFM*, *ALC*, *AU*; *Bk Leinster*, i, p. 190. **36** *AFM*, *ATig*. **37** *AFM*: '*ar lár Cille Caindigh*'; *ATig.*; *CS*; *Bk Leinster*, i, p. 190. **38** *AFM*; *Bk Leinster*, i, p. 190. **39** Ibid. **40** Donncha Ó Corráin, *Ireland before the Normans* (Dublin, 1972), pp 165–7; Orpen, *Normans*, i, pp 64–9. **41** *ATig.*, which does not specify Donnchad, but two years later, in 1168, he is named as the king of Osraige who blinded Diarmait Mac long, however. In August 1167 Diarmait returned and resumed his position as king of the ten cantreds of Uí Chennselaig.[42] As an indicator of his future good behaviour and the limitation of his ambitions, he gave Ruaidhrí Ua Conchobair seven hostages as security, one of whom was the ill-fated son of Murchad Ua Cáellaide, executed in 1170 when Diarmait, with Anglo-Norman support, reinstated himself as king of Leinster.

By the 1160s a pattern had been established. Although technically distinct, and still often referred to as 'Osraige and Leinster' as if they were separate, Osraige had in effect become a subordinate power within the ambit of the Uí Chennselaig kings of Leinster. These kings could impose their own nominees in the kingship of Osraige and partition it as they wished. There were three major political units, a northern kingdom based on Aghaboe, a southern kingdom with Kilkenny as its capital – both ruled by branches of the Mac Gilla Pátraics – and a disconnected eastern territory presided over by the Uí Cáellaide. No one could be a king in Osraige without external support and each king or *leth-rí* had to provide service, in the form of tribute, attendance and presence with supporters on their overlord's campaigns. The rulers of Osraige reigned only for as long as their over-kings consented; they had learned to accept diminished (and diminishing) territories, and they had adjusted to the constant presence of rivals, who might replace them at a whim. These developments ensured that rather than being an entity in its own right, Osraige would form part of Strongbow's (1171–6) and, later, William Marshal's (1189–1219) lordship of Leinster. They also meant that while the Anglo-Norman grants of fiefdoms might involve a new legal terminology, there was nothing new about them in practice. Indeed it could be argued that to an Osraige king in the 1170s an Anglo-Norman fief might look very attractive. It offered security, fixity of tenure and probable hereditary succession, while the terms of service were little more than what already existed, and, in the normal course of events, one did not have to surrender one's children as hostages.

II

The Anglo-Norman involvement with Kilkenny began in 1169. In May of that year three shiploads of mercenaries consisting of thirty knights, sixty mail-clad men and three hundred archers under the command of Robert fitz Stephen landed at Bannow Bay in Co. Wexford. They were joined by Diarmait Mac Murchada and five hundred of his supporters. Together they attacked the Hiberno-Scandinavian town of Wexford and compelled it to surrender. Mac Murchada already had a new order in mind because he immediately gave the town and its cantred to fitz Stephen and Maurice de Prendergast, while the

Murchada's son, Énna (*AFM*, *ATig.*). 42 *AFM*.

cantreds of Bargy and Shelburne were granted to Hervey de Montmorency.[43] Next he moved against Osraige, which he invaded with a large army of his Leinster men and Anglo-Norman allies, but they encountered stiff resistance.[44]

It is clear that a number (perhaps as many as two hundred) of Anglo-Normans stayed in Kilkenny for a time during the late summer or early autumn of 1169, when they defected from the service of Diarmait Mac Murchada, king of Leinster, to that of his rival Domnall Mac Gilla Pátraic, king of Osraige. Famously, according to 'The Song of Dermot and the Earl' (re-titled by its latest editor 'The Deeds of the Normans in Ireland'), they were lodged in the 'ostels' of Kilkenny.[45] It is equally clear, however, that this presence led to no permanent settlement because these Anglo-Normans later made their way to Waterford. The 'song' is specific that all of them left.[46]

Diarmait Mac Murchada with the support of his Anglo-Norman allies imposed Diarmait Ua Cáellaide as *leth-rí* in Osraige. The Leinster king died in 1171, however, and in the following year Domnall Mac Gilla Pátraic reasserted his authority by killing Diarmait Ua Cáellaide.[47] The grant of the Ua Cáellaide's lands to Adam de Hereford probably had the effect of stabilising Domnall Mac Gilla Pátraic's rule as king of Osraige.[48] The granting of Iverk (Overk) in *deisceart* (southern) Osraige to Milo fitz Bishop may have had a similar effect.[49]

The Kilkenny that the Anglo-Normans came to in 1169 would have included the church of Cainnech or St Canice (fig. 7.1), which was located on a low hill overlooking a major fording point on the River Nore, later marked by Green's Bridge. Nothing is known of the form of the early church.[50] The annals record the burning of Kilkenny in 1085, 1107 and 1114.[51] An examination of the modern street pattern suggests that by the twelfth century the church stood within a large enclosure with maximum dimensions of 300 by 225m, or roughly 6.5 hectares.[52] The curving alignment of Church Lane suggests that there may have been an inner enclosure and this is supported by the discovery of a ditch (which had been backfilled before the late ninth century) in the Deanery Orchard during excavations in 2006.[53] After 1111, when it was named at the Synod of Ráith Bressail as the episcopal seat of Ossory, it is likely that Kilkenny's elevation was expressed architecturally with a new suite of buildings, which would have

43 Giraldus, *Expugnatio*, pp 34–5. **44** Giraldus, *Expugnatio*, pp 34–9; *The Song of Dermot and the earl*, ed. G.H. Orpen (Oxford, 1892), pp 40–63, lines 520–823. **45** *Song of Dermot*, for the figure of 200, pp 80–1, line 1069; 'ostels', pp 100–1, line 1338; *Deeds of the Normans*, p. 87, line 1338; 'ostels' are also referred to at Ferns, Co. Wexford: *Song of Dermot*, pp 62–3, line 818; and beside a river: ibid., pp 72–3, line 956, which would suggest that some form of tent-like lodging is to be inferred. **46** Ibid., pp 100–3, lines 1356–73. **47** *AFM*. **48** *AFM*. **49** See Brooks, *Knights' fees*, p. 264; MacCotter, *Medieval Ire.*, pp 189, 183. **50** Bradley, *Kilkenny*, p. 1. **51** *AFM*, *A Tig.* **52** Bradley, *Kilkenny*, p. 1 and map 6; idem, 'Canice and Kilkenny' in John Bradley and Michael O'Dwyer (eds), *Kilkenny through the centuries: chapters in the history of an Irish city* (Kilkenny, 2009), pp 1–23 at p. 21. **53** Cóilín Ó Drisceoil, 'The Deanery Orchard, St Canice's Cathedral, Kilkenny', *Excavations 2006* (Dublin, 2009), no. 1062.

7.4 View of Kyteler's Inn, at site of St Ciaran's Chapel and Well, off St Kieran Street, Kilkenny (photograph: Cóilín Ó Drisceoil).

7.5 North view of Kilkenny Castle overlooking the River Nore. Extensively restored during the nineteenth century, incorporating the remains of William Marshal's early thirteenth-century masonry castle.

included the surviving round tower (fig. 7.1).[54] There were a number of churches in the vicinity beyond the outer enclosure, including St Brigid's to the north-west, near the junction of Granges Road and Lord Edward Street; St Maul's on the east side of Green's Bridge dedicated to Mella, the mother of Canice, which probably functioned as a nunnery, while further afield there was a chapel in proximity to Kyteler's Inn in St Kieran Street (fig. 7.4) dedicated to St Ciarán of Saighir (Seirkieran, Co. Offaly).[55]

The discovery of antler tines near the cathedral suggests the presence of craftspeople, comparable to the comb-makers that are known from contemporary Dublin, Kildare and Waterford.[56] The archaeological excavations at the junction of Irishtown and St Canice's Place revealed a layer of pre-Anglo-Norman debris 30cm thick, indicating that occupation extended southwards from the ecclesiastical enclosure.[57] Further afield to the south-east of the enclosure, excavations by Ben Murtagh at Kilkenny Castle (fig. 7.5) revealed evidence for bronze-working associated with a sod building pre-dating the initial Anglo-Norman earthwork fortress there.[58]

By the 1140s the Mac Gilla Pátraic kings of Osraige had a residence at Kilkenny in which they held court, and in which a deputy or seneschal acted during their absence.[59] When Gilla Pátraic mac Domnaill Mac Gilla Pátraic was assassinated in 1146, it was in his house 'in the middle of Kilkenny'.[60] The latter phrase would suggest that this house, which was the location of the court, was situated near the cathedral.[61] By 1169, then, Kilkenny consisted of a large

54 Bradley, *Discover Kilkenny* (Dublin, 2000), pp 106–7, 115–16; idem, 'Canice and Kilkenny', p. 21. 55 Ibid., pp 21–2; John Hogan, 'Notes on reputed holy wells of the city of Kilkenny, *Transactions of the Ossory Archaeological Society*, 3:1 (1883), pp 3–15 at pp 3–8. 56 *JRSAI*, 8 (1864–6), pp 411–12; Patrick Neary, 'Kilkenny main drainage: urban medieval', *Excavations 1997* (Bray, 1997), no. 291; Cóilín Ó Drisceoil, 'Archaeological test excavations in the Deanery Orchard, St Canice's Cathedral, Kilkenny', report 06E306 submitted to the National Monuments Service, Dublin (2006); idem, 'The Deanery Orchard, St Canice's Cathedral, Kilkenny', no. 1062. Dublin: A.B. Ó Ríordáin, 'Excavations at High Street and Winetavern Street, Dublin', *Medieval Archaeology*, 15 (1971), pp 73–85; Kildare: *FAI*, p. 167; Charles Doherty, 'The monastic town in early medieval Ireland' in H.B. Clarke and Anngret Simms (eds), *The comparative history of urban origins in non-Roman Europe: Ireland, Wales, Denmark, Germany, Poland and Russia* (BAR, Int. Ser. 255; Oxford, 1985), pp 45–75 at p. 67; Waterford: M.F. Hurley with Sarah McCutcheon and Margaret McCarthy, Section 17: i: 'Artefacts of skeletal material' in M.F. Hurley and O.M.B. Scully (eds), *Late Viking Age and medieval Waterford: excavations, 1986–1992* (Waterford, 1997), pp 650–99 at pp 659–62. Antler-working, and specifically comb-making, was an urban craft in the northern European world of the ninth to twelfth centuries and craftspeople were perceived as being a distinctive type of urban community: see Andrew Nicholson, 'The antler' in Peter Hill (ed.), *Whithorn and St Ninian: the excavation of a monastic town, 1984–91*(Stroud, 1997), pp 474–95 at p. 474. 57 Neary, 'Kilkenny main drainage', no. 291. 58 Ben Murtagh, 'Kilkenny Castle, Kilkenny', *Excavations 1992* (Bray, 1993), no. 115 at p. 39; Ben Murtagh, 'The Kilkenny Castle Archaeological Project, 1990–3: interim report', *OKR*, 45 (1993), pp 1101–17 at p. 1108 and fig. 4. 59 *Song of Dermot*, pp 95–105, esp. p. 101. 60 *AFM*; *BK Leinster*, i, p. 190. 61 Geophysical research has indicated the presence of a large hall-like structure south of the

ecclesiastical enclosure with some immediate settlement; this acted as the nucleus for a group of chapels, churches and manufacturing centres that were dotted along the ridges parallel to the River Nore. When the first Anglo-Normans arrived and were accommodated in its inns or 'ostels', Kilkenny was already the largest and most important inland settlement in the south-east of Ireland.[62]

Following the death of King Diarmait Mac Murchada, Osraige became part of Strongbow's lordship of Leinster (1171–6). During this period Strongbow made grants of outlying lands of this minor kingdom to some of his followers. These included the granting of Aghaboe in Upper Osraige to Adam de Hereford (1171x6) and Iverk (Overk) in the south to Milo fitz Bishop. Strongbow, while leaving Domnall Mac Gilla Pátraic in control of central Osraige, apparently built a castle at Kilkenny, which was destroyed in 1173 by Domnall Mór Ua Briain, king of northern Munster.[63] In a retaliatory raid against Ua Briain, Mac Gilla Pátraic guided the Anglo-Normans to Limerick, which resulted in its capture.[64] He was still in control of central Osraige following Strongbow's death in 1176, when he granted five carucates at Kilferagh to the south-east of Kilkenny to Christ Church Cathedral in Dublin with the consent of King Henry II.[65] Following Domnall's death in 1185, he was succeeded by Máel Seachlainn, his son or brother, who died in 1193x4.[66]

III

The lordship of Leinster, which included Osraige, was inherited by Strongbow's daughter, Isabel and, as she was a minor, her inheritance was held by the English crown until her marriage or majority.[67] In 1185, Henry II created his youngest son, John, lord of Ireland.[68] Subsequent to his marriage to Isabel in 1189, William Marshal was unable to gain seisin or possession of his Irish lands for some time, due to the opposition of John, his overlord in Ireland.[69] Furthermore, the English king's son made land grants in Osraige to his followers. One of these was Theobald Walter I, ancestor of the Butler family and future, earls, marquesses and dukes of Ormond.[70] During the episcopate of Bishop Felix Ua Duib Shláine (O'Dullany) of Ossory (*c*.1179–1202; fig. 7.3), Theobald took over

cathedral: see Cóilín Ó Drisceoil, 'Probing the past: a geophysical survey at St Canice's Cathedral', *OKR*, 56 (2004), pp 80–106. **62** Bradley, *Kilkenny*, p. 1; idem, 'Canice and Kilkenny', pp 22–3; *Song of Dermot*, pp 100–1, lines 1338–9. **63** *ATig.*; Giraldus, *Expugnatio*, p. 321n.222. **64** *AI*, 1176; Orpen, *Normans*, i, p. 348; *Song of Dermot*, pp 246–7, lines 3386–99. **65** *CAAR*, pp 24–5; *Crede Mihi: the most ancient register book of the archbishops of Dublin before the reformation*, ed. J.T. Gilbert (Dublin, 1897), p. 37. The grant was confirmed on 13 March 1190 by Pope Clement III (*CAAR*, p. 17). **66** *AFM*; *ALC*. **67** Orpen, *Normans*, ii, p. 5. **68** Orpen, *Normans*, i, pp 91–108. **69** Crouch, *William Marshal*, p. 70. **70** Bradley, *Discover Kilkenny*, pp 28–30, 71, 78.

church lands in eastern Osraige. These included Tullaherin, Kilfane, Ballynaboly (parish of Tullaherin) and others for which Theobald was excommunicated and fined.[71] In addition to Arklow in modern Co. Wicklow and Tullowphelim, Co. Carlow, John had granted to Theobald four knights' fees at Gowran (the land of Mactalewi) in eastern Osraige.[72] Theobald granted Clara to the east of Kilkenny to Jordan de Losche with fifteen carucates for the service of half a knight *c.*1190.[73] A knight's fee was given at Inistioge (Inistioche) with John's assent 'to the staff of Jesus' at Christ Church Cathedral, Dublin.[74] Theobald is referred to as 'pincerna' (butler) in a charter (15 May 1192) of John to the city of Dublin, when he was in England with the lord of Ireland.[75] A settlement was reached whereby on the insistence of King Richard I, of those granted lands by John, only Theobald was allowed to keep his, which he was to hold from William Marshal as he finally got seisin of his Irish lands.[76] Subsequent to Theobald's death (1205), a dispute arose over possession of his lands in April 1206 between the Marshal's bailiffs and those of King John's justiciar, Meiler fitz Henry.[77] This was resolved on 25 May when Theobald's land was delivered up to the earl.[78]

A castle is reputed to have been built at Kilkenny in 1192. The source for this information is James Ware (1594–1666) and it derives from an unfinished collection of annals of Ireland, covering the years between 1169 and 1485, which would have covered the period from the coming of the Anglo-Normans down to the commencement of his history of Ireland from the reign of Henry VII to Mary I.[79] These annals were issued after his death in an edition and translation prepared by his son, Robert.[80] Only the years between 1169 and 1202 were completed by Ware and Robert filled out the gap by using the chronicles of Hanmer and Marleburrough that his father had published in 1633. There is a noticeable decline in the quality of the entries after 1202, without, for instance, a single mention of William Marshal during the next two decades whereas Ware himself had noted the Marshal's visit to Ireland in 1200 and the foundation of Tintern Minor or *de Voto* in Co. Wexford (fig. 7.6). The 'Dublin Annals of Inisfallen' (TCD H.I.7) have been cited as the source for the 1192 date by Carrigan, G.H. Orpen and others, but these are in fact pseudo-annals.[81] The Dublin manuscript has nothing to do with the genuine Annals of Inisfallen, but is instead a hotchpotch of information from Giraldus, Camden, Hanmer and others, including a few genuine Irish annalistic entries, compiled in France in 1765 for John O'Brien, the Catholic bishop of Cloyne.[82] The 1192 date occurs in

71 *Ormond deeds, 1172–1350*, no. 23. **72** Brooks, *Knights' fees*, pp 79–80. **73** *Ormond deeds, 1172–1350*, no. 10. **74** '*Liber Niger*', p. 56; *CAAR*, p. 24; Carrigan, *Ossory*, iv, p. 103; *Crede Mihi*, p. 37. **75** '*Liber Niger*', pp 63–4, no. 117 (2). **76** Crouch, *William Marshal*, p. 70. **77** *CDI, 1171–1251*, nos 288, 292. **78** *CDI, 1171–1251*, no. 296. **79** *Rerum Hibernicarum Annales*, 1664. **80** [James Ware], *The annals of the affairs of Ireland from the first conquest by the English in the reign of King Henry II unto the end of the reign of Queen Elizabeth*, part 4 of *The antiquities and history of Ireland by the right honourable Sir James Ware, knight* [ed. Robert Ware] (Dublin, 1705). **81** Carrigan, *Ossory*, i, intr., p. 70; Orpen, *Normans*, ii, p. 225. **82** T.K. Abbott and E.J. Gwynn, *Catalogue of the Irish manuscripts in the library of Trinity*

7.6 North-west view of the former Cistercian abbey of Tintern *Parva* (Minor) or *de Voto*, Co. Wexford, founded by William Marshal *c.*1200 (photograph: Ben Murtagh).

these 'annals' simply because the compiler lifted it from the 1705 edition of Ware. The entry in Ware under 1192 states that in 'Leinster the castle of Kilkenny was built and another at Kilfeacle in Munster'.[83] That the annals (1169–1202) can be accepted as an authentic work of James Ware is reasonably certain. His son, Robert, stated that the manuscript was in the library of the late Dr John Madden and had come to him through Dr John Stearne. Presumably Ware had loaned it to Madden. *AFM* (1192) mentions that the English (of Leinster) erected the castles of Kilfeakle and Knockgraffon, while other annals merely refer to the building of many castles in Munster by the foreigners as they suffered a great defeat by Domnall Mór Ua Briain (d. 1194), king of Tuadmumu or northern Munster, in a battle at Thurles.[84]

As part of the Anglo-Norman lordship of Leinster, the Mac Gilla Pátraics had been left in relative control of their heartland in central Osraige since 1171 and the destruction of Kilkenny Castle in 1173, apart from some lands at the periphery that were granted by Prince John to his followers. It is apparent that this situation changed around 1192 as William Marshal finally got seisin of his Irish lands from John, who was then count of Mortain and lord of Ireland. This involved the Marshal apparently moving to expel the Mac Gilla Pátraics from their heartland and settling it with his followers, with Kilkenny at its centre.[85]

College Dublin (Dublin, 1921), p. 16. **83** Ware, *Annals*, p. 33. **84** *AI*; *MIA*. **85** See C.A. Empey, 'County Kilkenny in the Anglo-Norman period' in William Nolan and Kevin Whelan (eds), *Kilkenny: history and society* (Dublin, 1990), pp 75–95 at p. 77; Orpen, 'Castles in

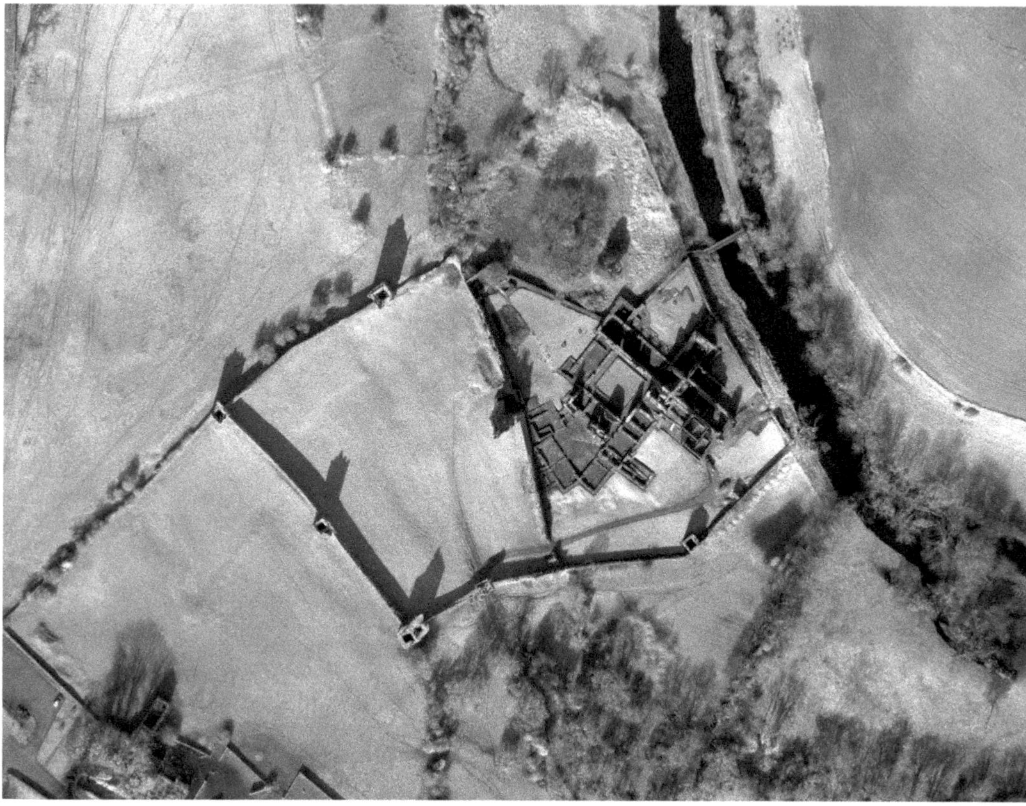

7.7 Aerial orthophoto of the ruins of the former Augustinian Kells Priory, Co. Kilkenny, founded in the 1190s by Geoffrey fitz Robert (courtesy of Simon Dowling).

These included those who became witnesses to the Marshal's charter to Kilkenny in 1207, such as the knight Geoffrey fitz Robert,[86] who quickly established himself at Kells, about 12km to the south of Kilkenny, where he built a castle and founded the nearby Augustinian priory (fig. 7.7).[87] It is possible that cantreds in central Osraige that were parcelled out by the Marshal to some of his household knights who were later also witnesses to the 1207 charter like Kells, Earley to John de Earley[88] and Ogenty to Thomas fitz Anthony[89] were demesne lands of

Ossory', pp 315–16, 333–4. **86** See sect. V, no. 6, below. **87** T.B. Barry, E. Culleton and C.A. Empey, 'Kells motte, County Kilkenny', *PRIA*, 35C (1984), pp 157–70 at p. 161; C.A. Empey, 'The sacred and secular: the Augustinian priory of Kells in Ossory, 1193–1541', *IHS*, 24 (1984), pp 131–51 at pp 139–40; idem, 'Section 1: The Augustinian priory of Kells: an historical introduction' in Miriam Clyne, *Kells Priory, Co. Kilkenny: archaeological excavations by T. Fanning and M. Clyne* (Dublin, 2007), pp 1–11 at pp 1–5; Orpen, 'Castles in Ossory', pp 325–8. See also sect. V, no. 6, below. **88** See sect. V, no. 3, below. **89** See sect. V, no. 9, below.

the Mac Gilla Pátraics. Their expulsion from their heartland involved transplanting them to Upper Osraige.[90]

The reference in Ware's annals to the building of a castle at Kilkenny in 1192 would have coincided with the establishment of a seigniorial centre there by William Marshal in conjunction with the commencement of the settlement of his followers in the surrounding heartland of the Mac Gilla Pátraics. This may have involved the building or rebuilding of the large earthwork castle found beneath the present masonry one by Murtagh during the 1990s.[91] At some time between *c.*1192 and 1202, William Marshal founded the first Augustinian house 'at the eastern end of the bridge of Kilkenny' and Bishop Felix Ua Duib Shláine (fig. 7.3) granted to Brother Osbert, prior of the hospital of St John, and the other brothers there, 'all the tithes of the provisions of the castle of Kilkenny'.[92] The Marshal did not go to Ireland during the 1190s to claim his fief, as he was largely engaged in matters of state in England and France.[93] Little is known of the process of subinfeudation in central Osraige during this period. In 1199, with the ascension of Prince John to the English throne and the elevation of William Marshal as earl of Pembroke, the latter appointed Geoffrey fitz Robert as seneschal of his lordship of Leinster to reorganise his estates there.[94]

The initial attraction that brought the Anglo-Normans to Kilkenny was the presence of a settlement that was a focus for both land and riverine routes. The pre-existing settlement, which became known as Irishtown, was under the authority of the bishop. So in order to avoid invoking the wrath of the church, as happened at Roscrea and Trim, the Marshal established a new town (known as Hightown) downriver and adjoining the castle on another knoll to the south of Irishtown, for which the new parish of St Mary was created.[95] It is clear from the Marshal's charter of 1207 that fitz Robert had previously given the burgesses of the new town privileges and had fixed their annual rent at twelve pence, payable half yearly (Appendix, item 23). St Mary's (fig. 7.8, pl. 22), as the parish church of the new Hightown, probably began as a chapel for those living near the

90 See n. 85 above and Carrigan, *Ossory*, i, intr., pp 70–1; Timothy O'Neill, 'Aghaboe, *c.*600–1800', *OLL*, 1 (2004), pp 19–27 at pp 23–4. 91 See Ben Murtagh, 'Kilkenny Castle', *Excavations 1991* (Bray, 1992), pp 29–30, no. 81 at p. 29; idem, 'Kilkenny Castle', *Excavations 1992*, pp 39–40; idem, 'Kilkenny Castle Archaeological Project', pp 1108–10; idem, 'Kilkenny Castle, the Parade, Kilkenny', *Excavations 1997* (Bray, 1998), no. 304, pp 102–4 at p. 103; idem, 'Kilkenny Castle, the Parade, Kilkenny', *Excavations 1999*, no. 449, pp 146–7; Orpen, 'Castles in Ossory', p. 316. 92 John Bradley, 'The priors of St John's Kilkenny (OSA) before the Reformation', *OKR*, 57 (2005), pp 62–72 at pp 62, 64; idem, 'The precinct of St John's Priory, Kilkenny, at the close of the Middle Ages', *Peritia*, 22–3 (2011–12), pp 317–45 at p. 318. 93 See Crouch, *William Marshal*, pp 77–86; Orpen, *Normans*, ii, pp 203–5. 94 John Bradley, 'Anglo-Norman Kilkenny' in John Bradley and Michael O'Dwyer (eds), *Kilkenny through the centuries: chapters in the history of an Irish city* (Kilkenny, 2009), pp 24–45 at p. 24. 95 Ibid., pp 25–6; idem, 'The early development of the medieval town of Kilkenny' in Nolan and Whelan, *Kilkenny: history and society*, pp 63–73 at pp 66–7; idem, *Kilkenny*, p. 2. 96 Ibid.; idem, 'Anglo-Norman Kilkenny', p. 31.

7.8 View of the remains of medieval St Mary's parish church, Kilkenny (photograph: Kilkenny County Council).

7.9 View of the church of the former Cistercian Duiske Abbey, Graiguenamanagh, Co. Kilkenny, founded *c.*1204 by William Marshal (photograph: Ben Murtagh).

castle.[96] By 1205 the church was sufficiently well established for the bishop of Ossory to convene an ecclesiastical court there.[97]

As noted above, William Marshal apparently briefly visited his Irish lordship in 1200, in the company of Countess Isabel, which resulted in new grants, including the foundation of the two Cistercian abbeys of Duiske or Graiguenamanagh (fig. 7.9, pl. 1) on the River Barrow and Tintern *de Voto* in Co. Wexford (fig. 7.6, pl. 2).[98] Another example of one of the grants at that time relates to an agreement between the earl and William, bishop of Glendalough (1192–1212), whereby the former gave three carucates in the fees at Castledermot, Moone and Kilcullen in modern Co. Kildare.[99] The bishop agreed to return (*reddet*) betaghs (*nativi*) and fugitives that pertained to his land (*illam terram*) according to the charter, which he already had of the Marshal since the first year of the earl's coming to Ireland (*Anno primus adventus ejusdem comitis de Hibernia*). Evidently the earl entered an agreement in 1200 and confirmed it *c.*1207, around the time of his second visit to his Irish lordship.[100] Although there is no record of the Marshal's itinerary during his first visit to Ireland, it is likely that he based himself at Kilkenny and in particular in what became his chief castle in Ireland (fig. 7.5). He would have had the opportunity to view his new town and to plan its future development with his seneschal, fitz Robert.

IV

The Marshal received permission from King John to travel to Ireland for his second visit on 19 February 1207, along with his knights, Henry Hose and John of Erlegh (de Earley).[101] The *Histoire de Guillaume le Maréchal*, which is an account of the earl's life compiled soon after his death in 1219, states that he set forth on his journey during Lent,[102] which began on 7 March, so it is likely that he arrived in Ireland in mid- to late March or perhaps early April.[103] The king apparently had a change of heart about allowing the earl to go to Ireland, but he went anyway, further incurring royal displeasure.[104] Since the loss of the duchy of Normandy to the French in 1204 and the Marshal's subsequent dealings to save his lands there with the victorious King Philip Augustus of France (r. 1180–1223), John's favour for the earl had noticeably ebbed.[105] Although there were

97 Ibid.; *Ormond deeds, 1172–1350*, no. 23. **98** Crouch, *William Marshal*, pp 87–8; Orpen, *Normans*, ii, pp 206–7. **99** *Crede Mihi*, p. 71; '*Liber Niger*', p. 46, no. 23. **100** Crouch, *William Marshal*, p. 103 would seem to date the reference to the Marshal's first visit to Ireland in the charter to 1207, rather than 1200, but it is unlikely that the earl's Irish clients would have made such a mistake. **101** *CDI, 1171–1251*, no. 313. **102** *HWM*, ii, p. 169, line 13350. **103** Easter Sunday fell on 22 April 1207. Crouch, *William Marshal*, p. 103 suggested that the earl's arrival took place in February or early March 1207. This overlooks the fact that the Marshal was still in Wales at the beginning of Lent, but Crouch corrects this in his note to line 13350 in *HWM*, iii, p. 151. **104** See Crouch, *William Marshal*, pp 101–2; *HWM*, ii, pp 169–73, lines 13355–423. **105** See Crouch, *William Marshal*, pp 93–9; W.L. Warren, *King John* those who welcomed the arrival of the lord of Leinster, there were others who did not. Chief among these was the king's justiciar (1199–1208), Meiler fitz Henry, who had arrived with the first wave of Anglo-Normans back in 1169 and who held Uí Fáelain (Offaly) from the lordship, which he disputed.[106] In the ensuing dispute, the Marshal incurred the wrath of his overlord and king, who backed his justiciar by recalling the earl forthwith to England.[107]

The Marshal left Ireland at the end of September to present himself before King John,[108] after spending about six months in the country during his second visit, which would have given him time to travel around Leinster and in particular to put in train his plans for the development and expansion of Kilkenny, which he chose as the chief centre of his Irish lordship. It is to the earl and his son William that the early greatness of the place is mainly due, as the rapid development of Osraige, or what became Co. Kilkenny, completely outstripped the other divisions of Leinster, progressive as they too were.[109] One example of the Marshal putting in train his plans for the development and expansion of his new town of Kilkenny that would appear to date to this time is the agreement that he made with the bishop of Ossory. This was Englishman Hugh le Rous (d. 1218), who had succeeded Felix Ua Duib Shláine (fig. 7.3) in 1202 and who became a close associate of the earl and a witness to his charter to the Hightown.[110] The agreement involved the acquisition of the episcopal land located between the old and new towns, which enabled the earl 'to enlarge his vill'.[111] The new town quickly expanded beyond its early boundaries, not just towards the north, but also to the south and east across the River Nore during the early thirteenth century.[112] Another development that would seem to have resulted from the earl's second visit to Kilkenny was the decision to commence the rebuilding of his castle there with stone (fig. 7.5), which was a major undertaking to strengthen its defences in its roles as an aristocratic residence, a major administrative and manorial centre, and seat of the seneschal's court and prison.[113]

The other logical step and a necessity for the Marshal would have been to support the rapidly growing and expanding chief town of his lordship by granting it a new charter,[114] particularly in the face of an ever-threatening environment from disloyal vassals like fitz Henry and a hostile king. The earl's

(new ed., New Haven and London, 1997), pp 113–15, 184–5. **106** Crouch, *William Marshal*, pp 102–3; *HMW*, ii, p. 173, lines 13427–34; ibid., iii, p. 152, line 13430; Orpen, *Norman*, ii, pp 209–10. **107** Crouch, *William Marshal*, pp 104–5; *HMW*, ii, p. 173, line 3437; ibid., iii, p. 152, line 13443; Orpen, *Normans*, ii, p. 210. **108** *HWM*, ii, p. 179, line 13553. **109** Orpen, *Normans*, ii, p. 222. **110** See sect. V, no. 1, below. **111** H.F. Berry, 'Ancient charters in the *Liber Albus Ossoriensis*', *PRIA*, 26C (1908), pp 115–25 at p. 124; Bradley, 'Anglo-Norman Kilkenny', p. 26; Carrigan, *Ossory*, i, p. 31. **112** Bradley, 'Anglo-Norman Kilkenny', pp 33–4; idem, 'The precinct of St John's Priory', p. 318; Ben Murtagh and Christiaan Corlett, 'St Patrick's Gate, Kilkenny', *JRSAI*, 137 (2007), p. 77. **113** Bradley, *Discover Kilkenny*, p. 70; idem, 'Anglo-Norman Kilkenny', p. 29; Murtagh and Corlett, 'St Patrick's, Kilkenny', p. 79; Orpen, 'Castles in Ossory', p. 316. **114** Bradley, 'The precinct of charter to the burgesses of Kilkenny must date to the time that he spent in Ireland during 1207 because virtually all of the witnesses, as will be seen below, were members of his household or *mesnie* and are known to have been present at Kilkenny in that year; furthermore, the grant was made 'with the council and advice and consent' of his wife, Countess Isabel, because it was by virtue of his marriage to her that he held the lordship of Leinster at that time.[115] In March 1208, however, prior to his return to Ireland, the earl was formally recognised by King John as lord of Leinster in his own right.[116]

The charter is also of interest because of the light that it sheds both on the constitution of the new town and on how it had developed during the preceding years. The document is not a foundation charter (see Appendix). Instead, it formalised the privileges of an existing settlement in which certain operational structures were taken for granted. The main concern was to establish that the earl's town and its inhabitants were entitled to special treatment in the eyes of the law (item 1). The concessions were designed primarily to protect the burgesses from arbitrary aristocratic or judicial pressure, but they also provided tax breaks and benefits in kind, while fixing a permanent rent (item 23). In addition, they permitted the burgesses to establish their own weekly court (item 6), known as 'the hundred', and to set the level of its fines (item 5); the burgesses, their sons, daughters and widows were entitled to contract marriages without the permission of their lord, unless they held land from him in chief (item 13); they could dispose of their burgages and personal possessions freely, except to members of religious orders (items 15–16); and while the number of burgesses was evidently limited, they were empowered to increase the privileged population by creating free tenants (item 19). It stipulated that their properties were to be twenty feet (6.1m) in width. The town's economic interests were also looked after. The burgesses were entitled to form a merchant guild to regulate their business (item 4); they could seize the goods of persistent debtors (item 9) and the trading licence of external merchants (specifically bakers and vintners) was limited to forty days (item 10).[117]

The charter permitted the burgesses to draw timber from the earl's woods outside the town (item 17) and it is likely that this provided the main building material for their housing. The same item states that the woods were located outside of his 'defensive enclosure', suggesting that his town was enclosed by defences by that time.[118] The Marshal also granted (item 22) the burgesses the right to grind corn in his mills for a reasonable toll, indicating that there was

St John's Priory', p. 318. **115** See first paragraph of the charter in the Appendix; also Bradley, 'Anglo-Norman Kilkenny', p. 24n.4; *HWM*, ii, p. 179, line 13544. **116** Crouch, *William Marshal*, p. 112; Orpen, *Normans*, ii, pp 216–17; Sidney Painter, *William Marshal: knight-errant, baron and regent of England* (new ed., Toronto, 1982), pp 159–60; see also sect. VI below. **117** Bradley, 'Anglo-Norman Kilkenny', pp 24–5, 28. **118** John Bradley, 'The town wall of Kilkenny revisited; a review article', *OKR*, 58 (2006), pp 185–97 at p. 187; idem, 'Anglo-Norman Kilkenny', p. 31; Murtagh and Corlett, 'St Patrick's, Kilkenny', pp 77–8.

more than one in or around the town. A century later, in the extent carried out after the death of Countess Joan de Clare, widow of Gilbert de Clare, late earl of Gloucester and Hereford (d. 1295), lord of Kilkenny and great grandson of William Marshal, she possessed '6 mills in bad condition', four of which can be confidently identified.[119]

Although it may seem that the charter provides little information on the administrative structure of the town, this was apparently viewed as an advantage and was clearly successful as a regulatory instrument because as late as 1366 an almost identical series of concessions was granted to Carrick-on-Suir, Co. Tipperary.[120] The lack of detailed regulations enabled the townspeople of Hightown in Kilkenny to develop the structure best suited to their needs and this process is exemplified in their 1231 decision to elect a principal officer, *le Sofreyn*, and four provosts annually who, lest the lord of the town might feel challenged by such developments, 'were to be profitable to the lord and commonalty'.[121]

Before he set off for England to face King John at the end of September 1207, the Marshal assembled his barons and knights in Kilkenny, presumably in his castle there (fig. 7.5). Eight of these are named in the *Histoire*, together with Mallard his standard bearer or 'banner carrier'.[122] Six were witnesses to the earl's new charter to the Hightown, supporting its dating to that time. These included John of Earley, Jordan de Sauqueville, Reinfrid (Ralph) fitz Payn, Geoffrey fitz Robert, Walter de Purcell and Thomas fitz Anthony.[123] Some of these like Geoffrey fitz Robert had been settled in Osraige for quite some years. In 1204, fitz Robert had been replaced as seneschal by the earl with his nephew, John Marshal,[124] another witness to the charter, together with a key Marshal ally, Bishop Hugh le Rous.[125]

The Marshal, fully aware of his precarious and insecure position, according to the *Histoire* informed his knights that of those he had brought over from England, only Henry Hose would be returning with him and that the rest were being left behind with his other household knights and barons as he announced in the presence of the pregnant countess, so as to protect their 'lady by birth', as 'I have no claim to anything here save through her'.[126] This alleged statement of recognition by the earl to his men of the debt of gratitude that he owed to Isabel for his position and status as a great lord in Ireland is replicated in the first paragraph of the charter (see Appendix). It differs from his status six months later following the defeat in his absence of his enemies in Leinster.[127] In the

119 Bradley, 'Anglo-Norman Kilkenny', p. 38; idem, Kilkenny, p. 4; *CDI*, *1302–7*, no. 653. **120** Bradley, 'Anglo-Norman Kilkenny', p. 25 and n. 6; Mac Niocaill, *Na buirgéisí*, pp 121–4. **121** Bradley, 'Anglo-Norman Kilkenny', p. 25; idem, *Kilkenny*, p. 2; *Liber Primus Kilkenniensis: the earliest of the books of the corporation of Kilkenny now extant*, ed. Charles McNeill (Dublin, 1931), p. 1. **122** *HWM*, ii, pp 174–7, lines 13464, 13473, 13490–1, 13496, 13502, 13505, 13507, 13510–13. **123** See sect. V, nos 3–6, 9 and 11, below. **124** See sect. V, no. 2, below. **125** See sect. V, no. 1, below. **126** *HWM*, ii, pp 176–9, esp. lines 13496–502, 13528–44. **127** See sect.

meantime, in addition to organising a plan with his men and allies to defend the lordship and the countess at Kilkenny Castle during his absence, if he had not done so already, the earl must have taken the opportunity to gather the group to witness his charter.

V

The witnesses

The charter was witnessed by a high-profile group of fourteen individuals. It is headed by Hugh le Rous, bishop of Ossory; seven of the witnesses were the Marshal's household knights – John Marshal, John de Earley, Jordan de Sauqueville, Ralph fitz Payn, Geoffrey fitz Robert, Thomas fitz Anthony and Walter de Purcell; the remaining six were his vassals – Gilbert de Vale, Milo fitz Bishop, Robert Smyth, Odo Archdeacon, Thomas de Druhull and Richard Fannyn.[128] Almost all (the exceptions were John Marshal, Jordan de Sauqueville (possibly) and Ralph fitz Payn) held, or were about to hold, estates granted by him in Osraige or what became medieval Co. Kilkenny.

1 – **Hugh le Rous**, bishop of Ossory (1202–18), was one of the four Augustinian canons of Bodmin, in Cornwall, introduced to Kells Priory in Osraige (fig. 7.7) by Geoffrey fitz Robert (no. 6 below).[129] The date is usually given as *c.*1193 but it may have been slightly later. This is because, on 30 March 1194, Henry Marshal, William's youngest brother, was installed as bishop of Exeter and the bishops of Exeter were the founders and patrons of the Augustinian house at Bodmin in Cornwall.[130] The family connection would explain why canons from an otherwise obscure house should turn up on Marshal lands in Osraige.[131] As

VI below. **128** Hugh le Rous, John of Earley, Geoffrey fitz Robert, Thomas fitz Anthony and Walter de Purcell were also tenants. **129** 'Register of Kells' in *IMED*, pp 300–13 at p. 311; Carrigan, *Ossory*, iv, pp 56–7. Between the seventeenth and nineteenth century the name was written as 'de Rous' but this form does not survive in any contemporary document. The Latin translation was Ruffus. Orpen, *Normans*, ii, p. 227n.3, restored the Old French 'le Rous', which, unknown to him, is found in the 'Register of Kells', p. 311, although in what appears to be a sixteenth-century context. **130** Frank Barlow, 'Marshal, Henry (d. 1206)' in *ODNB*, www.oxforddnb.com/view/article/94379, accessed 18 May 2010; Karen Jankulak, *The medieval cult of St Petroc* (Woodbridge, 2000), pp 136–9. William de Warelwast, bishop of Exeter (1107–37), introduced Augustinian canons to Bodmin in the 1120s: ibid., p. 137. **131** Nonetheless, the connection may have been earlier. In 1192 (or perhaps a little earlier), Hugh *canonico* witnessed Geoffrey fitz Robert's confirmation of land grants in Fotharta to St Thomas's Abbey, Dublin: *RAST*, p. 112, no. 129. Given the clientalist and cliquish nature of witness lists, it is tempting to think that this was the future bishop. The date of the grant may be deduced from the fact that it was witnessed by William Piro before his elevation to the see of Glendalough in 1192, a point noted by M.T. Flanagan, 'Fitzgerald, Raymond fitz William' in *ODNB*, 19, pp 843–4. The bishopric of Exeter was vacant from 1 June 1191 and it is puzzling that it took so long to make an appointment when other sees were rapidly filled: see plain Hugh Ruffus he was among the group of witnesses in *c.*1195, together with John Cumin, archbishop of Dublin (1181–1212), of the grant by Baldwin Niger of the church of Kilcash in Co. Tipperary to the Hospital of St John the Baptist, Dublin.[132] He appears to have been the third prior of Kells, succeeding Reginald de Aclond and Algar, his fellow Bodmin monks, before *c.*1200 when, as prior, he attested a grant of property to the new foundation by Baldwin de Hamptonsford.[133]

It was probably during his term as prior that he met William Marshal on the latter's visit to Leinster in 1200, although in view of the connections with Henry Marshal and Geoffrey fitz Robert (no. 6 below), he may well have met the earl before leaving England in the 1190s. In any event the meeting of minds was so successful that le Rous effectively became, if he was not already, one of the Marshal's men in Leinster.[134] Indeed, it is likely that, while he still enjoyed rights over the sees of Leinster, the earl played the key role in elevating Hugh to the episcopacy as bishop of Ossory in 1202.[135] It was probably shortly after his investiture that he witnessed a number of grants to St Mary's Abbey, Dublin, one of which specifically states that it was made at Dublin in the presence of Meiler fitz Henry, justiciar of Ireland.[136] Late in 1203 or early in 1204 Bishop Hugh attended on the Marshal at his castle of Hamstead Marshall in Berkshire; he was in England again (or perhaps still) in June 1204, and also in April 1207, when he received letters of protection to travel to Ireland.[137] It is likely that on each of these visits he reported to the earl on developments within Leinster.

Between 1204 and 1207 le Rous was a key figure in facilitating the Marshal's establishment of the Cistercian abbey at Duiske (fig. 7.9). He donated property and advowsons to the new foundation, he confirmed, witnessed and approved grants of lands to it by others, he attested quitclaims to the abbey's potential

R.V. Turner, 'Richard Lionheart and English episcopal elections', *Albion*, 29 (1997), pp 1–13. It may be that Henry Marshal, out of favour in York, where he had been dean, was already operating behind the scenes during the interepiscopate. **132** *RSJB*, p. 294, no. 458. Comin's active years as archbishop were 1191–6; he was forced into exile for nine years in 1197: see Margaret Murphy, 'Cumin [Comyn], John (d. 1212)' in *ODNB*, www.oxforddnb.com/view/article/6043, accessed 18 May 2010. **133** 'Register of Kells', p. 302; the period of nine years as prior credited to Hugh le Rous in the list of priors is too long: ibid., p. 212. The list, however, is full of inaccuracies. Algar is listed by Carrigan, *Ossory*, iv, p. 61. **134** Crouch, *William Marshal*, pp 88n.39, 212. **135** William Marshal claimed to the pope that he held the right of patronage of the diocese of Ossory: see John Watt, *The church in medieval Ireland* (Dublin, 1972), p. 94. **136** *CSMA*, i, pp 29–30, no. 2 (which must date to between 1202 and October 1204, when Robert, bishop of Waterford, died); pp 146–8, nos 125–6 (where 'Maurice', justiciar of Ireland, is a mistake for 'Meiler': see ibid., ii, p. 7, which would suggest that the original deed was witnessed by 'M.'). **137** 1203–4: 'Register of Kells', pp 301–2; Crouch, *William Marshal*, pp 88, 152, first spotted the significance of this entry. We are grateful to Prof. Crouch for pointing out that Bishop Hugh's visit to Hamstead Marshall can be placed between 5 December 1203 and 24 March 1204 because the Marshal was in Normandy until 3 December, when he crossed with King John. June 1204: 'Duiske charters', 24; April 1207: *CDI*, *1171–1251*, no. 326.

estates, and he wrote to the abbot of Cîteaux and the general chapter of the Cistercian order informing them of progress.[138] He was no less zealous in the cause of Kells Priory (fig. 7.7), for which he obtained three carucates of land from the earl in 1203 (which it is tempting to interpret as payment for services rendered), he witnessed Geoffrey fitz Robert's foundation charter of *c.*1204–6, and, subsequently, confirmed and attested further grants.[139] The letters of protection issued to him in April 1207 suggest that he returned independently of the Marshal and probably arrived a week or two after the earl's party. Nonetheless, he quickly joined the Marshal's entourage and, to judge from the witness lists, he remained close to the earl's side. Bishop Hugh attested the foundation charter of Duiske Abbey in the summer of 1207 and it was in that year or shortly afterwards that he granted the Marshal the land between St Kieran's Well (in the vicinity of the present Kyteler's Inn; fig. 7.4) and the River Bregagh in Kilkenny 'in order to expand the town'.[140]

About this time, he also witnessed the earl's grant of lands in the fee of Wicklow to the cathedral of Glendalough.[141] Between 1207 and 1213 he granted the Marshal the see-lands of Aghaboe in upper Osraige in exchange for four carucates at Ballinaslee, near the episcopal manor of Durrow, and four carucates at Grovine and Stonecarthy, just south of Kilkenny, as well as the advowson and appurtenances of the churches of St Mary (fig. 7.8) and St Patrick at Kilkenny.[142]

138 C.M. Butler and J.H. Bernard, 'The charters of the Cistercian abbey of Duiske in the county of Kilkenny', *PRIA*, 35C (1918–20), pp 1–187 at p. 14 (witness to a quitclaim, 1204); p. 19 (witness to the foundation charter, 1207); p. 22 (confirmation, *c.*1207); pp 23–4 (letter to Cîteaux, *c.*1207); p. 26 (approves a grant, *c.*1207; Bernard's suggested date of *c.*1216 for the latter deed and others below overlooks the fact, pointed out by Carrigan, *Ossory*, i, p. 25, that Odo was dean of Ossory before 1202: see *IMED*, pp 302, 307, while the presence of William Marshal as a witness places it between 1207 and 1213); p. 29 (confirmation, *c.*1207), p. 26 (approves a grant, *c.*1209), p. 28 (witness to a grant made in the presence of William Marshal and himself, probably *c.*1207). **139** 'Register of Kells', pp 301–2 (1203), 308 (1202x11), 309 (1208). **140** Duiske: 'Duiske charters', pp 18–19. The foundation charter can be dated to 1207 on the basis of the movements of one of the witnesses, John Marshal (see no. 2 below). Crouch, *William Marshal*, p. 212, suggests that the charter might be as late as 1210x12, when John Marshal may have rejoined his uncle's household. This is unlikely but, if so, it would have to be refined further to *c.*1212 because two of the witnesses to the charter – John de Earley (no. 3 below) and Thomas fitz Anthony (no. 9 below) – were imprisoned in England for much of 1210–11, and Earley was in England for part of 1212: see Crouch, *William Marshal*, pp 117–18; Sidney Painter, *William Marshal: knight errant, baron and regent of England* (Baltimore, 1933), p. 173. On the whole, a date of 1207, when at least five of the witnesses can be shown to have been in Kilkenny, seems more likely. Regarding the land grant in Kilkenny, see H.F. Berry, 'Ancient charters in the *Liber Albus Ossoriensis*', *PRIA*, 27C (1907–9), pp 115–25 at pp 123–5; *CDI, 1252–84*, no. 861. **141** *CAAR*, p. 36; the charter mentions John the canon, presumably an Augustinian, as Bishop Hugh's chaplain. **142** The text of William Marshal's side of the exchange was preserved in the White Book of Ossory: see Berry, 'Ancient charters in the *Liber Albus Ossoriensis*', pp 118–19, and in an inspeximus of 1577: *IMED*, pp 215–16. Bishop Hugh's text was preserved among the Ormond deeds and was edited and translated by James Graves and J.G.A. Prim, 'The history, architecture and antiquities of the city of Kilkenny', *JRSAI*, 5 (1858–9), pp 322–31 at pp 327–9. It seems likely that the grant

7.10 View of the remains of the former Augustinian priory of Inistioge, Co. Kilkenny, founded by Thomas fitz Anthony in the early thirteenth century (photograph: Ben Murtagh).

This exchange led Graves and Prim to conclude that le Rous was responsible for moving the cathedral of Ossory from Aghaboe to Kilkenny.[143] Such a move is contradicted by the wording of the charter itself, which mentions both the 'cathedral of Kilkenny' and the 'church of St Canice at Aghaboe' (fig. 7.2).[144] In fact, the so-called 'move' is an invention of much later times. It first appears in a sixteenth-century record noted for its inaccuracies.[145] Kilkenny was the

was made either in 1207, when the Marshal was trying to protect his northern frontier against Meiler fitz Henry, or in 1208, after he was confirmed with the lordship of Leinster. **143** Graves and Prim, *St Canice's, Kilkenny*, pp 29–32; as noted above, the simplicity of the theory has led many subsequent writers astray, among them Orpen, *Normans*, ii, p. 227; Neely, *Kilkenny: an urban history*, p. 9; Crouch, *William Marshal*, p. 152. Carrigan, *Ossory*, i, pp 24–6, demonstrated that the theory was wrong, but his views have been strangely ignored. **144** The site of the 'church of St Canice at Athaboe' is at the present Church of Ireland church, where the latter is apparently built on the foundations of the chancel of the medieval building: see Carrigan, *Ossory*, i, caption to pl. opp. p. 22; ibid., ii, pp 45–6; Peter Harbison, *Guide to national and historic monuments of Ireland* (Dublin, 1992), p. 207; P.D. Sweetman, Olive Alcock and Bernie Moran (comp.), *Archaeological inventory of County Laois* (Dublin, 1995), no. 688, pp 70–1 at p. 71. **145** '*Nomina reverendorum patrum episcoporum Ossoriensium*', ed. Carrigan, *Ossory*, i, pp 279–83 at p. 279, under Felix O'Dullanie. The manuscript, in the handwriting of David Rothe (1573–1650), ibid., pp xxii, 28–9, is probably a copy of a late sixteenth-century original because it trails off in 1567. James Ware also had access to this manuscript and it seems to be the foundation for his claim that Ua Duib Shláine (O'Dullany) moved the see from Aghaboe to Kilkenny: see his *De praesulibus Lageniae sive provinciae Dubliniensis* (Dublin, 1628), p. 70; idem, *De praesulibus Hiberniae, commentarius* (Dublin, 1665), diocesan see long before Bishop Hugh's time, having been named as such at the synod of Ráith Bressail in 1111, and there is no evidence at all that Aghaboe or Seirkieran (Co. Offaly) ever had cathedrals.[146] The Marshal also invested him, and the bishops of Ossory as his successors, with the manor of Durrow (in modern Co. Laois) and probably that of Freshford (Aghour), Co. Kilkenny.[147]

In 1208 together with Geoffrey fitz Robert and his wife Eva de Birmingham, as well as Baldwin de Hamptonsford, Bishop Hugh witnessed a grant of lands by Walter de Cantwell to Kells Priory (fig. 7.7).[148] He also played a role in the foundation of Thomas fitz Anthony's Augustinian house at Inistioge (fig. 7.10), when in *c.*1212 he petitioned the prior of Kells to appoint one of his monks as its prior. The choice fell upon Alured, who had accompanied le Rous (and Reginald de Aclond, the then prior of Kells) from Bodmin to Kells in *c.*1193.[149] Around this time he also confirmed the grant by Baldwin de Bret of the church of Kyllahet (perhaps Killahy, bar. Knocktopher, Co. Kilkenny) to Christ Church Cathedral, Dublin.[150] On his death in 1218 Bishop Hugh was buried not in his cathedral, but at Kells Priory, in the centre of the choir.[151]

2 – **John Marshal** (Johan le Mareschal), known from his marriage to Aline, the heiress of the Ryes family, as John Marshal of Hockering (Norfolk), was the illegitimate son of John Marshal of Hampstead Marshall and, as such, was William Marshal's nephew.[152] He was acknowledged by his father, but did not succeed to the estates, which were inherited by the Marshal, when his father died in 1194. John was compensated with other lands and entered William Marshal's household. He served with the Marshal in Flanders in 1197 and in Normandy in 1198. He accompanied the earl to Ireland in the winter of 1200 (see under Geoffrey fitz Robert, no. 6 below). He was in Normandy again in 1203 to meet the French advance at Falaise and was part of the withdrawal to England early in 1204.[153] The Marshal sent him to Leinster as his seneschal in April 1204.[154] During the following year he played an active role in the campaign between the

pp 139–40; this was popularised in the eighteenth century when these works were translated into English: see *A commentary of the prelates of Ireland, of the bishops of Dublin*, part 3 of *The antiquities and history of Ireland by the right honourable Sir James Ware, knight* [ed. Robert Ware] (Dublin, 1705), p. 29, and *The works of Sir James Ware concerning Ireland*, ed. Walter Harris (2 vols, Dublin, 1739), i, p. 403. The story of the 'move' was possibly invented as part of an attempt to validate claims to lands after the shiring of Laois (Queen's County) and Offaly (King's County) in 1556. **146** Graves and Prim did not have access to the information on the synod of Ráth Bressail, which later became available, see n. 4 above. **147** *CDI*, *1171–1251*, p. 364, no. 2437. **148** 'Register of Kells', p. 309. **149** Carrigan, *Ossory*, iv, p. 105. **150** *RSJB*, pp 271–2, no. 476; Baldwin's original grant was witnessed by Gilbert, Stephen and Hai de Valle: ibid., p. 271, no. 425. **151** Carrigan, *Ossory*, i, pp 33, 279. **152** His identity and that of his mother have been established by Crouch, *William Marshal*, p. 89n.40. **153** David Crouch, 'Marshal, Sir John (d. 1235)' in *ODNB*, 36, pp 812–13; Painter, *William Marshal*, pp 111–12, 116. **154** *CDI*, *1171–1251*, p. 32, no. 210; p. 33, no. 216; Painter, *William Marshal*, p. 153; Crouch, 'Marshal, Sir John (d. 1235)', p. 812.

earl's supporters and Meiler fitz Henry, the king's justiciar.[155] It seems likely that he remained in Ireland for the next two years and was on hand to meet the Marshal when he arrived in March or early April 1207.[156] During the summer of 1207, he witnessed the earl's grants to the Cistercian abbeys of Duiske (fig. 7.9) and Tintern *de Voto* in Co. Wexford (fig. 7.6).[157]

He travelled to England with his uncle when summoned by King John at the end of September 1207.[158] The meeting at Woodstock was a gradual, insidious assault on William Marshal's supporters in which they were winnowed away one by one. John Marshal was won over to the king's side by the offer of the position of marshal of Ireland and by a grant of land worth five knights' fees at Kylmien (probably Kilmeen, near Loughrea, Co. Galway).[159] This appears to have been part of a speculative grant of land in Connacht made to him jointly with one of the king's loyal men, Gilbert de Angulo, the former lord of Morgallion and a thorn in the side of the de Lacys.[160] John appears to have withdrawn from William Marshal's household and remained with the royal court between the autumn of 1207 and May 1213, the period when the earl was out of favour. It has been suggested that his alienation from the Marshal was more apparent than real because John's presence at court could have been useful to the earl by providing him with inside information and advance knowledge.[161] He returned to Ireland with the king on 20 June 1210, when the royal army landed at Crooke, Co. Waterford, and he accompanied King John throughout the whirlwind Irish campaign.[162] He served as a banneret, leading his own company of vassals, and played a role in capturing some of the de Lacy strongholds near Kells (Co. Meath) early in July of that year.[163] In August he seems to have returned to England with the king and he remained loyal during the subsequent baronial war.[164]

In 1215, in the aftermath of the granting of Magna Carta, when the king sought the pope's permission to have it annulled, John Marshal was sent on an embassy to Rome. He was with the king when the latter died at Newark on 19 October 1216. After William Marshal's restoration to favour John resumed 'with suspicious ease' his intimate association with the earl.[165] During the succeeding

155 Crouch, *William Marshal*, pp 102–3; Painter, *William Marshal*, p. 153, takes an opposite view. **156** Crouch, 'Marshal, Sir John (d. 1235)', pp 812–13; Crouch, *William Marshal*, p. 221, states that John was present in William Marshal's entourage in 1205, but presumably this is a misprint for 1207; cf. ibid., p. 102. According to the *Histoire*, only one (Henry Hose) of the household knights who had accompanied the Marshal to Ireland returned to England with him in September 1207. Since John Marshal also travelled back to England this would suggest that he was already in Ireland when the earl arrived: *HWM*, ii, pp 175–7, lines 13497–503. **157** *Chartae, privilegia et immunitates*, p. 80. **158** *Rotuli chartarum in turri Londinensi asservati* [1199–1216], ed. T.D. Hardy (London, 1837), pp 171b–173, quoted by Painter, *William Marshal*, p. 155. **159** Ibid., p. 156; Crouch, *William Marshal*, p. 106; Orpen, *Normans*, ii, p. 263. **160** Gilbert de Angulo was pardoned on 12 February 1207 and retained in the king's service: *CDI*, *1171–1251*, p. 46, no. 311; together with Theobald Walter *pincerna*, he had witnessed John's charter to Dublin on 15 May 1192: Mac Niocaill, *Na buirgéisí*, i, p. 81. **161** Crouch, 'Marshal, Sir John (d. 1235)', p. 812. **162** *CDI*, *1171–1251*, p. 59, no. 401. **163** Orpen, *Normans*, ii, p. 250. **164** Painter, *William Marshal*, pp 179–80. **165** The phrase

7.11 South-east view of the ruins of the thirteenth-century church of the former Augustinian St John's Priory, Kilkenny, founded on this site by William Marshal to replace the earlier St John the Evangelist's Hospital at Green's Bridge (photograph: Cóilín Ó Drisceoil).

years he campaigned with the Marshal on behalf of the royalist cause and was made justiciar of the forests, giving him custody of all royal manors pertaining to forests, as well as custody of 'a score of fees' in Dorset and Somerset.[166] He was at the earl's bedside when he died in 1219. Subsequently he formed a close political partnership with William Marshal II and later served as his executor. During the 1220s he was frequently engaged in Ireland, where he witnessed charters to Carlow, Kilkenny and St John's Priory, Kilkenny (fig. 7.11).[167] About this time also he provided the author of the *Histoire* with a considerable amount of the information that was used in the poem. He died in 1235.[168]

3 – **John de Earley** (Johan d'Erlee/of Earley/Erlegh) was William Marshal's closest friend and is referred to in the *Histoire* as his *carissimus* ('dearest', 'most intimate').[169] The family name derived from the manor of Earley (now Whiteknights Park) in Berkshire but the Earleys also held lands in Somerset. His

is that of Crouch, 'Marshal, Sir John (d. 1235)', p. 812. **166** Painter, *William Marshal*, p. 272. **167** Mac Niocaill, *Na buirgéisí*, i, pp 134 (Carlow, *c*.1223), 139 (Kilkenny, 1223); William Dugdale, *Monasticon Anglicanum*, ed. Roger Dodsworth, John Stevens, John Caley, Henry Ellis, Bulkeley Bandinel and R.C. Taylor (6 vols in 8, London, 1817–30), vi, pp 1143–4 (St John's Kilkenny, *c*.1223) trans. Carrigan, *Ossory*, iii, pp 248–9. **168** Crouch, 'Marshal, Sir John', p. 813. **169** Crouch, *William Marshal*, p. 166; the phrase is also used by William Marshal to describe William de St Leger (*carissimo et fideli militi meo*): *RAST*, p. 137, no. 160;

father, William, was a figure of baronial rank and had served as a titular royal chamberlain to King Henry II (r. 1154–89). He died soon after Christmas 1181 and the young John became a ward of court.[170] Around 1187, when he was about 14, the king placed John in the household of the Marshal, where he served as his squire.[171] He came of age in 1194, but instead of leaving William Marshal and dwelling on his estates, he became one of the Marshal's household knights.[172] The bond seems to have been strengthened by marriage because it is likely that his wife, Sybil, was William Marshal's illegitimate niece.[173] He served with the Marshal in France between 1195 and 1199, and brought the news of King Richard's death to the justiciar of England in the latter year.[174] In 1202 he was made sheriff of Devonshire and in 1204 he campaigned with the earl against the Welsh and was present at the capture of Cilgerran Castle (Pembrokeshire). He arrived in Ireland with the Marshal in late March or April 1207.[175] Shortly afterwards, if not before, he was granted the land that was to become known as Nova Villa de Erley (now the parish of Earlstown, consisting of almost 3,000 acres) for the service of three-quarters of a knight's fee.[176] He witnessed the charter to the Cistercian abbey of Tintern *de Voto*, Co. Wexford (fig. 7.6). Following the earl's recall, he was left in charge of Ossory and the southern half of Leinster during the winter of 1207–8.[177] In January 1208 he was summoned to England by King John, but famously refused to go, saying, according to the *Histoire*, that he had sworn to defend the Marshal's interests:

> My lords, it would be a most disgraceful thing to leave the earl's land, land which he has committed to us to guard. One should be concerned with his honour, so that no tale of our wrongdoing can be told; shame lasts longer than destitution. If the land is abandoned in this manner, our own honour will be diminished. So we are in a trap, for, on the one hand we lose honour and land, and, on the other, we lose land and honour and the love (*amor*) of our lord as well.[178]

p. 356, no. 399. **170** David Crouch, 'Earley, John (II) of (*c.*1173–1229)' in *ODNB*, 17, pp 574–5; elsewhere Crouch gives the date of William of Earley's death as 1180: *William Marshal*, p. 147, but cf. ibid., p. 217. **171** Crouch, *William Marshal*, p. 147. **172** Ibid., p. 11. **173** Ibid., p. 147. **174** Painter, *William Marshal*, pp 69, 116–21. **175** *CDI*, *1171–1251*, no. 313. **176** That the grant was made before William Marshal returned to England in September 1207 is indicated by King John's remark that he had confiscated the lands that Earley held from the earl: Crouch, *William Marshal*, p. 111; Brooks, *Knights' fees*, pp 243–5. The original grant may have consisted of the entire cantred of Earley, about 17,500 acres, including Coolaghmore (subsequently Marshal demesne land), Killamery (subsequently granted to the St Aubins or Tobins) and Mallardstown (granted to William Mallard, the Marshal's standard-bearer). See also Linda Shine, 'The manor of Earlstown, Co. Kilkenny: an interdisciplinary approach' in James Lyttleton and Tadhg O'Keeffe (eds), *The manor in medieval and early modern Ireland* (Dublin, 2005), pp 40–69. **177** *CDI*, *1171–1251*, no. 313; *HWM*, ii, p. 175, lines 13473–88. **178** Ibid., p. 187, lines 13721–32; see Crouch, *William Marshal*, pp 159–63, for an analysis of the insight this speech provides into the bonds of lordship and loyalty.

7.12 View of the ruins of the former Cistercian Dunbrody Abbey, Co. Wexford, founded in the 1180s by Hervey de Montmorency (photograph: Ben Murtagh).

His estates were confiscated and King John tried to rile William Marshal with the taunt that Earley's loyalty had ruined him.[179] Later the king went further and invented or spread the rumour that he had been killed in a siege of Kilkenny Castle (fig. 7.5).[180] The rumour was false, however, and Earley's lands were returned to him in March 1208. Together with Jordan de Sauqueville (no. 4 below), he met the Marshal at Glascarrig, near Gorey, Co. Wexford, upon the latter's return to Ireland in the summer of 1208.[181] It was probably about this time that he witnessed the earl's charter to the abbey of Dunbrody in Co. Wexford (fig. 7.12).[182] He probably spent the next two years in Ireland, but in August 1210 he was taken to England by King John as a hostage for the Marshal's good behaviour and was imprisoned for a number of months in Nottingham Castle. In 1212 he was entrusted with the shrievalty of Devon and

179 Ibid., pp 111, 162; Orpen, *Normans*, ii, p. 212n.27. **180** *HWM*, ii, p. 193, line 13842. **181** Ibid., p. 199, lines 13941–65. **182** J.T. Gilbert (ed.), '*Registrum Monasterii de Portu Sancte Marie, Dunbrothy*' in *CSMA*, ii, pp 97–208 at pp 158–9, no. iv. The absence of John Marshal's name suggests that it is later than 1207, while the presence of Henry Hose presumes his return with William Marshal in 1208. The charter must be earlier than August 1210, when John de Earley, Jordan de Sauqueville and Geoffrey fitz Robert were taken into custody by the king.

in the following year he was named a marshal (perhaps chamberlain) of the royal household.[183] He advised the earl against taking up the regency of England in 1216, probably because he was concerned about the stress it would cause to the Marshal's health (who was then aged about 69).[184] He was seneschal or bailiff of Striguil between 1217 and 1219. He attended the earl on his deathbed in his manor at Caversham (Berkshire) from mid-March until mid-May 1219 except for the time when he was sent to Chepstow to obtain the silken palls that the Marshal had acquired in Jerusalem and intended for his bier.[185] After the earl's death he served as an executor of his will and was an informant and financial supporter of the author of the *Histoire*.[186] He died before the month of May in 1229.[187]

4 – **Jordan de Sauqueville** (Jordan de Saukervile) was a member of an Anglo-Norman family that had estates at Sauqueville in Normandy, a short distance south of Dieppe, at Fawsley in Buckinghamshire, and at Buckhurst in Sussex.[188] The family had a long connection with the lords of Longueville, and Fawsley was held from William Marshal. Jordan joined the earl's household while he was campaigning in Normandy between 1195 and 1199.[189] He accompanied the Marshal to Ireland in 1207 and was made joint-seneschal of Leinster when the earl was recalled to England later that year.[190] He witnessed the charter to Tintern Abbey (fig. 7.6) in Co. Wexford during the summer of 1207. In January 1208 King John summoned him to England but, like John de Earley (no. 3 above) and Stephen d'Evereux, he refused to attend.[191] Instead, he sought and obtained the assistance of the earl of Ulster (from whom he held lands at Ardglass and Holywood, Co. Down) in the defence of the Marshal's lands in the baronial war of 1207–8.[192] The earl may also have granted him land at Rathemadon (unidentified) in Osraige for the service of one quarter of a knight's fee.[193] Jordan's lands were confiscated, but they were returned to him within a few months.[194] Together with John de Earley, as seen above, he was present to meet William Marshal at Glascarrig, Co. Wexford, when he arrived back in Ireland in the summer of 1208.[195] It was probably about this time that he witnessed the

183 Crouch, *William Marshal*, p. 118, but see p. 218 for alternative dates; Crouch, 'Earley', p. 574. **184** Painter, *William Marshal*, pp 195–6; Crouch, *William Marshal*, pp 126, 163. **185** Painter, *William Marshal*, pp 283–9; Crouch, *William Marshal*, p. 209. **186** Ibid., p. 2. **187** Ibid., p. 218. **188** The form 'Sanguill' in the text of the Kilkenny charter is clearly a scribal misreading of 'Sauqvill'. **189** David Crouch, 'Strategies of lordship in Angevin England and the career of William Marshal' in Christopher Harper-Bill and Ruth Harvey (eds), *The ideals and practice of medieval knighthood, 2: papers from the third Strawberry Hill conference, 1986* (Woodbridge, 1988), pp 1–25 at p. 22; Painter, *William Marshal*, p. 128. **190** *HWM*, ii, p. 175, lines 13464–72. **191** Ibid., p. 183, lines 13639–42; p. 189, lines 13745–52. **192** Ibid., p. 189, lines 13763–77; for the Co. Down lands, see Orpen, *Normans*, ii, pp 254, 260. **193** In 1299 'Rathemadon in Ossory' was held by the heirs of Bartholomew de Sakevill: see A.J. Otway-Ruthven, 'Knights' fees in Kildare, Leix and Offaly', *JRSAI*, 91 (1961), pp 163–81 at p. 180. **194** Orpen, *Normans*, ii, p. 212n.27; Painter, *William Marshal*, pp 158–9. **195** *HWM*, ii, p. 199, earl's charter to the abbey of Dunbrody in Co. Wexford (fig. 7. 12).[196] Jordan appears to have spent the next two years in Ireland, but King John removed him to England in August 1210 as a hostage for the Marshal's good behaviour. He was imprisoned at Gloucester Castle and remained in captivity until 1213.[197] On his release, he returned to the earl's service, in the office of seneschal of Pembroke in 1216 and he died in *c.*1233.[198]

5 – **Ralph fitz Payn** (Raol filz Paien): little is known about him.[199] He was a member of William Marshal's household and was left in Ireland when the earl was recalled to England in September 1207.[200] The implication of the text is that he had travelled with the Marshal's entourage to Ireland earlier that year. He was evidently a well-known supporter of the earl because, during the winter of 1207–8, King John taunted the Marshal with the rumour that fitz Payn had been killed in the siege of Kilkenny Castle.[201] The rumour was false, however. From the manner in which he is referred to in the *Histoire*, he clearly had control of an important fighting force, which was based at some distance from Castledermot, Co. Kildare, during the baronial war of 1207–8.[202] Judging from the charter evidence, Marshal seems to have deputed Ralph to liaise with Adam de Hereford in the contentious area of Uí Faeláin (Offaly). He held land in that cantred at Kill, Co. Kildare, and he was one of the witnesses to the deed drawn up to determine the boundary between Osraige and Uí Faeláin.[203] Together with his brother Walter, Ralph witnessed grants of lands, churches and tithes from Adam de Hereford, John de Hereford and Laurence of Castlemartin to St Thomas's Abbey, Dublin.[204] In the absence of his brother he attested grants to the same abbey by Thomas de Hereford and Richard de Lesse of churches and tithes in Uí Faeláin and in the other major Hereford holding in the cantred of Aghaboe, Co. Laois.[205] Unfortunately, these grants cannot be dated precisely, but probably fall into the period between 1207 and 1213. Together with Roger fitz Payn, probably another brother, he witnessed William Marshal's charter to the abbey of Dunbrody, Co. Wexford (fig. 7.12), which was probably made in the summer of 1208 and certainly before August 1210.[206]

lines 13941–65. **196** 'Registrum de Dunbrothy', pp 158–9, no. iv. **197** Crouch, *William Marshal*, p. 219. **198** Nigel Saul, 'Sackville [de Sackville] family (per. *c.*1066–*c.*1477)' in *ODNB*, www.oxforddnb.com/view/article/65281, accessed 18 May 2010; regarding the office in Pembroke, see Crouch, *William Marshal*, pp 173, 219, while ibid., p. 219, gives a death date of 1227x35. **199** The name is given as Ralph fitz Pagan in the text of the Kilkenny charter, which may be a mistake in transcription confusing 'ga' for 'y' or 'ya', although the form 'Pagan' also occurs in the *Ormond deeds, 1172–1350*, pp 30–1, no. 39, and in *RAST*, pp 74–5, nos 86–7. He is referred to both as Reinfrid and as Ralph fitz Payn in *HWM*, ii, p. 175, line 13496 (Reinfrid); pp 189, line 13749, 193, line 13840. **200** *HWM*, ii, p. 175, lines 13495–6. **201** Ibid., p. 193, line 13840; Crouch, *William Marshal*, p. 111. **202** *HWM*, ii, p. 189, line 13749; for Castledermot, see Orpen, *Normans*, ii, p. 213. **203** *RAST*, p. 299, no. 346; *Ormond deeds, 1172–1350*, pp 30–1, no. 39. **204** Ibid., pp 74–5, nos 86–7; pp 86–7, no. 99. **205** Ibid., pp 80–2, no. 93; pp 90–1, no. 104; p. 121, no. 139; pp 121–2, no. 140. **206** 'Registrum de

6 – **Geoffrey fitz Robert** (Guifrei filz Robert) was one of William Marshal's earliest household knights, a friend from the days when he still derived his income from tournament prowess. Geoffrey first appears in *c.*1187 when he witnessed the Marshal's earliest known charter.[207] His family origins are unclear. Crouch (who is probably right) suggests that he was the Geoffrey fitz Robert, *camerarius*, who succeeded to his brother's Wiltshire lands in *c.*1190, while Eric St John Brooks proposed that he was the Geoffrey who was lord of Villa Osmundi (Uzmaston, near Haverfordwest in Pembrokeshire) in *c.*1200.[208] He was almost certainly enfeoffed with the barony of Kells in Osraige, with a service of one-and-a-half knights' fees, in or soon after 1192.[209] About this time he married Basilia, Strongbow's sister, widow of Raymond le Gros, and aunt of William Marshal's wife Isabel. It was a marriage that made him part of the Marshal family. Together they confirmed land grants in Fotharta to St Thomas's Abbey, Dublin in *c.*1192.[210] At Kells, Geoffrey erected a motte and established a borough.[211] He also built a priory nearby for Augustinian canons (fig. 7.7). The monastery was founded not only to ensure his spiritual welfare in the next life, but also to aid the salvation of the souls of the lord of his lands, William Marshal, and his lady, Isabel; he discussed the foundation with the Marshal, obtained his permission and received a charter of confirmation.[212] In *c.*1193 or 1194, he introduced four monks from Bodmin in Cornwall.[213] In *c.*1198, together with Hamo de Valognes (d. 1202/3), Hugh Tyrell (d. 1199), Theobald Walter I and Meiler fitz Henry, he witnessed the grant of land at Palmerstown to the Hospital of St John the Baptist, Dublin.[214] The foundation charter of Kells Priory was not granted until between 1204 and 1206, at a time when John Marshal was in Ireland, but before the arrival of William Marshal, who would otherwise have been expected to be a testator.[215] He also held the lands of Dysart (Distermoholmoc) adjoining the River Nore in the cantred of Ogenty in eastern Osraige, which became an outlying grange of Kells Priory.[216]

Dunbrothy', pp 158–9, no. iv. **207** Crouch, *William Marshal*, pp 147–8. **208** Ibid., p. 219; Brooks, *Knights' fees*, pp 246–7. **209** Empey, 'Augustinian priory of Kells', p. 3; Orpen, *Normans*, ii, p. 225. **210** *RAST*, p. 112, no. 129; the charter is witnessed by William Piro before his elevation to the see of Glendalough in 1192, a point noted by Flanagan, 'Fitzgerald, Raymond fitz William', p. 844. **211** Orpen, 'Castles in Ossory', pp 325–8. **212** 'Register of Kells', pp 300–1, 311; William de St Leger granted the advowson of the church of St Nicholas and the tithes of the parish of Tullaghanbrogue, Co. Kilkenny, to St Thomas's Abbey, Dublin, 'for the salvation of his soul and that of his lord, William Marshal': *RAST*, p. 125, no. 145; similarly, Countess Isabel granted the church of Kilcullen, Co. Kildare, to Christ Church Cathedral, Dublin, probably in 1207–8, 'for the salvation of the soul of her father Earl Richard fitz Gilbert and that of her lord, William Marshal': *CCD*, p. 38, no. 13; '*Liber Niger*', p. 18, no. 30; pp 18–19, no. 21, pp 54–5, no. 85. For the date, see n. 246 below regarding Thomas fitz Anthony (sect. V, no. 9). **213** 'Register of Kells', p. 311; Empey, 'The Augustinian priory at Kells', p. 4. See also under Hugh le Rous (sect. V, no. 1, above) and n. 129. **214** *RSJB*, pp 197–8, no. 290; the charter may well date to 1194–5 because neither Hamo nor Meiler are styled justiciar, although Hamo is the first witness. **215** *IMED*, pp 1–3; *Ormond deeds, 1172–1350*, no. 30; reproduced in Clyn, *Kells Priory*, pl. 1.1. **216** Clyne, *Kells Priory*, pp 31–3;

On 14 October 1199, King John granted Geoffrey five knights' fees at Radoger in the cantred of Huhene (Uí Énna Áine, later the cantred of Any and Grene), which was centred on the manors of Grene and Asgrene (Pallas Green, Co. Limerick).[217] The grant was made when the Marshal was high in the king's favour but it was purely for Geoffrey's lifetime and reverted to the crown on his death. It is likely that the grant was purchased because on 18 June 1203 the king instructed the justiciar to acquit Geoffrey of a debt of three hundred marks but this seems to have been reversed because within a year Geoffrey's debt was to be assigned to the construction of Dublin Castle; on 2 March 1206 the order was given to seize Geoffrey's lands because of the debt of three hundred marks that was still owing to the king.[218] In all, between his properties in Cos Kilkenny and Limerick, he appears to have held about forty thousand acres.[219] His second wife, whom he married *c.*1203, was Eva de Birmingham, heiress of Robert de Birmingham, the first feoffee of Offaly (i.e., Tethmoy, immediately to the west of Uí Faeláin).[220] These marriages suggest that he was well aware of the social and political divide between the initial Anglo-Norman adventurers such as Meiler fitz Henry, who were successful frontiersmen, and the Marshal newcomers, who were regarded as effeminate courtiers intruding upon the hardy generation that had created the lordship. Indeed, in view of the subsequent war over Uí Faeláin between William Marshal and fitz Henry, it is likely that the marriage to Eva de Birmingham was one that the earl actively encouraged. In any event he could not have married Eva without the Marshal's permission. Geoffrey served as the earl's seneschal in Leinster between 1200 and 1202 and probably until the arrival of John Marshal in April 1204.[221] It was during this time that he presided over a

IMED, p. 2; Ben Murtagh, 'Archaeological investigations at Dysart, Co. Kilkenny, 1989–1994: an interim report', *OKR*, 46 (1994), pp 78–94 at pp 78–80 and fig. 1. **217** *CDI, 1171–1251*, p. 16, no. 103; 'Register of Kells', p. 311; Orpen, *Normans*, ii, p. 170; MacCotter, *Medieval Ire.*, pp 189–90. **218** *CDI, 1171–1251*, p. 28, no. 179; p. 35, no. 226; pp 43–4, no. 287. **219** C.A. Empey, 'The sacred and the secular: the Augustinian priory of Kells in Ossory, 1193–1541', *IHS*, 24 (1984–5), pp 131–51 at p. 140. **220** Brooks, *Knights' fees*, p. 247; Orpen, *Normans*, i, p. 381; *Song of Dermot*, pp 116–17, lines 3104–5; *Deeds of the Normans*, p. 132, lines 3102–3. **221** The date of Geoffrey's seneschalship has been something of a puzzle. It overlapped with part of the period when Meiler fitz Henry was justiciar of Ireland (*c.*1199–1200 with a gap in the latter year when he was recalled to England, then from October 1200 to at least June 1208 and perhaps early 1209: *NHI*, ix, p. 470; *HWM*, iii, pp 156–7). John Marshal (no. 2 above), who is known to have been in Ireland between 1204 and 1207, was a witness to deeds in which Geoffrey is styled 'seneschal of Leinster': *Ormond deeds, 1172–1350*, pp 19–20, no. 37; *RAST*, pp 125–6, nos 154–6; pp 355–6, no. 398. Accordingly, Empey suggested a date of *c.*1204–8 for the seneschalship: see Barry, Culleton and Empey, 'Kells motte, County Kilkenny', p. 168n.30; C.A. Empey, 'Callan in the Middle Ages' in Joseph Kennedy (ed.), *Callan 800, 1207–2007: history and heritage* (Callan, 2007), pp 17–37 at p. 28. Since John Marshal was seneschal of Leinster in 1204 and 1205, while John de Earley and Jordan de Sauqueville were joint seneschals in 1207–8 (see nos 3 and 4 above), this would confine Geoffrey to the seneschalship in *c.*1206 (or at its largest interpretation, because there are no sources, from possibly Oct. 1205 to possibly Sept. 1207). The solution is simpler, however. Fitz Robert was William Marshal's seneschal before December 1200: see J.H. Bernard, 'The foundation of Tintern Abbey, Co.

major reorganisation of the Marshal's Leinster holdings by establishing the burgess rent of Callan, Carlow, Coolaghmore, Kells, Kilkenny, Moone and Wexford.[222] He remained in Ireland when the earl was recalled to England in September 1207.[223] He witnessed the Marshal's charter to the Cistercian abbey of Dunbrody in Co. Wexford (fig. 7.12), as well as a deed of protection for its monks, which were made in 1208 and certainly before August 1210.[224] He was one of the hostages for the earl's good behaviour taken by John to England in August 1210 and he died in captivity at Hereford Castle in 1211 just before he was due to be released.[225]

7 – **Milo fitz Bishop**, also known as Milo (or Miles) fitz David, was one of the first Anglo-Norman adventurers to arrive in Ireland from Wales. He was the son of David fitz Gerald, bishop of St David's (1148–76), who was in turn the son of Gerald of Windsor (d. *c.*1130), the Norman castellan of Pembroke, and Nest (d. 1130), the daughter of Rhys ap Tewdwr, king of Deheubarth in south-west Wales (d. 1093).[226] Together with Meiler fitz Henry, Robert fitz Stephen and Maurice de Prendergast, Milo landed at Bannow Bay (Co. Wexford) in May 1169.[227] It is often

Wexford', *PRIA*, 33C (1916–17), pp 527–9. Further evidence that he was seneschal in 1200–1 is provided by the confirmation by King John, made on 1 March 1202, of the earl's grant of half a cantred in Uí Faeláin to Adam de Hereford: *Ormond deeds, 1172–1350*, pp 13–14, no. 29. The original Marshal grant to de Hereford is self-evidently the one published as no. 37 in the same volume to which the editor assigned the date 1207–13 because that was the period 'when William Marshal was in Ireland' (p. 20). Clearly, however, it can be dated to before March 1202 and must belong to the winter of 1200, when the Marshal was in Ireland. The witness list to the charter implies that the earl took with him to Leinster in 1200 a contingent consisting of Ralph de Sumeri, John Marshal, Hugh, Thomas and Reginald de Sandford, Ralph Bluet and his son (also Ralph Bluet), William Jardin, Reginald de Gosington and Warin de Ralegh. It is probably because of his service in Ireland during 1200, and not just due to the fact that he was redundant after the loss of Normandy, that John Marshal was appointed seneschal of Leinster in 1204. Fitz Robert's seneschalship evidently extended into 1202 and probably beyond because, while he was seneschal, he was also a co-witness with Hugh le Rous (no. 1 above), bishop of Ossory, of a grant to St Thomas's Abbey, Dublin: *RAST*, pp 355–6, no. 398. On the whole, it seems likely that Geoffrey was seneschal of Leinster from at least December 1200 until replaced by John Marshal in April 1204. This would give a succession list as Leinster seneschals of Geoffrey fitz Robert (1200–4), John Marshal (1204–7) and the joint seneschalship of John de Earley and Jordan de Sauqueville (1207–8, perhaps later). Brooks, *Knights' fees*, p. 202, suggested that the grant to Adam de Hereford was a confirmation made *c.*1207, after the conflict with Meiler fitz Henry, but if it was as late as this it should date to 1208, when William Marshal was confirmed as lord of Leinster. Since Adam de Hereford had gone over to the side of King John (*Ormond deeds, 1172–1350*, p. 20, no. 38; *CDI, 1171–1251*, no. 341) it is unlikely that the earl would have been in a rush to re-enfeof Adam: see Crouch, *William Marshal*, pp 88–9. **222** Mac Niocaill, *Na buirgéisí*, i, pp 112 (Callan), 134 (Carlow), 155 (Cooliagh), 129 (Kells), 138 (Kilkenny), 250 (Moone), 235 (Wexford). It is likely that the burgess rent of Bannow, New Ross and Thomastown was established at the same time. **223** *HWM*, ii, pp 176–7, lines 13503–6. **224** 'Registrum de Dunbrothy', pp 158–9, no. iv. **225** *HWM*, ii, pp 216–17, line 14325; pp 222–5, lines 14447–86; 'Registry of Kells', p. 311. **226** Giraldus, *Expugnatio*, p. 291n.20. **227** *Song of Dermot*, pp 34–5, lines 449–50; *Deeds of* pointed out that the initial landing was a family affair and Milo was related to several of the early invaders. Robert fitz Stephen was a maternal uncle while Meiler fitz Henry was a cousin, being Nest's grandson through her affair with King Henry I (r. 1100–35). Raymond le Gros was a first cousin as was Giraldus Cambrensis. A further connection was created by the marriage of Raymond le Gros to Strongbow's sister, Basilia, because after Raymond's death (1189x92) she married Geoffrey fitz Robert, thereby linking the generation of the invaders with that of William Marshal's knights. In 1169 Milo took part in Mac Murcadha's raid into central Osraige and the defeat there of King Domnall Mac Gilla Pátraic.[228] Together with Strongbow, Milo was one of the defenders of Dublin when it was besieged for two months by the army of Ruaidhrí Ua Conchobair, king of Connacht, in the summer of 1171.[229] In the following year he was one of the group of knights left behind by Henry II and assigned by him to secure Dublin.[230] He was a member of the attacking force that captured Limerick in 1175–6 and was left behind as custos of the garrison, a position he eventually had to give up.[231] Before 1176, Strongbow granted him the cantred of Iverk or Overk (comprising the modern barony of Iverk and the greater part of the barony of Ida), amounting to almost 100,000 acres in south Osraige, for the service of seven knights.[232] He was still alive in 1215.[233] Since William Marshal was Strongbow's successor as lord of Leinster, it was as his vassal that Milo fitz Bishop witnessed the charter to Kilkenny.

8 – **Gilbert de Valle** held a knight's fee at Ardristan in Co. Carlow and half a knight's fee at Castleinch or Inchyolaghan in the cantred of Shillelogher, immediately south of Kilkenny.[234] Brooks has pointed out that the name is the Latinised form of Dale, the place in Pembrokeshire from which the family took its name. In the 1190s, and probably for some time before, three de Valle brothers were active in Ireland: Gilbert, Stephen and Hay. All seem to have been attached to the household of Raymond le Gros (d. 1189x92) and were part of the subinfeudation of the areas of Fotharta, Uí Dróna in Co. Carlow, together with Glascarrig on the east coast of Co. Wexford.[235] This can be deduced not only from the fees they held but also from their association as testators with Raymond's widow, Basilia.[236] Stephen was granted Tulachany or Grange (now Cuffesgrange), Co. Kilkenny, while Hay was enfeoffed of Rathtoe, Co. Carlow.

the Normans, p. 64, lines 449–50. **228** *Song of Dermot*, pp 56–7, line 748; *Deeds of the Normans*, pp 72–3, line 748. **229** *Song of Dermot*, pp 132–3, line 1810; *Deeds of the Normans*, pp 98–9, line 1808. **230** *Song of Dermot*, pp 198–9, line 2722; *Deeds of the Normans*, pp 121–2, line 2720. **231** Giraldus, *Expugatio*, p. 159. **232** *Song of Dermot*, pp 226–7, lines 3108–11; *Deeds of the Normans*, pp 131–2, lines 3108–9; Brooks, *Knights' fees*, p. 264. **233** *CDI, 1171–1251*, no. 673. **234** Brooks, *Knights' fees*, pp 66–9, 242–3. **235** Ibid., p. 66; see also Billy Colfer, *Arrogant trespass: Anglo-Norman Wexford, 1169–1400* (Enniscorthy, 2002), p. 42. **236** *RAST*, p. 107, no. 122 (*c*.1192); p. 112, no. 129 (*c*.1192); *RSJB*, pp 262–3, no. 409 (1199x1201); pp 267–8, no. 418 (1199); p. 269, no. 421 (*c*.1199).

All were directly or indirectly tenants of William Marshal.[237] Gilbert was still alive *c*.1221.[238]

9 – **Thomas fitz Anthony** (Tomas filz Antonie) first appears in the records in 1204 when he witnessed the quit-claim of Geoffrey fitz Robert to lands at Duiske and Annamult in central Osraige.[239] It is likely that he had been sent to Ireland in the 1190s and that, in a move paralleling the development of Kells, as noted above (sect. III), William Marshal invested him with the pre-Anglo-Norman district or cantred of Ogenty in eastern Osraige.[240] There he proceeded to erect a castle with a commanding view of a bend on the River Nore at Grenan (fig. 7.13, pl. 25).[241] He also founded a town a short distance upriver to the north of it, with the eponymous name of Thomastown (*Baile Mhic Andáin*, 'fitz Anthony's town' in Irish).[242] He gave a charter to the new town 'of the usual Kilkenny type', but only fragments of the text are known.[243]

In February 1207 he travelled to Northampton in England, together with the king's clerk and the sergeant of Limerick, to deliver part of the treasure of Ireland to King John.[244] Whether he returned to Ireland in the Marshal entourage or travelled independently is unknown. He remained in Ireland, however, after the Marshal was summoned to England in September 1207. Indeed, in 1207–8, he was one of the handful of knights with experience of the Irish situation that William Marshal encouraged his freshly appointed seneschals

237 Brooks, *Knights' fees*, pp 66–9, 242–3. **238** 'Duiske charters', pp 30–1. **239** 'Duiske charters', p. 14; the charter is earlier than 6 June 1204 (ibid., p. 23) and later than April 1204, when John Marshal (no. 2 above), another witness, was given licence to travel to Ireland (*CDI, 1171–1251*, no. 210). **240** Empey, 'County Kilkenny in the Anglo-Norman period', p. 77; Brooks, *Knights' fees*, pp 254–5; see also MacCotter, *Medieval Ire.*, pp 180–1 and appendix 2 – atlas. **241** The remains of the thirteenth-century masonry castle (one of the few examples to be seen in Co. Kilkenny along with Kells and Kilkenny), overlies an earlier rectangular earthwork: see John Bradley and Ben Murtagh, 'Brady's Castle, Thomastown, Co. Kilkenny: a 14th-century fortified town house' in J.R. Kenyon and Kieran O'Conor (eds), *The medieval castle in Ireland and Wales* (Dublin, 2003), pp 194–216 at p. 216; Carrigan, *Ossory*, iv, pp 266–7; Orpen, 'Castles in Ossory', p. 321; Sweetman, *Medieval castles*, pp 74–5; D.M. Waterman, 'Rectangular keeps of the thirteenth century at Grenan (Kilkenny) and Glanworth (Cork)', *JRSAI*, 98 (1968), pp 67–73 at pp 67–72. **242** John Bradley, 'Planned Anglo-Norman towns in Ireland' in H.B. Clarke and Anngret Simms (eds), *The comparative history of urban origins in non-Roman Europe* (Oxford, 1985), pp 411–67 at p. 436; Carrigan, *Ossory*, iv, pp 256–7; Orpen, *Normans*, ii, p. 226; iii, p. 93. **243** Bateson, *Borough customs*, i, p. lii; the seven clauses she published from a patent roll of 32–3 Henry VIII (1541–2) then in PROI (destroyed in 1922) show that the Thomastown charter, like those of Callan, Carlow, Coolaghmore and Moone, derived verbatim from the Kilkenny charter: see ibid., i, p. 32 (Thos. cap. 3=Kk. cap. 3; duel); p. 115 (Thos. cap. 23=Kk. cap. 21; restoration of goods wrongly distrained); p. 120 (Thos. cap. 10=Kk. cap. 9; distraint if a toll is wrongly exacted); p. 167 (Thos. cap. 22=Kk. cap. 20; suit of lawful men); ibid., ii, p. 2 (Thos. cap. 67 [*sic*, clearly a mistake for 6 and 7]=Kk cap. 7 and 8; miskenning and pleading); p. 92 (Thos. cap. 17=Kk. cap. 15; disposal of burgage tenements). A further eleven clauses are summarised in *CPCRI, Hen. VIII–Eliz.* [1514–75], p. 78, no. 104; all are present in the Kilkenny charter. No witnesses are mentioned so the charter could date to anytime between *c*.1207–10 and *c*.1212–23. **244** *CDI, 1171–1251*, no. 321.

7.13 View of Grenan Castle, near Thomastown, Co. Kilkenny, commanding a bend on the River Nore with thirteenth-century donjon or 'hall house' built upon an earlier rectangular motte – manorial centre of lands in the cantred of Ogenty granted to Thomas fitz Anthony by William Marshal (photograph: Cóilín Ó Drisceoil).

to heed.[245] It was probably about this time that he witnessed Countess Isabel's grant of the church of Kilcullen (Co. Kildare) to Christ Church Cathedral in Dublin.[246] He served as a hostage for the earl's good behaviour in 1210–11, when he was held in captivity at Winchester in England.[247] At his inland port town of Inistioge on the River Nore, he founded the Augustinian priory of SS Mary and Columba (fig. 7.10) and endowed it with almost one-third of his lands in Ogenty.[248]

245 *HWM*, ii, pp 176–7, lines 13510–11. **246** *CCD*, p. 38, no. 13; that there is a separate charter from William Marshal ratifying the alienation of the lands suggests that Isabel's grant was made while her husband was out of the country: '*Liber Niger*', p. 18, no. 30; the confirmation by John Cumin, archbishop of Dublin, places it before November 1212 when he died '*senex et plenum dierum*', but since fitz Anthony was in England for much of 1210–11, the likely date is 1207–8: ibid., pp 18–19, no. 21, pp 54–5, no. 85. **247** *HWM*, ii, pp 224–5, line 14456. **248** Carrigan, *Ossory*, iv, pp 105–11; Adrian Empey, 'Inistioge in the Middle Ages'

By 1215 he was the Marshal's seneschal of Leinster and he held the post intermittently until 1223. In 1215 he obtained a hereditary grant of all the royal lands in the counties of Waterford and Desmond (Cork), including custody of the castle, but not the city of Waterford, the castle of Dungarvan and the castle and city of Cork.[249] It was probably about this time that he granted lands in the Knockmealdown Mountains to the abbey of Dunbrody, Co. Wexford (fig. 7.12).[250] He fell out of favour with the regency council of King Henry III in 1223 and was stripped of his estates when he failed to produce the charter by which they were held.[251] They were granted to John Marshal, but by 1225 he had received some of them back. Fitz Anthony died between August 1226 and April 1227.[252]

10 – **Robert Smyth** was a tenant of William Marshal's who held (or at least his descendants held) one, one-half and one-third fees at Coolcashin in the cantred of Galmoy in north-west Osraige.[253] In view of the longevity of Milo fitz Bishop (no. 7 above), Meiler fitz Henry and the Marshal himself, he may well be the same as the Robert Smiche, a follower of Maurice de Prendergast, who played a decisive role with his company of forty or fifty archers in the initial battle in Osraige in the summer of 1169.[254] Brooks, however, considered him to be a descendant.[255] Smyth witnessed several early thirteenth-century grants of land in the Kilkenny area.[256] He also held land in Cos Meath and Tipperary. His successor at Coolcashin, Richard Smyth, is first mentioned *c.*1224.[257] Together with Walter de Purcell (no. 11 below), Robert Smyth witnessed the grant by Manasser Arsic of Donaghmore and Tullabarry (both in northern Osraige) to St Thomas's Abbey, Dublin.[258]

11 – **Walter de Purcell** (Waltier, Watier or Gater Porcel) was one of William Marshal's household knights who was already pursuing the earl's interests in Ireland before 1205 and perhaps as early as 1200.[259] He witnessed the confirmation by Felix (O'Dullany) Ua Duib Shláine (fig. 7.3: bishop of Ossory *c.*1179–1202) of Manasser Arsic's grant of lands to St Thomas's Abbey, Dublin.[260] Between 1199 and 1204 he witnessed William de St Leger's grant of lands in Attanagh, on the modern border of Cos Kilkenny and Laois, to St Thomas's Abbey, Dublin.[261] By this time the Marshal had already invested him with a fief, for the service of one quarter of a knight's fee, at Kilmenan (Kilminan) in the northern part of the cantred of Odogh in northern

in John Kirwan (ed.), *Kilkenny: studies in honour of Margaret M. Phelan* (Kilkenny, 1997), pp 9–15 at pp 10–12. **249** Orpen, *Normans*, ii, p. 318; iii, p. 136. **250** 'Registrum de Dunbrothy', pp 190–5, nos 32.1, 32.5–7, 33. **251** David Beresford, 'Fitz Anthony, Thomas (d. *c.*1227)' in *DIB*, 3, p. 813. **252** Ibid. **253** Brooks, *Knights' fees*, p. 215. **254** *Song of Dermot*, pp 52–5, line 693; *Deeds of the Normans*, pp 70–1, lines 692–707. **255** Brooks, *Knights' fees*, p. 215. **256** Listed by Brooks, ibid., pp 215–16. **257** Ibid. **258** *RAST*, pp 129–30, no. 150; also Carrigan, Ossory, ii, p. 87 and Orpen, 'Castles in Ossory', p. 330 regarding Tullabarry. **259** *Chartae, privilegia et immunitates*, p. 12. **260** *RAST*, p. 311, no. 360. **261** Brooks, *Knights' fees*, pp 215–16.

Osraige.[262] He witnessed the earl's charter to Duiske Abbey in eastern modern Co. Kilkenny in 1207 as well as other grants to the abbey, also attested by the Marshal, made about the same time.[263] He also witnessed the charter to Tintern Abbey in Co. Wexford (fig. 7.6). After the earl's summons to England in September 1207, Purcell was left behind to act as an adviser to the new seneschals, indicating that he had considerable experience of the Irish situation.[264] He was sent to England as a hostage for the Marshal's good behaviour in August 1210, where he was entrusted to Peter fitz Herbert, a baron of Gloucestershire, who entertained him royally while in his custody.[265] He was seneschal of Leinster in 1219 and in *c.*1223 he witnessed the charters of Earl William Marshal II (d. 1231) to the Augustinian priory of St John's, Kilkenny (fig. 7.11), to Moone in Co. Kildare and the confirmatory charter to Duiske (fig. 7.9) by the same earl.[266] He was still alive in 1229–30.[267] Together with Robert Smyth, as seen above, he witnessed the grant by Manasser Arsic of Donaghmore and Tullabarry (both in north modern Co. Kilkenny) to St Thomas's Abbey, Dublin.[268] He also witnessed a grant of land at Malahide in north Co. Dublin to St Mary's Abbey, Dublin, bounded by lands which Hamon Mac Torcaill held (?holds), made by Richard Talbot.[269] Around 1220 he witnessed together with Thomas fitz Anthony (no. 9 above), then seneschal of Leinster, an agreement made with Christ Church Cathedral, Dublin.[270]

12 – **Thomas de Druhull** was a tenant of William Marshal's by 1202, when he held land in Osraige, amounting to one knight's fee in value at Dunmore (in the modern barony of Fassadinin) to the north of Kilkenny and Killahy (in the modern barony of Crannagh, north-west Co. Kilkenny).[271] He is likely to have been in Ireland when William Marshal arrived in 1207. He witnessed a charter to Duiske Abbey (fig. 7.9) *c.*1216 and he seems to have died shortly thereafter.[272] He also held land at Hacketstown, Co. Carlow.[273] Together with Meiler fitz Henry, Adam de Hereford and Geoffrey fitz Robert as seneschal of Leinster, he witnessed the grant of lands in Osraige by William de St Leger of Tullaghanbrogue, Rosconnell and Attanagh to St Thomas's Abbey, Dublin (*c.*1201–4).[274] He granted the advowson of the church of the Holy Trinity at Dunmore to St Thomas's.[275]

13 – **Odo Archdeacon** (Archiedekne), the first member of his family known in Ireland, witnessed the charter of Geoffrey fitz Robert to the Cistercian abbey of Duiske (fig. 7.9) in *c.*1204, together with other charters to same in the period

262 Ibid., p. 183. **263** 'Duiske charters', pp 19, 28, 29. **264** *HWM*, ii, p. 175, lines 13495–6. **265** Ibid., pp 222–5, lines 14447–68. **266** 'Duiske charters', pp 33–4; Brooks, *Knights' fees*, p. 183. **267** Ibid., p. 184. **268** *RAST*, pp 129–30, no. 150; see also n. 258 above. **269** *CSMA*, i, pp 129–30. **270** *CCD*, p. 40, no. 28. **271** Brooks, *Knights' fees*, pp 210–11. **272** Ibid., p. 211. **273** *RAST*, p. 128, no. 149. **274** Ibid., pp 125–6, nos 154–6; Brooks, *Knights' fees*, p. 231. **275** *RAST*, pp 310–11, no. 359.

from *c.*1207 to *c.*1216.[276] His descendants in Co. Kilkenny were also known as le Arcedekne Mac Odo and later Cody.[277] Stephen le Archiedekne, who appears to have been Odo's son, married Thomas fitz Anthony's daughter, Desiderata or Desiré through whom he inherited some of his father-in-law's estate in Ogenty, which became known as the manor of Dangan.[278] The Archdeacons also acquired lands in what is now the northern part of the present Co. Kilkenny, dating from at least Stephen's time and unconnected with Thomas fitz Anthony (no. 9 above), which included a holding near Donaghmore (modern barony of Fassadinin) and property in the barony of Galmoy, where they held knights' fees.[279]

14 – **Richard Fannyn** is first mentioned as a witness to Geoffrey fitz Robert's quit-claim to lands at Duiske and Annamult in 1204.[280] He was probably a tenant of William Marshal's by this time, holding half a knight's fee at Clomantagh in the modern barony of Crannagh in the north-west of present Co. Kilkenny.[281] He was killed fighting on the side of Richard Marshal, second son of William I, in the younger earl's abortive war of 1233–4 against Henry III and his French favourites. Following this, custody of his lands was given to the archbishop of Dublin 'to hold till Richard's heirs make a fine with the king for his transgression in standing against the king in the war'.[282] He was succeeded by his son, Thomas, who apparently recovered the manor of Clomantagh and continued to hold his father's fee.[283]

VI

Conclusion

As he had anticipated, once William had left for England at the end of September 1207, the rebel faction in Leinster, namely the adherents of the justiciar, Meiler fitz Henry, set to work attacking the earl's lands and properties.[284] A baronial war ensued in Ireland through the autumn and into the winter of 1207–8, while the earl languished in disgrace at the travelling royal court in England, even being taunted by King John with a story that the Marshal's forces had been routed in his absence and the countess was besieged at Kilkenny Castle.[285] By the spring of 1208, however, the true picture of the conflict in Ireland was filtering through to the royal court, whereby William Marshal's enemies had been routed by an alliance of his forces and those of

276 Brooks, *Knights' fees*, p. 177. **277** See Carrigan, *Ossory*, ii, pp 284–5; Brooks, *Knights' fees*, p. 177; Orpen, *Normans*, iii, p. 97n.64; p. 129n.41. **278** Ibid., p. 98n.64, p. 129n.41; Carrigan, *Ossory*, iv, pp 257, 267; Brooks, *Knights' fees*, pp 46–8, 254–6. **279** Carrigan, *Ossory*, ii, pp 87–8, 284–5; Brooks, *Knights' fees*, pp 176–8; Orpen, 'Castles in Ossory', p. 332; idem, *Normans*, iii, p. 97. **280** 'Duiske charters', p. 14. **281** Brooks, *Knights' fees*, p. 213. **282** *CDI*, *1171–1251*, no. 2212. **283** Brooks, *Knights' fees*, p. 213. **284** *HWM*, ii, pp 178–9, lines 13552–74. **285** Ibid., pp 188–93, lines 13575–843.

Hugh de Lacy, the earl of Ulster, which resulted in the defeat and capture of Meiler fitz Henry.[286] The king soon changed his tune by abandoning his discredited justiciar and returning the earl to royal favour.[287] On a practical level, this also involved John endeavouring to save face by regranting to the Marshal his Irish lordship to hold on new terms in his own right.[288]

In effect, William Marshal no longer owed his lordship and position in Ireland to his wife, as both the *Histoire* and the charter indicated had been the case previously. The wording of the charter referred to the then status of the earl when it was witnessed by the above fourteen individuals. This must have happened at some time subsequent to his second arrival in Ireland in the spring of 1207, before Bishop Hugh le Rous was out of the country and prior to the Marshal's departure for England about six months later. It is unstated where the charter was granted, but given the composition of the witness list there can be little doubt that it was at Kilkenny and probably in the earl's castle. In addition to organising a plan to defend his lordship with his men, allies and the countess at Kilkenny Castle during his absence, if he had not done so already the Marshal must have taken the opportunity of the assembled group to witness his charter in September 1207, prior to his departure for England to face an uncertain future. In such circumstances, it would have been a necessary step, as seen above (sect. IV), for him to support the rapidly growing and expanding chief town of his lordship by granting it a new charter, particularly in the face of an ever-threatening environment from disloyal vassals like the justiciar Meiler fitz Henry and a hostile overlord like King John, who was waiting upon his presence at court.

APPENDIX: CHARTER OF WILLIAM MARSHAL, EARL OF PEMBROKE, TO KILKENNY, 1207

Translation by John Bradley

The Latin text of the charter has been published several times.[289] As far as I am aware the only English translation is that of A.J. Otway-Ruthven.[290] The following translation is based upon hers, but I have tried to render it somewhat more fluently. This is not necessarily a recommendation because the charter is fundamentally a legal text and legal words require precise translation. I have tried, however, to maintain a balance between readability and legality. The clauses are numbered numerically according to Gearóid Mac Niocaill's edition.

286 Ibid., pp 194–5, lines 13867–82; ibid., iii, p. 155, line 13874; Crouch, *William Marshal*, pp 111–12. **287** *HWM*, ii, pp 196–7, lines 13903–30. **288** See n. 116 above. **289** *Chartae, privilegia et immunitates*, pp 33–4; Charles McNeill (ed.), *Liber primus Kilkenniensis* (Dublin, 1931), pp 71–4; Mac Niocaill, *Na buirgéisí*, pp 135–8. **290** A.J. Otway-Ruthven (trans.), *Liber primus Kilkenniensis* (Kilkenny, 1961), pp 5–7; sections were translated by Bateson, *Borough customs*, and Ballard, *British borough charters*, passim.

Be it known to all present and to come that I, William Marshal, earl of Pembroke, with the counsel and consent of my wife Isabella, have granted to my burgesses of Kilkenny all of the liberties that burgesses ought to have, insofar as it is in my power to confer them, to have and to hold for ever from me and my heirs to them and their heirs. Namely

1. Firstly, no burgess shall have to face a lawsuit in the castle or elsewhere, or respond to any charge relating to matters within the bounds of the borough, except in the hundred of the town, with the sole exception of lawsuits that are of the men of my household or of my bailiffs. This hundred shall be held in the town.

2. No homicide committed within the bounds of the town shall be deemed to be murdrum.

3. No burgess shall have to fight a duel for any appeal that may be made against him, except for the death of a man, or theft, or any other charge for which a duel may reasonably be fought.

4. The burgesses are free of toll and lastage and passage and pontage throughout all my land and power.

5. No burgess shall face a monetary fine except by the judgment of the hundred and that fine shall not exceed 10*s*. in greater lawsuits, of which half may be pardoned and the other half paid as a fine. In lesser lawsuits, such as bread and ale and things of that kind, the fine shall not exceed 2*s*. of which half may be pardoned and the other half paid as a fine. If, however, anyone incurs a fine for bread and ale or other similar penalty, the first time the fine shall not exceed 2*s*., of which half shall be pardoned, as mentioned already, and half paid as a fine. If he should incur the same penalty a second time, he shall pay 2*s*. If, however, he incurs it a third time he will accept the judgment or pay half a mark [3*s*. 8*d*.].

6. The hundred shall be held only once a week.

7. No burgess shall face a lawsuit by miskenning.

8. Every burgess may plead without using particular verbal formulas.

9. The burgesses may seize the goods of their debtors in the town of Kilkenny and if a lawsuit arises concerning pledges or goods seized for debt, then the trial shall be heard in the hundred. If, by chance, it happens that a toll is taken from any burgess in my land or power and if he who took it has been required to restore it and refuses, then his goods shall be seized until he pays back the toll at Kilkenny.

10. No outside merchant may bake bread or operate a wine tavern in the town of Kilkenny for more than forty days and if he wishes to remain longer it has to be with the common assent of the burgesses and to the profit of the town.

11. No burgess shall have his goods seized throughout my land and power for any external debt unless he is the security or the principal debtor.

12. No burgess shall be forced to act as a security to anyone, even if he holds [land] of him, unless he freely wills it.

13. I have granted also to the burgesses that they and their sons and daughters, and their widows, may freely enter marriage contracts without the permission of their lord unless they hold land directly from me [in chief] outside the borough. None of the lords from whom the burgesses of Kilkenny hold external properties [tenements] shall have the wardship or gift of them or of the sons or daughters or widows of such burgesses but only the custody of their property until those who were in ward have come of age, excepting those who hold land directly from me outside the borough.

14. My burgesses may have a merchant guild and other guilds together with the scot and all liberties pertaining to them as is the custom of other good towns.

15. The burgesses may dispose of their properties [tenements], held in burgage, whether buildings, gardens or orchards, as seems best to them unless it causes injury or injustice to their neighbours, and those who have properties [tenements] near the water may extend them by building over the water if they so wish.

16. I have granted to them also that they may give, sell or pledge all of their goods, saving the services due from them, except to religious men without my consent.

17. The burgesses may have common of my woods outside my defensive enclosure.

18. No burgess shall be forced to lend his chattels [i.e., any property or goods that are not free-hold] unless security is first given to restore them at a fixed time and, if any burgess should loan chattels, of his own accord, to the bailiffs of my castle, and if a fixed time was not established for payment, then full payment shall be made within forty days. And if, by chance, there was a change of bailiffs then I, or my bailiff, will compel the retiring bailiff to restore the debt that they can reasonably show is owing to them.

19. I have granted also to my burgesses that, by twenty feet of land, they may make their free tenants so that they may have common liberty with the burgesses.

20. My burgesses may also establish title and prove their debts by the suit of law-worthy men.

21. I have granted also to them that if any of their chattels are taken without cause because of an external penalty outside the borough, they shall be restored in so far as they can reasonably show that they are theirs.

22. I have granted to the burgesses that they may grind in my mills for a reasonable toll.

23. In addition, I have granted to the burgesses that they and their heirs shall have and hold their burgages with their appurtenances from me and my heirs, freely and quietly forever, for the rent that Geoffrey fitz Robert first established, namely a burgage with its appurtenances for a rent of twelve pence yearly, payable half at Easter and the other half at the feast of St Michael [29 September].

24. I will also that no assise of victuals shall be held in the borough unless it has the common assent of the burgesses and my bailiffs.

And in order that this grant may endure in future times I have strengthened this charter with my seal. Witness Lord Hugh [le Rous], bishop of Ossory, John Marshal, John de Earley, Jordan de Sauqueville, Ralph fitz Payan, Geoffrey fitz Robert, Milo fitz Bishop, Gilbert de Valle, Thomas fitz Anthony, Robert Smyth, Walter de Purcell, Thomas de Druhull, Odo Archdeacon and Richard Fannyn and many others.

Monastery and manor: William Marshal's settlement strategy in Co. Wexford

BILLY COLFER†

Following the death of Strongbow in 1176 the king appointed John, his youngest son, as lord of Ireland and gave William fitz Audelin the custody of Wexford.[1] Leinster remained in the king's hand until 1189 when William Marshal succeeded to the lordship by his marriage to Strongbow's daughter, Isabel, granddaughter of Diarmait Mac Murchada.[2] Prince John reluctantly agreed to give the Marshal possession of his lands in Ireland at the insistence of the king. However, the Marshal experienced considerable difficulty before eventually obtaining possession of Leinster.[3]

This essay outlines the Marshal's involvement in the development of the economy and settlement in the medieval county of Wexford, best represented by the modern diocese of Ferns, and the progress of the English colony in the county during the first half of the thirteenth century. The blood relationship between the Marshal's family and the Mac Murchadas was presumably exploited by both parties during that period. The Marshal's daughter, Maud, who acquired Carlow, with the manors of Old Ross and the Island in Co. Wexford, at the partition of Leinster in 1247, married Hugh Bigod, earl of Norfolk. In the late thirteenth century, her grandson Roger Bigod, lord of Carlow, still regarded the Mac Murchada as his kinsmen.[4]

The Marshal was made earl of Pembroke in 1199 and his first visit to Ireland in the following year resulted in the establishment of the Cistercian abbey of Tintern Minor on the shores of Bannow Bay. The Irish annals record that the Marshal founded the monastery in 1200, as a result of a vow made by him when the ship carrying his retinue from Pembroke was in danger of shipwreck.[5] They evidently succeeded in reaching the safety of Bannow Bay because it was there, at the head of a small inlet, that he endowed the foundation. It was colonised with Cistercian monks from Tintern Abbey in the Marshal's manor of Chepstow and named Tintern Minor or *de Voto* (of the vow) (fig. 8.1). King John's confirmation of the grant by the Marshal was made in 1200 but the Marshal's

1 Orpen, *Normans*, ii, p. 35. 2 Crouch, *William Marshal*, pp 68–9. 3 Orpen, *Normans*, ii, pp 202–3; for John's grant of Arklow, 'with the assent of his father', to Theobald Walter during Isabel's minority, see *Ormond deeds, 1172–1350*, p. 8, no. 17. 4 *CDI, 1252–84*, p. 352, no. 1716; p. 405, no. 1873. 5 *CSMA*, ii, pp 307–8.

8.1 Tintern Abbey (*de Voto*) (© National Monuments Service Photographic Unit).

actual charter can be dated to 1207–13 from the names of the witnesses.[6] The land granted to the Cistercians was part of Hervey de Montmorency's fief but it reverted to the Marshal after Hervey's death in 1205. This may have been the reason for the delay in the conferring of a foundation charter following the initial grant of land in 1200.

Of nine place-names mentioned in the charter to Tintern, four can be identified in the modern landscape.[7] The monastic estate, equivalent to the civil parishes of Tintern and Owenduff, contained almost 15,000 statute acres (allowing 300 statute acres to the carucate). According to the charter, part of the land had formerly been held by other individuals, presumably tenants-at-will, who were removed to make way for the Cistercians. It was not possible to displace all existing landholders because the grant to the Cistercians was divided in two by the episcopal manor of Kinnagh, an early example of a clash between the bishop of Ferns and the Marshal. The bishop's resistance to Anglo-Norman activity was epitomised by his opposition to early grants to Canterbury by Hervey de Montmorency. The granting by Hervey of nine church livings, and

6 Orpen, *Normans*, ii, p. 207. 7 Hore, *Wexford*, ii, p. 16; Marshal's charter to Tintern included 'one burgage in Ross': ibid., p. 19; the burgage lands of Clonmines, surrounded by the abbey lands, must have been retained at the time of the grant to the Cistercians.

other lands, in the south of the county to Canterbury was contested strongly by the bishop. Eventually, after about fifty years, an agreement was reached by which Canterbury retained eight of the churches in the barony of Bargy and the important manor of Fethard was restored to the bishop.[8]

Leaving Geoffrey fitz Robert in charge of Leinster, the Marshal was involved on the king's business in England and Normandy for the next six years until John eventually permitted him to return to Ireland in 1207. He received a mixed reception from the barons of Leinster who had been granted their lands from Strongbow and resented the new arrivals. Encouraged by the king, the justiciar, Meiler fitz Henry, opposed the Marshal; both men were recalled to England and fitz Henry's men began a campaign against the Marshal by attacking his recently established town of New Ross. They were successfully opposed by the earl's knights, led by John de Earley and Stephen d'Evereux, and the fitz Henry faction was defeated.[9] In 1208, the king instructed the justiciar to allow the Marshal to take possession of Leinster and to restore Offaly to him with its castles. Having received a new grant to Leinster by the service of one hundred knights,[10] the Marshal returned to Ireland and established his headquarters at Kilkenny. During the next five years, he was almost continually in Ireland planning the organisation of his Leinster lordship.[11]

THE MARSHAL'S LAND GRANTS

To facilitate administration, the liberty of Leinster was divided into the four shires or counties of Wexford, Kilkenny, Carlow and Kildare.[12] This arrangement was in place by at least the early thirteenth century as the county court of Wexford was in existence in 1204, with the centre of administration in Wexford Castle after its construction.[13] Strongbow had made considerable progress in the distribution of land-grants in Wexford and the process was completed under the Marshal's direction. The demesne manors already selected by Strongbow were retained by the Marshal (fig. 8.2). These were all located on sites with established settlement structures. Ross, Ferns and Taghmon were sites of early Christian monasteries and Wexford was a fortified Norse town.[14] A deforestation charter issued by Richard Marshal at Old Ross in 1233, defining the boundaries of the manors of Ross and Taghmon, indicated that the manorial boundaries corresponded substantially to the medieval parish boundaries later defined by the seventeenth-century Civil Survey.[15] In the case of Ferns, the parish also included

8 J.B. Sheppard (ed.), *Letter books of Christ Church, Canterbury* (3 vols, London, 1887–9), iii, pp 248, 363. 9 Crouch, *William Marshal*, pp 100–15. 10 *CDI, 1171–1251*, p. 56, nos 377, 378; p. 57, no. 381. 11 Crouch, *William Marshal*, pp 112–13. 12 Otway-Ruthven, *Medieval Ireland*, p. 186. 13 A.J. Otway-Ruthven, 'The medieval county of Kildare', *IHS*, 11 (1959), pp 181–99 at p. 185; 'Duiske charters', p. 16. 14 Colfer, *Arrogant trespass*, pp 39–42. 15 Eric St-J. Brooks and G.H. Orpen (eds), 'Charters of Earl Richard Marshal of the forests

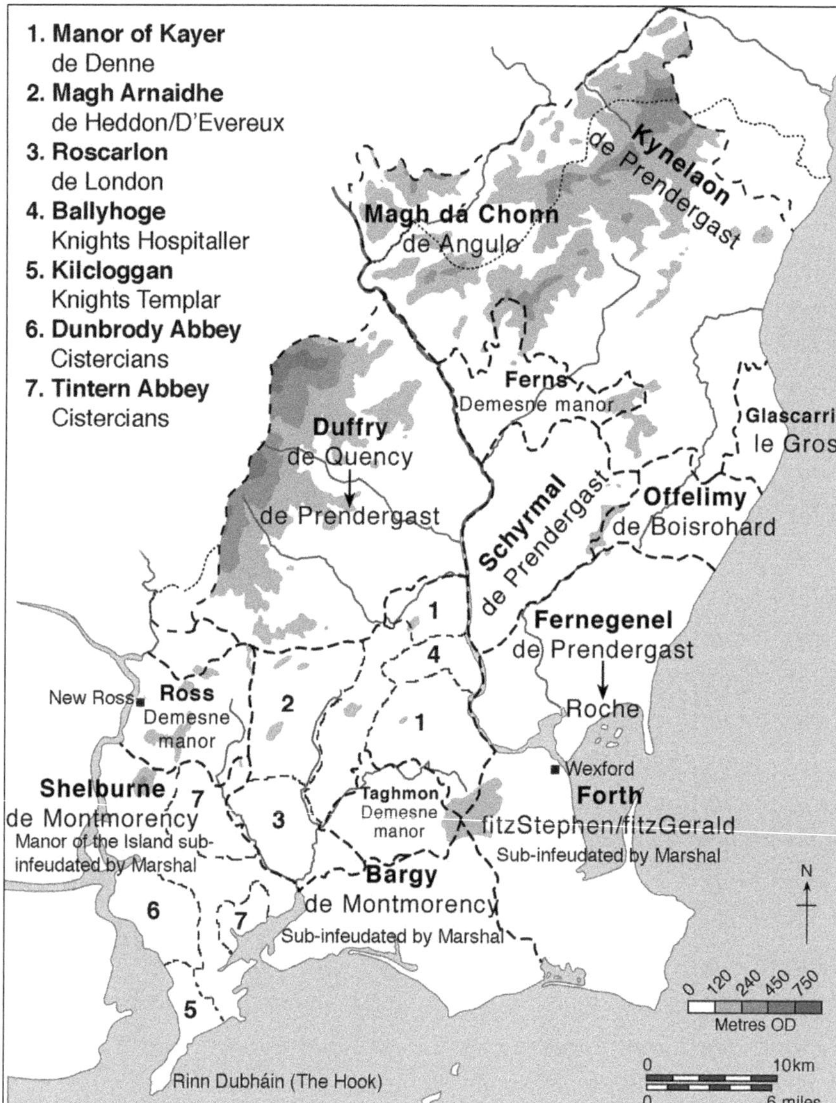

8.2 Outline of early Anglo-Norman land grants in medieval Co. Wexford.

an episcopal manor, possibly contributing to the endemic antagonism between the Marshal and successive bishops. Five knights from the Marshal's household received grants of land in Wexford.[16] The Prendergasts from Pembrokeshire acquired Fernegenel; the Rochfords from Gloucester succeeded to the Duffry by

of Ross and Taghmon', *JRSAI*, 64 (1934), pp 54–63. **16** Crouch, *William Marshal*, p. 148.

marriage to a Prendergast heir.[17] Members of the Bluet family from the manor of Striguil, on the River Severn, came to Ireland with Strongbow. They witnessed a number of charters, including one of Strongbow's to Dunbrody Abbey.[18] The family of Avenel, also from Striguil, came to Ireland with the Marshal. Andrew Avenel witnessed one of the earl's charters *c.*1207.[19]

CHANGES IN OWNERSHIP

The development of settlement in medieval Wexford was influenced to a considerable extent by changes in ownership of several early grants (fig. 8.2). Hervey de Montmorency's fief, represented by the modern baronies of Bargy and Shelburne, reverted to the Marshal following Hervey's death in 1205. Much of Shelburne had already been alienated to the church by grants by de Montmorency to the Cistercians at Dunbrody, by Henry II to the Knights Templar at Kilcloggan, and by the Marshal himself to the Cistercians at Tintern. The manorial centre was located on what is now Greatisland in the River Barrow (no longer an island due to reclamation). Originally called *Inis Teimle*, and occupied by the extensive early Christian foundation of Kilmokea,[20] the island was subsequently known as Hervey's Island. After its reversion to the Marshal the manor of the Island was administered with the demesne manor of Ross.[21] It is evident that Hervey de Montmorency had little success in colonising his fiefdom before entering Canterbury as a monk in 1185. He failed to attract a religious establishment to Bannow[22] and his grant to Buildwas at Dunbrody was rejected. A report prepared by a Brother Alan, who was sent by Buildwas to investigate the proposed grant, provides a description of the area in the late twelfth century that is perhaps somewhat prejudiced as the writer had to live in a hollow oak tree:

> A laybrother, Alan by name, found the place a solitary waste, took up his dwelling in a certain hollow oak and there made his abode during the time of his sojourn, and led a life of penury and toil; finally the bounds of the aforesaid lands and tenements being limited and assigned, he returned to us with speed, informing us to the full concerning the waste of the place, the sterility of the lands, and the wildness and ferocity of the neighbouring barbarians … We might incur no small damage or loss, if we should attempt to send any to those parts in order to inhabit and dwell.[23]

17 Brooks, *Knights' fees*, p. 140. **18** Hore, *Wexford*, iii, p. 43. **19** 'Duiske charters', p. 19. **20** Máirín Ní Dhonnchadha, 'Inis Teimle between Uí Chennselaig and the Déissí', *Peritia*, 16 (2002), pp 457–8. **21** Orpen, *Normans*, i, p. 393; *CIPM Edw. I*, iv [1300–7], pp 306–7. **22** J.C. Ward, 'Fashions in monastic endowment: the foundations of the Clare family, 1066–1314', *Journal of Ecclesiastical History*, 32 (1981), pp 427–52 at pp 445–6. **23** *CSMA*, i, p. 357.

As a result of this most unfavourable report, Buildwas declined the grant, passing it on to St Mary's Abbey in Dublin. Further proof of the difficulty in attracting settlers is provided in a recently published charter of Hervey de Montmorency, issued in the mid-1170s, which granted a large fief in Bargy to Osbert fitz Robert. Although he was offered very attractive terms the grant was not accepted and fitz Robert does not subsequently figure in the settlement history of the county.[24]

Because of de Montmorency's difficulty in attracting tenants before his departure to Canterbury, it is probable that the Marshal had to complete the subinfeudation of the three southern cantreds of Forth, Shelburne and Bargy (originally granted to Montmorency). Initially given to Robert fitz Stephen and Maurice fitz Gerald, Forth had reverted to Strongbow as a demesne manor attached to Wexford town and the Marshal presumably completed its organisation by granting a number of small military tenures, retaining some demesne land at Rosslare and Ballymore, in the south of the cantred. Similarly on the manor of the Island, a number of small sub-manors were created, held principally by the Suttons and Keatings. As in Forth, some demesne land was retained, principally represented by the parish of Kilmokea. Some of these grants created a narrow corridor between the lands of Tintern and Dunbrody, perhaps with the intention of creating a buffer zone between the two abbeys (fig. 8.2).

As well as installing new military tenants in the cantred of Bargy (including the Brownes of Mulrankin, the Marshal's men from south Wales and originally from Normandy), presumably due to the scarcity of suitable tenants, the Marshal granted much of the land in the cantred to holders of existing fiefs (de Heddon/Devereux, Boscher, de London, Keating) and in so doing created a complex system of 'split' manors.[25] Strongbow's early land grants, combined with the Marshal's, meant that much of the county was held by knight's fee, ensuring an essential military structure in what was in reality a frontier situation. Although the Marshal regime was involved in the settlement of the three southern cantreds, the settlement in each cantred, for various reasons, had a distinctive character. It is also clear that the dense settlement on small, more secure manors in the south of the county was quite different in character from the sprawling, thinly populated manors in the north where, as an incentive to settlers, knights' fees were up to four times bigger than those in the more secure south of the county (fig. 8.2). By the end of the thirteenth century, the northern 'land of war' had been overrun by the Irish. This is reflected in the distribution of various landscape features, including defensive earthworks, manorial villages, medieval parish churches and fifteenth-century tower houses.

24 M.T. Flanagan, 'An early Anglo-Norman charter of Hervey de Montmorency' in Marion Meek (ed.), *The modern traveller to our past: Festschrift in honour of Ann Hamlin* (Dublin, 2006), pp 232–42. 25 Brooks, *Knights' fees*, pp 96–116.

THE SITING AND DISTRIBUTION OF DEFENSIVE EARTHWORKS

The construction of defensive earthworks created the initial visual expression of Anglo-Norman activity in the Irish landscape (fig. 8.3). Castle-building was an integral part of Norman policy for the military domination of newly acquired lands. Giraldus Cambrensis recommended that 'the country should be secured and protected by the construction of many castles'.[26] The siting of castles was not regarded as a matter of random choice by individual manorial lords but was intended to be systematically planned for maximum efficiency. Twenty-nine defensive earthworks associated with early Anglo-Norman activity in Uí Chennselaig have been identified.[27] The significance of these sites becomes more obvious when they are viewed as part of an overall settlement pattern. The strategic and economic factors that influenced the location and morphology of defensive earthworks were obviously dependent on the status of the holding within the feudal hierarchy. Bigger fiefs offered a wider choice in the selection of a strategic site and more economic support. These factors had a bearing on the development of the site as a centre of long-term settlement.

The distribution of the defensive earthworks, integrated with thirteenth-century stone castles, reveals two distinctive alignments (fig. 8.3). As well as having individual defensive capabilities, the earthworks form a double protective line running diagonally across the county from south-west to north-east. This line marked the border within the region between the colonised south and east and the Gaelic-dominated district to the north-west. As well as providing a protective zone along the interface between native and settler, the defensive earthworks indicate the determination of the Anglo-Normans to occupy the best quality land, which also has a south-west to north-east orientation across the county.[28] The second obvious arrangement of earthworks is the alignment of eight mottes along the east coast, emphasising the importance of controlling access to vital strategic and economic sea routes with Britain and the Continent.

EARLY STONE CASTLES

The Marshal had started construction on Carlow Castle (pl. 5), built to control traffic on the River Barrow, in 1210–15,[29] so it is probable that he had initiated a

26 Giraldus, *Expugnatio*, p. 249. 27 Identification of mottes and ringwork castles is based on the following sources: Orpen, *Normans*, ii, distribution map of mottes; R.E. Glascock and T.E. McNeill, 'Mottes in Ireland: a draft list', *Bulletin of the Group for the Study of Irish Historic Settlement*, 3 (1972), pp 27–51 at p. 48; Geraldine Stout et al., *Sites and monuments record, County Wexford* (Dublin, 1987); Moore, *AI Wexford*, pp 90–4; T.B. Barry, *The archaeology of medieval Ireland* (London, 1987), pp 37–71; OS sheets County Wexford (1841) and fieldwork. 28 M.J. Gardiner and Pierce Ryan, *Soils of County Wexford* (Dublin, 1964). 29 Kieran O'Conor, 'The origins of Carlow Castle', *Archaeology Ireland*, 11:3 (1997), pp 13–16.

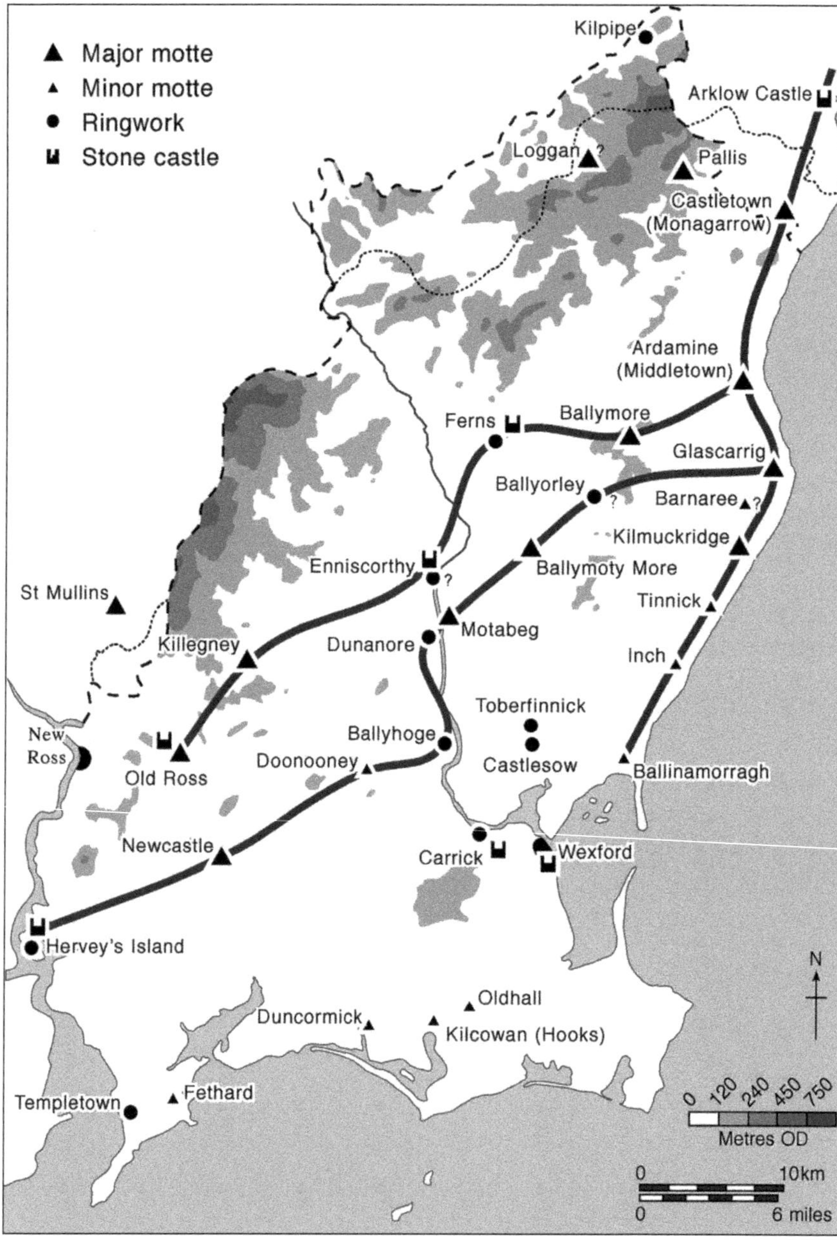

8.3 Defensive earthworks and thirteenth-century stone castles in Co. Wexford.

programme of stone castle-building in Co. Wexford before his death in 1219. His son, William II, was also engaged in castle-building, because in 1222 and 1225 the service that he owed to the king was cancelled to enable him 'to fortify a castle in Ireland'.[30] Stone castles on demesne land in the county had all been built by 1230: following the Marshal's death in that year, the castles of Wexford, Ross, Carrick-on-Slaney and the Island were taken into the king's hands and Ferns Castle (pl. 4) was given in dower to the Marshal's widow, the countess of Pembroke.[31] It is generally accepted that although the Marshals began the construction of the castle recorded at Ferns in 1231, further work was carried out later in the century (fig. 8.4). This may be attributed to William de Valence who succeeded to the lordship of Wexford by his marriage to a Marshal heiress.[32] The castle of Enniscorthy, built by the Prendergasts on a rock at the head of the tidal waters of the Slaney, is not mentioned in thirteenth-century records. It was first recorded when it was taken into the king's hands sometime between 1307 and 1327. After being destroyed by fire in 1569, it was 'repaired' in 1586 when it was given its present shape.[33] Ferns Castle, the only survivor of the six mentioned above, is one of a number of castles that are considered unique to south-east Ireland, sometimes classified as towered keeps or donjons (fig. 8.4).[34] However, this theory has been reviewed and questioned in recent times.[35] These castles consisted of a strong rectangular tower, two or three storeys in height, with a massive circular turret at each corner, a design possibly inspired by the Marshal's knowledge of castle construction in France, where the cylindrical keep was popular, inspired by castle design brought back by Crusaders from the Levant. Carlow Castle, where building may have started in the period 1210–15, is considered to be the earliest of this group.[36] Wexford Castle may have been of this type also as it was described in 1323 as 'a stone castle in which there are four towers roofed with shingles'. The mid-seventeenth-century Down Survey shows Wexford Castle with four conical-roofed towers.[37]

Although not strictly speaking a castle, the circular turret known as the Tower of Hook (pl. 12) belongs to the same period as the other Marshal castles (though see Murtagh, this volume, for a slightly later dating of the Tower of Hook) and was constructed using the same technology and, presumably, personnel (fig. 8.5). Realising the importance of Waterford Harbour and its river system for trade and shipping, the Marshal established the port of New Ross on the River Barrow, 40km from the open sea. Other towns in his lordship were also located on the rivers Barrow and Nore, principally Carlow and Kilkenny. Perhaps influenced by his own narrow escape from shipwreck, the Marshal knew that shipping needed to be guided safely into Waterford Harbour through the dangerous waters off the

30 *CDI, 1171–1251*, p. 158, no. 1030; p. 192, no. 1269. 31 Ibid., pp 278–9, no. 1872; p. 280, no. 1950. 32 Tadhg O'Keeffe and Margaret Coughlan, 'The chronology and formal affinities of Ferns donjon, Co. Wexford' in J.R. Kenyon and Kieran O'Conor (eds), *The medieval castle in Ireland and Wales* (Dublin, 2003), pp 133–48 at p. 145. 33 Hore, *Wexford*, vi, pp 351, 411. 34 H.G. Leask, *Irish castles and castellated houses* (Dundalk, 1941), p. 47; T.E. McNeill, *Castles in Ireland: feudal power in a Gaelic world* (London, 1997), p. 118. 35 O'Keeffe and Coughlin, 'Chronology of Ferns donjon', pp 133–48. 36 O'Conor, 'Origins of Carlow Castle', pp 13–16. 37 Billy Colfer, *Wexford: a town and its landscape* (Cork, 2008), pp 75–9.

8.4 Ferns Castle, Co. Wexford.

point of *Rinn Dubháin* (The Hook) if his new port of Ross was to be successful. As a navigation aid, he had a 36m-high circular tower constructed at the tip of the peninsula to act as a landmark by day and a fire-tower by night. The monks from the nearby monastery of Rinn Dubháin were involved in the construction of the tower and acted as lightkeepers; in 1247, the custodian and chaplains of St Saviour's of Rinn Dubháin 'who there built a tower as a beacon for ships' were granted maintenance in 'money and otherwise' from the Pembroke estate, with 'all arrears due to them', indicating that the tower had been in operation for some time.[38] As the construction would have taken some years, it was presumably started in the early decades of the century. The Marshal's idea for a light-tower may have been inspired by Mediterranean examples, such as the crusader lighthouse at Acre or the Pharos lighthouse in Alexandria, which he presumably saw when on crusade to the Holy Land.[39] The Tower of Hook was also based on the cylindrical castles, which were popular in France, where the Marshal spent many years. His castles at Chepstow, Pembroke, Ferns, Carlow and Kilkenny also had circular towers (see Murtagh, this volume, and pls 4, 5, 8, 9, 11). The monks

38 *CDI, 1171–1251*, p. 420, no. 2811; p. 429, no. 2872. 39 Crouch, *William Marshal*, p. 55.

8.5 Thirteenth-century Tower of Hook, Co. Wexford.

lived in the tower, which served as a monastery as well as a lighthouse. Thirty statute acres around the tower (still known locally as 'the tower lands') were reserved for the use of the light-keepers. These lands had been included in the Knights Templar manor of Kilcloggan, granted by Henry II in 1172,[40] but were apparently requisitioned for the development of the light-tower. This was presumably facilitated by the Marshal's close connection with the Templars as evidenced by his burial in London's Temple Church (pl. 28). For centuries after its construction, the Tower of Hook remained in the control of the Marshal's town of Ross. In 1411, the sovereign and community of the town of Ross held the Tower of Hook, with twelve acres of adjoining land.[41] Now serving as a base for a modern lantern, the thirteenth-century tower survives intact, still serving its original function as a lighthouse. Following automation, the complex was developed as a visitor attraction with guided tours of the unique medieval tower, which can claim to be the oldest intact operational lighthouse in the world.

40 Billy Colfer, *The Hook Peninsula* (Cork, 2006), pp 47–50, 55–61. 41 Hore, *Wexford*, iv, pp 405, 409.

BOROUGHS

The concept of the chartered town was introduced into Ireland by the Anglo-Normans who were subsequently responsible for most of the towns and boroughs established in Ireland in the twelfth and thirteenth centuries. The recipients of large fiefs, who needed settlers for their newly acquired lands, offered the bait of burgess status as a strategy to attract colonists from Britain.[42] The continuity that can be demonstrated in the use of land divisions in Co. Wexford was also apparent in the selection of some urban sites as the Anglo-Normans were inevitably attracted to the infrastructure associated with the Scandinavian towns and early Christian monastic centres.[43] The Marshal was directly involved with nine chartered boroughs in the county. He inherited Ferns, Old Ross, the town of the Island, Bannow and possibly Taghmon and Carrick-on-Slaney. He granted charters for New Ross, Clonmines (pl. 26) and the Scandinavian town of Wexford. Four of these – Wexford, New Ross, Taghmon and Ferns – survive as settlements in the modern landscape. The town of Wexford was the first settlement in Ireland to be taken over by the Anglo-Normans and became the administrative centre of the county. However, the charter of 1307 records that the town was not created a borough until about 1200, when Geoffrey fitz Robert, the Marshal's seneschal, granted it a charter.[44] Under the Marshal regime, Wexford became the administrative centre of a county of the same name.

Three early medieval monastic centres were selected as sites for early boroughs on demesne land, presumably because of the existing settlement structure and strategic possibilities. Ferns, the most substantial monastic centre, with the added attraction of being the headquarters of the Uí Chennselaig dynasty, was chosen by Strongbow as one of his demesne manors, and was created a borough by him as there were burgesses there by 1176.[45] The monastic centre of Taghmon was reserved as a demesne manor and was also granted borough status. The town of the Island, probably located beside deep water where the modern pier stands, and where some archaeological remains survive, was associated with the monastic centre of Kilmokea on *Inis Teimle*, now known as Greatisland.[46] The island, located in the River Barrow where it enters Waterford Harbour, was ideally positioned as a trading centre. It also straddled

42 A.J. Otway-Ruthven, 'The character of Norman settlement in Ireland' in *Historical studies*, 5, ed. J.L. McCracken (London, 1965), pp 75–84 at p. 79; John Bradley, 'Planned Anglo-Norman towns in Ireland' in H.B. Clarke and Anngret Simms (eds), *The comparative history of urban origins in non-Roman Europe* (Oxford, 1985), pp 411–67 at pp 414–21. 43 Charles Doherty, 'Exchange and trade in medieval Ireland', *JRSAI*, 110 (1980), pp 67–89 at pp 81–2. 44 Hore, *Wexford*, v, pp 102–3. 45 Edward Culleton, *Celtic and early Christian Wexford* (Dublin, 1999), p. 104; *Calendar of the ancient deeds and muniments preserved in the Pembroke Estate Office, Dublin* (Dublin, 1891), p. 11. 46 Ní Dhonnchadha, 'Inis Teimle', p. 451; Moore, *AI Wexford*, p. 117, no. 1163; Culleton, *Celtic and early Christian Wexford*, pp 152, 210.

the road from Wexford to Waterford, which crossed the river by ferry at this point. The town must have been founded by Hervey de Montmorency who established his caput on the island, subsequently known as Hervey's Island, and was taken over by the Marshal after Hervey's death in 1205.[47] The town of the Island, located beside deep water in a sheltered area on the River Barrow, continued in use as a port throughout the thirteenth century but was eventually abandoned in favour of Ross.[48]

Hervey de Montmorency's attempt to found a monastery at Bannow is a strong indication that he was the founder of the borough.[49] Located on the south coast, Bannow was well placed for overseas trade but the harbour, like that of Wexford, was shallow and difficult for shipping. Bannow survived until the middle of the seventeenth century when it was still functioning as a settlement with streets and house plots.[50] Clonmines (pl. 26), at the head of Bannow Bay, was one of two boroughs founded by the Marshal himself (fig. 8.6).[51] The relationship between the lands of Clonmines and the surrounding lands of Tintern Abbey indicates that the land for Clonmines was reserved before, or contemporaneous with, the founding of the abbey in 1200. It is difficult to reconcile the establishment of Clonmines at the head of Bannow Bay by William Marshal with the development of New Ross as the port of Leinster, because Clonmines, on a tortuous channel and with a limited hinterland, was inevitably at a disadvantage. Indeed, this proved to be the case, leading ultimately to its abandonment. However, other factors influenced his decision to establish the borough, at least in the short term. One of these is related to the Marshal's narrow escape from shipwreck on the occasion of his first visit to Leinster and the subsequent construction of the Tower of Hook as a navigational aid. In bad weather, it is notoriously difficult for boats and smaller ships coming from the east to round the point of Hook and gain entrance to Waterford Harbour. By avoiding the dangers off the Hook, a port at Clonmines gave the Marshal's officials a sheltered alternative to New Ross during the winter months. There may also have been a political factor in the Marshal's decision to establish Clonmines. From the early thirteenth century, continuous directives were issued to shipping entering Waterford Harbour to land at the king's port of Waterford instead of the Marshal's ports of Ross and the Island.[52] The Marshal provided his shipping with an alternative by establishing the port of Clonmines, which was well placed to take advantage of the trade generated by the monastic estates of Tintern, Dunbrody and Kilcloggan.

47 Orpen, *Normans*, i, p. 393. 48 *CDI, 1171–1251*, p. 136, no. 912; p. 351, no. 2361. 49 Ward, 'Monastic endowment', p. 445. 50 Hore, *Wexford*, iv, p. 459; in the mid-seventeenth-century survey of the town of Bannow, the following street names are given: Lackey, High, New, Little, Lady, Weavers; a church, castle, dovecote and market cross are also mentioned. 51 *CDI, 1252–84*, pp 246–7, no. 1330. 52 Colfer, *Arrogant trespass*, pp 178–9.

8.6 Deserted medieval town of Clonmines, Co. Wexford.

Documentation for Clonmines is scarce, possibly because it was economically detached from the rest of the county at the partition of Leinster.[53] It was functioning as a town in the fourteenth century; in 1356, the provost, bailiff and community were fined for having the pillory broken and in 1364 a sheriff for the county was elected there. In the early fifteenth century, it was the venue for a number of inquisitions and in the late sixteenth century Clonmines was still referred to as a town. In the seventeenth century, the town had a portreeve, and burgage lands 'within and without' the town.[54] In 1684, however, it was described as 'a place of great trade in times passed, and a harbour for shipping of indifferent bulk until the sand filled up the ancient passage near the town of Bannow, which was the destruction of both these towns [Clonmines and Bannow]'.[55]

The surviving remains include an Augustinian priory, two tower houses, a fortified church, the parish church of St Nicholas and the ruins of a Jacobean house (fig. 8.6).[56] J.N. Brewer's account from 1826, which described 'the foundations of numerous other buildings throughout an extent of at least twenty acres', has been supported by a limited resistivity survey carried out in the early 1990s that identified a number of underground features.[57] Part of the town

53 *CDI, 1252–84*, pp 160–1, no. 933. 54 Hore, *Wexford*, ii, pp 211–62. 55 H.F. Hore (ed.), 'A chorographic account of the southern part of the county of Wexford, written anno 1684: by Robert Leigh esq. of Rosegarland in that county', *JRSAI*, 5 (1858–9), pp 451–67 at p. 455. 56 Moore, *AI Wexford*, pp 153–4. 57 M.E. Byrne, 'The results of a resistivity survey

defences, described as a 'vallum and fosse' in 1837,[58] may be represented by a large bank and ditch, running northwards from the parish church, which, when it was complete, protected the landward side of the headland on which the town was situated.[59] Clonmines has been described as the best example in Ireland of a deserted medieval borough.[60]

The Marshal's decision to relocate the borough of Ross may have been influenced by current developments in England: the town of Hull, like New Ross located on an estuary, had recently been founded and Liverpool, also on a tidal estuary, received its first charter in 1207.[61] The Marshal, no doubt briefed by officials who had been administering the lordship in his absence, was determined to exploit the potential of the rivers and the Waterford Harbour estuary. The communications network provided by the Barrow and Nore meant that New Ross could become the port of Leinster; the Barrow, for example, was navigable as far as Athy.[62] The concentration of medieval towns and boroughs founded along the two rivers as part of the development of Leinster is a clear indication of their economic significance. The Marshal probably initiated the foundation of the port of New Ross during his first visit to Ireland in 1200. In 1207 it was referred to as *la novele ville* and at the same period 'one burgage of Ross, on the south side of the bridge' is mentioned in the Marshal's charter to Tintern Abbey.[63] When King John visited Ireland in 1210, he stayed at New Ross, referred to as *Pons novus, villa Willielmi Marescalli* (a new bridge, the town of William Marshal).[64] The building of the bridge, which facilitated a road link between Wexford and the Marshal's caput of Kilkenny, was obviously a crucial element in the infrastructure of the lordship, and indicated the Marshal's commitment to the development of the site. The most dramatic symbol of his determination to create an international port was the construction, early in the thirteenth century, of the massive Tower of Hook as a light-tower and navigation aid at the entrance to Waterford Harbour, previously mentioned. The town, known as Ross or Rospont, took its name from the initial land-locked borough, located about 10km to the east, which came to be known as Old Ross. The older foundation, which never achieved more than rural borough status, continued to function as the centre of the manor of Old Ross and its significance was

undertaken at Clonmines, County Wexford', *Journal of the Wexford Historical Society*, 15 (1994–5), pp 67–73. **58** J.N. Brewer, *The beauties of Ireland, being original delineations, topographical, historical and biographical, of each county* (2 vols, London, 1826), i, pp 362–3. **59** Samuel Lewis, *A topographical dictionary of Ireland* (2 vols, London, 1837), i, p. 372. **60** R.E. Glasscock, 'Moated sites and deserted boroughs and villages; two neglected aspects of Anglo-Norman settlement in Ireland' in Nicholas Stephens and R.E. Glasscock (eds), *Irish geographical studies in honour of E. Estyn Evans* (Belfast, 1970), pp 162–77 at p. 170. **61** Maurice Beresford, *New towns of the Middle Ages* (London, 1967), pp 515, 461; R.E. Glasscock, 'Some parallels to New Ross', *Journal of the Old Wexford Society*, 7 (1978–9), pp 31–4 at pp 32–3. **62** *Calendar of the justiciary rolls, Ireland* [1295–1303], ed. James Mills (Dublin, 1905), p. 202. **63** *HWM*, ii, line 13569; G.H. Orpen, *New Ross in the thirteenth century* (Dublin, 1911), p. 7. See also Ó Drisceoil, this volume. **64** Ibid., p. 3.

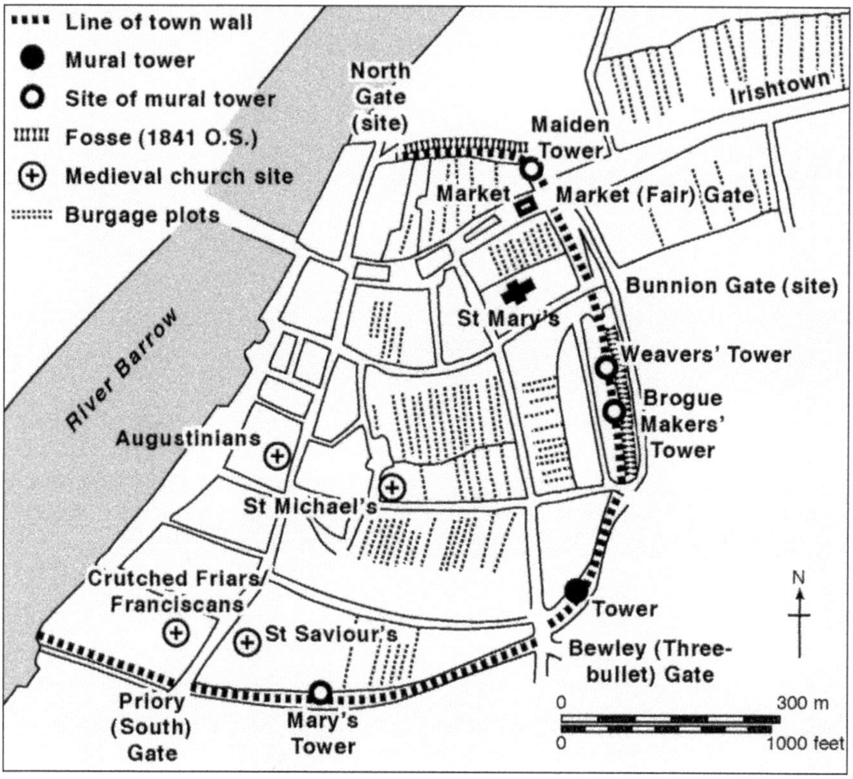

8.7 Map of medieval New Ross, Co. Wexford.

emphasised by the construction of an early thirteenth-century castle, which succeeded the original motte castle.

The location of New Ross, a carefully planned commercial venture on a 'green-field' site, was dictated by the commercial potential of the river system associated with Waterford Harbour (fig. 8.7). The site of the town, sloping from the river to a height of 60m within 1km, and situated between a steep cliff to the north and extensive marshes to the south, was not ideal for development. The problems associated with the site were compensated for by the quality of the sheltered harbour. Located 40km from the open sea, it was described as 'one of the best harbours for shipping in the kingdom', with deep water close to the shore where a 'ship of 500 tons burden could ride afloat fast by the quay'. As many as 400 ships could be accommodated at the same time; 100 at anchor and 300 by the quay.[65] The location of the town, at a point just above the widening of the river, making it possible to construct a bridge, must also have been taken into consideration. The potential earning power of a successful port was reflected

65 Hore, *Wexford*, i, p. 289; Leigh, 'Chorographic account', p. 451.

8.8 St Mary's Church, New Ross, Co. Wexford.

throughout the century in a bitter dispute that persisted between the Marshal's port of Ross and the king's port of Waterford. Directives issued by the king ordering that the Marshal's own ships could trade freely with Ross, with all other ships entering the estuary diverting to Waterford, proved ineffective. Although the bitter rivalry continued, both ports prospered and by the end of the century, Ross was one of the principal ports in Ireland.[66]

Information on the early development of the town relates mostly to ecclesiastical affairs. In contrast to Wexford, Ross, with its lands, consisted of one large parish of 4,922 statute acres. The construction of the early thirteenth-century parish church of St Mary's, near the top of the slope on which the town was built, is attributed to William Marshal and his wife Isabel.[67] Extensive remains survive, part of which has been converted for use as a modern church (fig. 8.8, pl. 27).[68] Of other medieval churches, only the sites are known. The construction of the town wall in the 1260s was celebrated in a Norman-French poem entitled 'The walling of Ross'.[69]

66 For a more complete account of the port, see Colfer, *Arrogant trespass*, pp 171–82 and Ó Drisceoil, this volume. 67 H.G. Leask, *Irish churches and monastic buildings* (3 vols, Dundalk, 1955–60), ii, p. 85. 68 Moore, *AI Wexford*, p. 158, no. 1457. 69 Hugh Shields, '"The walling of Ross": a thirteenth-century poem in French', *Long Room*, 12–13 (1975–6), pp 24–33.

CONCLUSION

The broad outline of Anglo-Norman settlement in Co. Wexford had been established before Strongbow's death in 1176 but remained incomplete until the Marshal's arrival in the early thirteenth century. The Marshal initiated an ambitious programme to develop the colony and to exploit the economic possibilities of his lordship. In theory at least, the feudal model of settlement introduced by the Anglo-Normans, based on the economic unit of the manor, should have resulted in a standardised development of all fiefs. This was not the case, however, as the settlement structure that evolved in each cantred depended on the status of the manorial lord, as well as location, soil type, security and trade routes. The demesne manors provide the best example of the diverse nature of settlement. In theory, the manors of Taghmon, Ferns and Old Ross (all located on soils with a wide use range) should have evolved along similar lines but due to geographical, political and military factors, each manor developed in a distinctive way.

As the organisation of manorial development, including the introduction of settlers, was the responsibility of the immediate overlord, different levels of ambition, ability and resources resulted in the creation of a varied manorial structure. Due to geographical and political factors, the comprehensive organisation of settlement in the southern cantreds for which the Marshal was responsible contrasted sharply with the uneven level of settlement on secondary land-grants. The nature of manorial organisation can be assessed from the contemporary emergence of the parochial structure, which provides an index to the density and permanence of settlement. The small parishes created by the complex colonisation of south-east Co. Wexford contrasted dramatically with the large sprawling parishes associated with sporadic speculative settlement in the wooded uplands bordering the Blackstairs and Wicklow Mountains. There is an obvious change in parochial size north of a line running approximately from New Ross to Cahore Point. By 1325, all of the identified manors north of this line were abandoned due to pressure from the Mac Murchadas and their allies.

Because of the significance of his ecclesiastical status within the feudal system, the bishop was the only landowner in Uí Chennselaig who was in a position to protect his rights during the process of sub-infeudation and settlement. There is evidence to show that Bishop Ailbe Ua Maelmhuidhe (the last pre-Reformation Gaelic-Irish bishop) was at least partly successful in challenging grants of land that he considered to rightfully belong to the diocese.[70] Ua Maelmhuidhe was also in dispute with William Marshal concerning diocesan lands that the Marshal had appropriated, possibly in the process of developing the demesne manor of Ferns. The bishop took the

70 *Letter books of Christ Church, Canterbury*, iii, pp 248, 363.

extreme step of obtaining a letter from Rome threatening the Marshal with excommunication if the lands were not returned. This ultimate sanction did not, apparently, have the desired effect because when the Marshal died in 1219 he was under excommunication by the bishop of Ferns for seizing and keeping two episcopal estates.[71] The determination of the bishop to protect the diocesan lands did not depend on the ethnic background of the incumbent because Ua Maelmhuidhe's successor, John de St John, treasurer of Ireland and the first Anglo-Norman bishop of Ferns, whose family later occupied land at Tomhaggard in the south of the county, successfully continued the same policy.[72]

The premature demise of all five Marshal brothers was rendered even more extraordinary by the fact that all died childless, which had a dramatic impact on the subsequent development of the lordship. Following the demands of feudal practice, Leinster was divided among his five daughters or their representatives. This event, which divided counties as well as Leinster, created a fragmented political, administrative and economic situation in Co. Wexford, which, inevitably, contributed to the gradual disintegration of the colony. The Marshal's activities in Co. Wexford were interpreted rather bizarrely by contemporary commentators. The deaths of his five sons without heir – and the consequent partition of Leinster – was attributed to the excommunication of the elder Marshal by the bishop of Ferns. For example, Matthew Paris, the St Alban's chronicler, recorded the extinction of the Marshals in the male line as the result of the episcopal 'curse'.[73] Perhaps the Marshal's most enduring legacy in the county was the granting of lands to the families of Browne, Codd, Devereux, Esmonde, Hore, Keating, Lamport, Pettit, Rossiter, Stafford, Wadding, Whitty and many others – surnames that are now synonymous with the history and heritage of the county.

The stability and success of the colony in Co. Wexford under the Marshal regime was not sustained. By the early fourteenth century, the English settlement in Co. Wexford, weakened by internal conflict, was under severe pressure from the resurgent Irish. The disruptive impact of the Bruce invasion and famine in the early part of the century, followed by the devastating Black Death in mid-century, helped to determine the ultimate extent of the colony in the county. By the end of the fourteenth century, the north of the county had been abandoned by the settler community and was controlled by the Irish. Co. Wexford was ultimately divided into 'an enduring trilogy of regions'; a Gaelic north, an English south, with a hybrid region in between.[74] Evidence for these divisions is abundantly visible in the settlement and landscape of the modern county.

71 Orpen, *Normans*, iii, p. 29; Crouch, *William Marshal*, p. 114. 72 Hore, *Wexford*, vi, p. 343. 73 J.F. Lydon, 'The expansion and consolidation of the colony, 1215–54' in *NHI*, ii, pp 156–78 at p. 158. 74 W.J. Smyth, *Map-making, landscape and memory: a geography of colonial and early modern Ireland, c.1530–1750* (Cork, 2006), p. 201.

Pons Novus, villa Willielmi Marescalli: New Ross, a town of William Marshal

CÓILÍN Ó DRISCEOIL

On the summer solstice of the year 1210, King John and his 7,000-strong army descended on William Marshal's port town of New Ross.[1] This was the second day of the king's two-month 'shock and awe' campaign to restore royal authority over his insubordinate barons in Ireland and William would have been well aware that he was considered to be of this ilk. For although the Marshal had come to a measure of *rapprochement* with John following a particularly stormy period between the two, he was still a thorn in the royal side. Most recently William had harboured the estranged William and Maude de Braose from the king's wrath and so the fact that John's first major stop-off was at the earl's prestigious new town – then in only its first decade of existence – indicates a singular intention: to remind him who was really boss in Leinster.[2] We know nothing of what transpired between the two men at Ross but the earl must have done enough to restrain John's ire, for the borough was left untouched and the next day the king left for Kilkenny.[3] An entry in the royal military accounting records known as the *Presitia roll* contains mention of John's visit to New Ross and pointedly calls the town *Pons Novus, villa Willielmi Marescalli*.[4]

LOCATION AND GEOLOGY

New Ross is located in the south-east of Ireland, in the county of Wexford, the barony of Bantry and the civil parish of St Mary (NGC 272000 127550)

1 T. Duffus Hardy (ed.), *Rotuli de liberate ac de misis et praestitis* (London, 1884), pp 178–9; G.H. Orpen, *Ireland under the Normans, 1169–1333* (repr., 4 vols, Oxford, 1968), ii, pp 245–6; Seán Duffy, 'King John's expedition in Ireland, 1210: the evidence reconsidered', *IHS*, 30:117 (May 1996), pp 1–24; S.D. Church, 'The 1210 campaign in Ireland: evidence for a military revolution?' in Christopher Harper-Bill (ed.), *Anglo-Norman Studies: Proceedings of the Battle Conference, 1997* (Woodbridge, 1998), pp 45–58. 2 Sidney Painter, *William Marshal: knight-errant, baron and regent of England* (Baltimore, 1933), pp 161–6. 3 Orpen, *Normans*, ii, p. 246. *HWM*, ii, 14258–9 notes that King John was in Kilkenny with William Marshal on St John's day, 24 June, rather than 22 June. The *HWM* was written at some remove from the events they describe and therefore the date of 22 June in the near-contemporary *Presitia roll* can be considered more accurate. According to Hore, John also confirmed the privileges of New Ross at this time but no source is cited for this nor could any corroboration be found: Philip Herbert Hore, *History of the town and county of Wexford: Old and New Ross* (London, 1900), p. 50. 4 *Praestitis*, p. 178. The roll also refers to the town as

(figs 9.1–9.2). It is 40km from the Irish Sea on the east bank of the tidal estuary of the River Barrow as it flows into Waterford harbour, at the lowest point before the sea where a bridge could be built. The urban area covers a steep escarpment that overlooks the river; the ground rises at a gradient of 1:10 from 2m OD at the river to 60m OD 1km away at the western limit of the town. The site is further constrained by precipitous river-cliffs to the north and a wide marshy floodplain to the south. Three kilometres to the north-west is the confluence of the Nore and Barrow river systems and the River Suir is accessible via Waterford, 20km to the south-west (fig. 9.1). The bedrock geology below the town is the grey slates and siltstones of the Oaklands Formation[5] and rock is rarely more than 2m from the surface beyond the waterfront. The soils to the west of the town are derived from this parent bedrock and are well-drained brown earths, the Clonroche series, which has a range of uses but is mainly suitable for cultivated crops, pasture and forestry.[6] By way of contrast, the poorly drained alluvial soils of the floodplain to the south are wholly unsuitable for agriculture.[7]

EARLY MEDIEVAL ORIGINS?

There is some evidence that William Marshal's New Ross did not occupy a 'green-field' site but was instead prefaced by at least one monastic foundation that was situated on the junction of two significant land routes.[8] These roadways were the *Slighe Chualann*, which probably marks the north–south axis of the town (the modern North Street/South Street/Priory Street), and a second east–west road that was aligned on an early fording point of the River Barrow and was to become the main market place at the Bullawn and Irishtown. The various *Vitae* of Abbán[9] record that this *Dál Chormaic* saint founded a monastery 'near

'pontem novum': ibid., p. 179. The entry translates at 'the New Bridge, a town of William Marshal'. 5 Daniel Tietzsch-Tyler and A.G. Sleeman, *Geology of south Wexford* (Sligo, 1994), p. 44. 6 M.J. Gardiner and P. Ryan, *Soils of County Wexford* (Dublin, 1964), 2, fig. 2. 7 Ibid., p. 65. 8 Colm Ó Lochlainn, 'Roadways in ancient Ireland' in John Ryan (ed.), *Féilsgríbhinn Éoin Mhic Néill* (repr., Dublin, 1995), pp 465–74; Linda Doran, 'New Ross in maps: an enduring image, 1590–1900' in Tom Dunne (ed.), *New Ross. Rosponte. Ros Mhic Treoin: an anthology celebrating 800 years* (Wexford, 2007), p. 7. 9 J.F. Kenney, *Sources for the early history of Ireland, 1: ecclesiastical* (New York, 1929), pp 318–19; W.W. Heist, 'Over the writer's shoulder: St Abban', *Celtica*, 11 (1976), pp 76–84. The *Vitae* survive in five manuscripts: two sister manuscripts in Irish, copied by Michael O'Clery (Plummer's O'Clery, in the Bibliothèque Royale, Brussels) – and by Donnell Dinneen (vol. ix of the Stowe MSS, A.4.1 in the Royal Irish Academy); two sister MSS in Latin, a Marsh Library MS and a Trinity College Dublin MS, both of about 1400 (known collectively as *Codex Kilkenniensis*); and the *Codex Salamanticensis*, a fourteenth-century MS now in the Bibliothèque Royale, Brussels. All these MSS are late recensions of an original compilation that Kenney suggests dates between the mid-eighth and the mid-ninth century.

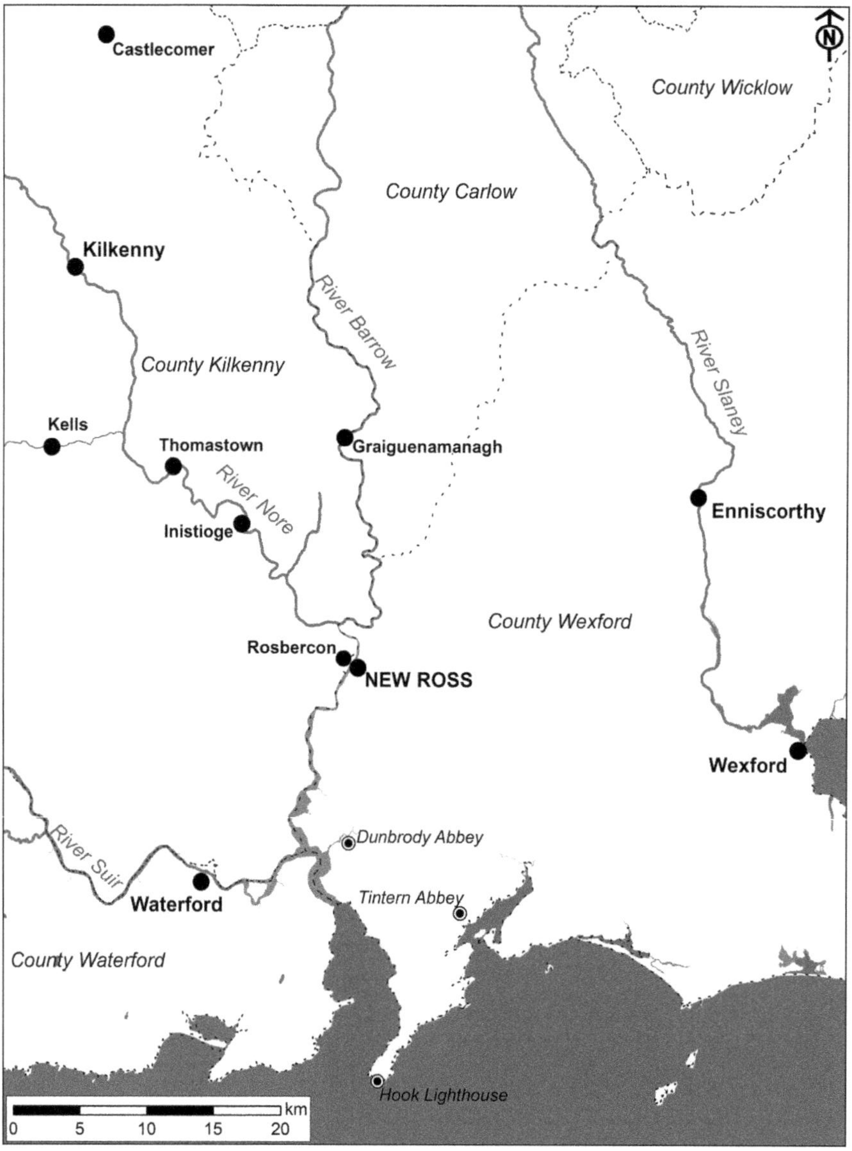

9.1 Location of New Ross (Barry Fitzgibbon, Kilkenny Archaeology).

the barrow' at *Ros Mhic Thriúin*.[10] This translates as 'the wood(s) of the son of Tréan', Tréan being presumably a Gaelic sept who inhabited the area of modern

10 'And Abban and the king parted in great amity, and Abban went to Ros mac Triuin': Charles Plummer, *Lives of Irish saints*, 1 (Oxford, 1922), p. 8; *Magnum siquidem monasterium prope flumen Berbha quod vocatur Roismictruin*, John Colgan, *The* 'Acta Sanctorum Hiberniae' *of John Colgan* (Dublin, 1948), pp 26, 617; *magnum siquidem monasterium prope flumen Berbha*,

9.2 Aerial photograph of New Ross from south-west (Cóilín Ó Drisceoil/Pat Nolan).

New Ross.[11] The monastery's exact location has never been satisfactorily determined but the place-name can be identified with the general area of the modern town because the 'Ros' element was incorporated into its name from at least the end of the thirteenth century.[12] P.H. Hore was the first to place the monastery at John Street (on the north side of the town) but he did not offer any reliable evidence for his suggestion.[13] Another, more likely, possibility is St

quod uocatur Ross meic Treoin in quo iacet beatissimus abbas sanctus Emenus: Richard Sharpe, *Medieval Irish saints' Lives* (Oxford, 1991), p. 350; *E quibus unum fuit prope Berba, quod vocatur Ross Mac Troin, in quo iacet abbas Emenus …*: C. De Smedt and J. De Backer, *Acta Sanctorum Hiberniae* (London, 1888), p. 525; *Aliquando sanctus Molua uisitauit sanctum Emenum, abbatem in regione Cennselach, non longe a flumine Berua, in monasterio Ross meic Treoin, quod sanctissimus senex Abbanus fundauit, habitantem …*: *Medieval saints' Lives*, p. 351; *S. vero Eminus, qui and corruptè Euinus appellatur contulit fe ad fines Lageniae, and ad ripá fluminis Berbha, ubi in oppido extruxit monasterium in loco prifcis Ros-mic-treoin*: *Acta Sanctorum of John Colgan*, pp 3, 751. **11** Dónall Mac Giolla Easpaig, Irish Placenames Commission, pers. comm. **12** For example, in the later thirteenth century the town is variously referred to as 'Rospont' and 'Novem Rospentem', to distinguish it from Old Ross: Hore, *Ross*, pp 20, 35. The identification of the place-name with New Ross is beyond doubt in later sources such as the 1541 *Fiants*, which refer to the town as *New Ross alias Rospont alias Rossincrowne*. By the seventeenth century, this had simplified to 'Rosse': Simington, *CS Wexford*, p. 233. **13** Hore, *Ross*, p. 42n.; P.H. Hore, *History of the town and county of Wexford: Duncannon Fort, Kilclogan or Templetown, Fethard*

9.3 Aerial photograph of St Stephen's graveyard, Irishtown, New Ross from north east (Cóilín Ó Drisceoil/Pat Nolan).

Stephen's graveyard at the east end of the suburb of Irishtown where there was almost certainly a parish church dedicated to the Irish St Evin in the thirteenth century (fig. 9.3).[14] This seems to have been on the site of an earlier foundation as evidenced by a pair of bullaun stones and perhaps a holy well within the cemetery (fig. 9.4).[15] Whether this was Abbán's monastery is not clear but the fact that Evin was, according to the hagiography, a contemporary of Abbán and became abbot of, and was subsequently buried in, the latter's monastery at *Ros*

(London, 1904), p. 404. **14** The street-name 'St Evin's Street' is recorded from the late thirteenth to the sixteenth century: *Ormond deeds*, i, pp 301, 832 – which suggests that it led to St Evin's chapel. Since the modern graveyard of St Stephen is located at the end of Irishtown Street and the name 'St Stephen's' is considered to be a corruption of the name St Evin – W.H. Grattan Flood, *History of the diocese of Ferns* (Waterford, 1915), p. 86 – St Evin's chapel can be placed in St Stephen's cemetery with some confidence. St Evin's was also the parish church for the separate parish of the same name until at least the fifteenth century (see below). **15** Moore, *AI Wexford*, no. 1168. Moore has also suggested that the curving boundary for the graveyard is of early medieval origin but there is no evidence to back this up and, despite archaeological investigations having taken place within the putative enclosure, nothing of early medieval date has been found. There are also local reports of a stone souterrain having been found in the vicinity of the graveyard though these have never been

9.4 A granite bullaun stone with a single basin built into the top of a grave enclosure-wall in St Stephen's graveyard, Irishtown, New Ross. Another bullaun is located nearby.

Mhic Thriúin, suggests Abbán's foundation may have been renamed for Evin to commemorate his burial in the place.[16] Certainly the location of the cemetery on the top of a prominent ridge with good views of the surrounding countryside would have been less vulnerable for a monastery than the John Street area, which is hemmed in between a steep cliff to the east and the river on the west.

The grafting of the Anglo-Norman town onto an earlier monastic foundation occurred at other Marshal boroughs such as Kilkenny, Inistioge, Naas, Kildare and Thomastown, and it seems to have formed part of his modus operandi for town development. While it undoubtedly would have had the advantage of providing a degree of infrastructure, and in the case of larger centres such as Kilkenny what was in effect already a quasi-urban settlement, the seizure of monastic land was not done lightly as William learnt to his cost when he confiscated 'in a time of war' two manors belonging to the then bishop of Ferns, Ailbe Ó Máelmuaid.[17] This act provoked an angry response from the bishop

substantiated: Sinéad Marshal, pers. comm. **16** Sharpe, *Medieval saints' Lives*, p. 350. Linda Doran also raises the possibility of the monastery having been located in St Stephen's: Doran, *New Ross*, pp 111, 117. Likewise Patrick Donovan suggested it was located in the Irishtown/Bullawn area: see Tom Dunne, *New Ross. Rosponte. Ros Mhic Treoin: an anthology celebrating 800 years* (Wexford, 2007), p. 18. **17** H.R. Luard (ed.), *Matthew Paris, Monachi Sancti Albani, Chronica Majora, iv* (London, 1877), pp 492–4; Pádraig Ó Néill, 'The impact of the Norman invasion on Irish literature' in Christopher Harper-Bill (ed.), *Anglo-Norman Studies: Proceedings of the Battle Conference*, 20 (London, 1997), p. 178. The Marshal's enmity towards Ailbe probably has its roots in the latter's support for Meiler fitz Henry and probably which culminated in his excommunication in 1218 and despite the attempts of Henry III to have the interdict lifted it was with him until his death in 1219.[18] The nature of the infrastructure that early medieval *Ros Mhic Thriúin* contributed to the new town was probably minimal, however, and there is no suggestion that there was a quasi-urban nucleus here or any form of market place. The impression, and that is all it is, is instead of a small and relatively insignificant monastic settlement that was subsumed into the Anglo-Norman town.

THE MANOR OF ROSS

New Ross was located at the west end of the manor of Ross. After the Anglo-Norman conquest the manor was held as a demesne manor of the cantred of Shirebryn. The cantred, one of eight in Wexford, is likely to correspond to the later deanery of Shelburne and has its origin in the two early medieval local kingdoms of Loígis and Beanntraige.[19] The cantred flanked the Barrow estuary and stretched from Hook Head in the south to the confluence of the Nore and Barrow in the north. Hervey de Montmorency was granted Shirebryn along with Bargy by Diarmait Mac Murchada and the grant was later confirmed by Strongbow.[20] The medieval extent of the manor of Ross can be established from a 1234 charter of Richard Marshal which provided supports for deforestation within its bounds:[21] it corresponded closely with the civil parishes of St Mary's and Oldross[22] and the demesne lands were probably the one-thousand-acre townland of Old Ross that was recorded in 1654–6 by the Civil Survey (fig. 9.5).[23] The strategic importance of the manor to the economic development of the lordship of Leinster was recognised from the beginning of the conquest for it was retained in demesne by Strongbow from about 1175.[24]

The manor's agrarian workings are brought to light vividly by the remarkably detailed financial records of the various provosts known as the 'Ministers' Accounts' (1280–94).[25] These show that the manor was a centre for wool and grain (primarily oats) farming, the production of which had expanded

in the fact that he was Irish. **18** Orpen, *Normans*, iii, pp 29–31; Crouch, *William Marshal*, pp 106–7, 132, 142. The Marshal would no doubt have been somewhat reassured though that his excommunication was not a major concern as Ailbe's interdict had been trumped by a plenary indulgence from the papal legate Gualo. Not content to leave well enough alone following the death of William Marshal, Ailbe in 1220 or 1221 visited the earl's grave in the Temple Church, London, and 'damned him as a despoiler of the church': M.T. Clanchy, *England and its rulers, 1066–1307* (3rd ed., London, 2006), p. 175. **19** MacCotter, *Medieval Ire.*, p. 252. **20** Orpen, *Normans*, i, p. 393. **21** G.H. Orpen and Eric St-J. Brooks, 'Charters of Earl Richard Marshal of the forests of Ross and Taghmon', *JRSAI*, 7th ser., 4:1 (1934), pp 54–63. **22** *CSMA*, ii, p. 154; Hore, *Ross*, p. 3. **23** Colfer, *Arrogant trespass*, pp 117–18. **24** Ibid., p. 40. **25** Hore, *Ross*, pp 2, 14, 35, 39; Mary C. Lyons, 'An account for the manor of Old Ross, September 1284–September 1285, part I', *Decies*, 18 (1981), pp 33–40; idem, 'An account for the manor of Old Ross, September 1284–September 1285, part 2', *Decies*, 19 (1982), pp 18–31; Margaret Murphy, 'The profits of lordship: Roger Bigod, earl of Norfolk,

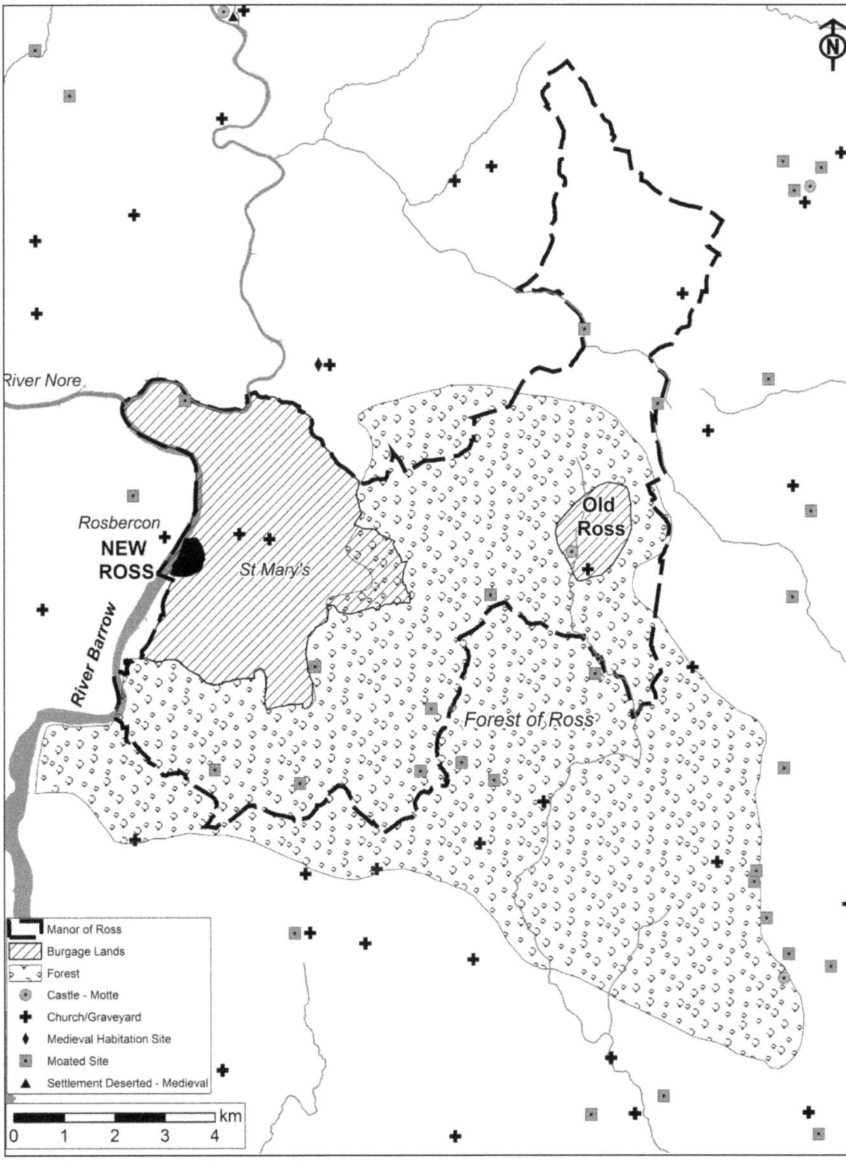

9.5 The manor of Ross in the thirteenth century (Barry Fitzgibbon, Kilkenny Archaeology).

dramatically in the 1280s to provision Edward I's Welsh wars. Three manorial mills processed the grain that was harvested and managed through a network of out-farms and granges throughout the estate.[26]

and the lordship of Carlow, 1270–1306' in Linda Doran and James Lyttleton (eds), *Lordship in medieval Ireland: image and reality* (Dublin, 2007), p. 87. **26** Murphy, 'Profits of lordship', pp 86–7.

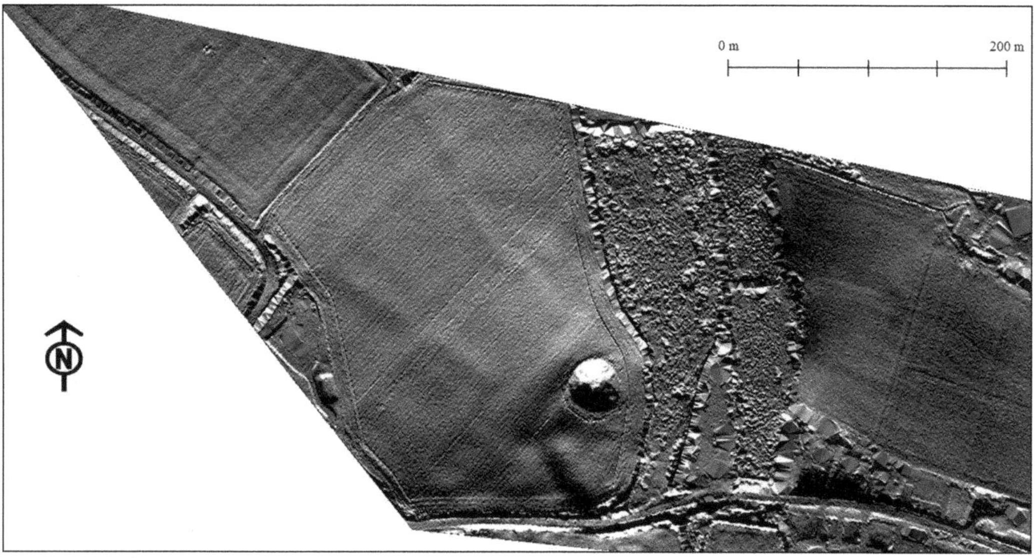

9.6 LiDAR image of the motte and bailey at Old Ross (courtesy of Sinéad Marshal and Tori McMorran (Old Ross Research Project) and Steve Davis (School of Archaeology, UCD)).

While New Ross was by far the most significant urban centre in the manor, the seigniorial caput remained throughout the Middle Ages at Old Ross, 7.5km to the east of the town. Here a motte and bailey was erected, probably by Strongbow, to defend the north of the manor, which was then on the border with the Marches (fig. 9.6).[27] It was most likely William Marshal who replaced or at least augmented this earth-and-timber castle with a stone edifice, to which occasional references occur throughout the first half of the thirteenth century.[28] In 1230 the castle of Ross was one of four in Wexford that were taken into the king's hands following the death of William Marshal the younger and it is again mentioned in Richard Marshal's 1234 deforestation charter.[29] At the partition of Leinster in 1247 the castle was retained, along with the burghs of New Ross and Carlow by William Marshal's eldest daughter Maud (Matilda) and was valued at a healthy £72 3*s*. 4½*d*.[30] In 1281 repairs were carried out to the 'palisade about the castle'[31] and in 1284–5 the 'new hall' and repairs by a mason to the 'hall and moat' were noted.[32] The castle comprised in 1307 the decayed remains of 'one

27 Billy Colfer and Edward Culleton, 'The Norman motte at Old Ross: method of construction', *Journal of the Old Wexford Society*, 10 (1974), pp 69–78; Moore, *AI Wexford*, no. 955; Sinéad Marshal and Tori McMorran, 'People and places: a bird's-eye view of medieval Old Ross' in Ian Doyle and Bernard Browne (eds), *Medieval Wexford: essays in memory of Billy Colfer* (Dublin, 2016), pp 241–61. 28 For example, William Marshal the younger and his brother Richard both utilised the fortification as a residence and signed a number of charters from it: Hore, *Ross*, pp 2 and 2n.3. 29 *CDI*, *1171–1251*, nos 1030, 1269. 30 Ibid., no. 933. 31 Hore, *Ross*, p. 15. 32 Ibid., p. 34.

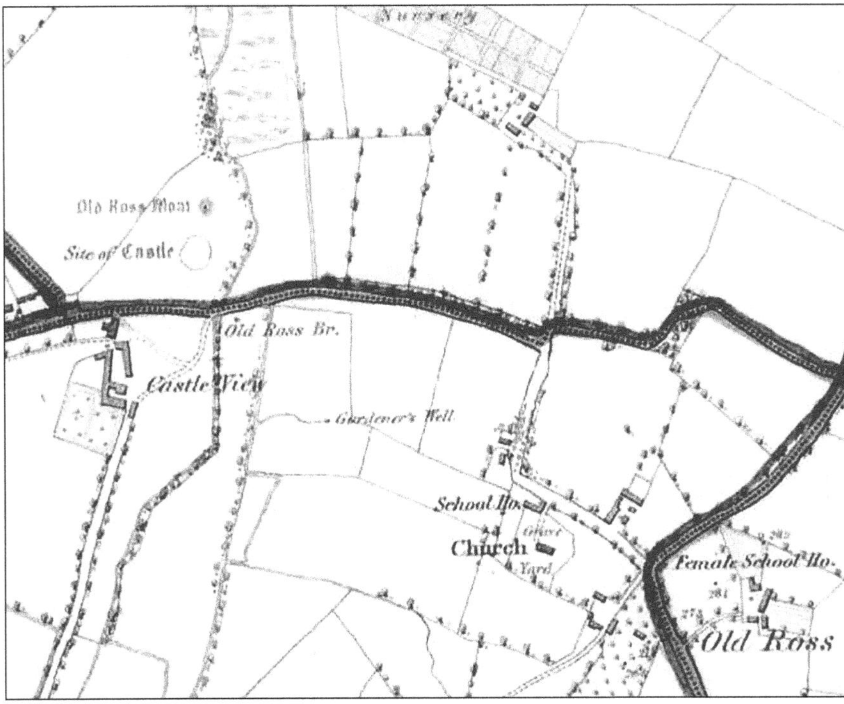

9.7 First-edition Ordnance Survey map of Old Ross (sheet 30, surveyed 1840, published 1841) (Trinity College Dublin Map Library).

old hall surrounded with a stone wall', beside which was a 'smaller hall' and a chapel.[33] The various allusions to the castle as a 'hall' within a bawn wall suggest it may have been of similar design to Grenan (pl. 25), Thomastown, built *c.*1210 by Thomas fitz Anthony.[34] In 1684 the castle was still standing, though 'quite oute of repayre' and nothing survives today of it; even its exact whereabouts is not known for certain.[35] A pair of thirteenth-century gargoyles recovered from the fosse of the motte *c.*1850 are reputed to have belonged to the stone castle and would indicate it was sited somewhere nearby.[36] A parish church, dedicated to the Blessed Virgin Mary, was situated 450m south-east of the motte, in the present Church of Ireland graveyard.[37] The borough of Old Ross developed around the castle and church and brought in a total of 58*s.* 10*d.* each year in fixed

33 *CDI, 1302–7*, no. 617; Hore, *Ross*, p. 170. 34 Sweetman, *Medieval castles*, pp 74–5. 35 Hore, *Ross*, p. 2n. 36 'Donations to the museum', *JRSAI*, 1:2 (1850), p. 120; Hore, *Ross*, p. 1n.; Bernard Browne, *Old Ross: the town that never was* (Wexford, 1993), p. 19; Colfer, *Arrogant trespass*, p. 66; the gargoyles may be viewed in the collection of the Royal Society of Antiquaries of Ireland, 63 Merrion Square, Dublin. The first-edition Ordnance Survey map of Old Ross places the castle immediately to the south of the motte. 37 The church was largely destroyed in 1798: Hore, *Ross*, p. 39n. Only the fragmentary remains of an L-shaped wall of the church survive within the graveyard: Moore, *AI Wexford*, no. 1276.

rents. What may be remnant burgage plots can be seen between the motte and the church on the first-edition Ordnance Survey map (fig. 9.7).

THE BEGINNINGS OF WILLIAM MARSHAL'S NEW TOWN

The formal establishment of the borough of New Ross may be dated to 1207 when its first charter of incorporation was issued by William Marshal (see below) but the preparation work and initial construction probably preceded this by some years, perhaps commencing at the time of the first visit by William and Isabel in 1200. It is unlikely to have been included in the 'first wave' of Marshal boroughs in the 1190s, however, as there is no mention in its foundation charter of the rent having been previously set at one shilling by Geoffrey fitz Robert, as was the case with the charters to Kilkenny, Callan, Carlow, Cooliagh, Kells, Moone and Wexford (and probably Bannow and Thomastown).[38] In the *Histoire de Guillaume le Maréchal*, the events of late 1207 are recounted when Meiler fitz Henry had orchestrated (with the assent of the king) the burning of 'la Novele vile', its barns (*les granges*) and the murder of twenty of the Marshal's men:

> The week after the feast day,
> on the first Sunday,
> they set fire to the earl's barns
> in Newtown,
> reducing them to ashes.
> They also killed twenty of his men,
> and carried before them all the booty
> they had taken in the town as they went on their way.
> So started throughout the land
> Upheaval and war on a grand scale.[39]

This was a pointed attack on the earl's prestige project and the description in the *Histoire* is suggestive of an established, functioning town in 1207 and certainly much more than a building site. This is also borne out by the charter to the monks of Tintern that granted them *burgagium de Weiseford et vnum burgagium de Ros ex australi parte pontis* ('a burgage in Wexford and another at New Ross to the south of the bridge').[40] The charter has been dated by G.H. Orpen to

38 Bradley and Murtagh, this volume. 39 *HWM*, ii, 13564–74. There can be little doubt that *la Novele vile* refers to New Ross since it is the only one of the Marshal's towns that could be so called. Similarly named places like Newtown Jerpoint and Newtown Early were promoted by his household knights. Orpen was the first to realise this connection: G.H. Orpen, *New Ross in the thirteenth century* (Dublin, 1911), p. 7; Orpen, *Normans*, ii, p. 212. 40 *Chartae, privilegia et immunitates*, p. 80. A translation of a 1382 transcript of the charter is contained in P.H. Hore, *History of the town and county of Wexford: Tintern Abbey, Rosegarland and Clonmines* (London,

between 1207 and 1213[41] but can be assigned to 1207 from its list of witnesses and its close similarity to the charter to Duiske Abbey of more-or-less the same date.[42] The abbey had been established by the Marshal in late 1200 and King John issued letters patent for it in December of that year,[43] on the occasion of the Marshal's first visit to Ireland, and it is conceivable the 1207 grant of the burgage in New Ross was a confirmation of an award originally made at this time.

THE ROLE OF ISABEL DE CLARE

Following its foundation, the Marshal took to the challenge of making New Ross work with some gusto, and so when the earl returned to the king's favour free passage was quickly obtained past Waterford for ships bound for New Ross, and additional privileges were granted to merchants trading with Leinster when he became regent.[44] The rationale for the new town's foundation was simple: the Marshal needed control of a port to serve his Leinster lordship and because Waterford had been lost to the crown since 1171 New Ross was its audacious surrogate. The town, inside the Marshal's demesne manor, with a deep harbour, ready riverine access into the heart of Leinster via the Nore and Barrow river systems, and a bridging link between Cos Wexford and Kilkenny was ideally sited as an outport for the earl's lordship.[45] And, critically, it allowed the Marshal and his vassals to supply the lordship directly from the family's estates at Chepstow and Pembroke without incurring the royal taxation that would have been levied at Waterford.

1901), p. 19, and an Elizabethan transcript is to be found in the Colclough family papers: NLI MS 24445(4). I am grateful to Prof. David Crouch for providing me with a new transcript and translation of the charter from the National Archives at Kew (PRO): C66/312 (patent roll of 5 Ric. II, pt 2, inspeximus dated 12 June 1382), m. 2. **41** Orpen, *Normans*, ii, p. 207. In his paper on New Ross in the thirteenth century, Orpen dates the charter to 1207–8 but does not give reasons: Orpen, *New Ross*, p. 7. **42** The Tintern charter was witnessed by among others John Marshal (the illegitimate son of John Marshal II and nephew of the Marshal) and Jordan de Sauqueville. The only time that William, John and Jordan were in Ireland together before the Marshal's return to court in England in 1213 was between February/March and September 1207: Crouch, *William Marshal*, pp 97–8, 99, 101. It is possible that the charter was issued in England after 1213 but the common set of exemptions with the 1207x8 charter to Duiske Abbey (including items that were antiquated and not relevant to Leinster circumstances such as 'tithingpenny', 'blodwite', 'flemeneswite') strongly suggests the same English scribe drafted the two charters at more or less the same time. **43** J.H. Bernard, 'The foundation of Tintern Abbey, Co. Wexford', *PRIA*, 33 (1916/17), pp 527–9. The Cistercians held onto their property in New Ross until at least 1540: *EIMP*, p. 358. **44** *CDI, 1252–84*, nos 648, 725, 862. **45** The Nore was navigable as far as Kilkenny (at a minimum) and the Barrow to Monasterevin: Colfer, *Arrogant trespass*, p. 177. This was critically important as water transport was preferred to road throughout the Middle Ages. It has been estimated that the cost of carrying goods on water was half that incurred over land: Heather Swanson, *Medieval British towns* (Basingstoke, 1999), p. 36.

There may also have been another, subtler, motivation at play behind the development of the new port, one which suggests the Marshal's wife the countess Isabel de Clare was an important figure in the venture. As already mentioned, she had probably accompanied William on his first voyage to Ireland in 1200 and it is not unreasonable to suggest that she would have played a role in the discussions around the foundation and siting of the new town.[46] Isabel's 'counsel and consent' is explicitly referred to in many of her husband's charters indicating that her opinion and judgment were sought and valued when it came to the management and development of the family's Irish estates. The location of the new town on the Wexford bank of the Barrow rather than the opposite side is also a strong indication of Isabel's influence. Both banks were held in demesne by the earl and, on the face of it, it would seem that the Kilkenny bank would have made for a far more attractive proposition. On the Wexford side the ground was precipitous and inconvenient for developing a town, while the opposite bank with its flatter terrain was more suitable. Either side could have accommodated a new quay as there was little difference in the depth of the river. The decision to site the town on the Wexford bank meant, therefore, that one of the largest bridges ever built in medieval Ireland had to be constructed across the Barrow, presumably at enormous cost to the founder of the town.

So if the economics of siting New Ross on the Wexford side did not quite make sense the politics most certainly did. Wexford was the centre of the former kingdom of Isabel's grandfather, Diarmait Mac Murchada, and she had a vested interest in making the project work for the benefit of her ancestral lands; in so doing holding in check any sparks of resistance that may have been ruminating among her kinfolk. There may also have been an element of defiance against the king at play. Fearing a loss of royal authority, John had done his utmost to thwart the development of her dower lands in Leinster and the foundation on Isabel's lands of a new town in direct opposition to the royal port of Waterford was a strategic strike at the heart of royal power in Ireland. The decision to found the town on the Wexford bank can thus be seen as a political move infused with the authority of one of the most powerful women of the day. The early success of the venture undoubtedly afforded Isabel more than a slight degree of pleasure.

WILLIAM MARSHAL'S CHARTER TO NEW ROSS, 1207

Charters of incorporation formed the commonest means used by feudal lords to ensure new sources of profit from urban development, by which a migratory population was enticed with the promise of economic and judicial autonomy, and

46 The evidence for Isabel's presence in Ireland comes from her 'counsel and consent' being affirmed in William Marshal's reconfirmation of lands at Aghaboe to Adam de Hereford: *Ormond deeds*, i, p. 37. This was dated by Curtis to the occasion of the Marshal's second visit to Ireland in 1207–13, but the list of witnesses is completely different from the 1207–13 suite of

freedom from the vast bulk of feudal labour services. Many such charters were issued in Ireland during the 1200s and in this sense Ireland was being brought into the mainstream of European urban development, albeit playing a minor role in the 'widespread migration of people moving into the wastelands and peripheral regions of medieval Europe'.[47] The original New Ross charter of incorporation has been lost but it is possible to reconstruct its contents from the town's earliest extant charter of 1283x6, which was granted by William's grandson Roger Bigod,[48] and further details can be gleaned from Richard II's 1389 inspeximus of Bigod's charter, which included an inspection of the liberties and customs licensed by William Marshal's original charter.[49] Both sources confirm that New Ross's first charter was almost identical to that granted by the Marshal to Kilkenny in 1207 and it stands to reason that it was issued around the same time.[50]

The majority of the New Ross document deals with the three essential liberties offered to entice settlers to the new chartered boroughs of the early thirteenth century – burgage tenure, an autonomous legal system and freedom from tolls. These freedoms were granted to the townspeople primarily to foster a profitable trading class, the tolls and taxes from which entered the lord's coffers. By far the most important privilege was the right to hold property from the lord 'freely and quietly forever' (that is, by fee farm) and to dispose of it 'as seems best to them [the burgesses]', without the feudal custumaries that pertained outside the town.[51] Burgages were granted on the basis that 'by twenty feet of land, they may make their free tenants so that they may have common liberty with the burgesses' and each plot was rented at 12*d.* per annum. Tenants who had properties 'near the water' were allowed to extend their plots 'by building over the water if they so wish'. Burgesses were also ensured of trial in the town hundred rather than the lord's castle for crimes committed within the liberty and the profits from the court were given to the town. Exemptions from 'toll and lastage and passage and pontage' were granted throughout all of the Marshal's 'land and power' and lesser privileges included the 'common' of the lord's forests for firewood and building timber and the right to grind in the lord's mills for a 'reasonable toll'. No outside merchant was allowed to bake bread or to operate a wine tavern for more than forty days without the assent of the town

charters and must instead date to the 1200 visit: John Bradley, 'Pulp facts and core fictions: translating a cathedral from Aghaboe to Kilkenny' in Emer Purcell, Paul MacCotter, Julianne Nyhan and John Sheehan (eds), *Clerics, kings and Vikings: essays on medieval Ireland in honour of Donnchadh Ó Corráin* (Dublin, 2015), pp 169–84. See Crouch, this volume. 47 B.J. Graham, 'Urbanisation in the high Middle Ages' in T.B. Barry (ed.), *A history of settlement in Ireland* (London and New York, 2000), p. 128. 48 Mac Niocaill, *Na buirgéisí*, pp 300–4; *Chartae, privilegia et immunitates*, pp 84–6; Orpen, *New Ross*, p. 22. Roger Bigod was the son of Hugh Bigod and Matilda, eldest daughter of William Marshal. 49 Mac Niocaill, *Na buirgéisí*, pp 304–15. Ballard and Tait date the charter to *c.*1279, 'when he [Roger Bigod] was in Ireland': Adolphus Ballard and James Tait (eds), *British borough charters, 1216–1307* (Cambridge, 1923), p. xlv. 50 See John Bradley and Ben Murtagh, this volume. 51 The fee farm grant is a feature of almost every borough charter in the reign of King John: Adolphus Ballard, 'The English authorities. Burgesses could form merchant guilds and they were granted the right to sell goods (with certain caveats) without the lord's consent. Burgesses and their families were also granted the right to 'enter marriage contracts without the permission of their lord', subject to certain conditions.

THE TOPOGRAPHY OF EARLY THIRTEENTH-CENTURY NEW ROSS

The preceding sections have provided something of the background to the formation of New Ross, its setting within the manor of Ross, the rationale for its location and an overview of its foundation charter. But what exactly constituted the new town? Previous studies have focused in the main on the late thirteenth- to mid-fourteenth-century town, which is much better served by documents and archaeology, but it must be realised that by this stage the 'original' Marshal town had undergone a significant expansion and transformation under William's grandson Roger Bigod II (fig. 9.8).[52] Another focus has been on the role played by the town in national and international trade and the intense rivalry between the port of New Ross and the king's port at Waterford.[53] By way of contrast, relatively little has been written about the first half-century or so of the town's existence (*c.*1200–50) – the 'Marshal period' – and this is the chronological focus for this essay. Recreating the physical layout of the earliest town is severely hampered by a lack of written and material sources: only about fifteen historical references from the first half of the thirteenth century are known for New Ross and of these just four provide any direct topographical information,[54] though some of the gaps can be filled by later records.[55] Elements of the medieval town's

boroughs in the reign of John', *English Historical Review*, 14 (1899), pp 93–104. 52 Orpen, *New Ross*; Colfer, *Arrogant trespass*, pp 171–82; Linda Doran, *New Ross, c.1200 to c.1900: seven hundred years in the making* (Dublin, 2008), pp 6–11. 53 Orpen, *New Ross*, pp 9–10; Timothy O'Neill, *Merchants and mariners in medieval Ireland* (Dublin, 1987), pp 81, 107–12; A.F. O'Brien, 'Commercial relations between Aquitaine and Ireland, *c.*1000 to *c.*1550' in J.M. Picard (ed.), *Aquitaine and Ireland in the Middle Ages* (Dublin, 1995), pp 31–80; O'Brien, 'Politics, economy and society'. Dispute with Waterford: Eamonn McEneaney, 'Waterford and New Ross trade competition, *c.*1300', *Decies*, 12 (1979), pp 16–24; Colfer, *Arrogant trespass*, pp 178–82; Mac Niocaill, *Na buirgeisí*, pp 456–7. 54 The remaining early/mid-thirteenth-century documentary references deal with the disputes with Waterford over trading rights. A concise overview of these is provided in Colfer, *Arrogant trespass*, pp 178–82; and see Hore, *Ross*, pp 134–5. 55 Most of the historical records for New Ross were compiled in the nineteenth century by P.H. Hore, *Ross*. The other major source is the *Ormond deeds, 1172–1350* [etc.], the largest single collection of medieval deeds and records in Ireland. Three of New Ross's charters and a charter to Rosbercon are reproduced in Mac Niocaill, *Na buirgéisí*, pp 296–319. The Middle French poem 'The walling of New Ross', one of the few surviving pieces of Irish literature in French from the thirteenth century, recounts the construction of the town wall in 1265: Hugh Shields, 'The walling of New Ross: a thirteenth-century poem in French', *Long Room*, 12–13 (1976–7), pp 24–33. *CDI* has information on ecclesiastical foundations and a market grant to Rosbercon, *CDI*, ii, no. 2145, iii, no. 109, iv, no. 260. *EIMP* parish church, dedicated to the Blessed Virgin Mary,[56] represent the only standing remains from the 'Marshal period' and excavations have yet to recover anything of substance for this earliest phase of the town's development.[57] Nonetheless, the sources that are available do permit to a certain extent reconstruction of the layout and topography of the Marshal's town.

Streets and property plots

The modern street pattern of the town is largely of medieval origin.[58] The 650m-long quayside (see below) was an important factor that determined the layout of

contain much information regarding the form and layout of the religious houses of New Ross at the Dissolution of the monasteries: *EIMP*, pp 180, 184, 355, 363–4, 208, 365. The *Civil Survey of Wexford* has some information on the medieval topography albeit in a seventeenth-century guise: pp 223, 233–55. The later seventeenth- and eighteenth-century corporation books of New Ross are a useful source for identifying disappeared street names and public utilities: P.D. Vigors, 'Extracts from the books of the old corporation of Ross, Co. Wexford', *JRSAI*, 21 (1892), pp 171–6; idem, 'Extracts from the books of the old corporation of Ross, Co. Wexford', *JRSAI*, 22 (1892), pp 288, 290; idem, 'Extracts from the books of the old corporation of Ross, Co. Wexford', *JRSAI*, 24 (1894), pp 176–9; idem, 'Extracts from the old corporation books of New Ross, Co. Wexford', *JRSAI*, 31 (1901), pp 55, 58, 59, 60. Two seventeenth-century maps of New Ross are important in examining the growth of the town, street-names and the make-up of the defences – the 1649 'Design for the recovery of town of Ross' and the Anglesey Estate map (1666x99): see n. 79. New Ross has received fleeting attention from antiquarians and historians from the sixteenth century onwards, beginning in 1577 with Richard Stanihurst whose account in Holinshed's *Irish chronicle* gives an important insight into the state of the town at the end of the Middle Ages: L. Miller and E. Power (eds), *Holinshed's Irish chronicle* (repr. 1st ed., 1577) (Dublin, 1979), pp 56–8. In 1684 a brief description of New Ross was written by Robert Leigh and transcribed: H.F. Hore, 'A chorographic account of the southern part of the county of Wexford, written anno 1684: by Robert Leigh esq. of Rosegarland, in that county', *JRSAI*, 5 (1858–9), pp 451–4, and Samuel Lewis's description is useful for ecclesiastical history: *A topographical dictionary of Ireland*, 2 (London, 1837), pp 531–3. 56 Leask, *Irish churches*, ii, pp 84–5; Moore, *AI Wexford*, no. 1457; Jill Unkel, 'An enduring monument', *Irish Arts Review*, 22:3 (autumn 2005), pp 100–3; idem, 'Architectural patronage', pp 223–60. I am indebted to Jill Unkel for providing me with a copy of her doctoral thesis. 57 The only substantive work regarding the archaeology of New Ross was completed in 1990: John Bradley and H.A. King, 'Urban Archaeology Survey, 5: Old and New Ross (unpublished report for Office of Public Works, 1990). Michael Moore briefly describes all the surviving medieval buildings in the town and identifies a number of sites which are no longer extant: Moore, *AI Wexford*, nos 1453–64. A synthesis of the historical and archaeological data for New Ross was presented by the author in an MA thesis: Cóilín Ó Drisceoil, 'The layout, topography and archaeology of medieval New Ross, County Wexford' (2 vols, MA, UCD, 1996). A preliminary overview of seventy-seven archaeological excavations that have taken place in New Ross has been completed by Linda Doran, 'Archaeological investigations in New Ross and Rosbercon, 1994–2006: analysis and classification' (Heritage Council unpublished report, 2009). The town defences have also been a focus and illustrations of the surviving mural tower and two mural gates were included in J.S. Fleming's *The town wall fortifications of Ireland* (Dublin, 1914), pp 38–41. A description of the walls as well as an inventory of the historical and archaeological sources was published in 1992: Avril Thomas, *The walled towns of Ireland*, 2 (Dublin, 1992), pp 175–9 and more recently a Heritage Council conservation plan has been completed: Alastair Coey, *New Ross town walls conservation plan* (Kilkenny, 2008). 58 John Bradley, 'Planned Anglo-Norman towns in Ireland'

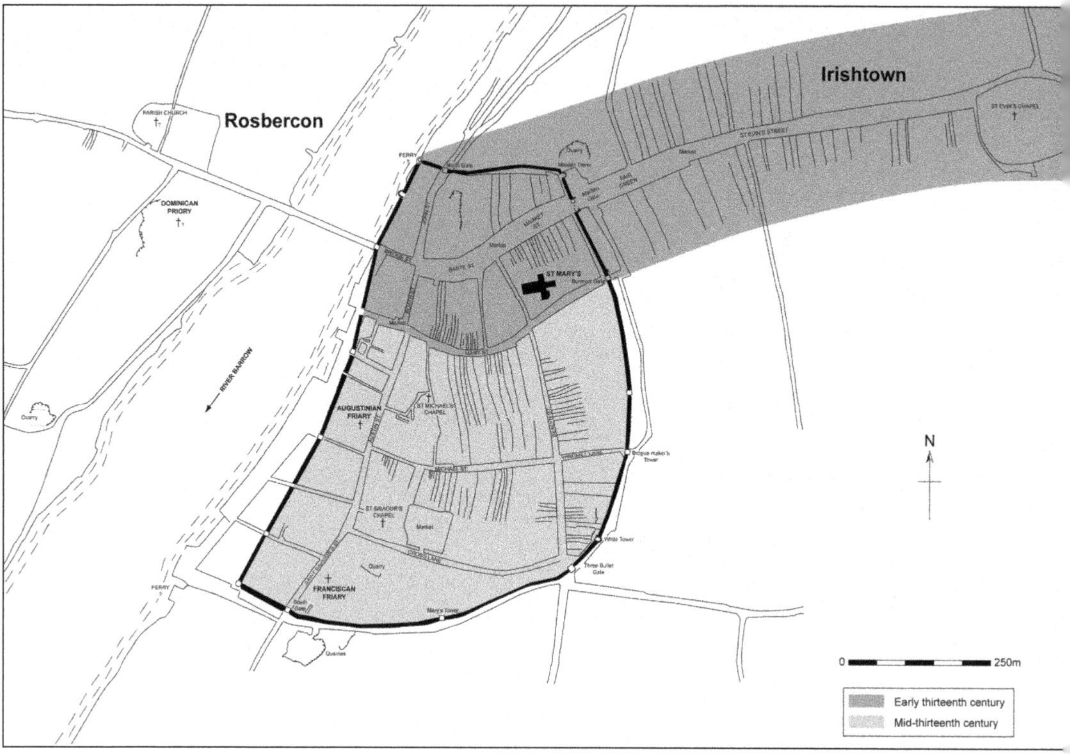

9.8 Map of medieval New Ross, *c.*1300, with the projected outline of the primary core marked (map by Cóilín Ó Drisceoil; digitised by Philip Kenny, Kilkenny Archaeology).

the streets and three streets run parallel (north–south) to the quays; these are in turn intersected by seven cross (east–west) streets forming an irregular chequer pattern of eight squares – *insulae* – similar to that found at Drogheda and Clonmel (fig. 9.8).[59] The streets follow the natural contours of the ground as best they can though the site, as already mentioned, was far from ideal for this purpose. The density of the street pattern has a distinct northern bias to it and in the northern quarter a long and broad thoroughfare – in effect a simple linear street pattern – links the probable site of St Evin's monastery (modern St Stephen's graveyard) in Irishtown to the bridge and quays. It broadened in the area of the Bullawn into a wide rectangular market place that was the main market and that also contained the parish church of St Mary. It is to here that we should look for the core of William Marshal's town (figs 9.8 and 9.12).[60] This core occupied about half of the area that was walled by *c.*1300 and it was not until

in H.B. Clarke and Anngret Simms (eds), *The comparative history of urban origins in non-Roman Europe, pt 2* (BAR, Int. Ser. 255), pp 449–50. **59** The north–south streets are North Street, South Street and Church Lane in the west, Bewley Street and Neville Street in the centre and Cockpit Lane, Nunnery Lane and Town Wall in the east. The east–west streets, beginning in the north of the town, are Goat Hill, Bridge Street and Maiden Lane, High Hill Street and the Bullawn, Quay Street and Mary Street, Michael Street and Windmill Lane, Cross Lane and William Street. **60** That this was the older part of the town may also be

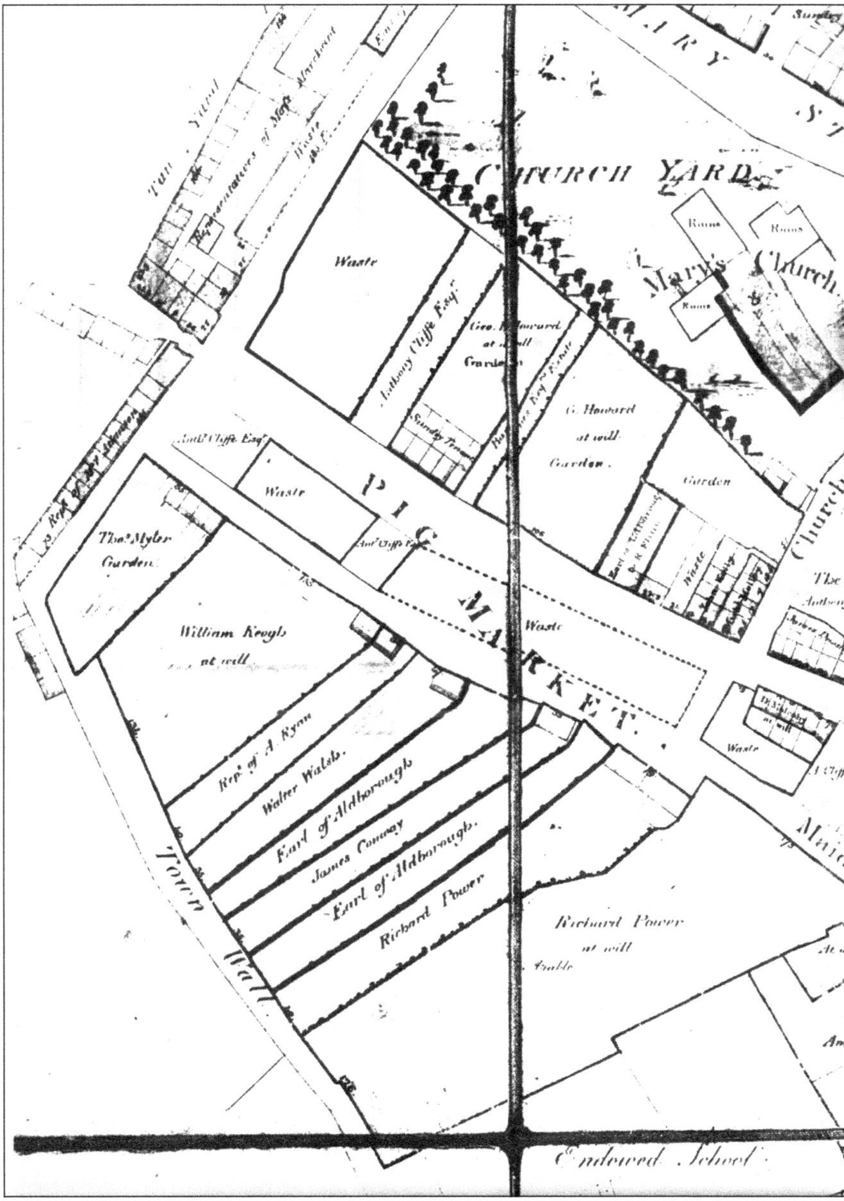

9.9 Extract from 'Survey of the estate of Charles Tottenham esq. in the town of New Ross and county of Wexford' by Sherrard, Brassington and Gale, 1827 (courtesy of the Tottenham Estate Office, Priory Street, New Ross). The map shows the burgage-plot framework on the north side of the Bullawn.

the Bigod earls gained seisin of the town that the other half to the south became the focus for intensive development, much of it at the behest of the church: the Franciscans established their extensive friary in Priory Street by 1256; a chapel dedicated to St Michael was located off Michael Street before 1280; and the Augustinians were in South Street by 1319 (fig. 9.8). Since it is improbable that numerous burgage plots would have been cleared to make way for the large precincts of these religious houses, there is unlikely to have been any substantive pre-existing settlement in these areas.

Once the basic street pattern was in place the next stage in the development was to divide the town into property plots – burgages – on which a house, working yard and garden could be built. A 12*d.* burgage rent was payable to the lord of the borough (via his provost)[61] on an annual basis; the amount was on a par with most of the Anglo-Norman towns in Ireland, Cork, Drogheda, Kilkenny and Carlow being other examples of such 'shilling boroughs'.[62] Though the burgage rent had a relatively low nominal value (equating to around €30 in today's terms or three days work for a craftsman in the 1200s),[63] with the various liberties granted to burgesses it was one of the few concrete ties that remained between the lord and his land and as such was a powerful symbol of the feudal system in its urban form. In certain cases the burgage rent was higher, presumably reflecting the amalgamation of messuages; for example, William de Gloucester paid 2*s.* per annum in 1235,[64] John Slim paid 3*s.* 4*d.* for the 'square' house in the Bullawn in 1280–1 and the vicar's house in Market Street was rented at 4*s.* per annum in the same years.[65] At the lower end of the scale messuages were subdivided, such as the tenements in Michael Street and John Street, which were rented at 3*d.* per annum.[66] Apart from the Tintern charter's reference to burgages, the only other early allusion occurs in 1235 when William Marshal's son Gilbert, then lord of Leinster, granted to 'William de Gloucester, burgess of Kilkenny, half a plot (*placea*) in the town of the new bridge of Ross which the bailiffs of Leinster have retained to build a house for his [the Earl Marshal's] use. To have and to hold ...paying 2*s.* per annum'.[67]

The 1827 Tottenham Estate map of New Ross, which precedes the six-inch first-edition Ordnance Survey map by thirteen years and is at a much larger scale of eighty feet to an inch (1:9600), provides an important record of its burgage-plot framework (fig. 9.9).[68] Of great benefit is the fact that almost all of the

reflected in a document from 1289 which refers to the 'community of the street called Market Street [Bullawn]', perhaps an indication that the people living here saw themselves as distinct from the rest of the townsfolk: Hore, *Ross*, p. 161. **61** Hore, *Ross*, p. 143. **62** The 'shilling boroughs' tended to be the new towns of the thirteenth century: Morley De Wolf Hemmeon, *Burgage tenure in medieval England* (Cambridge, 1914), pp 67–8. **63** Figures obtained from the UK National Archives 'currency converter': www.nationalarchives.gov.uk/ currency/defaulto.asp#mid (accessed 12 Jan. 2010). **64** *Ormond deeds*, i, p. 86. **65** Hore, *Ross*, p. 143. **66** Ibid., p. 151. **67** *Ormond deeds*, i, p. 86. The Ormond deeds and Hore, *Ross*, contain additional references to plots from the later thirteenth to the sixteenth century. **68** The map confines itself to the walled town and does not include Irishtown or Rosbercon. It is the

9.10 First-edition Ordnance Survey map of New Ross (sheet 29, surveyed 1840, published 1841) (Trinity College Dublin Map Library).

housing stock in the town at the time was in the possession of the Tottenham Estate and each of their street frontages was measured and their width in feet recorded on the map. In total 288 plots are marked within the town wall and of these, notwithstanding a certain degree of variation, 80 per cent show a remarkable fidelity to the 20-foot standard as set out in the Marshal's original charter.[69] The northern third of the town contains the greatest density of plots, reflecting its status as the main market area and 'core' of the medieval town. The value of the 1827 Tottenham Estate map is further emphasised by the fact that only fifty-two burgage plots may be identified on the first-edition Ordnance Survey map (fig. 9.10). None of the medieval houses that would have occupied the front of the plots are known to survive and archaeological excavations have yet to uncover any such evidence.[70] Likewise, little is known about the types of

property of the Tottenham Estate Office, South Street, New Ross. My thanks to Sinéad Marshal, New Ross, for bringing this map to my attention and to the Tottenham Estate Office for allowing me make a copy of the document. **69** This accords with the five-sixths of plots in the oldest part of Alnwick that conformed to a standard burgage width of 8.5–9.8m or units thereof: M.R.G. Conzen, *Alnwick, Northumberland: a study in town plan analysis* (London, 1960). **70** There exists quite a range of written evidence for housing, though little detail, in the later thirteenth and fourteenth centuries: for example, Hore, *Ross*, pp 143, 150, 151;

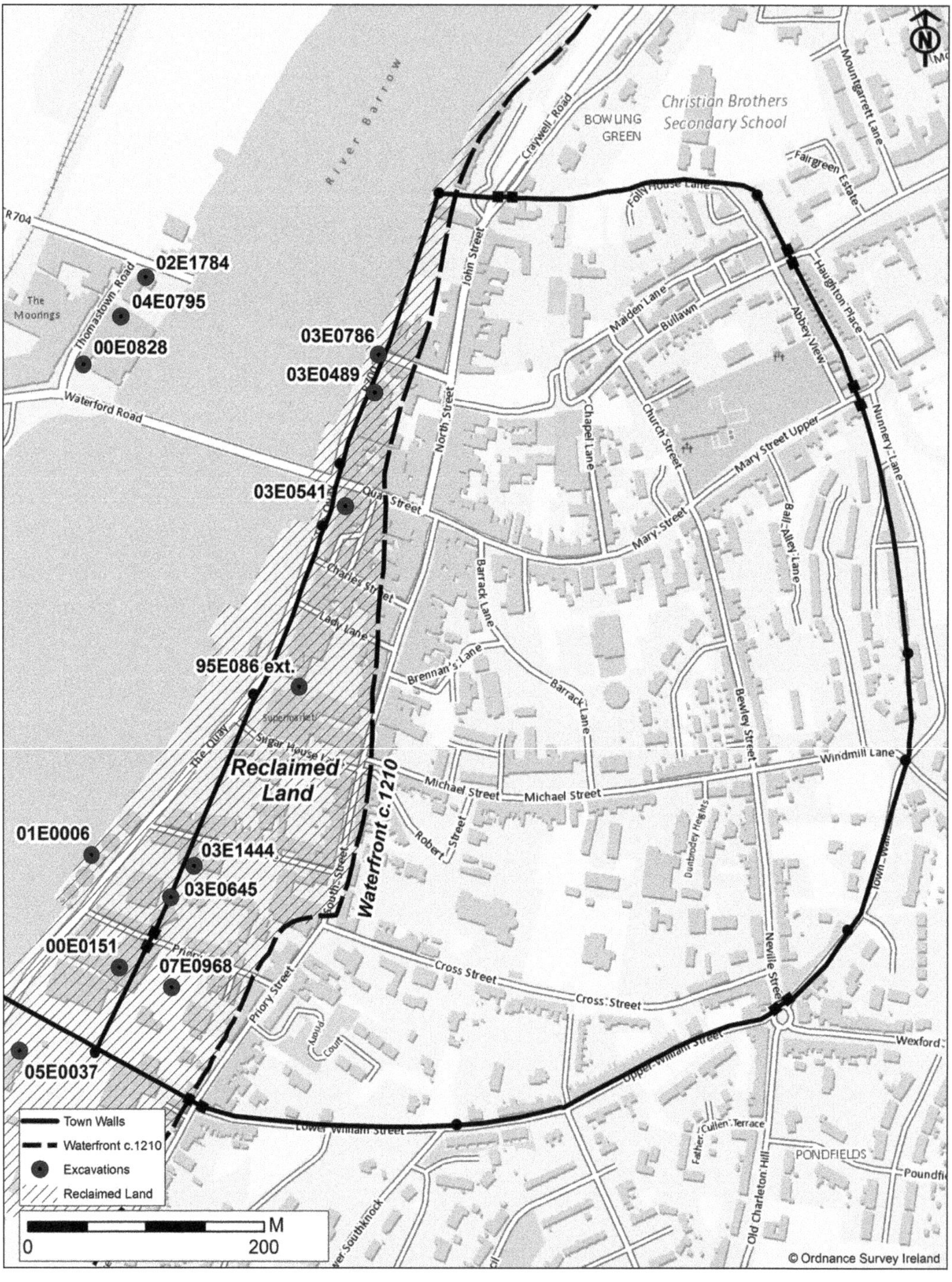

9.11 Estimated extent of the waterfront at New Ross prior to *c.*1210 and extent of reclamation zone (Barry Fitzgibbon, Kilkenny Archaeology).

industries, crafts and horticulture that were being undertaken within the plots, although a limited excavation at 6–8 the Bullawn uncovered an 11m wide by 0.6m deep quarry pit, a refuse pit and an area of burning, possibly the remains of a destroyed building, associated with Wexford-type pottery of mid-thirteenth- to fourteenth-century date.[71]

The quayside

The hub of the town was at the waterfront, away from the property plots, and since economic stimulus came via ship, a large, well-functioning quayside was a necessity from the beginning and the deep-water port afforded by the tidal River Barrow was evidently an important consideration in the town's siting. By plotting the occurrences of alluvial material in the various archaeological investigations that have taken place along the quays and relating them to the town's natural topography it is possible to estimate the extent of the river prior to its reclamation and extrapolate from this the approximate whereabouts of the early waterfront (fig. 9.11).

Ten excavations, all of which were testing or monitoring projects, led to the recovery of estuarine silts and/or reclamation material along the town's quayside (table 9.1; fig. 9.11). Within the town, all of the alluvial material occurred on the river side of the 6m contour and this can therefore be used as a marker for the location of the original high-tide shoreline (fig. 9.11). This shore followed a low bluff which ran from John Street in the north for 5–10m inside the current waterfront until the Quay Street area where it widened by around 200m to form a broad pool of slack water (as evidenced by the low-energy peat and marl deposits recorded in the various Priory Lane excavations).[72] This included most of the area to the south of Quay Street and the west of South Street and Priory Street.

To provide a new quayside, however, required a major re-engineering of the waterfront and to maximise the capacity of the town to accommodate ships in deep water it was necessary to extend into the Barrow; this would have been achieved following a process of reclamation of the foreshore. Urban excavations in Ireland have regularly unearthed evidence for the reclamation process, which generally took the form of timber and stone revetments with which the waterfront was advanced and behind which refuse, rubble and clay from the town

Ormond deeds, 1172–1350, pp 300, 386, 450, 508, 614. **71** Catherine McLoughlin, 'The Bullawn, New Ross, Wexford', *Excavations 2003*, 2021; Catherine McLoughlin, 'The Bullawn, New Ross, Wexford', *Excavations 2004*, 1814; Catherine McLoughlin, 'Archaeological assessment report: 16–18 the Bullawn, New Ross (03E962)' (Stafford McLoughlin Archaeology unpublished report, 2003); Catherine McLoughlin, 'Archaeological monitoring: 16–18 the Bullawn, New Ross (03E962)' (unpublished report, Stafford McLoughlin Archaeology, 2004). I am grateful to Catherine McLoughlin (Stafford McLoughlin Archaeology) for furnishing me with a copy of her Bullawn report. **72** Cóilín Ó Drisceoil, 'Priory Lane, New Ross', *Excavations 2003*, 2028; *2005*, 1658; *2007*, 1973. The Brayford Pool, Lincoln, around which the later city developed, provides a good parallel: Michael J. Jones, David Stocker and Alan Vince, *The city by the pool: assessing the archaeology of the city of Lincoln* (Lincoln, 2003).

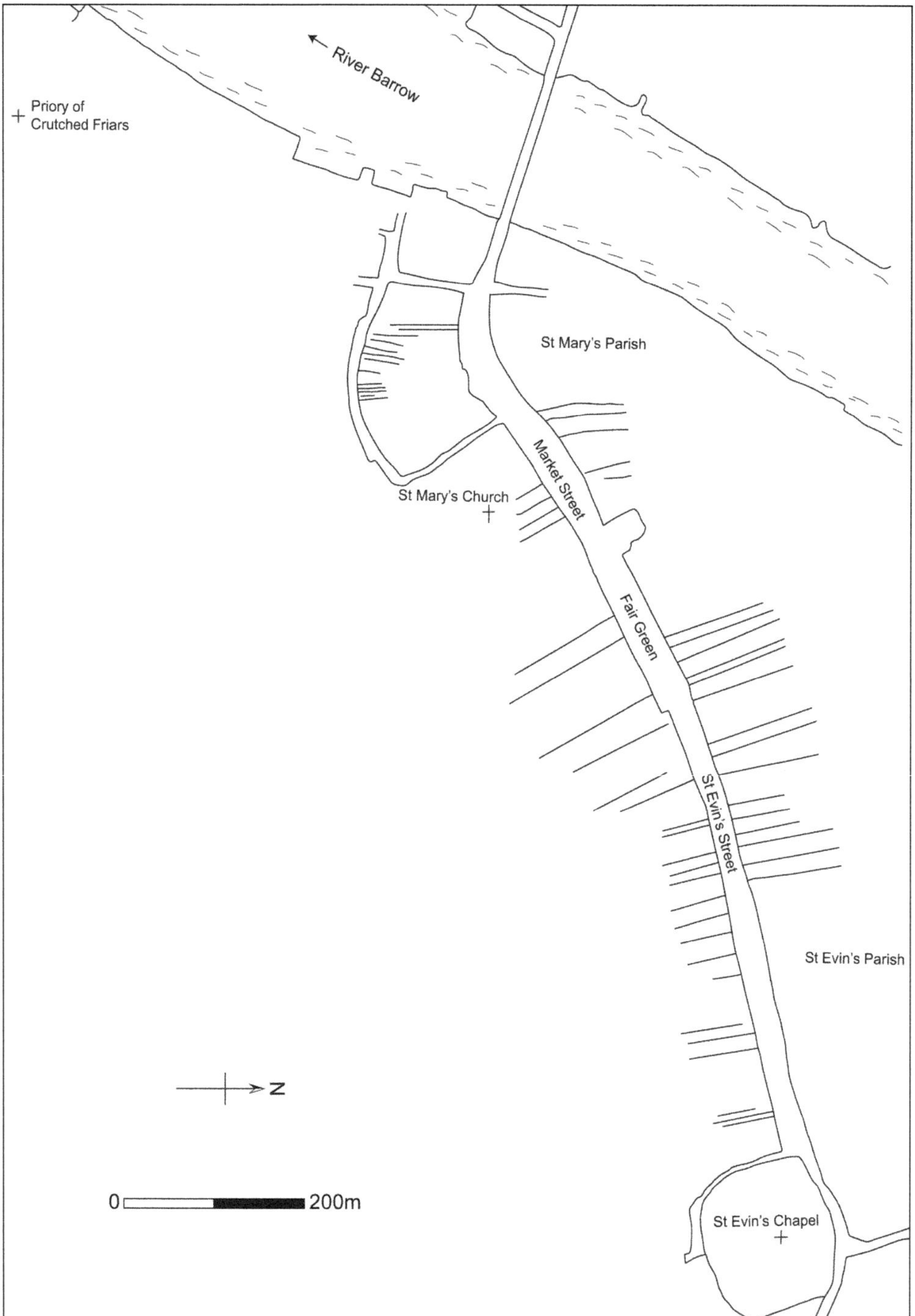

9.12 Map of medieval New Ross, *c.*1210 (map by Cóilín Ó Drisceoil; digitised by Philip Kenny, Kilkenny Archaeology).

Table 9.1 Archaeological investigations in New Ross that have produced evidence of reclamation/estuarine clays/silts.

Excavation licence/ excavator	Site location	Description	Reference
95E086 ext. Sarah McCutcheon	New Ross Main Drainage Scheme, south of bridge on quay	Estuarine silts with medieval pottery at 0.88m and 1.49m OD	*Excavations 1997*, 601
00E0151 Martin Byrne	'Lidl' Carpark Priory Lane/ South Quays	Marl at 2.5m depth, below estuarine silt which was in turn beneath post-medieval gravel and shale reclamation fills	*Excavations 2000*, 1065; *2001*, 1312
01E006 Maurice Hurley	South Quay	Estuarine silts recorded below post-medieval clay and coal ballast reclamation infill	*Excavations 2001*, 1313
03E0489 Daniel Noonan	North Quay	Reclamation dump at 1.64m OD with medieval pottery, beneath 1m-thick redeposited yellow natural clay	*Excavations 2003*, 2025
03E0541 Emmet Stafford	48 The Quays	Estuarine silt below post-medieval reclamation dumps	*Excavations 2003*, 2032
03E0645 Cóilín Ó Drisceoil	Priory Lane	Bedrock at 7.5m depth (–4m OD) below *c.*2.5m deep estuarine peat deposit with unworked timbers and plant macro-fossils. The medieval archaeological level commenced at –1.5m OD and comprised a 0.9m deep dark silty peat with wooden planks and boat timbers, leather and animal bone. It was sealed beneath a 0.8m deep 'garden soil' horizon with medieval pottery and animal bone. 1.2m of post-medieval rubble covered the deposit	*Excavations 2003*, 2028
03E0786 Catherine McLoughlin	Bridge Street	Timber plank (possibly relating to medieval bridge) discovered at 10.5m depth, sealed by silty gravel layer with medieval pottery	*Excavations 2003*, 2030
03E1444 John Tierney	Marsh Lane/ The Quay	Estuarine clays at a depth of 1.6–1.9m, below post-medieval reclamation dumps	*Excavations 2003*, 2031
05E0037 Niall Gregory	South Quay	2.5m deep grey estuarine marl at 2m depth, below post-medieval rubble	*Excavations 2005*, 1658
07E0968 Orla Scully	Priory Street/ Priory Lane	1m of post-medieval rubble overlying estuarine silts	*Excavations 2007*, 1973

was dumped and sealed with gravel/stone to provide a quayside.[73] While there is little by way of direct archaeological evidence for such reclamation from New Ross, the fact the Augustinian house was in place by 1319 and the Franciscan gardens and quay sometime before 1338 infers that reclamation had occurred in the area between South Street/Priory Street and the river by at least the beginning of the fourteenth century, and probably before this.[74] That this area was primarily given over to the precincts of the Franciscan and Augustinian orders is repeated at Kilkenny where the bulk of its reclamation zone, which took in nearly half the area of the walled town, was occupied and presumably engineered by the religious houses.[75] Private efforts at reclamation were also supported as set out originally in the Marshal's charter.

The Civil Survey records that ships of three hundred tons could safely berth on its two 'faire stronge keys maid of lime and stone'[76] and writing thirty years later in 1684 Robert Leigh noted that 'there are two keays now in good repaire where a ship of 500 Tunns may (at ye grand one of them) ride afloat at low water and discharge her loading mely'.[77] Unfortunately there is no direct documentary or archaeological evidence for the medieval quays and very little can be stated with certainty regarding their form.[78] The reconstruction of the old shoreline set out above has pointed to the existence of a deep-water pool in the southern half of the town and it is possible that this was the focus for the earliest quays. The seventeenth-century maps[79] show the quays extending along the riverfront for around 650m, from the bridge to the Franciscan friary which controlled a private

73 Irish examples include Wood Quay, Dublin: Patrick Wallace, 'Dublin's waterfront at Wood Quay, 900–1317' in G. Milne and B. Hobley (eds), *Waterfront archaeology in Britain and northern Europe* (London, 1981), pp 109–18; Wexford: Colfer, *Arrogant trespass*, pp 165, 169n. 74 Hore, *Ross*, p. 181; *Ormond deeds*, i, p. 715. 75 Cóilín Ó Drisceoil, 'Kilkenny reclaimed: the archaeological evidence for medieval reclamation in Kilkenny city', *OKR*, 55 (2003), p. 64. 76 Simington, *CS Wexford*, p. 233. 77 Hore, *Ross*, p. 368. As a comparison, the average tonnage of ships trading across the Irish sea was around 200: Timothy O'Neill, *Merchants and mariners in medieval Ireland* (Dublin, 1987), pp 107–12 and see Paul Gosling, 'From Dún Delca to Dundalk', *County Louth Archaeological and Historical Journal*, 22 (1991), p. 318. 78 Archaeological monitoring of the dredging of sections of the River Barrow at New Ross recovered a range of artefacts, some of which may have originated from the medieval quayside, including three stone anchors, a number of boat frames and strakes, clinker and carvel, seine netting weights, gaming-pieces, nails, bone, leather and small wooden tools: Eoghan Kieran, 'Archaeology sinks to new depths in the River Barrow', *Archaeology Ireland*, 13:4 (winter 1999), p. 21. Thanks to Eoghan Kieran for additional information regarding the finds. 79 'Design for the recovery of town of Ross', 1649 map and Anglesey Estate map. The 1649 map is a hasty sketch of the town to inform the earl of Ormonde of a means of re-taking New Ross from the Confederates. It was contained in 'An aphorismical discovery of treasonable faction', which is a narrative by an unknown Irish Royalist and reproduced in J.T. Gilbert (ed.), *A contemporary history of affairs in Ireland, from 1641 to 1652* (Dublin, 1879–80), ii, p. 312 (facing). For an account of the 'Aphorismical discovery …', see Deana Rankin, *Between Spenser and Swift: English writing in seventeenth-century Ireland* (Cambridge, 2005), pp 117–49. The 1649 map is traced (and the text copied) and reproduced in Hore, *Ross*, p. 329. The quay nearest the bridge is marked the 'Custom House Quay' on the map; that to the south is the 'Block House Quay' in reference to a nearby seventeenth-century fortification. The

9.13 Trace of the 'Design for the recovery of town of Ross', 1649 map of New Ross (reproduced in Hore, *Ross*, p. 329).

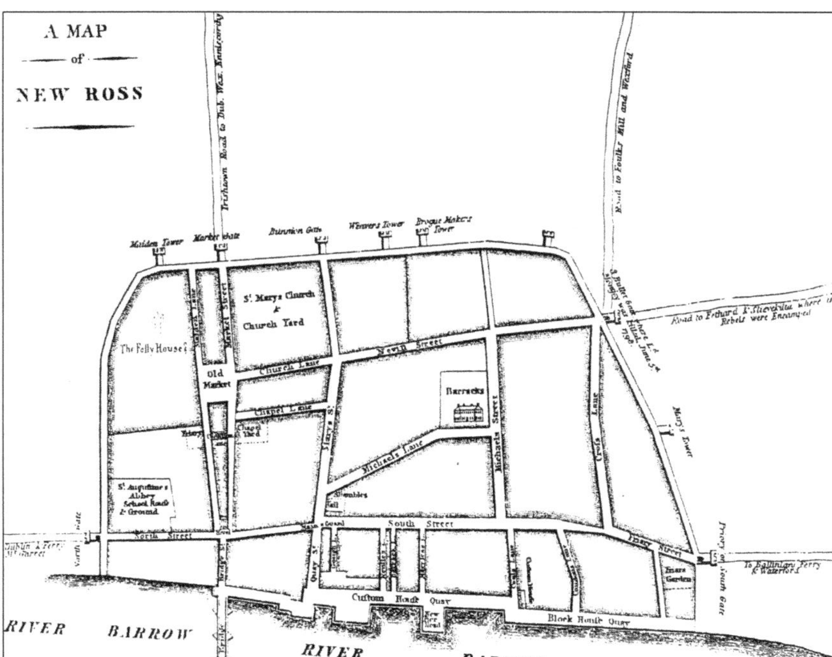

9.14 Anglesey Estate map of New Ross, *c.*1675, reproduced in Carroll, *Memoir*.

9.15 View of New Ross from west by W.H. Bartlett, 1831 (NLI ET 1792TA).

pill and quayside on which they allowed (for a fee) boats to offload their goods (figs 9.13, 9.14).[80] If this is accurate it would make it one of the longest quays in Ireland and larger than that of its great rival at Waterford. The friars had been given an exemption from customs in their foundation charter and not surprisingly this was a recipe for conflict with the port authorities.[81] In the mid-1600s, and perhaps earlier, the quays were protected by a stone parapet: both the seventeenth-century maps depict a river wall as part of the town defences and jetties (marked 'gates upon the water') as well as a postern gate, a bridge gate and a flanking tower are shown jutting from the quays on the 1649 map (fig. 9.13). W.H. Bartlett's 1831 view of New Ross also shows jetties and a river wall to the north of the bridge (fig. 9.15).[82]

Anglesey Estate map is held in the Tottenham Estate Office, Priory Street, New Ross, and was drawn for the earl of Anglesey, who had obtained a large grant of property in New Ross in 1666: Hore, *Ross*, p. 366. Reproductions of the map are contained in W.G. Carroll, *A memoir of the Right Rev. James Thomas O'Brien DD* (London, 1875); Hore, *Ross*, p. 51 and T.C. Butler, *Near restful waters: the Augustinians in New Ross and Clonmines* (Dublin, 1975), pp 88–9. At the base of the reproduction in Carroll it is stated that the map is a nineteenth-century copy of an original which the earl of Anglesey presented to the town in 1699. The map, it is stated, 'is believed to represent New Ross as it stood 200 years ago' (*c.*1675). This would date the map to between 1666, when the earl was granted his property, and 1699, when he presented the map to the town. **80** *Ormond deeds*, i, p. 303. **81** For example, in 1295 the friars were cited as having in their possession the goods of two merchants from Flanders: *CDI, 1293–1301*, no. 260; *MHFPI*, pp 179–80. **82** NLI ET 1792 TA.

Mills

Milling was an important element in the town economy and many of the mills were located on the waterfront, perhaps functioning as tidal mills.[83] One of these was at the bridge crossing and was farmed by one William Serveren in 1279.[84] There is little direct evidence for milling from before 1250 but the *Histoire*'s notice of the Marshal's barns (*granges*) being set alight in 1207 infers that mills were in place to process the grain held in this facility.[85] It is also of interest to note that the stores were not out in the countryside, as might be expected. This suggests they were stores of grain intended for export, and perhaps near the quays. In 1286, there were at least five watermills at New Ross, one of which was in ruins.[86] Milling was controlled by the lord of the town, as initially set out in the charter of incorporation, and in 1247 the mills were worth 5*s.* to Hugh Bigod.[87] A *c.*1292 grant of land to John Kempe makes mention of 'the mill pools of the Earl Marshall on the west'.[88]

Bridge and ferry

Traffic on the land route between Kilkenny and Wexford was facilitated by a bridge and a ferry. The town's medieval bridges spanned the Barrow and joined Bridge Street with the Thomastown road on the Rosbercon (west) side of the river (fig. 9.8).[89] It presently spans a distance of 180m over the river, but it was almost certainly longer, perhaps as much as 250m, in the early thirteenth century. The bridgehead on the New Ross side was placed at the narrowest point in the river, immediately above the broad pool to the south. Construction of the bridge was a major undertaking and it is no surprise that the structure was memorialised in the name of the town, 'Rospont' (the bridge of Ross), throughout the Middle Ages.[90] Today the official seal of the town council carries a representation of the bridge.[91] The first bridge appears to have been destroyed sometime before 1270–90 when the Dominicans of Rosbercon petitioned the crown for murage money to be spent on the construction of a new bridge between their abbey and New Ross.[92] It is not known if their request was acceded to but in 1313 pontage was granted to Thomas Bigod, Gilbert de Clare and

83 The Maudlins to the east of Irishtown was another important area for milling: A. O'Sullivan, 'Industrial archaeology' in M. Tubridy and E. Culleton (eds), *Traces of County Wexford's past* (Wexford, 1994), pp 60–75. 84 Hore, *Ross*, p. 142. 85 *HWM*, ii, lines 13564–72. 86 Hore, *Ross*, p. 157. 87 Ibid., p. 136. 88 *Ormond deeds*, i, p. 301; iv, p. 98. 89 The Anglesey Estate map shows a bridge at this location and the street-name 'Bridge Street' is recorded in 1543: *Ormond deeds*, iv, p. 290. The modern bridge is 100m downstream (south) from its medieval precursors. 90 For example, Hore, *Ross*, pp 20, 35, 154, 178. 91 Hore states that image on the town's seal, a greyhound pulling down a stag on a bridge, was derived from that of William Marshal: Hore, *Ross*, pp 54n., 267. William Marshal's seal was however a typical thirteenth-century equestrian device of a knight on horseback: Crouch, *William Marshal*, p. 200. An example can be seen on the base of the 1217 reissue of Magna Carta: MS Ch. Oxon. Oseney 142b. 92 National Archives (UK) SC 8/53/2639; T.S. Flynn, *The Dominicans of Rosbercon (1267–c.1800)* (Kilkenny, 1981), p. 17n.

Aylmer de Valence, for the second of at least three bridges constructed prior to 1649.[93] Virtually nothing is known about the form of the Marshal's bridge. It was presumably of timber for a stone structure would have been prohibitively expensive and technically impractical to construct. It is possible that at least some of the bridge timbers that have been noted occasionally within the river belonged to this first crossing. Stanihurst in 1577 recorded that New Ross

> was no more famoused for these wals than for a notable bridge that stretched from the towne unto the other side of the water, which must have been by reasonable survey 12 score if not more. Diverse of the poales, logs and stakes with which the bridge was underpropt, sticke to this daie in the water.[94]

In 1795 and 1825 large oak bridge timbers were found in the river beneath Bridge Street and, from their description, they appear to have been scribed timbers, typical of Anglo-Norman carpentry.[95] In 2003 archaeological monitoring of geotechnical investigations in advance of a main drainage scheme at the bridgehead at Bridge Street recovered a piece of a timber plank at a depth of 10.5m from the surface (table 9.1). The overlying deposit of silty gravel contained thirty-five sherds of medieval pottery and the excavator was of the view that it was a bridge timber that had been recovered.[96]

The transportation of goods and people over the River Barrow by bridge was supplemented by a ferry that ran between New Ross and Rosbercon throughout the Middle Ages. The economic viability of the ferry was probably due to lower tolls and levies being placed on it than those levied on goods that were transported across the bridge. The first historical reference to a ferry at New Ross occurs in 1246–7 when the rent charged was 5*s*. per annum.[97] A document from 1686 provides an indication of the types of materials transported: 'we present that ye antient duty of ye ferry at Ross was ½*d*. for every man or woman, 1*d*. for every horse, cow or bullock, ¼*d*. for every sheep or goat, for every stone of wool ¼*d*., for every barrell of corn ½*d*.'[98] The need to facilitate carrying the maximum tonnage across the river infers that the ferries were of log platform/raft construction.[99] The income generated by the ferry was quite

93 *CPR, 1313–17*, p. 43; Bradley and King, 'Urban Archaeological Survey of New Ross', p. 106. 94 L. Miller and E. Power (eds), *Holinshed's Irish chronicle* (Dublin, 1979, repr. of 1577 ed.), p. 56. 95 H. Martin, 'Ancient bridge at New Ross: monuments of New Ross', *JRSAI*, 5 (1858–9), pp 204–7; Hore, *Ross*, p. 112n. Hore also noted that the timbers recovered in 1825 were sold to John Rossiter, of Abbeybreny, who made furniture from them. As there is no Abbeybreny in Wexford it is almost certainly Kilbraney (civil parish of Clongeen) that is being referred to. In 1853 according to Griffith's Valuation a John Rossiter, landlord, had a house here with 237 acres. My thanks to the late Billy Colfer and Hilary Murphy for this information. 96 Catherine McLoughlin, 'The Quays/Marshmeadows, New Ross, Wexford', *Excavations 2003*, 2030. 97 Hore, *Ross*, p. 136. 98 Ibid., p. 357. 99 European examples of log rafts have been published by A. Eskeröd, 'Early Nordic arctic boats', *Arctica* (1956), pp 59–61

substantial: for instance in 1285–6 its keeper returned the substantial sum of £7 16*s*. 8*d*. for three-quarters of a year.[100] In the sixteenth and seventeenth centuries a dedicated 'ferry quay' was provided, away from the main port, and this is likely to have also been the case in earlier years.[101]

St Evin's parish

If economic fulfilment was provided for the new urban community at the waterfront, the main centre for spiritual fulfilment was the splendid parish church dedicated to the Blessed Virgin Mary (fig. 9.16, pl. 27). St Mary's served the large urban parish of the same name, which is today the sole parish in the town. Until at least the fifteenth century, however, before it was subsumed into the parish of St Mary's, a separate parish of St Evin's existed outside the town wall and though its parochial bounds are difficult to reconstruct it seems to have included the suburb of Irishtown and perhaps a portion of the eastern extent of the civil parish of St Mary's.[102] The church was in what is now St Stephen's graveyard (see above) (fig. 9.12); a thoroughfare called 'St Evin's Street' led up to it[103] and tenements belonging to the foundation were rented in *c.*1292.[104] In 1224 it was appropriated to St John's, Kilkenny, along with St Mary's and it formed a parcel of the possessions of that priory at the Dissolution.[105] Nothing survives of the structure but the Archaeological Survey of Ireland recorded a 5.8m long wall within the graveyard that may be associated with the former church.[106]

St Mary's parish church

St Mary's Church was sited at the highest point within the town, making what must have been a remarkable sight from the bustling port below. St Mary's, when completed around 1250, was one of the largest parish churches in medieval Ireland and comparable to some of the country's biggest monastic churches and cathedrals.[107] Its medieval plan was cruciform with a long rectangular chancel, a simple rectangular north transept, an aisled south transept with two eastern chapels and an aisled nave at the west end of which was a rectangular residential tower (probably a late medieval addition) (fig. 9.17). A crypt – one of the few in an Irish parish church – extends under the south transept (and may have gone further prior to its collapse at the north end). The west aisle of the south transept and the nave as far as the east side of the crossing were pulled down in 1812–13

and D. Ellmers, *Fruhmittelalterliche Handelsschiffahrt in Mittel und Nordeuropa* (Neumunster, 1972), pp 106, 112–16. **100** Hore, *Ross*, p. 153. **101** *Ormond deeds*, v, p. 297. A separate ferry quay is marked on the 1649 and Anglesey maps. **102** *Ormond deeds*, i, pp 301, 828, 838; ii, p. 80; iii, pp 89, 128. **103** Ibid., i, p. 843; iv, p. 98. **104** Ibid., i, p. 301. **105** William Dugdale, *Monasticon Anglicanum* (3 vols, London, 1818–30), ii, p. 1042; Hore, *Ross*, p. 246. **106** Moore, *AI Wexford*, no. 1168. There is no trace today of this wall. **107** It measured 41.45m north–south and some 56m east–west. Leask calculated that it was slightly smaller east–west at 47m though this figure would appear to have been based on the length of the shortened nineteenth-century nave: Leask, *Irish churches*, ii, p. 85.

9.16 The parish church of the Blessed Virgin Mary (St Mary's) from east.

to make way for the existing Church of Ireland edifice and today the unroofed chancel, transepts and crossing arches survive to near their full heights.[108] A *c*.1799 engraving is the only known illustration of the now-lost western half of the church (fig. 9.18).[109] It shows the south aisle of the nave with its three blocked pointed arches, the original south wall, which would have stood in front of the arches, has been removed.[110] The drawing also depicts the nave's parapet as crenelated and a ruined rectangular tower is attached to the west end – this is the 'strong Norman tower' described by Hore.[111] The cemetery that surrounds the church is rectangular and is bounded by stone walls; these revet about 2m of a

108 A. Marmion, *The ancient and modern history of the maritime ports of Ireland* (London, 1860), p. 576. This was the last in a long series of misfortunes to befall the church: it was dissolved in 1541 because it was monastic property: *EIMP*, p. 180; badly burnt in 1636: *Chorographic account*, p. 452; badly despoiled in the Cromwellian attack on the town: ibid.; and in 1763 a newly built steeple 'contiguous to the church' fell down: *FJ*, 25–29 Oct. 1763. **109** NLI ET 1791 TA; the print is from an engraving by Joseph Walker after a painting by G. Holmes and was first published in Joseph Walker (ed.), *The Copper Plate Magazine; or, Monthly Cabinet of Picturesque Prints, Consisting of Views in Great Britain and Ireland*, 4 (London, 1799). **110** The blocked pointed arches in the west walls of the transepts are of similar style and would have led into the side aisles. **111** Hore, *Ross*, p. 93n. There were also clerestory windows, according to Cullen, though he does not record the source of this information: J.B. Cullen, 'The Canons Regular in Ireland: St Mary's Church, New Ross', *Irish Ecclesiastical Record*, 16 (1920), p. 43.

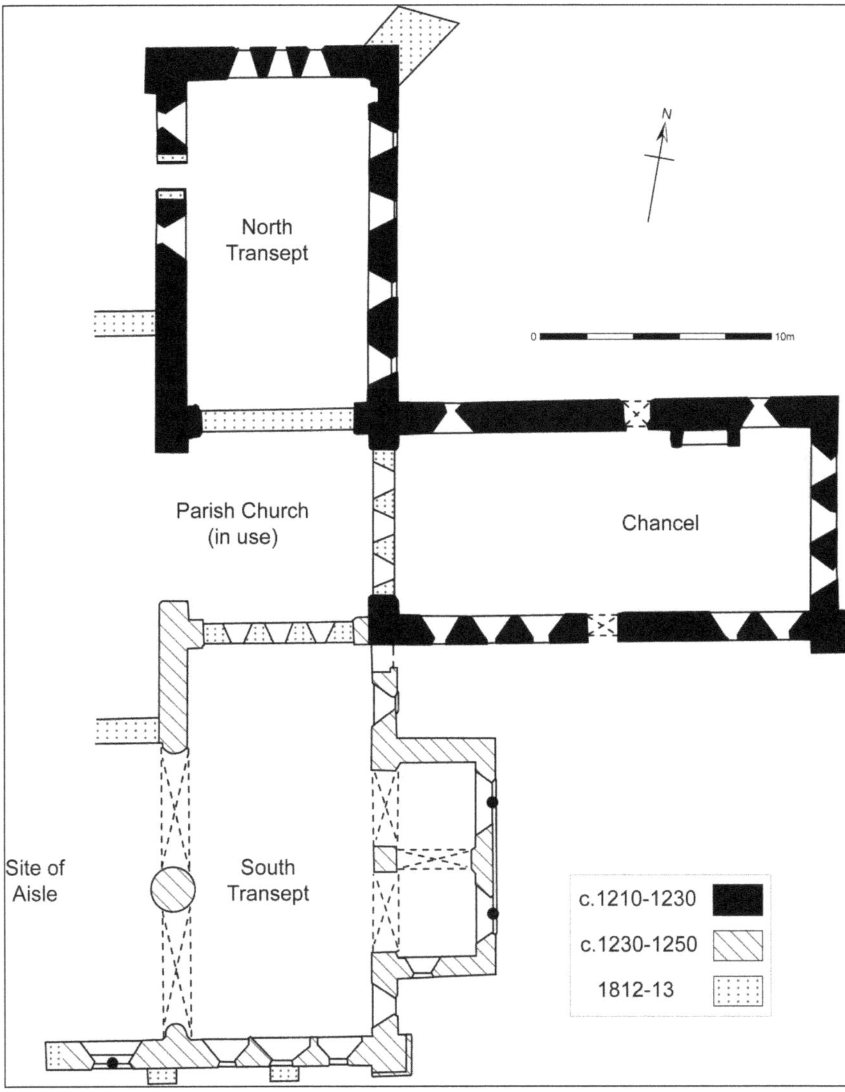

9.17 Ground plan of St Mary's Church, New Ross.

'graveyard earth' to street level. Originally the graveyard appears to have been larger for there are local reports of skeletal remains having been found in the mid-1900s at the top of Mary Street, *c.*20m outside the present boundary walls.[112] A breakdown in the burgage-plot pattern on the south-east side of the Bullawn also indicates that the churchyard may have originally extended further to the north and into this area (figs 9.9 and 9.10).

112 Mr P. Reid, Mary Street, New Ross, pers. comm.

A folk tradition in New Ross links William Marshal and more particularly Isabel de Clare with the foundation of St Mary's.[113] However, the earliest known documentary record for the church does not occur until 1224 (after both William and Isabel's deaths) when William Marshal the younger issued a charter to St John's Augustinian priory in Kilkenny granting it the patronage and tithes of St Mary's.[114] St John's was founded before 1211 and it had been provided with a (now lost) foundation charter by William Marshal: its 1224 charter from William Marshal the younger confirmed an earlier grant and it can be speculated that St Mary's was among its original benefices.

If the historical sources linking William and Isabel with St Mary's are somewhat vague, there are Early English Gothic architectural details that can be used to date the beginnings of the church to their time.[115] These include the typical early thirteenth-century triplet of graduated tall lancets in the east wall of the chancel, the use of small rolls with banded shafts of Dundry stone in the north transept and chancel (fig. 9.19),[116] and the presence in the south wall of the chancel of a semi-circular round-headed doorway with Dundry mouldings.[117] The medieval capitals in the chancel and transepts use 'stiff-leaf' design and a number are decorated on their abacus with a narrow panel of barley twist and/or

113 The earliest written mention of the tradition can be traced to 1607: William Camden, *Britannia* (1607), p. 696 (English trans. Philemon Holland: www.philological. bham.ac.uk/ cambrit/) (accessed 6 June 2010); see also Orpen, *New Ross*, p. 7. Indeed Leask proposed that a thirteenth-century head-slab in the chancel of St Mary's was a cenotaph to Isabel, the countess herself having been buried with her mother in Tintern, Wales: H.G. Leask, 'A cenotaph of Strongbow's daughter at New Ross, County Wexford', *JRSAI*, 78 (1948), pp 65–7. Leask read the inscription on the tomb as ISABEL: LAEGN … GIST ICI … (Isabel of Leinster) while it is actually inscribed 'ISABEL: LA FEMME DE …GIST ICI …' (Isabel the wife of … lies here). John Hunt has also pointed out that the head-slab in question would be more appropriate for a middle-class burgess rather than a lady of Isabel's standing: Hunt, *Figure sculpture*, i, p. 238, nos 263, 264. **114** William Dugdale, *Monasticon Anglicanum* (3 vols, London, 1818–30), ii, p. 1042. Around 1227, William Marshal the younger notified John, bishop of Ferns, that he had appropriated to the prior of St John's the parish churches of St Mary and St Evin of New Ross: Orpen, *New Ross*, p. 11n. For a short time after 1279 St Mary's appears to have been the property of Christ Church Canterbury: Charles McNeill, 'Harris: *Collectanea de rebus hibernicis*', *Analecta Hibernica*, 6 (Nov. 1934), pp 312–13; *CDI, 1252–84*, no.2145, but by 1308 St John's had regained their rights over the church when they were sued by the abbot of Tintern, Co. Wexford, for its advowson, large debts due by Tintern to Canterbury were probably the cause of Tintern's involvement in the dispute: P.H. Hore, *History of the town and county of Wexford: Tintern etc.*, 2 (London, 1901), pp v–xv, 30–66, 47. Tintern's claim appears to have been unsuccessful because St John's still held possession of the church when it was dissolved in 1540–1: Hore, *Ross*, p. 246. **115** Unkel, 'Architectural patronage', pp 223–60. **116** Leask, *Irish churches*, p. 34; D.M. Waterman, 'Somersetshire and other foreign building stone in medieval Ireland, *c.*1175–1400', *Ulster Journal of Archaeology*, 33 (1970), p. 68. Jill Unkel has pointed out that one of the Marshal's caputs was at Chepstow, close to the Dundry quarries and Bristol from where the stone was exported: Unkel, 'Architectural patronage', p. 259. **117** Another round-headed Dundry-built doorway is present in the east wall of the north transept but it has brick in its lower courses and has clearly been reset from elsewhere. These are the sole rounded medieval arches in the church; the remainder are pointed.

9.18 'New Ross, Co. Wexford', *c.*1799 illustration, from an engraving by Joseph Walker after a picture by G. Holmes (NLI 1791TA; National Library of Ireland).

dog-tooth, a motif that is also to be found in the early thirteenth-century east end of St Canice's Cathedral, Kilkenny,[118] and in the transept crossings at St Patrick's Cathedral, Dublin (*c.*1225).[119] The equal lengths of the north and south transepts (7.6m) suggest they were laid out at the same time and the similarities in arch mouldings between the south transept chapels and those in the north transept and chancel also indicate broad contemporaneity, though the decreasing use of Dundry stone in the south transept has been taken to imply a slightly later date.[120] A number of other architectural features support this view: the shaft mouldings in the south transept show a move away from those set between pairs of small rolls to larger rolls being placed on either side of the shafts. A sexfoil window above the projecting side chapels in the south transept is paralleled in the mid-thirteenth-century parish churches of Gowran (*c.*1250–60) and Thomastown (*c.*1250) and in the Cistercian foundation at Dunbrody (*c.*1210–40)

118 Siuban Barry, 'The architecture of the cathedral' in Adrian Empey (ed.), *A worthy foundation: the cathedral church of St Canice, Kilkenny, 1285–1985* (Mountrath, 1985), pp 28, 33. **119** E.C. Rae, 'The medieval fabric of the cathedral church of St Patrick in Dublin', *JRSAI*, 109 (1979), p. 52, fig. 15a4. **120** Leask, *Irish churches*, p. 55; B. De Breffny and G. Mott, *The churches and abbeys of Ireland* (London, 1976), p. 78.

9.19 Detail of early thirteenth-century mouldings in Dundry stone on lancet in north wall of north transept, St Mary's, New Ross.

and the placement of double lancets into a single embrasure is a post mid-thirteenth-century feature. The broad consistency of the architectural details throughout St Mary's can be used to verify that at a minimum the entirety of the east of the church was completed by *c.*1220, with the south transept having been finished slightly later, perhaps by mid-century.

Comprising some forty burial monuments in total, St Mary's Church contains the third largest collection of medieval funerary monuments – figure sculptures, recumbant graveslabs and altar-tombs – in Ireland.[122] The one

122 The largest collection resides at St Canice's Cathedral, Kilkenny, where there are eighty-one monuments pre-dating 1600: John Bradley, 'The medieval tombs of St Canice's' in Adrian Empey (ed.), *A worthy foundation: the cathedral church of St Canice, Kilkenny, 1285–1985* (Mountrath, 1985), pp 49–103. St Patrick's graveyard, Kilkenny, has sixty-six monuments: Michael O'Dwyer, *St Patrick's, Kilkenny: graveyard* (Kilkenny, n.d.), p. 3, and St Mary's medieval church in Kilkenny has thirty-nine: Cóilín Ó Drisceoil, 'A collection of previously

a b c d

9.20 Some of the thirteenth-century burial monuments at St Mary's Church, New Ross: *top left*: fragment of female effigy carved in oolitic limestone (*c.*1200–50); *top right*: Alis La Kerdif (*c.*1280–1300); *bottom left*: 'Cristiana' slab (*c.*1280–1320); *bottom right*: effigy of a layman (*c.*1280–1300).

unpublished medieval burial monuments from Saint Mary's Church, Kilkenny', *OKR*, 58 (2006), pp 29–44. There are twenty-five monuments at St Patrick's Cathedral, Cashel: Denise Maher, *Medieval grave slabs of County Tipperary, 1200–1600AD* (BAR, Brit. Ser. 262, Oxford, 1997), pp 69–74. It should be noted that, to date, there has been no nationwide survey of medieval burial monuments and these figures, while generally accurate for their respective sites, may be superseded by future surveys. The fine collection of medieval and early modern

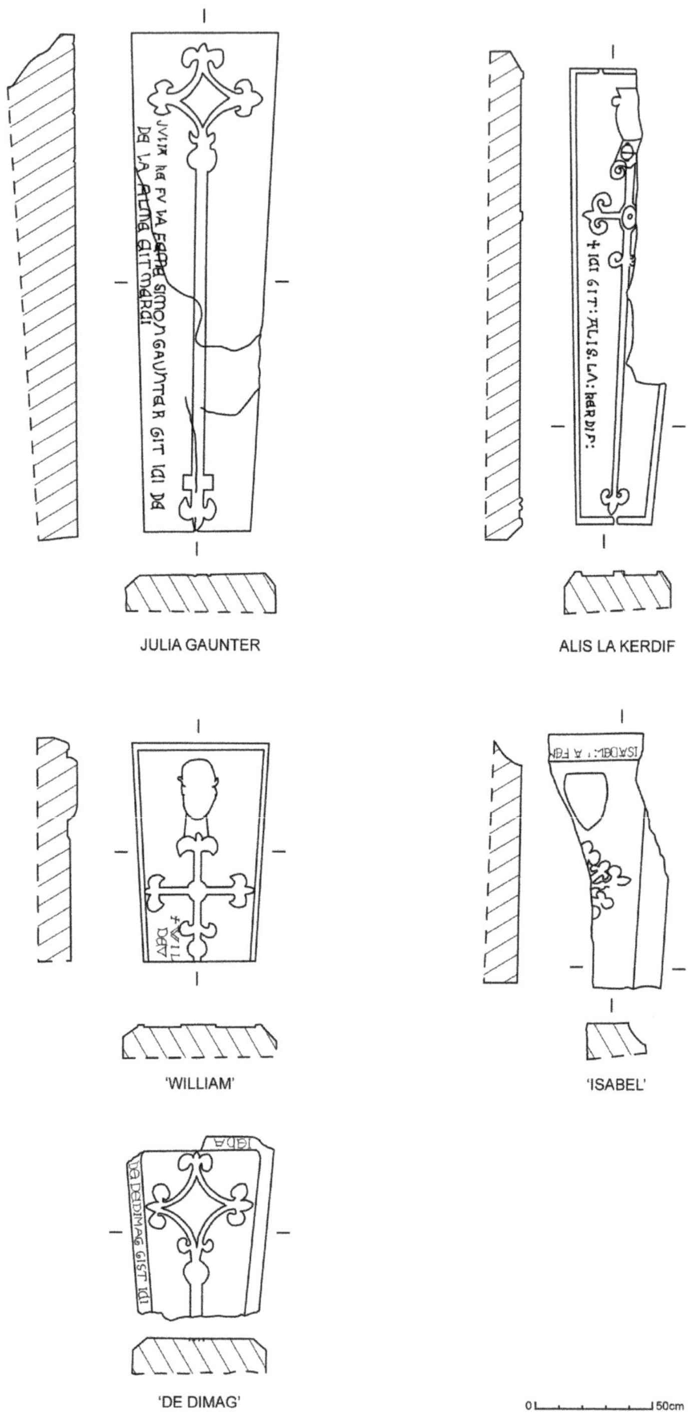

9.21 Thirteenth-century graveslabs from St Mary's, New Ross (drawings: Cóilín Ó Drisceoil, digitised by Philip Kenny): *top left*: Julia Gaunter (*c.*1280–1300); *top right*: Alis La Kerdif (*c.*1280–1300); *middle left*: 'William' head-slab (*c.*1200–1300); *middle right*: 'Isabel' head-slab (*c.*1200–1300); *bottom left*: 'De Dimag' graveslab (*c.*1280–1300).

example that can be dated to the first half of the thirteenth century – the lower half of a female effigy carved in an oolitic limestone[123] – was described by John Hunt as a 'very beautiful and well-carved figure, and is one of the most important remaining in the south-east of Ireland' (figs 9.20–9.21).[124] Twelve of the plainly carved graveslabs and two head-slabs can be assigned broadly to the thirteenth/fourteenth century but not more closely.

Hospital of the Fratres Cruciferi and Franciscan friary

Before *c.*1250 New Ross possessed just one religious house, the hospital of the Fratres Cruciferi. The Fratres were the main Hospitaller order in medieval Ireland and were charged with providing monastery-hospitals for the poor, travellers and pilgrims.[125] Hore was the first to state that their hospital was established around 1195 by the Marshal and this has been repeated by subsequent authors.[126] Such an early date – at least five years before the town was founded – has always been doubtful, particularly because the order would have required the presence of a relatively large dependent community. The basis for Hore's 1195 date was the occurrence of 'peculiar lettering on some ancient tombs', which he noted on the site of the order's former monastery in Priory Street.[127] This is clearly not sufficient reason to posit such an early date, and in the absence of any supporting evidence, it must be discounted.

Only one medieval document exists linking the Fratres Cruciferi with New Ross. This is a 1435 bull from Eugenius IV to the bishop of Ferns in which he reiterated a 1412 statement that the inhabitants of New Ross were absolved from a papal interdict of excommunication that had been placed upon them after

> the inhabitants of Rosponte rose against a brother of the Order of Crossbearers or Crouched Friars (Cruciferorum) who had killed one of the

funerary monuments at St Mary's has been studied intermittently since the nineteenth century: P.D. Vigors, *APMDI*, 4 (1899–1900), pp 328–31, 497; idem, 5 (1901–3), pp 125–33; G.J. Hewson, 'Proceedings', *JRSAI*, 12 (1872–3), p. 199; J.F.M. Ffrench, 'New Ross: St Mary's graveyard', *JRSAI*, 26 (1896), pp 193–6, J.F.M. Ffrench, *APMDI*, 6 (1904–6), p. 411; J.R. Garstin, *APMDI*, 4 (1899–1900), pp 332–7, 501, idem, *APMDI*, 5 (1901–3), pp 125–6; M.J.C. Buckley, 'The Bambino of New Ross', *JRSAI*, 28 (1898), pp 250–3 and see Peter Harbison, 'Some medieval sculpture in Kerry', *Journal of the Kerry Archaeological and Historical Society*, 6 (1973), p. 10; G.H. Orpen, *APMDI*, 6 (1904–6), pp 165–6; H.G. Leask, 'A cenotaph of Strongbow's daughter at New Ross, County Wexford', *JRSAI*, 78 (1948), pp 65–7; Hunt, *Figure sculpture*, i, pp 238–40; Áine O'Mahony, *The monuments of St Mary's Church, New Ross* (New Ross, 1987). The majority of the pre-1600 funerary monuments were drawn and catalogued in Ó Drisceoil, 'Medieval New Ross', 1, pp 59–63, 212–66. **123** Waterman tentatively identified the geology as Bath stone: Waterman, *Foreign building stone*, p. 68, but Hunt prefers Dundry: Hunt, *Figure sculpture*, i, p. 238, no. 263. **124** Both head-slabs are published in Hunt, *Figure sculpture*, i, p. 238, nos 264–5. These and all the medieval graveslabs are also catalogued in Ó Drisceoil, 'Medieval New Ross', 1, pp 213–14, 232–41. A selection is also to be found in O'Mahony, *Monuments of St Mary's Church*. **125** *MRHI*, pp 208–9. **126** Hore, *Ross*, pp 74, 94n., 96. **127** Ibid., p. 96.

> inhabitants, slew him and other brethren of the Order and confiscated their house, though this was afterwards allocated to the use and habitation of the Friars Minor.[128]

The Franciscans had taken over the friary of the Fratres Cruciferi before 1256, when a provincial chapter was held to collect crusading money.[129] Nothing remains above ground of their friary – its conventual buildings were torn down in 1732[130] – and even its exact site has been the subject of some confusion. Most authors have placed it between Priory Street and the river[131] but this area has been the subject of several archaeological excavations and no structures that could be associated with the friary have been found.[132] In addition, the seventeenth-century Anglesey Estate map marks it as the 'Friars Gardens'[133] rather than the site of the friary proper (fig. 9.14); this is borne out by the discovery of medieval garden soils in an excavation on the north side of Priory Lane.[134] In the nineteenth century four medieval graveslabs and two 'stone coffins' were found at a place called 'Dowsly's Garden, Priory Street'.[135] A 'Dowsley' is marked on the 1827 Tottenham Estate map as occupying a house in front of a large area of open ground called 'Priory Field', *c.*30m inside the South Gate, on the east side of Priory Street rather than the west and therefore this would seem to be a more likely location for the Franciscan friary and presumably the house of the Crutched Friars that preceded it.[136] At the Dissolution the

128 *MHFPI*, p. 188. **129** Ibid., pp 23–5. The money was presumably being collected for the Crusade for the reconquest of Padua, which was proclaimed by Innocent IV in 1256. According to James Ware, the founder of the monastery was Sir John Devereux who may have been acting lord of New Ross in the mid-thirteenth century: James Ware, *De Hibernia et antiquitatibus eius, disquisitions* (London, 1654), p. 278; Hore, *Ross*, pp 64, 200n. **130** Hore, *Ross*, p. 94. A description of the site from 1684 records that much of the friary was 'turned into dwelling houses': *Chorographic account*, p. 452. **131** The site currently occupied by Steele and Co. manufacturing engineers. **132** Mary O'Donnell, 'Priory Street, New Ross', *Excavations 2001*, 1311; Ó Drisceoil, 'Priory Lane, New Ross', *Excavations 2003*, 2028; Orla Scully, 'Priory Street/Priory Lane', *Excavations 2007*, 1973. **133** Anglesey Estate map. **134** Ó Drisceoil, 'Priory Lane, New Ross', *Excavations 2003*, 2028. **135** The slabs commemorate high-ranking burgesses such as the constable of New Ross, Gaylard de Rise, and the provost's wife, Alis La Kerdif. Gaylard de Rise: Hore, *Ross*, p. 95; J.R. Garstin, *APMDI*, 4 (1899), pp 332–7. An uninscribed slab is also illustrated in Carroll, *Memoir*. A rubbing of the Gaylard de Rise slab by Vigors is held by the Royal Society of Antiquaries of Ireland, 63 Merrion Square, Dublin. Alis la Kerdif: *APMDI*, 6 (1904–6), p. 165; Orpen, *New Ross*, p. 27; John Bradley and Heather King, 'Urban Archaeological Survey of New Ross' (Office of Public Works, unpublished report 1990), p. 116. The slab is now in the chancel of St Mary's. De Altibilaris slab: Carroll, *Memoir*; Hore, *Ross*, p. 95. 'Two stone coffins': Vigors, *APMDI*, 5 (1901–3), p. 130. **136** This area is currently occupied by housing and back gardens. A site directly to the north, 'Priory Place', was archaeologically test-trenched and medieval soil horizons were recorded, though nothing structural was noted: Clare Mullins, 'Priory Street, New Ross', *Excavations 1998*, 674. The friary's precinct occupied an area of around two acres and originally it was outside the town wall. In 1308–9, presumably as a consequence of the frequent attacks on the town, the friars petitioned, successfully as it turned out, to be enclosed within the defences: *MHFPI*, pp 89–90. A section of the southern part of church, kitchen, cemetery, two small gardens, a watermill and a salmon weir were noted as well as 'other buildings suitable for the farmer'.[137] In 1574 the ruined church, cloisters, dormitory and half an acre were granted to Thomas Butler, tenth earl of Ormond.[138]

Town defences

New Ross did not enjoy the security of a castle. This was at Old Ross and the defence of the town must have therefore been a concern from its inception. The unique poem, written around 1265 and known as 'The walling of Ross', explicitly states that the townsfolk were living in fear because they 'had no town walls' and were solely reliant on the keeping of a 'watch' at night as a means of defence.[139] There is also no indication from the poem that the new defences replaced or augmented an existing palisade and fosse circuit, such as that built in the early 1200s at Kilkenny,[140] and it can be concluded that in the absence of any evidence to the contrary, the Marshal town was not defended by a town wall. That is not to say that there was not some form of an urban boundary or demarcation but this may have taken a less substantive form, perhaps a simple bank with guarded entries such as at Ely.[141] This situation was not unique to New Ross and many medieval towns, both in Ireland and in Britain, prospered without recourse to a town wall,[142] and in this sense New Ross had much in common with other Marshal boroughs such as Carlow, Kildare and Naas, all of which were without a town wall during their first generation or two of existence.[143] The absence of a town wall (and castle) at New Ross provides a good indication of the relative security that must have been felt within the borough during its early years. This may have been in no small part due to the strong familial links, through Isabel

this town wall, standing to a height of 1.2m, was unearthed in excavations on the south side of Priory Lane: Scully, 'Priory Street/Priory Lane', 1973. Another possible section of the western river-wall was noted in excavations adjacent to the Lidl car park: Martin Byrne, 'The Quay, New Ross', *Excavations 2000*, 1065. **137** *EIMP*, pp 363–4. **138** Hore, *Ross*, p. 258. **139** Frederick Madden (ed.), 'Poem on the erection of the walls of New Ross, in Ireland', *Archaeologia*, 22 (1829), pp 307–22; trans. in T. Crofton Croker (ed.), *Popular songs of Ireland* (London, 1886), pp 275–87; Shields, 'The walling of Ross', pp 24–33; William Sayers, 'Anglo-Norman verse on New Ross and its founders', *IHS*, 28:110 (Nov. 1992), pp 113–23. The line of the circuit, the largest single stretch in Ireland, can be determined with a fair degree of accuracy from historic maps, upstanding remains and a small number of archaeological excavations: Thomas, *Walled towns*, 2, pp 175–9; Ó Drisceoil, 'Medieval New Ross', 1, pp 41–51. **140** Recent archaeological excavations at Talbot's tower, Kilkenny (E3646), have confirmed that an earth-and-timber 'town wall' was replaced by stone defences at this site in the later thirteenth century: Cóilín Ó Drisceoil, *Excavations 2007*, 967. **141** Oliver Creighton and Robert Higham, *Medieval town walls: an archaeology and social history of urban defence* (Stroud, 2005), pp 26, 207. **142** Ibid., pp 22, 26. **143** Thomas, *Walled towns*, 2, pp 36, 124–5, 168–9. In general, responsibility for constructing the town wall was left with the urban community rather than the lord, which may often explain the lag between the inception of a town and its eventual encirclement with a town wall. Thus at Dundalk, for example, the walls came about a generation after the borough was developed: ibid., pp 97–8.

de Clare, between the Mac Murchada Kavanaghs and the Marshals, and it can be no co-incidence that the commencement of Mac Murchada attacks on New Ross coincided with the cessation of direct ties between the Marshals and the town following the death of the last of William's children in 1248.

Civic institutions

William Marshal's charter facilitated the establishment of civic institutions and 'The walling of Ross' makes it clear that a range of guilds existed by at least 1265.[144] As with other towns the administrative buildings would have been positioned near the market or the bridge crossing. In 1280–1 there was an exchequer, when 'a carpet' (*tapetum*) was bought for the fair,[145] and certainly the large volume of trade that went through New Ross in the medieval period meant that a custom house would have been necessary to enforce the collection of tolls and levies from visiting merchants: in 1280–1 when repairs were carried out 'to a certain house in which the [New] custom was received'.[146] The town hundred is also occasionally referred to in the thirteenth-century documents and a pillory was repaired in 1284–5.[147]

Suburbs and liberties

The attractions of the burgeoning port and market would have drawn a substantial population – for which estimates are given below – and many of these individuals would typically have lived at the fringes of the town.[148] Very little evidence exists for suburbs from the first half-century of New Ross's existence but it is possible that the area that was to be eventually enclosed with walls around 1265 – at thirty-nine hectares the largest unitary walled town in Ireland – included a substantial suburban population around the Bullawn-Irishtown core and in the southern part of the town. Directly across the bridge from New Ross another suburb was located at Rosbercon from at least the later thirteenth century, and this was granted its own charter of incorporation *c.*1294 (fig. 9.8).[149] In all likelihood there was a pre-existing suburban settlement here that was being given formal recognition. There was also a suburb in the Irishtown that was at least partially within the separate parish of St Evin in the early thirteenth century and may have enveloped the pre-existing monastic settlement (figs 9.8 and 9.12).[150]

The liberties of New Ross were carved from the seigniorial manor of Ross and stretched far beyond the urban core.[151] On the *c.*1654 Down Survey map the borough is recorded as having comprised fifty-eight acres, and its liberties

144 For example, it includes reference to 'the commons' assembling and sixteen different guilds: Shields, 'The walling of Ross', p. 151. **145** Hore, *Ross*, p. 144. **146** Ibid., p. 145. In 1588 the structure was located 'close to St Saviour's'. **147** Hore, *Ross*, pp 145, 151. **148** Derek J. Keene, 'Suburban growth' in M.W. Barley (ed.), *The plans and topography of medieval towns in England and Wales* (London, 1976), pp 71–82. **149** Mac Niocaill, *Na buirgéisí*, p. 296. **150** Hore, *Ross*, p. 150. **151** Colfer, *Arrogant trespass*, p. 99, fig. 38.

covered 3,799 acres, equivalent to the civil parish of St Mary's (fig. 9.5).[152] In 1688, and presumably reflecting their medieval extent, the urban privileges also extended within the rivers Nore and Barrow as far as Inistioge to the north of the town and to the Hook lighthouse in the south.[153] Inches, meadows and woodland also surrounded the town and at the 1247 partition the inquisition into the lands of Hugh Bigod recorded that each had a rental value of 5*s.* per annum.[154] The inches – water-meadows used for summer grazing of cattle – were an important economic resource for the town and presumably extended along the broad floodplain of the Barrow to the south of the town. Each burgess probably held lands outside the town and many of the long narrow fields to the north and south of the Irishtown marked on the first-edition Ordnance Survey map are probably enclosed relics of medieval openfield strip holdings.[155]

THE POPULATION OF THE MARSHAL'S NEW ROSS

New Ross had become a thriving port by *c.*1250 but providing accurate estimates of its population in these early years is problematical.[156] The burgage rent in 1279 and 1307 was £25 6*s.* 8*d.* indicating that, on the basis that the rent was habitual from the time of the town's foundation and that each burgage produced one shilling, some 506 burgages were provided for by the Marshal.[157] This is an extraordinarily high figure – higher than any other Irish or Welsh borough of the period – and should thus be treated with a degree of caution. Certainly it includes separate rental income from agricultural holdings that were 'outside the walls' which would decrease the figure somewhat but nevertheless it gives a good idea of the scale of the project that was envisaged by the earl.[158] A further difficulty is that we have no indication of how many of the plots provided were actually taken up in the early 1200s.[159] Estimating population numbers in medieval towns is generally difficult, even where relatively good documentary coverage exists. By using J.C. Russell's model of average population density per hectare at between 100 and 120 people, New Ross's later thirteenth-century walled extent at thirty-nine hectares leads to a figure of between 3,900 and 4,680 people, on a par with Kilkenny or the more substantial 'country towns' of

152 Down Survey map, *c.*1654–6. 153 *Reports from commissioners, corporations Ireland*: appendix, parts 1 and 2, vol. 28, p. 561; Hore, *Ross*, p. 174. 154 The Marshal of England's lands in Ireland: Carew MS 611, fo. 14b [n.d.]. 155 A.J. Otway-Ruthven, 'The organisation of Anglo-Irish agriculture in the Middle Ages', *JRSAI*, 81 (1951), pp 1–13; John Feehan, *Farming in Ireland: history, heritage and environment* (Dublin, 2003), p. 78. 156 B.J. Graham, 'The towns of medieval Ireland' in R.A. Butlin (ed.), *The development of the Irish town* (London, 1977), p. 44. 157 *CIPM*, iv, no. 434, p. 306; Hore, *Ross*, p. 142. 158 Maurice Beresford, *New towns of the Middle Ages*: *town plantation in England, Wales and Gascony* (London, 1967), p. 255. 159 At Drogheda the dating of waterfront timbers to *c.*1200 has been taken to infer the town had filled up quite quickly following its foundation, but no such dates are available for New Ross: John Bradley, 'Recent archaeological research on the Irish

England.[160] Brian Graham, on the other hand, has suggested multiplying the number of burgage holdings by a factor of five, which in the case of New Ross produces a population of some 2,530 individuals.[161] As Graham admits, this method does not take into account burgage amalgamations or subdivisions, something that was happening in New Ross from an early date and nor does it provide for the problem of agricultural holdings.[162] Neither method is reliable but there is one intimation that the town had attracted a large population from close to its inception, and that is the grand scale at which its parish church was built, and in particular its spacious nave, infers that it served as a preaching house to a large population. In sum, it is more than a possibility that there were over five thousand inhabitants within a few decades of its foundation, which would place New Ross within the top twenty or so towns of Britain and Ireland in terms of population size.[163] Whatever the true figure, 'The walling of Ross' provides an impression of a large, vibrant, diverse and self-confident urban community and perhaps its claim that there were 4,667 men in the town who could bear arms is not the major exaggeration it was once thought to be.[164]

NEW ROSS AND THE LORDSHIP OF LEINSTER

Although New Ross had some form of minor monastic antecedent – whose scale and even exact location is far from clear – to all intents and purposes it was a plantation town and as such formed part of the boom in new town foundation, most of it seigniorial in origin, that was taking place throughout Europe in the decades either side of 1200. This boom was occurring within the context of a doubling of the population and a growing commercialisation of society.[165] In Ireland most of the fifty-six towns associated with the Anglo-Normans were established between 1190 and 1230; the fact that forty-nine new towns were founded throughout the whole of England (and none in Wales) during this period is a reflection of the gusto with which the Anglo-Normans took to settling towns in Ireland.[166] New Ross was founded in a 'second wave' of new towns after *c.*1200, along with places like Carrick-on-Suir, Clonmel, Carlow, Kinsale and Youghal.

town' in Helmut Jäger (ed.), *Stadtkernforschung* (Cologne, 1987), p. 336. **160** J.C. Russell, *Medieval regions and their cities* (London, 1972), p. 137. **161** Graham, 'Towns of medieval Ireland', p. 44. **162** B.J. Graham, 'Urbanisation in the high Middle Ages' in T.B. Barry (ed.), *A history of settlement in Ireland* (London and New York, 2000), p. 136. **163** Swanson, *British towns*, p. 14. **164** The 1265 poem records the presence of 600 seamen in the town with a further 500 at sea, as well as vintners, mercers, merchants, drapers, mariners, tailors, cloth-workers, tent-makers, fullers, saddlers, cordwainers, tanners, butchers, priests, fishermen, hucksters, carpenters, blacksmiths, masons, goldsmiths, wimplers, nappers, spicers and glovemakers: Shields, 'Walling of Ross', pp 24–33. **165** Swanson, *British towns*, p. 10; Beresford, *New towns*, pp 329, 335. **166** Beresford, *New towns*, pp 328–31, 338.

William Marshal's Irish estates were the only ones where he undertook town foundation with vigour, no doubt a reflection of the relatively unstable conditions in his Welsh and Norman estates and the fact that the period saw much of eastern and southern Ireland pacified to the extent that towns could be founded as commercial rather than wholly military entities. New Ross, with no castle or administrative function for the manor, is a case in point. New Ross was also the entrepôt for one of the few urban hierarchies of medieval Ireland.[167] This comprised a network of towns and markets that were strung out along the Nore and Barrow river-catchments, from which the products for export – fish, wool, wool-fells and hides and cereals (wheat and oats) – were funnelled through the new port.[168] Ireland's largest inland town at the time, Kilkenny was the location for the Mashal's 'court' and provided a ready market for the imports that returned with the ships; luxury goods, wine and English woollen cloth being the main commodities.[169] New Ross was in effect an outport to Kilkenny in the same manner as Boston was to Lincoln, Hull was to York and Southampton was to Winchester. That the beginnings of most of the Leinster boroughs in the Nore and Barrow catchments can be associated with the Marshal implies he had a grand plan to structure and control the urban network. But this was not confined to the boroughs, for they were of little use without the availability of a large agricultural surplus for export.[170] Thus the Marshal harnessed the manorial economy through extensive land-grants to lesser seigniors and the Cistercian order to facilitate what Alfie O'Brien has termed 'a revolution in pastoral husbandry and arable agriculture'.[171]

The success of the Marshal's venture was quickly realised and New Ross became one of the five main ports of thirteenth-century Ireland – with Drogheda, Dublin, Waterford and Cork.[172] Edward I's 'great custom' on wool, the king's most valuable export, allows the ports to be ranked in terms of the volume of trade they enjoyed (though it did not include taxes on all tradable activities). This shows that between 1275 and 1279 New Ross was by far the busiest port in Ireland for wool.[173] In the years 1276–1333, the town yielded

167 A similar commercial network can be seen with the trading route between Cork and the town of Kilmallock, Co. Limerick: O'Brien, 'Politics, economy and society', p. 95. **168** On the River Nore and its tributaries these towns included Inistioge, Newtown Jerpoint, Thomastown, Kilkenny Hightown, Dunmore, Odagh (Threecastles), Moatpark, Castlecomer, Callan, Kells, Knocktopher, Palmerstown, Loughmerans and Coolaghmore: see Adrian Empey, 'County Kilkenny in the Anglo-Norman period' in William Nolan and Kevin Whelan (eds), *Kilkenny: history and society* (Dublin, 1990), p. 80; Swanson, *British towns*, pp 15, 25; Graham, 'Urbanisation in the high Middle Ages', pp 133–5; Colfer, *Arrogant trespass*, p. 140–1. **169** O'Brien, 'Politics, economy and society', pp 92, 97–9. **170** Ibid., p. 92. **171** Ibid., p. 98. **172** Graham, 'Towns of medieval Ireland', pp 40, 132. In 1278 the ports of Ireland are listed as New Ross, Waterford, Wexford, Dublin, Drogheda, Carrickfergus, Galway, Cork, Youghal and Limerick: *CDI, 1171–1251*, no. 1429. **173** Mac Niocaill, *Na buirgéisí*, ii, pp 526, 528. £2,079 was the total return for 1275–9, about a fifth of that from England's busiest port at Boston: A.L. Brown, *The governance of late medieval England, 1272–*

£5,928 in customs, representing 26 per cent of the total duties from Ireland.[174] At this time New Ross was an international trading centre and the presence of Florentine middle-men in the town as early as 1217 is an indication that this was the Marshal's intention from the beginning.[175]

William Marshal's eldest son William succeeded as lord of Leinster following the death of his father in May 1219, and his tenure was marked by a period of further stability and economic development in the lordship.[176] For New Ross it meant that its role as chief port was secured and enhanced, most notably by Henry III's grant to William in 1227 of a (shortlived) concession that permitted shipping to land at Ross.[177] On William's death in 1231 the castle of Old Ross was seised by the king[178] but was wrested back by Richard Marshal who subsequently issued from the castle the charter for the deforestation of the manor of Ross.[179] Richard died from wounds received on the Curragh in 1234 and his successor Gilbert was killed in a tournament in 1241; with the death of Walter and Anselm in 1245 the male line was terminated without a male heir.[180] The lordship was two years later divided according to feudal custom into five equal shares among the daughters of William Marshal the elder (or their representatives).[181] Old Ross, New Ross and the Island were assigned with the shire of Carlow, presumably with the intention of providing it with a port, to the sole surviving daughter Matilda (Maud) upon whose death the following year it passed to her son Roger Bigod, earl of Norfolk. While the partition undoubtedly weakened the lordship New Ross continued to thrive in its role as outport and it saw sustained economic development that led to the enlargement of the town, its walling from 1265 and the establishment of new religious houses, chapels and hospitals before the turn of the century, all of which was based on the urban foundations that had been put in place by William Marshal at the beginning of the century.

CONCLUSION

The study of early New Ross is based on a mixture of scrappy documentary records and the evidence from urban topography. Many questions remain unanswered about the Marshal's town; these may be divided into three main categories that relate to its origins, its landscape and its society. Regarding its

1461 (Stanford, 1989), p. 66. **174** Graham, 'Towns of medieval Ireland', p. 41 (table 3). **175** T.J. Westropp, 'Early Italian maps of Ireland from 1300 to 1600, with notes on foreign settlers and trade', *PRIA*, 30C (1912–13), p. 381; Wendy Childs and Timothy O Neill, 'Overseas trade' in Art Cosgrove (ed.), *NHI*, ii: *Medieval Ireland, 1169–1534* (Oxford, 1993), p. 494. **176** James Lydon, 'The expansion and consolidation of the colony, 1215–54', *NHI*, ii, pp 166–7. The impact of the partition of Leinster on Wexford has been recounted in considerable detail by Colfer, *Arrogant trespass*, pp 71–82. **177** *CDI, 1171–1251*, no. 1552. **178** Ibid., no. 1872. **179** *CSMA*, ii, p. 160. **180** Orpen, *Normans*, iii, pp 73–5. **181** Ibid., pp 79–110.

origins, the settlement that preceded the town is poorly understood. Where exactly was the early medieval monastery of *Ros Mhic Thriúin* and what was its topography? Was it in existence when the new town was founded? The townscape of the Marshal's primary urban settlement is also far from clear. What was the full extent of the early town and its suburbs? What was the character of its private, public, defensive and ritual landscapes? What was the form of the early quayside and where exactly was it? What was the chronology of its development? What was the form of the original bridge? What was the town's broader landscape context? What were the rural settlement forms and patterns of the period 1200–50 in the hinterland? How did the town interface with the surrounding landscape? Perhaps the aspect of the Marshal's New Ross about which we know least is the nature of the society that colonised the town. From where did the first settlers come? Were they enticed solely from the earl's estates in Ireland, Wales and Normandy? Or was there a mass movement from the rural areas of Old Ross? Was there a place for the Gaelic Irish in the town? What were the living conditions, lifestyles, health and diet of the early settlers? What were the agencies that shaped town society and what were the origins of the town oligarchy? What was the nature and extent of urban occupations and industry?

A paucity of written evidence makes archaeology vital for addressing these questions and fully understanding the early town; as Maurice Beresford so aptly put it, 'the silence of documents is the classic moment for the archaeological intervention. All power to the spade and trowel'.[182] It is salutary at this point to note that the archaeological agenda for the town first set out by John Bradley and Heather King in 1990 has seen little progress despite over twenty-five years of investigation.[183] The key reason for this is the fact that all archaeological excavation has been determined by the requirements of development compliance rather than the needs of research. In the reclamation zone, for instance, where deeply stratified waterlogged deposits and structures are known to exist, most developments are by necessity placed on pile foundations, which leaves little or no opportunity for excavation of these areas. The need for a substantial excavation of the medieval waterfront, which was some 100m from the present east bank of the River Barrow, must be re-emphasised as a research priority (fig. 9.11). This was one of the most extensive and elaborate quaysides in Ireland and there is no reason why timber (and possibly stone) quays, river walls, docks, reclamation revetment sequences, warehouses and dwellings would not survive beneath the present townscape between North Street/South Street/Priory Street and the river. The waterfront also most probably acts as a repository for an enormous wealth of artefacts, many of which would be preserved by the waterlogged conditions. These would provide important insights into the local industries – shipwrighting for instance – that utilised the foreshore as well as a

182 Beresford, *New towns*, p. 321. **183** Bradley and King, 'Urban Archaeology Survey', pp 125–33.

far greater understanding of the chronology, topography and economy of the early town, its trade connections and the nature of its society.[184]

This essay aimed to set out the current state of knowledge regarding the first half-century of William Marshal's town of New Ross and to place it in the broader context of contemporary urbanism and the development of the Leinster lordship. The creation of the town had three main aims: economic, strategic and political. The Marshal sought to usurp Waterford as the port for the south-east and succeeded with aplomb through the formation of a hierarchical urban network that had New Ross at its fulcrum. This facilitated the new town's entry to the international economy and its rise as one of Ireland's major urban centres. At New Ross we also see in clear focus the Marshal as a master strategist, a conquistador and entrepreneur whose assets harmonised feudal lordship and urbanisation for a private enterprise that underscored the autonomy of his Irish 'empire'. And, lastly, the foundation of New Ross can be viewed as an overtly political act, a symbolic gesture towards the ancestral lands of Isabel de Clare, a gesture with a peace dividend that allowed the port to thrive and prosper.

184 For overviews of port archaeology, see Helen Clarke, *The archaeology of medieval England* (London, 1984), pp 181–7; J.M. Steane, *The archaeology of medieval England and Wales* (London, 1984), pp 131–7.

The wife's tale: Isabel Marshal and Ireland

GILLIAN KENNY

The marriage of Isabel de Clare and William Marshal is often viewed as a perfect example of the ascent of a man through his marriage to an important heiress.[1] The lands that he received in various countries after his marriage are enumerated in other essays in this collection and so need not be listed here. Certainly the material benefits to him were enormous, as is well known. The Marshal's life is one of the best known in medieval history, but what about Isabel? Like most medieval women, very little of her life is known to us. An exception to this paucity of information is revealed in descriptions of her conduct in Ireland after 1207 and especially centring on her doings in Kilkenny. From the available evidence I hope to reveal a little about one of the most important and least written about heiresses in medieval Irish history.

Isabel was not born to be an heiress. The death of her older brother Gilbert in 1185 meant that the heir to Leinster was to be a woman. The choice of her husband, then, was of supreme importance in Ireland with regard to how the lordship of Leinster would survive and develop. Through choosing her husband, Isabel's guardian (the king) could control the passage of lands and affect the balance of power in an Ireland where colonisation was still in its very early stages. There may have been some in Ireland who harboured ambitions towards bidding for her themselves and were disappointed and embittered when she was given in marriage to the Marshal, an outsider. Unfortunately it appears that, despite his fame (or perhaps because of it), Isabel's new husband was not a particularly popular choice among the barons of Leinster as their new overlord (judging by subsequent rebellious developments in Leinster that will be examined further on in this essay).

The thoughts of Isabel herself on her new husband are unknown. She must, though, have been acutely aware that her marriage to William Marshal was not the first time that a woman from her family had been used as a reward for an ambitious man. She herself was the product of such a match because her mother Aoife had married Richard de Clare, earl of Striguil, and otherwise known as Strongbow. He, while not quite as penurious as his future son-in-law, was not a favourite of King Henry II, having opted for the losing side in the recent civil war, and according to Giraldus Cambrensis, when Strongbow agreed to Diarmait

1 Jessie Crosland, *William the Marshal: the last great feudal baron* (London, 1962), p. 63.

Mac Murchada's terms, 'he had a great name rather than great prospects, ancestral prestige rather than ability, he had succeeded to a name rather than possessions'.[2]

Strongbow had welcomed a chance to redeem his fortunes and escape from the watchful eye of the king by taking his chances with Diarmait in Ireland. The marriage between Strongbow and Aoife sealed the alliance made between this Cambro-Norman adventurer who chose to aid Isabel's grandfather, Diarmait Mac Murchada, in his quest to win back his kingdom. After the death of Diarmait, the deal he had made with Strongbow came into effect and Strongbow claimed his lands by right of his wife Aoife. Through her, Diarmait had granted to Strongbow most of his kingdom of Leinster, which went completely against traditional Irish inheritance law and practice.

Under Gaelic law, the inheritance rights of the heiress (*banchomarba*) were very different to the Anglo-Norman practice and legislation concerning heiresses.[3] The Gaelic-Irish law relating to women and property was that a woman could only inherit from her father if there were no male heirs and in that case she could hold only a life-interest in land belonging to her own family or land settled on her by her husband. If there were male heirs in her family then she was entitled either to only *lanna*, *ranna* and *bregdha* or to a share of the movables but not of the paternal land.[4] In Aoife's case there were viable male heirs to Leinster and therefore Aoife was not eligible as an heiress, a fact that was ignored by her father and her husband.

Regarding the inheritance from her mother (because Isabel inherited from Aoife), a daughter could inherit a life-interest of hereditary land from her mother, if there were no sons to succeed. This would revert to her mother's family after her death. A woman could also inherit a separate type of land-holding, namely 'land of hand and thigh'. This was land granted to a daughter by her father, which could then be inherited by her lawful heirs. If her heirs were daughters they could inherit if they undertook to provide military service in time of war, or they could inherit half the land without such an undertaking. The daughters could inherit all of such land for the usual limited life-interest but if a woman's sons were her heirs, they had to share her inheritance with members of her own family (*fine*). Thus, as Myles Dillon pointed out, daughters inherited more easily from their mother than from their father.[5]

Transmission of land to an heiress was unusual in Irish society due to the absence of primogeniture and the consequent acceptability of varying male relatives as heir. The major disadvantage of the Irish heiress was her lack of the

2 Giraldus, *Expugnatio*, pp 54–5. 3 Myles Dillon, 'The relationship of mother and son, of father and daughter, and the law of inheritance with regard to women' in Rudolph Thurneysen, N. Power, M. Dillon, K. Mulchrone, D.A. Binchy, A. Knoch and J. Ryan, *Studies in early Irish law* (Dublin, 1936), pp 133–4. 4 Ibid.; the definition of *lanna* as 'gold' or perhaps 'griddle', *ranna* as possibly 'of silver' and *bregdha* as 'the speckled cloth' are cited in the same article on pp 169 and 171n.3. 5 Ibid., p. 175.

right to transmit her own inheritance. It betrays a real reluctance on the part of male kin to see any part of their patrimony disappear outside their *fine* (kin group) through outside marriage. Therefore, an heiress could keep the land only if she married within the family. Such measures ensured that women never posed any real long-term political threat within Gaelic Ireland. Thus Diarmait's decision to ignore Irish legal tradition and settle his lands on his daughter and her husband met with opposition in Leinster. Strongbow did not enjoy his new-found prosperity for too long because he died in 1176 and he left as his heir a son, Gilbert, who was to die in 1185, eventually leaving his sister, Isabel, as the heiress.

In the late summer of 1189, the Marshal arrived back in London from France ready to meet and then marry the teenager who was to be his wife.[6] Like the marriage of Isabel's mother and father, this marriage involved a disparity in ages as the Marshal was born in around 1147 and Isabel was born presumably sometime quite soon after 1170. Through the Marshal and his new wife it is possible to glimpse the international, trans-continental nature of complex Anglo-Norman family structures. William was an Anglo-Norman knight married to an Anglo-Irish heiress of extensive lands in Ireland, England, France and Wales.[7] Through marriage to her, this Anglo-Norman knight was related to the Irish Mac Murchadas and through her husband's sisters Isabel was related to the families of de Pont l'Arche and Crassus who the Marshal's two sisters married into.[8] After the marriage this once cash-strapped knight was now a landowner on a large scale, which was quite an achievement for him. He also became lord of Striguil but he did not succeed to the earldom of Pembroke for over a decade.[9] Furthermore, he experienced difficulties trying to extricate Isabel's inheritance of Leinster from Prince John and eventually had to appeal to King Richard for help.[10] Despite such problems though, William was right to claim that he had nothing 'save through her'.[11]

As I have stated, Isabel, like many of the wives of great medieval men, is a shadowy figure but it is possible to gain some insights into her life and activities particularly in Ireland from some contemporary sources. This daughter of a Gaelic-Irish mother does not appear to have experienced any significant Gaelic influences on her life. As a child (and a very valuable heiress) she was taken into the king's custody in England and stayed there until she married. She was then part of the royal household and, as such, was immersed in an aristocratic French-speaking world.[12] Marriage to the most famous knight in that world (even if he was much older than her) must have been an almost overwhelming prospect for a young girl from such a milieu. They appear to have made a successful match,

6 Crouch, *William Marshal*, pp 68–9. 7 Brooks, *Knights' fees*, p. 72; Daniel Power, 'The French interests of the Marshal earls of Striguil and Pembroke, 1189–1234', *Anglo-Norman Studies*, 25 (2003), pp 199–225. 8 Brooks, *Knights' fees*, p. 73. 9 Crouch, *William Marshal*, pp 69–70, 86. 10 Ibid., pp 70–1. 11 *HWM*, ii, line 13544. 12 *CSMA*, ii, p. 141.

however, based on mutual affection. Isabel duly became pregnant before the end of 1189 and they eventually produced ten living children.[13]

Upon marriage, Isabel's authority over her lands was transferred to her husband. Once married, a woman was legally treated as a minor who was under the authority of her husband.[14] Most husbands, however, were careful to include their wives' assent in the documents recording the deals relating to land owned by them, in case a contest later arose if she was a widow.[15] In medieval society the husband was pre-eminent and his authority was paramount and thus the subordination of the wife's role, even though she may have been the owner of the land, was considered normal and natural. However, it appears that Isabel was an active participant in the governance of her ancestral lands in Ireland and, certainly, she was active in their defence during the thirteenth century.

Over the following years many children were conceived and born in various areas of William and Isabel's lordship because, like all other great landowners, they led peripatetic lives. Their lands and interests stretched over several countries and, as a consequence, travel was a necessary element in their lives. It seems that Isabel and William were first in Ireland together in 1200. This was probably her first return journey to the land of her birth since she left it as a child and it does not seem to have been an unqualified success because her husband failed to impress the marcher barons there.[16]

She did manage with her husband to found the abbey of Tintern in Wexford in thanks for a safe journey across the Irish Sea.[17] Another, later, opportunity to impress the battle-hardened veterans of Irish warfare and colonisation was to come several years later and, this time, Isabel herself took it. In 1207–8 the Marshal was severely tested by a rebellion against his authority in Leinster while at the same time his relations with the king were rapidly deteriorating. He and Isabel arrived in Ireland with their entourage in late March or early April 1207 to a mixed reception that was heavily influenced by the plotting of Meiler fitz Henry.[18] The situation deteriorated to the extent that the Marshal was recalled to England by the king and he left behind him his pregnant wife. The *Histoire de Guillaume le Maréchal* describes the situation thus:

13 Crouch, *William Marshal*, p. 69. 14 According to common law, wives were not entitled to hold property by themselves: see Kenneth Nicholls, 'Irishwomen and property in sixteenth-century Ireland' in Margaret MacCurtain and Mary O'Dowd (eds), *Women in early modern Ireland* (Edinburgh, 1991), pp 17–31 at p. 17. 15 Peter Fleming, *Family and household in medieval England* (Basingstoke, 2001), p. 38. Husbands assumed control of all their wives' property but safeguards eventually were put in place so that a husband could not alienate his wife's lands without her permission; if he did not gain her permission and sold or leased her land, then, after his death, a wife could contest his actions. 16 Crouch, *William Marshal*, pp 87–9. 17 *CSMA*, ii, pp 307–8. 18 Crouch, *William Marshal*, pp 102–5.

In Kilkenny on the day set
they were all there with him
and once they had arrived on that day,
the Marshal said: 'My lords,
here you see the countess whom I have brought
here by the hand into your presence.
She is your lady by birth,
the daughter of the earl who graciously,
in his generosity, enfieffed you all,
once he had conquered the land.
She stays behind here with you as a pregnant woman.
Until such time as God brings me back here,
I ask you all to give her unreservedly
the protection she deserved by birthright,
for she is your lady, as we well know:
I have no claim to anything here save through her'.[19]

With these words the Marshal left to return to his displeased king and Isabel stepped into the spotlight at last. She was undoubtedly a figure of respect to the barons of Leinster, a living link to the strong men who enabled the Anglo-Norman colonisation to proceed – her maternal grandfather, Diarmait Mac Murchada, and her father, Strongbow. Her presence may have been designed to inspire some of the old loyalties to her family felt by the fractious lords of Leinster. The fact of her pregnancy and her need for protection and aid would also have made sufficient impression on the warriors around her. Indeed she must have consented to be left in Ireland even though she was heavily pregnant.[20] Isabel was well aware of the symbolic power of her presence as well as that of her unborn child to warriors who had followed her father and she used this power to bolster her husband's position as lord of Leinster. The presence and the ordering of such armed men would not have fazed her. As the daughter of a noble house, Isabel would have been exposed to militarism from very early on and during her life may have learned about armed defence or, more significantly, how to command and control soldiers; skills that she would display in the defence of her rights in Leinster. She was a woman well used to military life and strategy and this would serve her well in the coming crisis in Leinster.

She stayed there, in her capacity as both heiress and countess, to defend both her and her husband's rights and she proved to be a formidable defender of those rights in the face of concerted military opposition organised by her principal enemy, Meiler fitz Henry. War broke out in Leinster in 1207 after the departure

19 *HWM*, ii, lines 13529–44. **20** It is unlikely that the health considerations of an advanced pregnancy on their own influenced her decision to stay. She had travelled to Normandy with William in 1190, while heavily pregnant: see Crouch, *William Marshal*, p. 107.

of William to England and Isabel soon found herself besieged in an undermanned Kilkenny Castle by fitz Henry who had returned in January 1208 with the backing of King John. Her husband was forced by the king to stay in England while acutely conscious of the danger both his wife and his lands were in.

Rather than hand the castle over to this enemy of her husband she ordered a man to be lowered from the castle battlements to inform her followers of her plight which they promptly responded to and thus saved both her and the castle.[21] This showed a level of resourcefulness appropriate to a woman in her position and illustrated the considerable responsibility she exercised in her husband's absence. She was aided, of course, by loyal and experienced soldiers but it was Isabel who was responsible for the victory and who showed remarkable courage not only by staying in Ireland as a physically vulnerable, pregnant, woman but also by refusing to submit to the martial pressure of her husband's (and her own) enemies. The humiliation for fitz Henry was profound. Not only was he defeated by the courage and cunning of a woman ('he had made his peace, first with the countess, and then with the earl's men')[22] but she also demanded that he submit to her and give his son as a hostage for his future good behaviour. She had also forced the other rebel knights of Leinster to come to terms and surrender their children, or brothers if they had none, as hostages to her.[23] Her decisive actions restored her family's firm grip on Leinster and forced an unhappy king to impart the 'good and welcome news' of her victory and of her own 'good health and spirits' to her husband waiting in England.[24] With fitz Henry defeated in Leinster, John had no choice but to permit the Marshal to return to Ireland where he was warmly welcomed by his countess whose reaction to her husband's return was reported thus:

> The countess came up
> for the encounter was much to her liking[25]

A rather laconic description for what must have been a much-anticipated reunion for the relieved couple after months of intense stress.

Countess Isabel was clearly a woman of courage and resilience but, perhaps, an even more telling key to her character comes a little later in the *Histoire* when her reactions to her husband's conciliatory actions to his rebellious vassals are recounted. At Kilkenny the rebels are described as coming to him and begging for mercy and he, as the ideal, compassionate knight, forgave them and returned the hostages taken on the orders of his wife. The author of the *Histoire* described Isabel's reaction to all this:

21 *HWM*, ii, lines 13820–37. 22 Ibid., lines 13875–6. 23 Ibid., lines 13879–87. 24 Ibid., lines 13912–15. 25 Ibid., lines 14021–2.

> Once the countess was informed of this,
> I can tell you that she was not at all pleased,
> for they had done her many a wrong and hurt,
> and their crimes were many.
> I can assure you that, had he listened to her,
> the earl would have exacted revenge on them.[26]

Yet the *Histoire*'s picture of events, portraying Isabel as out for vengeance in the face of her husband's magnanimity, is not entirely accurate. Punishments were, in fact, severe for the principal rebels. Fitz Henry, having been forced to hand over his castle of Dunamase and his son to the countess, also had to pledge the surrender of his lands after his death to the Marshal. Other rebels were also harshly treated for a time.[27] So Isabel's desire to make her enemies suffer, in this instance, seems to have been at least partly sated. She, after all, was the one who had been attacked and had successfully beaten the rebels – therefore, her desire for vengeance can be understood in those terms. Politically, though, she must have been well aware of the need to temper the punishments lest her tenants be tempted to revolt again.

The failed attack on Kilkenny Castle in the face of Isabel's determination to hold onto it illustrates the type of tough, resourceful woman she must have been. Yet her ability and desire to aid her husband in governing their holdings is also illustrated in other areas of Leinster, particularly in Wexford. She is reputed to have directed the erection of a motte at Old Ross and, along with the Marshal, she is credited with founding New Ross in the early years of the thirteenth century.[28] The years after 1207 that they spent together in Ireland were marked by their activities in building, endowing and regulating castles, churches and boroughs.

Before she died, Isabel had to endure the death of her husband. Her distress at his sufferings and eventual death are vividly portrayed in the *Histoire*:

> It was observed that the countess
> could not walk without danger of coming to grief,
> for her heart and body, her head and limbs
> had suffered from her exertions,
> her weeping and her vigils.[29]

The marriage of Isabel and William Marshal appears to have involved mutual affection. Now, with her husband dead, Isabel was weak with grief and had to face into old age alone. Not only that but she also had a battle before her to claim control over her own lands in Ireland, which was denied to her by the justiciar.

26 Ibid., lines 14095–100. 27 Crouch, *William Marshal*, pp 113–14. 28 For the early development of New Ross, see Ó Drisceoil, this volume. 29 *HWM*, ii, lines 18992–6.

Isabel, however, was not a woman to run from a battle and so she proved again as she fought for control of her lands. In April/May 1219 she petitioned to have seisin of her lands, which was continually being denied her by the justiciar, Geoffrey de Marisco.[30] The justiciar was ordered to give her possession of her lands in Ireland in June 1219 but she did not enjoy them for long because she died sometime in 1220.[31] Multiple childbirths, a peripatetic lifestyle and, perhaps, physical exhaustion due to grief, the barely fifty-year-old Isabel followed her husband into the grave and was buried at Tintern Abbey in Wales.[32] She left behind a surfeit of heirs and surely died in the knowledge that, in part thanks to her efforts, her inheritance was secure.[33] The reality was to prove very different, however.

Amazingly, all five sons of William and Isabel died without legitimate heirs. At the death of the last Marshal brother in 1245, eleven days after his brother Walter, a totally unexpected dilemma was revealed, the partition of the huge Marshal inheritance between their five sisters or their heirs. The five daughters who inherited married into some of the most powerful families in Ireland and England (table 10.2). By the time the partition was completed in 1247 only Matilda Marshal, widow of Roger Bigod, earl of Norfolk, and William, earl of Warenne, was alive. The children of the heiresses who could make claim were Joan de Munchensy, Aylmer de Valence, Richard, earl of Gloucester, Maud, Eva and Eleanor de Braose and the seven daughters of Sibyl de Ferrers.

Table 10.1 The male line of the inheritance of William Marshal.

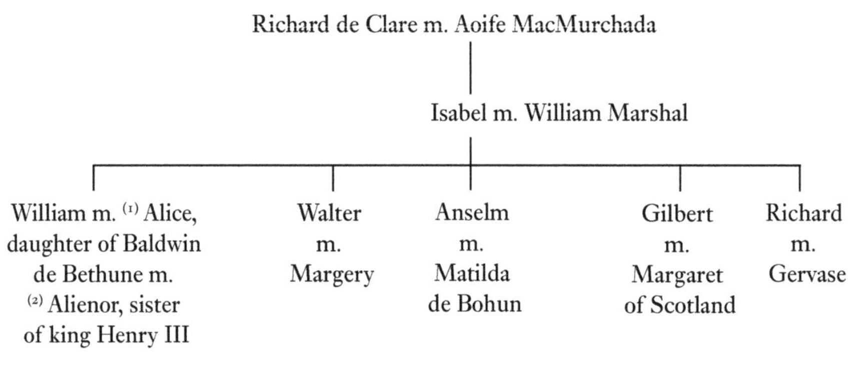

30 *CDI, 1171–1251*, p. 130, no. 877; p. 131, no. 880. 31 *CSMA*, ii, p. 142. 32 *CSMA*, ii, p. 142. 33 Ibid., pp 312–13.

Table 10.2 The female heirs of William Marshal (* indicates heirs in 1247).

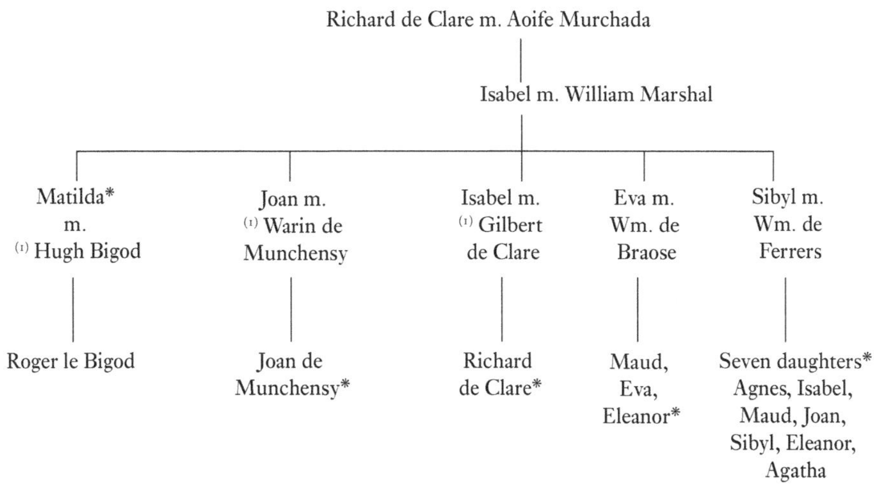

So it was that for a third successive generation, the lands of Leinster descended solely through the female line. With this latest descent, however, the patrimony was broken up and it signalled a new interest in Ireland from the great English families these women had married into. The once-enormous lordship of Leinster was divided up and changed forever from the lordship that Isabel had once fought to defend.

By the time of the division of Leinster in 1247, the families of Richard de Burgh, Walter de Lacy and Hugh de Lacy were without male representatives. Leinster was not the only once-huge lordship debilitated by partition. It was, however, the only one in which three generations of heiresses had enriched their husbands by their links to it. It was also the only one that was once a Gaelic kingdom that had passed out of Gaelic hands due to the inheritance of a woman. That the daughter of that woman was then married to the most famous knight in the medieval West ensured that of all the women whose lives were linked with Leinster, Isabel's is the best documented. That is not saying a lot because for as much as her actions can be examined in Leinster, particularly after 1207, there are great swathes of her life as a young heiress, a married woman and eventually a widow that will always remain hidden. What can be said with certainty though is that, like many women of her class, she was willing and able to experience hardship and danger, in a highly militarised society, in order to defend what was hers. That she earned the respect and admiration of her husband and his battle-hardened knights is without question, as is her courage and tenacity as defender of her family's rights. The activities celebrated by the author of the *Histoire* give us a brief insight into the personality of one of the more extraordinary women of the early days of the Anglo-Norman colonisation of Ireland. Accident, warfare and bad luck meant that her lands were eventually denuded of their power and parcelled up between her many heirs but her death before that event saved her from the grief and disappointment of such a development. Hers was a life well lived by the standards of the time (as far as we can tell). Blessed with a devoted husband, many children and a determined disposition, Isabel Marshal was a woman who was every bit a match for her illustrious husband – a fact that, one suspects, was not lost on William.

Bibliography

PRIMARY SOURCES: UNPUBLISHED

Bradley, John and King, Heather A., 'Urban Archaeology Survey, 5: Old and New Ross' (Office of Public Works, 1990).

C66/312 (patent roll of 5 Ric. II, pt 2, inspeximus dated 12 June 1382), m.2. The National Archives (PRO), London.

Doran, Linda, 'Archaeological investigations in New Ross and Rosbercon, 1994–2006: analysis and classification' (Heritage Council report, 2009).

Earthsound Archaeological Geophysics, 'Kilkenny Castle grounds, Kilkenny: archaeological geophysical survey'. Report for Kilkenny Archaeology (7 November 2010).

Marshal of England's lands in Ireland, Carew MS 611, fo. 14b [n.d.].

McLoughlin, Catherine, 'Archaeological assessment report: 16–18 the Bullawn, New Ross (03E962)' (Stafford McLoughlin Archaeology, 2003).

MS H.1.7: 'The Dublin Annals of Inisfallen' (TCD).

Ó Drisceoil, Cóilín, 'Archaeological test excavations in the Deanery Orchard, St Canice's Cathedral, Kilkenny' (report 06E306 submitted to the National Monuments Service, Dublin, 2006).

Ó Drisceoil, Cóilín, 'The layout, topography and archaeology of medieval New Ross, County Wexford' (2 vols, MA, UCD, 1996).

Unkel, Jill, 'Architectural patronage in Ireland: the early Anglo-Norman lords' (PhD, TCD, 2010).

PRIMARY SOURCES: PUBLISHED

Abbott, T.K. and Gwynn, E.J., *Catalogue of the Irish manuscripts in the library of Trinity College, Dublin* (Dublin, 1921).

Acta Sanctorum Hiberniae, C. De Smedt and J. De Backer (London, 1888).

Annála ríoghachta Éireann: annals of the kingdom of Ireland by the Four Master, from the earliest period to the year 1616, ed. John O'Donovan (7 vols, Dublin, 1851; 3rd repr. with intro. by K.W. Nicholls, Dublin, 1990).

Annála Uladh: Annals of Ulster, otherwise Annála Senait, chronicle of Irish affairs, 431–1131, 1155–1541, ed. William Hennessy and Bartholomew Mac Carthy (4 vols, Dublin, 1887–1907; vol. i ed. Hennessy, vols ii–iv ed. Mac Carthy).

The Annals of Inisfallen: MS Rawlinson B503, ed. Seán Mac Airt (Dublin, 1951).

The Annals of Loch Cé: a chronicle of Irish affairs, 1014–1590, ed. William Hennessy (2 vols, London, 1871; repr. in reflex facsimile, Dublin, 1939).

The Annals of Tigernach, ed. Whitley Stokes. In *Revue Celtique*, 16 (1895), pp 374–419; 17 (1896), pp 6–33, 119–263, 337–420; 18 (1897), pp 9–59, 150–97, 267–303 (repr., Llanerch, 2 vols, 1993).

Archdall, Mervyn, *Monasticon Hibernicum; or, An history of the abbies, priories and other religious houses in Ireland* (Dublin, 1786).

Berry, H.F., 'Ancient charters in the *Liber Albus Ossoriensis*', *PRIA*, 26C (1908), pp 115–25.

— (ed.), *Statute rolls of the parliament of Ireland, 1–12 Edward IV* (Dublin, 1914).

Book of Leinster formerly Lebor na Núachonghála, ed. R.I. Best, Osborn Bergin, M.A. O'Brien and Anne O'Sullivan (6 vols, Dublin, 1954–83).

Byrne, N.J. (ed.), *The Great Parchment Book of Waterford* (Dublin, 2007).

Calendar of Archbishop Alen's register, c.1172–1534, ed. Charles McNeill (Dublin, 1950).

Calendar of documents relating to Ireland, 1171–1251 [etc.], ed. H.S. Sweetman (5 vols, London, 1875–86).

Calendar of inquisitions post mortem and other analogous documents preserved in the Public Record Office [1236–1432] (23 vols, London, 1904–2004), 2nd ser. [1485–1509] (3 vols, London, 1898–1955).

Calendar of the ancient deeds and muniments preserved in the Pemboke Estate Office, Dublin (Dublin, 1891).

Calendar of the Gormanston register, ed. James Mills and M.J. McEnery (Dublin, 1916).

Calendar of the justiciary rolls: or; Proceedings in the court of the justiciar of Ireland [1295–1303] [etc.], ed. James Mills, Herbert Wood and A.E. Langman, rev. M.C. Griffith (3 vols, Dublin, 1905–56).

'Calendar of the *Liber Niger* and *Liber Albus* of Christ Church, Dublin', ed. H.J. Lawlor, *PRIA*, 27C (1907–9), pp 1–93.

Calendar of the patent and close rolls of chancery in Ireland [1514–75] [etc.], ed. James Morrin (3 vols, Dublin, 1861–3).

Calendar of the patent rolls, 1216–25 [etc.] (London, 1901–).

Chartae, privilegia et immunitates: being transcripts of charters and privileges to cities, towns and other bodies corporate [...], 1171–1395 (Dublin, 1829–30; pub. 1889).

'Charters of Earl Richard Marshal of the forests of Ross and Taghmon', ed. Eric St-J. Brooks and G.H. Orpen, *JRSAI*, 64 (1934), pp 54–63.

Chartularies of St Mary's Abbey, Dublin, with the register of its house at Dunbrody and Annals of Ireland, ed. J.T. Gilbert (2 vols, London, 1884–6).

Christ Church deeds, ed. M.J. McEnery and Raymond Refaussé (Dublin, 2001).

Chronicum Scotorum: a chronicle of Irish affairs from the earliest times to AD1135, with a supplement, AD1141–50, ed. William Hennessy (London, 1866; repr., Wiesbaden, 1964).

Civil Survey, AD1654–6, ed. R.C. Simington (10 vols, Dublin, 1931–61).

Colgan, John, *The 'Acta Sanctorum Hiberniae' of John Colgan* (Dublin, 1948).

Crede Mihi: the most ancient register of the archbishops of Dublin before the Reformation, ed. J.T. Gilbert (Dublin, 1897).

Deeds of the Normans in Ireland, La geste des Engleis en Yrlande: a new edition of the chronicle formerly known as the Song of Dermot and the earl, ed. Evelyn Mullally (Dublin, 2002).

Dugdale, William, *Monasticon Anglicanum*, ed. by Roger Dodsworth, John Stevens, John Caley, Henry Ellis, Bulkeley Bandinel and R.C. Taylor (6 vols in 8, London, 1817–30).

'Duiske charters': 'The charters of the abbey of Duiske', ed. C.M. Butler and J.H. Bernard, *PRIA*, 35C (1918–20), pp 1–187.

Extents of Irish monastic possessions, 1540–1, ed. N.B. White (Dublin, 1943).

Fragmentary annals of Ireland, ed. Joan Radner (Dublin, 1978).

Gilbert, J.T. (ed.), *Historic and municipal documents of Ireland, AD1170–1320* (Dublin, 1870).

Gilbert, J.T. (ed.), '*Registrum Monasterii de Portu Sancte Marie, Dunbrothy*' in *CSMA*, ii, pp 97–208.

Giraldus Cambrensis: *Expugnatio Hibernica: the conquest of Ireland by Giraldus Cambrensis*, ed. and trans. A.B. Scott and F.X. Martin (Dublin, 1978).

Harris: '*Collectanea de rebus Hibernicis*', Charles Mc Neill, *Analecta Hibernica*, 6 (November 1934), pp 312–13.

Histoire des ducs de Normandie et des rois d'Angleterre, ed. Francisque Michel (Paris, 1840).

History of William Marshal, ed. A.J. Holden and David Crouch, trans. Stewart Gregory (3 vols, London, 2002–6).

Holinshed's Irish Chronicle, L. Miller and E. Power (eds) (repr. of 1st ed. 1577) (Dublin, 1979).
Irish monastic and episcopal deeds, AD1200–1600, ed. N.B. White (Dublin, 1936).
Keating, Geoffrey, *Foras feasa ar Éirinn: the history of Ireland*, ed. David Comyn and P.S. Dinneen (4 vols, London, 1902–14), iii, pp 304–5.
Knights' fees in Counties Wexford, Carlow and Kilkenny (13th–15th century), ed. Eric St-J. Brooks (Dublin, 1950).
Leabhar mór na ngenealach: The great book of Irish genealogies compiled (1645–66) by Dubhaltach Mac Fhirbhisigh, ed. and trans. Nollaig Ó Muraíle (5 vols, Dublin, 2003).
Leigh: 'A chorographic account of the southern part of the county of Wexford, written anno 1684 by Robert Leigh esq. of Rosegarland in that county', ed. H.F. Hore, *JRSAI*, 5 (1858–9), pp 451–67.
Letter books of Christ Church, Canterbury, ed. J.B. Sheppard (3 vols, London, 1887–9).
Liber primus Kilkenniensis: the earliest of the books of the corporation of Kilkenny now extant, ed. Charles McNeill (Dublin, 1931).
Liber primus Kilkenniensis, trans. A.J. Otway-Ruthven (Kilkenny, 1961).
L'histoire de Guillaume le Maréchal, comte de Striguil et de Pembroke, regent d'Angleterre de 1216 à 1219, ed. Paul Meyer (3 vols, Paris, 1891–1901).
Marsan: *L'ensenhamen ou code du parfait chevalier du troubadour Gascon Arnaut Guilhem de Marsan*, trans. Jacques de Cauna (Mounenh en Biarn, 2007).
Marshal: *The acts and letters of the Marshal family, marshals of England, and earls of Pembroke, 1145–1248*, ed. David Crouch (London, 2015).
Matthew Paris, Monachi Sancti Albani, Chronica Majora, iv, Henry Richards Luard (ed.) (London, 1877).
Miscellaneous Irish Annals, AD1114–1437, ed. Séamus Ó hInnse (Dublin, 1947).
Na buirgéisí, xii–xv aois, ed. Gearóid Mac Niocaill (Dublin, 1964).
'O'Clery book of genealogies', ed. Seamus Pender, *Analecta Hibernica*, 18 (1951), pp 1–198.
Ormond deeds, 1172–1350 [etc.], ed. Edmund Curtis (6 vols, Dublin 1932–43).
Petty, William, *Hiberniae delineatio: atlas of Ireland* (London, 1685, repr. Shannon, 1969).
Pipe rolls: 'The Irish pipe roll of 14 John, 1211–1212', ed. Oliver Davies and D.B. Quinn, supplement to *Ulster Journal of Archaeology*, 3rd ser., 4 (1941).
Red Book of Ormond, ed. N.B. White (Dublin, 1932).
'Register of Kells', ed. N.B. White, in *IMED*, pp 300–13.
Register of the abbey of St Thomas the Martyr, Dublin, ed. J.T. Gilbert (London, 1889).
Register of the hospital of St John the Baptist without the New Gate, Dublin, ed. Eric St-J. Brooks (Dublin, 1936).
'*Registrum monasterii de Portu Sancte Marie, Dunbrothy*', ed. J.T. Gilbert, in *CSMA*, ii, pp 97–208.
Reports from commissioners, corporations Ireland: appendix, parts 1 and 2, vol. 28.
Roger of Howden: *Chronica magistri Rogeri de Houedene*, ed. William Stubbs (4 vols, London, 1868–71).
Rotuli chartarum in turri Londinensi asservati [1199–1216], ed. T.D. Hardy (London, 1837).
Rotuli litterarum patentium in turri Londonensi asservati [1201–1316], ed. T.D. Hardy (London, 1835).
Rymer, Thomas, *Foedera, conventions, litterae et acta publica*, ed. Adam Clarke, John Caley and Frederick Holbrooke (4 vols in 7; London, 1816–69).
'Short annals of Leinster', ed. Pól Breatnach, *Irish Book Lover*, 24 (1936), pp 58–60.
Song of Dermot and the earl, ed. G.H. Orpen (Oxford, 1892).
The topographical poems of John O'Dubhagain and Gilla na Naomh O'Huidhrin, ed. John O'Donovan (Dublin, 1862).
'"The walling of New Ross": a thirteenth-century poem in French', ed. Hugh Shields, *Long Room*, 12–13 (1975–6), pp 24–33.

Topographical poems by Seán Mór Ó Dubhagáin and Giolla-na-naomh Ó hUidhrín, ed. James Carney (Dublin, 1943).

Ware, James, *De Hibernia et antiquitatibus eius, disquisitions* (London, 1654).

Ware: *A commentary of the prelates of Ireland, of the bishops of Dublin*, part 3 of *The antiquities and history of Ireland by the right honourable Sir James Ware, knight* [ed. Robert Ware] (Dublin, 1705).

Ware: *The works of Sir James Ware concerning Ireland*, ed. Walter Harris (2 vols, Dublin, 1739).

[Ware, James], *The annals of the affairs of Ireland from the first conquest by the English in the reign of King Henry II unto the end of the reign of Queen Elizabeth*, part 4 of *The antiquities and history of Ireland by the right honourable Sir James Ware, knight* [ed. Robert Ware] (Dublin, 1705).

SECONDARY SOURCES: PUBLISHED

Aalen, Fred, Whelan, Kevin and Stout, Matthew, *Atlas of the Irish rural landscape* (Cork, 1997).

Allen Brown, R. and Curnow, P.E., *Tower of London* (London, 1984).

Anonymous, *The Dublin Penny Journal*, 1:38 (16 March 1833).

Asbridge, Thomas, *The greatest knight* (London, 2015).

Aurell, Martin, *Le chevalier lettré: savoir et conduite de l'aristocratie aux xiie et xiiie siècles* (Paris, 2006).

Avent, Richard, *Dolwyddelan Castle, Dolbadarn Castle, Castle y Bere* (Cardiff, 2010).

— *Laugharne Castle* (Cardiff, 1995).

— 'The twelfth-century gatehouse at Chepstow, Monmouthshire, Wales', *Château Gaillard*, 20 (2002), pp 27–40.

— 'William Marshal's building works at Chepstow Castle, Monmouthshire, 1189–1219' in Kenyon and O'Conor (eds), *The medieval castle in Ireland and Wales*, pp 50–71.

— 'William Marshal's castle at Chepstow and its place in military architecture' in Turner and Johnson (eds), *Chepstow Castle*, pp 81–90.

— and Miles, Daniel, 'The main gatehouse' in Turner and Johnson, *Chepstow Castle*, pp 51–62.

Ballard, Adolphus, *British borough charters, 1042–1216* (Cambridge, 1913).

— 'The English boroughs in the reign of John', *English Historical Review*, 14 (1899), pp 93–104.

— and Tait, James (eds), *British borough charters, 1216–1307* (Cambridge, 1923).

Barry, Siuban, 'The architecture of the cathedral' in Adrian Empey (ed.), *A worthy foundation: the cathedral church of St Canice, Kilkenny, 1285–1985* (Mountrath, 1985), pp 25–48.

Barry, T.B., 'The chronology and development of medieval rural settlement in Munster', *Journal of the Cork Historical and Archaeological Society*, 105 (2000), pp 191–8.

— *The archaeology of medieval Ireland* (London, 1987).

— *The medieval moated sites of S.E. Ireland: Counties Carlow, Kilkenny, Tipperary and Wexford* (BAR, Brit. Ser. 35, Oxford, 1977).

— Culleton, Edward and Empey, C.A., 'Kells motte, Co. Kilkenny', *PRIA*, 84C (1984), pp 157–70.

Bateson, Mary, *Borough customs* (2 vols, London, 1904–6).

Beresford, David, 'Fitz Anthony, Thomas (d. *c.*1227)', *DIB*, iii, p. 813.

Beresford, Maurice, *New towns of the Middle Ages: town plantation in England, Wales and Gascony* (London, 1987).

Bernard, J.H., 'The foundation of Tintern Abbey, Co. Wexford', *PRIA*, 33C (1916–17), pp 527–9.

Bond, C.J., 'Water management in the rural economy' in Roberta Gilchrist and Harold Mytum (eds), *The archaeology of rural monasteries* (BAR, Brit. Ser. 227, Oxford, 1989), pp 83–111.

Bracken, Damien and Ó Riain-Raedel, Dagmar (eds), *Ireland and Europe in the twelfth century* (Dublin, 2006).

Bradbury, Jim, *Philip Augustus, king of France, 1180–1223* (London and New York, 1998).

Bradley, John, 'Anglo-Norman Kilkenny' in John Bradley and Michael O'Dwyer (eds), *Kilkenny through the centuries: chapters in the history of an Irish city* (Kilkenny, 2009), pp 24–45.

— 'Canice and Kilkenny' in John Bradley and Michael O'Dwyer (eds), *Kilkenny through the centuries: chapters in the history of an Irish city* (Kilkenny, 2009), pp 1–23.

— *Discover Kilkenny* (Dublin, 2000).

— *Kilkenny* (Irish Historic Towns Atlas 10, Dublin, 2000).

— 'Planned Anglo-Norman towns in Ireland' in H.B. Clarke and Anngret Simms (eds), *The comparative history of urban origins in non-Roman Europe: Ireland, Wales, Denmark, Germany, Poland and Russia* (BAR, Int. Ser. 255; Oxford, 1985), pp 411–67.

— 'Pulp facts and core fictions: translating a cathedral from Aghaboe to Kilkenny' in Emer Purcell, Paul MacCotter, Julianne Nyhan and John Sheehan (eds), *Clerics, kings and Vikings: essays on medieval Ireland in honour of Donnchadh Ó Corráin* (Dublin, 2015), pp 169–84.

— 'Recent archaeological research on the Irish town' in Helmut Jäger (ed.), *Stadtkernforschung* (Cologne, 1987), pp 321–70.

— (ed.), *Settlement and society in medieval Ireland: studies presented to F.X. Martin OSA* (Kilkenny, 1988).

— 'The creation of the Parade: Ormond's deal with Kilkenny Corporation, 1677', *OKR*, 58 (2006), pp 77–116.

— 'The early development of the medieval town of Kilkenny' in Nolan and Whelan (eds), *Kilkenny: history and society*, pp 63–73.

— 'The medieval tombs of St Canice's' in Adrian Empey (ed.), *A worthy foundation: the cathedral church of St Canice, Kilkenny, 1285–1985* (Mountrath, 1985), pp 49–103.

— 'The precinct of St John's Priory, Kilkenny, at the close of the Middle Ages', *Peritia*, 22–3 (2011–12), pp 317–45.

— 'The priors of St John's Kilkenny (OSA) before the Reformation', *OKR*, 57 (2005), pp 62–72.

— 'The town wall of Kilkenny', *OKR*, new ser., 1:2 (1975), pp 209–18.

— 'The town wall of Kilkenny revisited: a review article', *OKR*, 58 (2006), pp 185–95.

— *Walled towns in Ireland* (Dublin, 1995).

— Fletcher, A.J. and Simms, Anngret (eds), *Dublin in the medieval world: studies in honour of Howard B. Clarke* (Dublin, 2009).

— and Halpin, Andrew, 'The topographical development of Scandinavian and Anglo-Norman Waterford' in William Nolan and T.P. Power (eds), *Waterford: history and society* (Dublin, 1992), pp 105–29.

— and Murtagh, Ben, 'Brady's Castle, Thomastown, Co. Kilkenny: a 14th-century fortified town house' in Kenyon and O'Conor (eds), *The medieval castle in Ireland and Wales*, pp 194–216.

— and O'Dwyer, Michael (eds), *Kilkenny through the centuries: chapters in the history of an Irish city* (Kilkenny, 2009).

Brewer, J.N., *The beauties of Ireland, being original delineations, topographical, historical and biographical of each county* (2 vols, London, 1826).

Brewer, R.J., *Caerwent Roman town* (Cardiff, 3rd ed., 2006).

Briais, Bernard, *Loches through history* (Monts, 2012).

Brindle, Steven, 'The keep at Conisbrough Castle, Yorkshire', *Château Gaillard*, 25 (2012), pp 61–74.

Brooks, Eric St-J., *Knights' fees in Counties Wexford, Carlow and Kilkenny (13th–15th century)* (Dublin, 1950).

Brown, A.L., *The governance of late medieval England, 1272–1461* (Stanford, 1989).

Brown, R.A., *Castles from the air* (Cambridge, repr. 1992).

Browne, Bernard, *Old Ross: the town that never was* (Old Ross, 1993).

Buckley, M.J.C., 'The Bambino of New Ross', *JRSAI*, 28 (1898), pp 250–3.

Butler, T.C., *Near restful waters: the Augustinians in New Ross and Clonmines* (Dublin, 1975).

Byrne, F.J., *Irish kings and high-kings* (London, 1973; repr. Dublin, 2001).

Byrne, Martin, 'The Quay, New Ross', *Excavations 2000* (Bray, 2001), 1065.

— 'The Quay, New Ross', *Excavations 2001* (Bray, 2002), 1312.

Byrne, M.E., 'The results of a resistivity survey undertaken at Clonmines, County Wexford', *Journal of the Wexford Historical Society*, 15 (1994–5), pp 67–73.

Campbell, D.B. and Delf, Brian, *Roman legionary fortresses, 27BC–AD378* (Oxford, 2006).

Campbell, Kieran, 'The floor tiles' in Clyne, *Kells Priory*, pp 234–61.

Caple, Chris, 'Nevern Castle: searching for the first masonry castle in Wales', *Medieval Archaeology*, 55 (2011), pp 326–34.

— 'News – Wales – Nevern Castle – Pembrokeshire', *CSGJ*, 23 (2009–10), pp 140–4.

Carrigan, William, *The history and antiquities of the diocese of Ossory* (4 vols, Dublin, 1905; repr. 1981).

Carroll, W.G., *A memoir of the Right Rev. James Thomas O'Brien DD* (London, 1875).

Cathcart King, D.J. and Cheshire, Mark, *Pembroke Castle and the town walls of Pembroke* (1987, repr. from *Archaeologia Cambrensis*).

Childs, Wendy and O'Neill, Timothy, 'Overseas trade' in Art Cosgrove (ed.), *NHI*, ii: *Medieval Ireland, 1169–1534* (Oxford, 1993), pp 492–524.

Church, Stephen, *King John and the road to Magna Carta* (London, 2015).

— 'The 1210 campaign in Ireland: evidence for a military revolution?' in Christopher Harper-Bill (ed.), *Anglo-Norman Studies: Proceedings of the Battle Conference, 1997* (Woodbridge, 1998), pp 45–58.

Clanchy, M.T., *England and its rulers, 1066–1307* (London, 2006; 3rd ed.).

Clyne, Miriam, *Kells Priory, Co. Kilkenny: archaeological excavations by T. Fanning and M. Clyne* (Dublin, 2007).

Coey, Alastair, *New Ross town walls conservation plan* (Kilkenny, 2008).

Coldstream, Nicola, *Medieval craftsmen: masons and sculptors* (London, 1991).

Colfer, Billy, *Arrogant trespass: Anglo-Norman Wexford, 1169–1400* (Enniscorthy, 2002).

— 'New Ross: a chartered town' in Tom Dunne (ed.), *New Ross. Rosponte. Ros Mhic Treoin: an anthology celebrating 800 years* (Wexford, 2007), pp 55–9.

— 'The Hook, County Wexford' in Aalen et al., *Atlas of the Irish rural landscape*, pp 262–76.

— *The Hook Peninsula* (Cork, 2004).

— *Wexford: a town and its landscape* (Cork, 2008).

— and Culleton, Edward, 'The Norman motte at Old Ross: method of construction', *Journal of the Old Wexford Society*, 10 (1974), pp 69–78.

Conzen, M.R.G., *Alnwick, Northumberland: a study in town plan analysis* (London, 1960).

Creighton, Oliver and Higham, Robert, *Medieval town walls: an archaeology and social history of urban defence* (Stroud, 2005).

Crofton Croker, T. (ed.), *Popular songs of Ireland* (London, 1886), pp 275–87.

Crosland, Jessie, *William the Marshal: the last great feudal baron* (London, 1962).

Crouch, David, 'Chepstow under the Marshals' in Turner and Johnson, *Chepstow Castle*, pp 43–50.
— 'Earley, John (II) of (*c*.1173–1229)' in *ODNB*, 17, pp 574–5.
— 'Marshal, Sir John (d. 1235)' in *ODNB*, 36, pp 812–13.
— 'Strategies of lordship in Angevin England and the career of William Marshal' in Christopher Harper-Bill and Ruth Harvey (eds), *The ideals and practice of medieval knighthood, 2: papers from the third Strawberry Hill conference, 1986* (Woodbridge, 1988), pp 1–25.
— 'The complaint of King John against William de Briouze (*c*.September 1210)' in Janet Loengard (ed.), *The England of King John and Magna Carta* (Woodbridge, 2010), pp 168–79.
— *The English aristocracy, 1070–1272: a social transformation* (New Haven, 2010).
— *William Marshal: knighthood, war and chivalry, 1147–1219* (2nd ed., Harlow, 2002; 3rd ed., 2016).
— 'Writing a biography in the thirteenth century: the construction and composition of the "History of William Marshal"' in David Bates, Julia Crick and Sarah Hamilton (eds), *Writing medieval biography, 750–1250: essays in honour of Professor Frank Barlow* (Woodbridge, 2006), pp 221–35.
Cullen, J.B., 'The Canons Regular in Ireland: St Mary's Church, New Ross', *Irish Ecclesiastical Record*, 16 (1920).
Culleton, Edward, *Celtic and Early Christian Wexford* (Dublin, 1999).
Davies, R.R., *Conquest, coexistence and change: Wales, 1063–1415* (Oxford, 1987).
Davis, P.R., *Castles of the Welsh princes* (Ceredigon, 2011).
De Breffny, Brian and Mott, George, *The churches and abbeys of Ireland* (London, 1976).
De Wolf Hemmeon, Morley, *Burgage tenure in medieval England* (Cambridge, 1914).
Dictionary of Irish biography, ed. James McGuire and James Quinn (9 vols, Cambridge, 2009).
Dillon, Myles, 'The relationship of mother and son, of father and daughter, and the law of inheritance with regard to women' in Rudolph Thurneysen et al. (eds), *Studies in early Irish law* (Dublin, 1936), pp 129–79.
Doherty, Charles, 'Exchange and trade in early medieval Ireland', *JRSAI*, 110 (1980), pp 67–89.
— 'The monastic town in early medieval Ireland' in H.B. Clarke and Anngret Simms (eds), *The comparative history of urban origins in non-Roman Europe: Ireland, Wales, Denmark, Germany, Poland and Russia* (BAR, Int. Ser. 255; Oxford, 1985), pp 45–75.
Doran, Linda, 'Medieval settlement hierarchy in Carlow and the "Carlow Corridor", 1200–1500' in McGrath and Nolan (eds), *Carlow: history and society*, pp 173–212.
— *New Ross,* c.*1200 to* c.*1900: seven hundred years in the making* (Dublin, 2008).
— 'New Ross in maps: an enduring image, 1590–1900' in Tom Dunne (ed.), *New Ross. Rosponte. Ros Mhic Treoin: an anthology celebrating 800 years* (Wexford, 2007), pp 107–19.
Downham, Clare, 'The career of Cearbhall of Osraighe', *OLL*, 1 (2004), pp 1–18.
Doyle, Ian, 'Excavation of a riverside circular tower in College Park, Kilkenny city', *OKR*, 57 (2005), pp 32–42.
Duby, Georges, *Guillaume le Maréchal, ou le meilleur chevalier du monde* (Paris, 1984).
— *William Marshal: flower of chivalry*, trans. Richard Howard (London, 1986).
Duffy, Seán, 'John and Ireland' in S.D. Church (ed.), *King John: new interpretations* (Woodbridge, 1999), pp 238–42.
— 'King John's expedition in Ireland, 1210: the evidence reconsidered', *IHS*, 30:117 (May 1996), pp 1–24.
Dugdale, William, *Monasticon Anglicanum* (3 vols, London, 1818–30).
Dunboyne, Lord, *Butler family history* (7th ed., Kilkenny, 1991).

Dunne, Tom, *New Ross. Rosponte. Ros Mhic Treoin: an anthology celebrating 800 years* (Wexford, 2007).
Ellmers, D., *Fruhmittelalterliche Handelsschiffahrt in Mittel und Nordeuropa* (Neumunster, 1972).
Empey, C.A., 'A case study of the primary phase of Anglo-Norman settlement: the lordship of Kells', *OKR*, new ser., 3:1 (1984), pp 32–40.
— 'Callan in the Middle Ages' in Joseph Kennedy (ed.), *Callan 800: 1207–2007, history and heritage* (Callan, 2007), pp 17–37.
— 'Conquest and settlement: patterns of Anglo-Norman settlement in north Munster and south Leinster', *Irish Economic and Social History*, 13 (1986), pp 5–31.
— 'County Kilkenny in the Anglo-Norman period' in Nolan and Whelan (eds), *Kilkenny: history and society*, pp 75–95, 646–9.
— 'County Waterford: 1200–1300' in William Nolan and T.P. Power (eds), *Waterford: history and society, interdisciplinary essays on the history of an Irish county* (Dublin, 1992), pp 131–46.
— 'Inistioge in the Middle Ages' in John Kirwan (ed.), *Kilkenny: studies in honour of Margaret M. Phelan* (Kilkenny, 1997), pp 9–15.
— 'Medieval Knocktopher: a study in manorial settlement', *OKR*, new ser., 2:4 (1982), pp 329–42; 2:5 (1983), pp 441–52.
— 'Medieval Thurles: origin and development' in William Corbett and William Nolan (eds), *Thurles: the cathedral town: essays in honour of Archbishop Thomas Morris* (Dublin, 1989), pp 31–9.
— 'The Anglo-Norman community in Tipperary and Kilkenny in the Middle Ages: change and continuity' in Gearóid Mac Niocaill and P.F. Wallace (eds), *Keimelia: studies in medieval archaeology and history in memory of Tom Delaney* (Galway, 1988), pp 449–67.
— 'The Anglo-Norman settlement in the cantred of Eliogarty' in Bradley (ed.), *Settlement and society in medieval Ireland*, pp 207–39.
— 'The Augustinian priory at Kells: an historical introduction' in Clyne, *Kells Priory*, pp 1–11.
— 'The cantreds of the medieval county of Kilkenny', *JRSAI*, 101 (1971), pp 128–34.
— 'The layperson in the parish: the medieval inheritance, 1169–1536' in Raymond Gillespie and W.G. Neely (eds), *The laity and the Church of Ireland, 1000–2000: all sorts and conditions* (Dublin, 2002), pp 7–48.
— 'The liberty and counties of Carlow in the high Middle Ages' in McGrath and Nolan (eds), *Carlow: history and society*, pp 153–71.
— 'The Norman period: 1185–1500' in Nolan and McGrath (eds), *Tipperary: history and society*, pp 71–91.
— 'The origins of the medieval parish revisited' in H.B. Clarke and J.R.S. Phillips (eds), *Ireland, England and the Continent in the Middle Ages and beyond: essays in memory of a turbulent friar, F.X. Martin OSA* (Dublin, 2006), pp 29–50.
— 'The sacred and the secular: the Augustinian priory of Kells in Ossory, 1193–1541', *IHS*, 24 (1984–5), pp 131–51.
— 'The settlement of the kingdom of Limerick' in J.F. Lydon (ed.), *England and Ireland in the Later Middle Ages: essays in honour of Jocelyn Otway-Ruthven* (Blackrock, 1981), pp 1–25.
Eskeröd, A., 'Early Nordic arctic boats', *Arctica* (1956), pp 59–61.
Feehan, John, *Farming in Ireland: history, heritage and environment* (Dublin, 2003).
Fenlon, Jane, *Kilkenny Castle: a visitor's guide* (Dublin, 2007).
Ffrench, J.F.M., 'New Ross: St Mary's graveyard', *JRSAI*, 26 (1896), pp 193–6.
— *APMDI*, 6 (1904–6), p. 411.
Fitzmaurice, E.B. and Little, A.G. (eds), *Materials for the history of the Franciscan province of Ireland, AD1230–1450* (Manchester, 1920).

Flanagan, M.T., 'An early Anglo-Norman charter of Hervey de Montmorency' in Marion Meek (ed.), *The modern traveller to our past: Festschrift in honour of Ann Hamlin* (Dublin, 2006), pp 232–42.

— 'Fitzgerald, Raymond fitz William' in *ODNB*, 19, pp 843–4.

— 'Henry II and the kingdom of Uí Fáeláin' in Bradley (ed.), *Settlement and society in medieval Ireland*, pp 229–38.

— 'Irish church reform in the twelfth century and Áed Ua Cáellaide, bishop of Louth: an Italian document' in Michael Richter and J.M. Picard (eds), *Ogma: essays in Celtic studies in honour of Próinséas Ní Chatháin* (Dublin, 2002).

— (ed.), *Irish royal charters: texts and contexts* (Oxford, 2006), p. 73.

— *Irish society, Anglo-Norman settlers, Angevin kingship: interactions in Ireland in the late twelfth century* (Oxford, 1989).

— 'Strategies of lordship in pre-Norman and post-Norman Leinster', *Anglo-Norman Studies*, 20 (1998), pp 107–26.

— *The transformation of the Irish church in the twelfth century* (Woodbridge, 2010).

Fleming, J.S., *The town wall fortifications of Ireland* (Dublin, 1914).

Fleming, Peter, *Family and household in medieval England* (Basingstoke, 2001).

Fleury, M. and Kruta, V., *The castle of the Louvre* (Dijon, 2000).

Florençon, Patrick, *The city of Aigues-Mortes* (Paris, 2001).

Flynn, T.S., *The Dominicans of Rosbercon (1267–*c.*1800)* (Kilkenny, 1981).

Friel, Paddy, *Kilkenny Castle* (Dublin, 1989).

Gardiner, M.J. and Ryan, Pierce, *Soils of County Wexford* (Dublin, 1964).

Garstin, J.R., *APMDI*, 4 (1899–1900), pp 332–7, 501.

— *APMDI*, 5 (1901–3), pp 125–6.

Gilbert, J.T. (ed.), *A contemporary history of affairs in Ireland, from 1641 to 1652. Now for the first time published, with an appendix of original letters and documents* (Dublin, 1879–80).

Gillingham, John, *Richard I* (New Haven and London, 1999).

— *The Angevin empire* (2nd ed., New York, 2001).

Gladstone, E.W., *Hawarden Old Castle* (privately published, 2003).

Glasscock, R.E., 'Moated sites and deserted boroughs and villages: two neglected aspects of Anglo-Norman settlement in Ireland' in Nicholas Stephens and R.E. Glasscock (eds), *Irish geographical studies in honour of E. Estyn Evans* (Belfast, 1970), pp 162–77.

— 'Some parallels to New Ross', *Journal of the Old Wexford Society*, 7 (1978–9), pp 31–4.

Gleeson, D.F. and Leask, H.G., 'The castle and manor of Nenagh', *JRSAI*, 66 (1966), pp 247–69.

Goodall, John, *The English castle* (New Haven and London, 2011).

Gosling, Paul, 'From Dún Delca to Dundalk', *County Louth Archaeological and Historical Journal*, 22 (1991), pp 225–353.

Graham, B.J., 'The towns of medieval Ireland' in R.A. Butlin (ed.), *The development of the Irish town* (London, 1977), pp 28–60.

— 'Urbanisation in the high Middle Ages' in T.B. Barry (ed.), *A history of settlement in Ireland* (London and New York, 2000), pp 124–39.

Grattan Flood, W.H., *History of the diocese of Ferns* (Waterford, 1915).

Graves, James and Prim, J.G.A., *The history, architecture and antiquities of the cathedral church of St Canice, Kilkenny* (Dublin, 1857).

— 'The history, architecture and antiquities of the city of Kilkenny', *JRSAI*, 5 (1858–9), pp 322–31.

Gravett, Christopher and Hook, Adam, *Norman stone castles, 2: Europe, 950–1204* (Oxford, 2004).

Greene, J.P., *Medieval monasteries* (Leicester, 1992).

Gregory, Niall, 'Quayside, New Ross', *Excavations 2005* (Bray, 2006), 1658.

Grose, Francis, *Antiquities of Ireland* (2 vols, London, 1791–5).

Guy, Neil et al., 'Castle Studies Group Conference, Abergavenny, April 2008', *CSGJ*, 22 (2008–9), pp 4–127.

— 'Castles of north Munster', *CSGJ*, 23 (2009–10), pp 4–116.

Gwynn, Aubrey, 'The Black Death in Ireland', *Studies*, 24 (1935), pp 25–42.

— *The Irish church in the eleventh and twelfth centuries*, ed. Gerard O'Brien (Dublin, 1992).

— and Hadcock, R.N., *Medieval religious houses: Ireland* (Dublin, 1970).

Hall, Hamilton, 'The Marshal pedigree', *JRSAI*, 43 (1913), pp 1–29.

Harbison, Peter, 'Barralet and Beranger's antiquarian sketching tour through Wicklow and Wexford', *PRIA*, 104C (2004), pp 184–5.

— *Cooper's Ireland: drawings and notes from an eighteenth-century gentleman* (Dublin, 2000), pp 144–5.

— *Guide to National and Historic Monuments of Ireland* (Dublin, 1992).

— 'Some medieval sculpture in Kerry', *Journal of the Kerry Archaeological and Historical Society*, 6 (1973), pp 9–25.

Harris, Walter (ed.), Item IV – 'The story of King Richard the Second: his last being in Ireland' in *Hibernica; or, Some ancient pieces relating to Ireland* – part 1 of 2.

Hayward, Paul, 'The earls of Leicester, Sygerius Lucanus and the death of Seneca: some neglected evidence for the cultural agency of Norman aristocracy', *Speculum*, 91 (2016), pp 328–55.

Heist, W.W., 'Over the writer's shoulder: St Abban', *Celtica*, 11 (1976), pp 76–84.

Hennessy, Mark, 'Manorial organisation in early thirteenth-century Tipperary', *Irish Geography*, 29:2 (1996), pp 116–25.

— 'Parochial organisation in medieval Tipperary' in Nolan and McGrath (eds), *Tipperary: history and society*, pp 60–70.

Hewson, G.J., 'Proceedings', *JRSAI*, 12 (1872–3), p. 199.

Hill, Peter, *Whithorn and St Ninian: the excavation of a monastic town, 1984–91* (Stroud, 1997).

Hilling, J.B., *Cilgerran Castle, St Dogmaels Abbey etc.* (Cardiff, rev. 2000).

Hodkinson, B.J., 'Excavations in the gatehouse of Nenagh Castle, 1996 and 1997', *Tipperary Historical Journal* (1999), pp 162–82.

Hore, P.H., *History of the town and county of Wexford: Duncannon Fort, Kilclogan or Templetown, Fethard* (London, 1904).

— *History of the town and county of Wexford: Old and New Ross* (London, 1900).

— *History of the town and county of Wexford: Tintern Abbey, Rosegarland and Clonmines* (London, 1901).

— 'The barony of Forth', *The Past*, 1 (1920), pp 62–106; 2 (1921), pp 38–99.

Hulme, Richard, 'The impact of Château Gaillard and crusading on English castle architecture', *CSGJ*, 27 (2013–14), pp 203–33.

Hunt, John, *Irish medieval figure sculpture* (2 vols, Dublin, 1974).

Hurley, Maurice, 'The bone artefacts' in Clyne, *Kells Priory*, pp 415–23.

— 'The Quay, New Ross', *Excavations 2001* (Bray, 2002), 1313.

— and Scully, Orla M.B. (eds), *Late Viking Age and medieval Waterford: excavations 1986–1992* (Waterford, 1997).

— with McCutcheon, Sarah and McCarthy, Margaret, Section 17: i: 'Artefacts of skeletal material' in M.F. Hurley and O.M.B. Scully (eds), *Late Viking Age and medieval Waterford: excavations 1986–1992* (Waterford, 1997), pp 650–99.

Impey, Edward and Parnell, Geoffrey, *The Tower of London: the official illustrated history* (London, 2006).

Innes-Smith, Robert, *Pembroke Castle: birthplace of the Tudor dynasty* (Derby, 1996).

Jaeger, C.S., *The origins of courtliness: civilising trends and the formation of courtly ideals, 939–1210* (Philadelphia, 1985).

Jankulak, Karen, *The medieval cult of St Petroc* (Woodbridge, 2000).
Jarman, T.J., *William Marshal, first earl of Pembroke and regent of England* (Oxford, 1930).
Johns, C.N., *Caerphilly Castle, Mid Glamorgan* (Cardiff, 1978).
Johnson, D.N., *The Irish castle* (Dublin, 1985).
Jolliffe, J.E.A., *The constitutional history of medieval England from the English settlement to 1485* (4th ed., London, 1961).
Jones, M.J., Stocker, David and Vince, Alan, *The city by the pool: assessing the archaeology of the city of Lincoln* (Lincoln, 2003).
Keene, D.J., 'Suburban growth' in M.W. Barley (ed.), *The plans and topography of medieval towns in England and Wales* (London, 1976), pp 71–82.
Kenealy, Mary, 'Plan of Kilkenny Castle, 1767', *OKR*, new ser., 2:4 (1982), pp 343–6.
Kenny, Colum, 'New Leighlin: an Anglo-Norman settlement' in McGrath and Nolan (eds), *Carlow: history and society*, pp 213–34.
Kenney, J.F., *Sources for the early history of Ireland, 1: ecclesiastical* (New York, 1929).
Kenny, Michael, 'The coins, tokens and jetons' in Clyne, *Kells Priory*, pp 406–14.
Kenyon, J.R., *The medieval castles of Wales* (Cardiff, 2010).
— and O'Conor, Kieran (eds), *The medieval castle in Ireland and Wales: essays in honour of Jeremy Knight* (Dublin, 2003).
Kerrigan, P.M., *Castles and fortifications, 1485–1945* (Cork, 1995).
Kieran, Eoghan, 'Archaeology sinks to new depths in the River Barrow', *Archaeology Ireland*, 13:4 (winter 1999), p. 21.
Knight, J.K., *The three castles: Grosmont Castle, Skenfrith Castle, White Castle. Hen Gwart moated site* (Cardiff, 1991).
— 'Welsh space and Norman invader: Usk Castle, 1136–1245' in J.K. Knight and Andy Johnson (eds), *Usk Castle, priory and town* (Logaston, 2008), pp 55–78.
Lahert, Richard, *The history and antiquities of the parish of Dunnamaggan, including a full history of the great monastic foundation of Kells in the diocese of Ossory* (Tralee, 1956).
Leask, H.G., 'A cenotaph of Strongbow's daughter at New Ross, County Wexford', *JRSAI*, 78 (1948), pp 65–7.
— *Irish castles and castellated houses* (2nd ed., Dundalk, 1951).
— 'Irish castles, 1180 to 1310', *Archaeological Journal*, 93 (1937), pp 143–99.
— *Irish churches and monastic buildings* (3 vols, Dundalk, 1955–60).
Lewis, Samuel, *A topographical dictionary of Ireland* (2 vols, London, 1837).
Litoux, Emmanuel, 'La construction de la forteresse du XIIIe siècle: un château Philippien' in Société Française d'Archéologie, *Le château et la citadelle de Saumur: architectures du pouvoir.* Supplement au *Bulletin monumental*, 3 (2010), pp 39–48.
Loftus, Simon, *The invention of memory: an Irish family scrapbook, 1560–1934* (London, 2014).
Loyn, H.R., *The Norman conquest* (London, 1967).
Ludlow, Neil, 'Pembroke Castle: discoveries in the Outer Ward', *Castle Studies Group Bulletin*, 18 (Sept. 2014), pp 2–6.
Lydon, J.F., 'Richard II's expeditions to Ireland', *JRSAI*, 93 (1963), pp 135–49.
— 'The Bruce invasion of Ireland' in *Historical Studies*, 4, ed. G.A. Hayes-McCoy (London, 1963), pp 111–25.
— 'The expansion and consolidation of the colony, 1215–54', *NHI*, ii, pp 156–78.
Lynch, Ann and Manning, Conleth, 'Excavations at Dublin Castle, 1985–7' in Seán Duffy (ed.), *Medieval Dublin II* (Dublin, 2001), pp 169–204.
Lyons, M.C., 'An account for the manor of Old Ross, September 1284–September 1285, part I', *Decies*, 18 (1981), pp 33–40.
— 'An account for the manor of Old Ross, September 1284–September 1285, part 2', *Decies*, 19 (1982), pp 18–31.
MacCotter, Paul, *Medieval Ireland: territorial, political and economic divisions* (Dublin, 2008).

MacErlean, John, 'Synod of Ráith Bresail: boundaries of the dioceses of Ireland', *Archivium Hibernicum*, 3 (1914), pp 1–33.
Mackay, Ronan and Beresford, David, 'Marshal, William (I)', *DIB*, vi, pp 372–6.
Madden, Frederick (ed.), 'Poem on the erection of the walls of New Ross in Ireland', *Archaeologia*, 22 (1829), pp 307–22.
Maher, Denise, *Medieval grave slabs of County Tipperary, 1200–1600AD* (BAR, Brit. Ser. 262, Oxford, 1997).
Manning, Conleth, 'Clogh Oughter Castle, Co. Cavan, and thirteenth-century circular towers in Ireland', *Château Gaillard*, 25 (2012), pp 223–32.
— 'Dublin Castle: the building of a royal castle in Ireland', *Château Gaillard*, *18* (1996), pp 119–22.
— 'The 1653 survey of the lands granted to the countess of Ormond in Co. Kilkenny', *JRSAI*, 129 (1999), pp 40–66.
— 'The Record Tower, Dublin Castle' in Kenyon and O'Conor (eds), *The medieval castle in Ireland and Wales*, pp 72–95.
Marmion, A., *The ancient and modern history of the maritime ports of Ireland* (London, 1860).
Marshall, Pamela, 'Making an appearance: some thoughts on the phenomenon of multiple doorways and large upper openings in Romanesque donjons in western France and Britain', *Château Gaillard*, 25 (2012), pp 233–42.
Marshal, Sinéad and McMorran, Tori, 'People and places: a bird's eye view of medieval Old Ross' in Ian Doyle and Bernard Browne (eds), *Medieval Wexford: essays in memory of Billy Colfer* (Dublin, 2016), pp 241–61.
Martin, F.X., 'Diarmait Mac Murchada and the coming of the Anglo-Normans', *NHI*, ii, pp 43–66.
— 'John, lord of Ireland, 1185–1216', *NHI*, ii, p. 151.
Martin, G.H., 'The English borough in the thirteenth century', *Transactions of the Royal Historical Society*, 13 (1963), pp 123–44.
Martin, H., 'Ancient bridge at New Ross: monuments of New Ross', *JRSAI*, 5 (1858–9), pp 204–7.
McCormick, Finbar, 'The faunal remains' in Clyne, *Kells Priory*, pp 477–82.
McCutcheon, Clare, 'The medieval pottery' in Clyne, *Kells Priory*, pp 316–42.
McCutcheon, Sarah, 'New Ross main drainage scheme', *Excavations 1997* (Bray, 1998), p. 601.
— 'The small stone artefacts' in Clyne, *Kells Priory*, pp 424–33.
McEneaney, Eamonn, 'Waterford and New Ross trade competition, *c*.1300', *Decies*, 12 (1979), pp 16–24.
McGrath, Thomas and Nolan, William (eds), *Carlow: history and society, interdisciplinary essays on the history of an Irish county* (Dublin, 2008).
McLoughlin, Catherine, 'The Bullawn, New Ross, Wexford', *Excavations 2003* (Bray, 2004), 2021.
— 'The Bullawn, New Ross, Wexford', *Excavations 2004* (Bray, 2005), 1814.
— 'The Quays/Marshmeadows, New Ross, Wexford', *Excavations 2003* (Bray, 2004), 2030.
McNeill, T.E., *Castles in Ireland: feudal power in a Gaelic world* (London, 1997).
— 'Squaring circles: flooring round towers in Wales and Ireland' in Kenyon and O'Conor (eds), *The medieval castle in Ireland and Wales*, pp 96–106.
Mesqui, Jean, *Châteaux forts de la guerre à la paix* (Paris, 1995).
— *Châteaux forts et fortifications en France* (Paris, 1997).
Mills, James, 'Accounts of the earl of Norfolk's estates in Ireland, 1279–94', *JRSAI*, 22 (1892), pp 50–62.
Monk, Mick, 'The plant remains' in Clyne, *Kells Priory*, pp 483–4.
Monson, D.A., *Les ensenhamens occitans: essai de definition et delimitation du genre* (Paris, 1981).
Montague, John, 'The cloister arcade' in Clyne, *Kells Priory*, pp 187–206.

Moody, T.W., Martin, F.X. and Byrne, F.J. (eds), *NHI*, ix: *maps, genealogies, lists: a companion to Irish history, part ii* (Oxford, 2011).
Moore, Michael, *Archaeological inventory of County Waterford* (Dublin, 1999).
— *Archaeological inventory of County Wexford* (Dublin, 1996).
Moran, Josephine, 'The window glass' in Clyne, *Kells Priory*, pp 261–316.
Morris, Marc, *King John: treachery, tyranny and the road to Magna Carta* (London, 2015).
Morton, Karena, 'The wall painting fragments' in Clyne, *Kells Priory*, pp 206–25.
Mullins, Clare, 'Priory Street, New Ross', *Excavations 1998* (Bray, 1999), p. 674.
Munby, Julian and Tyler, Ric, *Kilkenny city walls conservation plan* (Kilkenny, 2005).
Murphy, Margaret, 'The profits of lordship: Roger Bigod, earl of Norfolk, and the lordship of Carlow, 1270–1306' in Linda Doran and James Lyttleton (eds), *Lordship in medieval Ireland: image and reality* (Dublin, 2007), pp 75–98.
Murtagh, Ben, 'Archaeological investigations at Dysart, Co. Kilkenny, 1989–1994: an interim report', *OKR*, 46 (1994), pp 78–94.
— 'Enniscorthy Castle, Co. Wexford: an Elizabethan castle on the borderland with Gaelic Ireland', *Château Gaillard*, 26 (2014), pp 271–82.
— 'Kilkenny Castle, Kilkenny', *Excavations 1991* (Bray, 1992), pp 29–30.
— 'Kilkenny Castle, Kilkenny', *Excavations 1992* (Bray, 1993), pp 39–40.
— 'Kilkenny Castle, the Parade, Kilkenny', *Excavations 1997* (Bray, 1998), pp 102–4.
— 'Kilkenny Castle, the Parade, Kilkenny', *Excavations 1999* (Bray, 2000), pp 146–7.
— 'Reginald's Tower, the Quay, Waterford', *Excavations 1997* (Bray, 1998), pp 186–7.
— 'The Kilkenny Castle Archaeological Project, 1990–1993: interim report', *OKR*, new ser. 4:5 (1993), pp 1001–17.
— 'The medieval tower of Hook: a review of its dating and history' in Bernard Browne and Ian Doyle (eds), *Medieval Wexford: essays in honour of Billy Colfer* (Dublin, 2016), pp 124–80.
— 'The medieval tower of Hook, Co. Wexford: a beacon of commerce and symbol of Marshal power and wealth in Ireland', *Château Gaillard*, 27 (2016), pp 223–36.
— and Corlett, Christiaan, 'St Patrick's Gate, Kilkenny', *JRSAI*, 137 (2007), pp 70–100.
Neary, Patrick, 'Kilkenny main drainage', *Excavations 1997* (Bray, 1997), 291.
Neely, W.G., *Kilkenny: an urban history, 1391–1843* (Belfast, 1989).
Nicholls, Kenneth, 'Irishwomen and property in sixteenth-century Ireland' in Margaret MacCurtain and Mary O'Dowd (eds), *Women in early modern Ireland* (Edinburgh, 1991), pp 17–31.
Nicholson, Andrew, 'The antler' in Peter Hill, *Whithorn and St Ninian: the excavation of a monastic town, 1984–91* (Stroud, 1997), pp 474–95.
Ní Dhonnchadha, Máirín, 'Inis Teimle between Uí Chennselaig and the Déissí', *Peritia*, 16 (2002), pp 451–8.
Nolan, William and McGrath, Thomas (eds), *Tipperary: history and society, interdisciplinary essays on the history of an Irish county* (Dublin, 1985).
— and Whelan, Kevin (eds), *Kilkenny: history and society, interdisciplinary essays on the history of an Irish county* (Dublin, 1990).
Noonan, Daniel, 'North Quay, New Ross', *Excavations 2003* (Bray, 2004), 2025.
Nugent, Patrick, 'The dynamics of parish formation in high and late medieval Clare' in Elizabeth FitzPatrick and Raymond Gillespie (eds), *The parish in medieval and early modern Ireland: community, territory and building* (Dublin, 2006), pp 91–123.
O'Brien, A.F., 'Commercial relations between Aquitaine and Ireland, *c.*1000 to *c.*1550' in J.M. Picard (ed.), *Aquitaine and Ireland in the Middle Ages* (Dublin, 1995), pp 31–80.
— 'Politics, economy and society: the development of Cork and the Irish south-coast region, *c.*1170 to *c.*1583' in Patrick O'Flanagan and C.G. Buttimer (eds), *Cork: history and society* (Dublin, 1993), pp 83–154.

O'Byrne, Emmett, *War, politics and the Irish of Leinster, 1156–1606* (Dublin, 2003).

Ó Ciobháin, Brendan, 'Deoisí na hÉireann i ndiaidh Shionaid Cheanannas, 1152 – teacsanna [text]', *Dinnseanchas*, 5:2 (1972), pp 52–6.

— 'Foinsí éagsúla [various sources]', *Dinnseanchas*, 5:3 (1973), pp 71–85.

— 'Nótaí téacsa [textual notes]', *Dinnseanchas*, 5:4 (1973), pp 119–28.

O'Conor, Kieran, 'The origins of Carlow Castle', *Archaeology Ireland*, 11:3 (1997), pp 13–16.

Ó Corráin, Donncha, *Ireland before the Normans* (Dublin, 1972).

— 'The education of Diarmait Mac Murchada', *Ériu*, 28 (1977), pp 71–81.

O'Donnell, Mary, 'Priory Street, New Ross', *Excavations 2001* (Bray, 2002), 1311.

Ó Drisceoil, Cóilín, 'A collection of previously unpublished medieval burial monuments from Saint Mary's Church, Kilkenny', *OKR*, 58 (2006), pp 29–44.

— 'Kilkenny reclaimed: the archaeological evidence for medieval reclamation in Kilkenny city', *OKR*, 55 (2003), pp 58–69.

— 'Priory Lane, New Ross', *Excavations 2003* (Bray, 2004), 2028.

— 'Probing the past: a geophysical survey at St Canice's Cathedral', *OKR*, 56 (2004), pp 80–106.

— 'Talbot's Tower, Ormond Road, Kilkenny', *Excavations 2007* (Bray, 2008), 967.

— 'The Deanery Orchard, St Canice's Cathedral, Kilkenny', *Excavations 2006* (Bray, 2009), 1062.

O'Dwyer, Michael, *St Patrick's, Kilkenny: graveyard* (Kilkenny, n.d.).

O'Flanagan, Patrick and Buttimer, C.G. (eds), *Cork: history and society* (Dublin, 1993).

O'Keeffe, Tadhg, 'Dublin Castle's donjon in context' in John Bradley, A.J. Fletcher and Anngret Simms (eds), *Dublin in the medieval world: studies in honour of Howard B. Clarke* (Dublin, 2009), pp 277–94.

— *Medieval Ireland: an archaeology* (Stroud, 2000).

— and Coughlan, Margaret, 'The chronology and formal affinities of Ferns donjon, Co. Wexford' in Kenyon and O'Conor (eds), *The medieval castle in Ireland and Wales*, pp 133–48.

Ó Lochlainn, Colm, 'Roadways in ancient Ireland' in John Ryan (ed.), *Féilsgríbhinn Éoin Mhic Néill* (repr. Dublin, 1995), pp 465–74.

O'Mahony, Áine, *The monuments of St Mary's Church, New Ross* (New Ross, 1987).

O'Meara, Brenda, 'Nenagh Castle, Nenagh', *Excavations 2006*, 509.

Ó Néill, Pádraig, 'The impact of the Norman invasion on Irish literature' in Christopher Harper-Bill (ed.), *Anglo-Norman Studies: Proceedings of the Battle Conference*, 20 (London, 1997), pp 171–85.

O'Neill, Timothy, *Merchants and mariners in medieval Ireland* (Dublin, 1987).

— 'Aghaboe, *c.*600–1800', *OLL*, 1 (2004), pp 19–27.

Ó Riain, Pádraig, *A dictionary of Irish saints* (Dublin, 2011).

Ó Ríordáin, A.B., 'Excavations at High Street and Winetavern Street, Dublin', *Medieval Archaeology*, 15 (1971), pp 73–85.

Orpen, G.H., *APMDI*, 6 (1904–6), pp 165–6.

— 'Dundrum Castle, County Down, identified with the "Castrum de Rath"', *JRSAI*, 39 (1909), pp 23–9.

— *Ireland under the Normans* (4 vols, Oxford, 1910–20; repr. Dublin, 2005).

— 'Motes and Norman castles in Ossory', *JRSAI*, 39 (1909), pp 313–42.

— *New Ross in the thirteenth century* (Dublin, 1911).

— and St-J. Brooks, Eric, 'Charters of Earl Richard Marshal of the forests of Ross and Taghmon', *JRSAI*, 7th ser., 4:1 (1934), pp 54–63.

Otway-Ruthven, A.J., *A history of medieval Ireland* (2nd ed., London, 1980).

— 'Knight service in Ireland' in Peter Crooks (ed.), *Government, war and society in medieval Ireland: essays by Edmund Curtis, A.J. Otway-Ruthven and James Lydon* (Dublin, 2008), pp 155–68.

— 'Knights' fees in Kildare, Leix and Offaly', *JRSAI*, 91 (1961), pp 163–81.

— 'Parochial development in the rural deanery of Skreen', *JRSAI*, 94 (1964), pp 111–22.
— 'The character of Norman settlement in Ireland', *Historical Studies*, 5, ed. J.L. McCracken (London, 1965), pp 75–84.
— 'The medieval county of Kildare', *IHS*, 11 (1958–9), pp 181–99.
— 'The organisation of Anglo-Irish agriculture in the Middle Ages', *JRSAI*, 81 (1951), pp 1–13.
Oxford dictionary of national biography, ed. H.C.G. Matthew and Brian Harrison (60 vols, Oxford, 2004).
Painter, Sidney, *William Marshal: knight-errant, baron and regent of England* (Baltimore, 1933; repr. Toronto, 2001).
Panouillé, Jean Pierre, *Les châteaux forts dans la France au Moyen Âge* (Rennes, 2015).
Perfect, Vicky, *Flint Castle: the story of Edward I's first Welsh castle* (Mold, Flintshire, 2012).
Picard, J.M. (ed.), *Aquitaine and Ireland in the Middle Ages* (Dublin, 1995).
Plummer, Charles, *Lives of Irish saints* (Oxford, 1922).
Pollock, Dave, 'Dungarvan Castle', *Excavations 1995* (Bray, 1996), pp 84–5.
— 'Dungarvan Castle', *Excavations 1998* (Bray, 2000), pp 206–7.
Postan, M.M., *The Cambridge economic history of Europe, 1: the agrarian life of the Middle Ages* (2nd ed., Cambridge, 1966).
Pounds, N.J.G., *An historical geography of Europe* (Cambridge, 1990).
Power, Daniel, 'The French interests of the Marshal earls of Striguil and Pembroke, 1189–1234', *Anglo-Norman Studies*, 25 (2003), pp 199–225.
Rae, E.C., 'The medieval fabric of the cathedral church of St Patrick in Dublin', *JRSAI*, 109 (1979), pp 28–73.
Rankin, Deana, *Between Spenser and Swift: English writing in seventeenth-century Ireland* (Cambridge, 2005).
Renn, Derek, *Caerphilly Castle* (2nd ed., Cardiff, 1997).
Richter, Michael and Picard, J.M. (eds), *Ogma: essays in Celtic studies in honour of Próinséas Ní Chatháin* (Dublin, 2002).
Robertson, J.G., 'Architectural notes on Kilkenny Castle', *JRSAI*, 2 (1852–3), pp 115–18.
Russell, J.C., *Medieval regions and their cities* (London, 1972).
Rynne, Colin, 'The Patrick Street watermills, their technological context and a note on the reconstruction' in Claire Walsh, *Archaeological excavations at Patrick, Nicholas and Winetavern Streets, Dublin* (Dingle, 1997), pp 81–101.
Salter, Mike, *The castles of south-west Wales* (Malvern, 1996).
Saul, Nigel, 'Sackville [de Sackville] family (per. *c.*1066–*c.*1477)' in *ODNB*, www.oxforddnb.com/view/article/65281.
Sayers, William, 'Anglo-Norman verse on New Ross and its founders', *IHS*, 28:110 (Nov. 1992), pp 113–23.
Schweitz, Daniel, *Châteaux et forteresses du Moyen Âge en Val de Loire* (Tours, 2006).
Scully, O.M.B., 'The ferrous artefacts' in Clyne, *Kells Priory*, pp 353–80.
— 'The non-ferrous metal artefacts' in Clyne, *Kells Priory*, pp 383–405.
— 'Priory Street/Priory Lane, New Ross', *Excavations 2007* (Bray, 2008), 1973.
Sharpe, Richard, *Medieval Irish saints' lives* (Oxford, 1991).
Simms, Anngret, 'Irland: Überformung eines keltischen Siedlungsraumes am Rande Europas durch externe Kolonisationsbewegungen' in Juergen Hagedorn, Juergen Hövermann and H.J. Nitz (eds), *Gefügemuster der Erdobefläche: d. genet. Analyse von Reliefkomplexen und Siedlungsräumen: Festschrift zum 42. deutschen Geographentag* (Göttingen, 1979), pp 285–312.
Smyth, W.J., *Map-making, landscape and memory: a geography of colonial and early modern Ireland,* c.*1530–1750* (Cork, 2006).
Stacey, Nicola, *Framlingham Castle* (London, 2009).
Stafford, Emmet, '48 The Quays, New Ross', *Excavations 2003* (Bray, 2004), 2032.
Stalley, Roger, *The Cistercian monasteries of Ireland* (London and New Haven, 1987).

Stout, Geraldine et al., *Sites and monuments record, County Wexford* (Dublin, 1987).

Sweetman, P.D., 'Archaeological excavations at Ferns Castle, Co. Wexford', *PRIA*, 79C (1979), pp 217–45.

— *Medieval castles of Ireland* (Cork, 1999).

— Alcock, Olive and Moran, Bernie (comp.), *Archaeological inventory of County Laois* (Dublin, 1995).

Taylor, A.J., *The king's works in Wales, 1277–1330* (London, 1974).

Thomas, Avril, *The walled towns of Ireland* (2 vols, Dublin, 1992).

Tierney, John, 'Marsh Lane/The Quay, New Ross', *Excavations 2003* (Bray, 2004), 2031.

Tietzsch-Tyler, Daniel, 'Roscommon Castle: staged construction, unrealised vision' in Ben Murtagh (ed.), *Castles and defences in Ireland and beyond: studies in honour of David Newman Johnson* (forthcoming).

— *The Augustinian priory of Kells, Co. Kilkenny: an exploration* (Stonyford, 1993).

— and Sleeman, A.G., *Geology of south Wexford* (Sligo, 1994).

Tubridy, M. and Culleton, E. (eds), *Traces of County Wexford's past* (Wexford, 1994).

Turner, Rick, *Chepstow Castle* (2nd ed., Cardiff, 2006).

— and Johnson, Andy, *Chepstow Castle: its history and buildings* (Logaston, 2006).

Turner, R.V., 'Richard Lionheart and English episcopal elections', *Albion*, 29 (1997), pp 1–13.

Unkel, Jill, 'An enduring monument', *Irish Arts Review*, 22:3 (autumn 2005), pp 100–3.

Veach, Colin, 'King John and royal control in Ireland', *English Historical Review*, 129 (2014), pp 1051–78.

— *Lordship in four realms: the Lacy family, 1166–1241* (Manchester, 2014).

Vigors, P.D., *APMDI*, 4 (1899–1900), pp 328–31, 497.

— *APMDI*, 5 (1901–3), pp 125–33.

— 'Extracts from the books of the old corporation of Ross, Co. Wexford', *JRSAI*, 21 (1892), pp 171–6, 287–90.

— 'Extracts from the books of the old corporation of Ross, Co. Wexford', *JRSAI*, 24 (1894), pp 176–9.

— 'Extracts from the old corporation books of New Ross, Co. Wexford', *JRSAI*, 31 (1901), pp 48–64.

Walker, Joseph (ed.), *The Copper Plate Magazine; or, Monthly Cabinet of Picturesque Prints, Consisting of Views in Great Britain and Ireland*, 4 (London, 1799).

Wallace, Patrick, 'Dublin's waterfront at Wood Quay: 900–1317' in G. Milne and B. Hobley (eds), *Waterfront archaeology in Britain and northern Europe* (London, 1981), pp 109–18.

Walton, Julian, *The royal charters of Waterford* (Waterford, 1992), pp 17–18.

Ward, J.C., 'Fashions in monastic endowment: the foundations of the Clare family, 1066–1314', *Journal of Ecclesiastical History*, 32 (1981), pp 427–52.

Warren, W.L., *King John* (New Haven and London, 1997).

Waterman, D.M., 'Rectangular keeps of the thirteenth century at Grenan (Kilkenny) and Glanworth (Cork)', *JRSAI*, 98 (1968), pp 67–73.

— 'Somersetshire and other foreign building stone in medieval Ireland, *c.*1175–1400', *Ulster Journal of Archaeology*, 33 (1970), pp 63–75.

Watt, John, *The church in medieval Ireland* (Dublin, 1972).

Westropp, T.J., 'Early Italian maps of Ireland from 1300 to 1600, with notes on foreign settlers and trade', *PRIA*, 30C (1912–13), pp 361–428.

Whelan, Kevin (ed.), *Wexford: history and society* (Dublin, 1987).

Wiggins, Kenneth, *Anatomy of a siege: King John's Castle, Limerick, 1642* (Bray, 2000).

— 'King John's Castle, St Mary's parish', *Excavations 1990* (Bray, 1991), 43–4.

Wiles, John, 'Marshal towers in south-west Wales: innovation and mimicry', *CSGJ*, 27 (2013–14), pp 181–202.

Wren, Joanna, 'The roof tiles' in Clyne, *Kells Priory*, pp 225–34.

Index